1/00

Biography Today

Profiles of People of Interest to Young Readers

1999
Annual
Cumulation

Laurie Lanzen Harris
Executive Editor

Cherie D. Abbey
Associate Editor

Omnigraphics

615 Griswold • Detroit, Michigan 48226

Laurie Lanzen Harris, *Executive Editor*
Cherie D. Abbey, *Associate Editor*
Kevin Hillstrom, Laurie Hillstrom, and Sue Ellen Thompson, *Sketch Writers*
Joan Margeson and Barry Puckett, *Research Associates*

Omnigraphics, Inc.

* * *

Matt Barbour, *Vice President, Operations*
Laurie Lanzen Harris, *Vice President, Editorial Director*
Peter E. Ruffner, *Senior Vice President*
Thomas J. Murphy, *Vice President, Finance*
Jane Steele, *Marketing Coordinator*

* * *

Frederick G. Ruffner, Jr., Publisher

This book is printed on acid-free paper meeting the ANSI Z39.48 Standard. The infinity symbol that appears above indicates that the paper in this book meets that standard.

Printed in the United States

Contents

5

Preface

Biography Today is a magazine designed and written for the young reader—ages 9 and above—and covers individuals that librarians and teachers tell us that young people want to know about most: entertainers, athletes, writers, illustrators, cartoonists, and political leaders.

The Plan of the Work

The publication was especially created to appeal to young readers in a format they can enjoy reading and readily understand. Each issue contains approximately 10 sketches arranged alphabetically; this annual cumulation contains 30 entries. Each entry provides at least one picture of the individual profiled, and bold-faced rubrics lead the reader to information on birth, youth, early memories, education, first jobs, marriage and family, career highlights, memorable experiences, hobbies, and honors and awards. Each of the entries ends with a list of easily accessible sources designed to lead the student to further reading on the individual and a current address. Obituary entries are also included, written to provide a perspective on the individual's entire career. Obituaries are clearly marked in both the table of contents and at the beginning of the entry.

Biographies are prepared by Omnigraphics editors after extensive research, utilizing the most current materials available. Those sources that are generally available to students appear in the list of further reading at the end of the sketch.

New Index

Beginning with the January 1999 issue, a new Index appeared in *Biography Today*. In an effort to make the index easier to use, we have combined the **Name** and **General Index** into one, called the **General Index**. This new index contains the names of all individuals who have appeared in *Biography Today* since the series began. The names appear in bold faced type, followed by the issue in which they appeared. The General Index also contains the occupations, nationalities, and ethnic and minority origins of individuals profiled. The General Index is cumulative, including references to all individuals who have appeared in the *Biography Today* General Series and the *Biography Today* Special Subject volumes since the series began in 1992.

In a further effort to consolidate and save space, the Birthday and Places of Birth Indexes will be appearing only in the September issue and in the Annual Cumulation.

Our Advisors

This publication was reviewed by an Advisory Board comprised of librarians, children's literature specialists, and reading instructors so that we could make sure that the concept of this publication — to provide a readable and accessible biographical magazine for young readers — was on target. They evaluated the title as it developed, and their suggestions have proved invaluable. Any errors, however, are ours alone. We'd like to list the Advisory Board members, and to thank them for their efforts.

Sandra Arden, *Retired*
Assistant Director
Troy Public Library, Troy, MI

Gail Beaver
Ann Arbor Huron High School Library
and the University of Michigan School
of Information and Library Studies
Ann Arbor, MI

Marilyn Bethel
Pompano Beach Branch Library
Pompano Beach, FL

Eileen Butterfield
Waterford Public Library
Waterford, CT

Linda Carpino
Detroit Public Library
Detroit, MI

Helen Gregory
Grosse Pointe Public Library
Grosse Pointe, MI

Jane Klasing, *Retired*
School Board of Broward County
Fort Lauderdale, FL

Marlene Lee
Broward County Public Library System
Fort Lauderdale, FL

Judy Liskov
Waterford Public Library
Waterford, CT

Sylvia Mavrogenes
Miami-Dade Public Library System
Miami, FL

Carole J. McCollough
Wayne State University School of
Library Science, Detroit, MI

Deborah Rutter
Russell Library, Middletown, CT

Barbara Sawyer
Groton Public Library and Information
Center, Groton, CT

Renee Schwartz
School Board of Broward County
Fort Lauderdale, FL

Lee Sprince
Broward West Regional Library
Fort Lauderdale, FL

Susan Stewart, *Retired*
Birney Middle School Reading
Laboratory, Southfield, MI

Ethel Stoloff, *Retired*
Birney Middle School Library
Southfield, MI

Our Advisory Board stressed to us that we should not shy away from controversial or unconventional people in our profiles, and we have tried to follow their advice. The Advisory Board also mentioned that the sketches might be useful in reluctant reader and adult literacy programs, and we would value any comments librarians might have about the suitability of our magazine for those purposes.

New Series

In response to suggestions from our readers, we have expanded the *Biography Today* family of publications. So far, we have published special subject volumes in the following categories: **Artists, Authors, Scientists and Inventors, Sports Figures, and World Leaders**. Each of these hardcover volumes is approximately 200 pages in length and covers about 15 individuals of interest to young readers.

Your Comments Are Welcome

Our goal is to be accurate and up-to-date, to give young readers information they can learn from and enjoy. Now we want to know what you think. Take a look at this issue of *Biography Today*, on approval. Write or call me with your comments. We want to provide an excellent source of biographical information for young people. Let us know how you think we're doing.

And here's a special incentive: mail or fax us the names of people you want to see in *Biography Today.* If we include someone you suggest, your library wins a free issue, with our thanks.

And take a look at the next page, where we've listed those libraries and individuals who received a free issue of *Biography Today* for 1999 for suggesting people who appeared this year.

Laurie Harris
Executive Editor, *Biography Today*
Omnigraphics, Inc.
615 Griswold
Detroit, MI 48226
Fax: 1-800-875-1340

Congratulations!

Congratulations to the following individuals and libraries, who received a free copy of *Biography Today* for suggesting people who appeared in 1999:

Sarah Beam, Woodville, OH
Belle River Elementary School,
   Marine City, MI
Brian Carlo, East Providence, RI
Central Montcalm Middle School,
   Stanton, MI
Charlene Chan, Scarsdale, NY
Joe Christian, Mt. Pocono, PA
Megan Donnell, Birmingham, MI
Sonja Durham, Dover, DE
Adam Finkel, Bloomfield Hills, MI
Goodwin Elementary School,
   Cicero, IL
Dwayne Helm, Alex, OK
Erica Hunter, Camp Springs, MD
Mercedes Jones, Toledo, OH
Debra Longstreet, Kentwood, MI
Gabriela Magda,
   Middle Village, NY
Connie Mahautmr, Bartlett, TN
Manhasset Public Library,
   Manhasset, NY

Colleen McKernan,
   Lathrup Village, MI
Helen Mengstu, Florissant, MO
Bethany Palmer, Plymouth, MI
Roosevelt Elementary School,
   Mankato, MN
Roosevelt Middle School,
   Coffeyville, KS
Martha Tilton
St. Clair Shores Public Library,
   St. Clair Shores, MI
Dale Humeston
Rosemary Orlando
Rose Sibble, Ames, IA
Marcellos Stanford,
   Chatsworth, CA
Kera Toler, Salt Lake City, UT
Sacheen A. Torres,
   Pico Rivera, CA
Jim Tucker, Lakewood, CO
Marjorie Wright, Manassas, VA
David Xiao, New York, NY

Ben Affleck 1972-

American Actor and Screenwriter
Co-Wrote the Screenplay for *Good Will Hunting* and
Co-Starred in *Armageddon* and *Shakespeare in Love*

BIRTH

Benjamin Geza Affleck was born on August 15, 1972, in Berkeley, California. His mother is Chris Affleck, a sixth-grade teacher. His father is Timothy Affleck, a former bartender, auto mechanic, janitor, and actor who now works in a drug rehabilitation center. Ben has one brother, Casey, also an actor, who has appeared in *To Die For* and *Good Will Hunting*.

YOUTH

Affleck and his family moved from California to Cambridge, Massachusetts, when he was about three years old. Cambridge is a suburb of Boston that is home to the world-renowned schools Harvard University and Massachusetts Institute of Technology (MIT). There, he grew up in a financially comfortable, middle-class environment.

But the Affleck family also struggled through some tough times when Ben was a kid. His father, Timothy Affleck, supported the family with a series of blue-collar jobs, including a stint as a janitor at Harvard University. But his real work was as an actor with the Theater Company of Boston, a prestigious group that featured such acting talents as Dustin Hoffman, James Woods, and Robert Duvall. Tim Affleck was also an alcoholic, though, and his drinking put a strain on family life. He and Chris, Ben's mother, divorced around 1984, when Ben was about 11 or 12. Their two boys, Ben and Casey, stayed in Massachusetts with Chris, while Tim moved back to California. There, he eventually entered a drug rehabilitation center to fight his addiction. Now sober, he works at the rehab center counseling others with substance abuse problems.

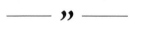

> *Matt Damon once characterized his friendship with Affleck like this: "If one kid had enough for a candy bar, then the candy bar was bought and split in half—that's just the way it's been."*

Ben Affleck started acting when he was very young. He was six when he appeared in his first TV commercial, one for Burger King, and after that he went on to appear in several TV commercials, in an independent film called *The Dark End of the Street,* and in the PBS documentary series, "The Voyage of the Mimi," an educational public television series that featured lessons on a boat. "The Voyage of the Mimi" is still sometimes shown in classrooms today. Affleck continued to act throughout his childhood, winning parts on commercials, TV shows, TV movies, and even small roles in feature films.

Meeting Matt Damon

Ben was eight when he met Matt Damon, another Cambridge boy who lived two blocks away. They were brought together by their mothers, good friends who both worked in the field of education. According to Ben, "My mom was trying to get me to do more work around the house and would say, 'Well, Matt's mom makes *him* cook once a week.' So I first knew him as a guy who was really setting a bad precedent in the neighborhood." Although Matt was two years older than Ben, they soon discovered they shared several passions: playing Little League baseball, playing Dungeons and Dragons, watching Godzilla and Kung Fu movies, reading superhero comic books, and acting. By that point, Ben had already had a couple of acting parts. So it seemed only natural that his friend, who also liked acting, would go along to auditions and to meetings with his agent. Soon Damon was landing small parts as well.

Affleck and Damon developed a close, sharing friendship that continues to this day. Here's how Damon once characterized their friendship: "If one kid had enough for a candy bar, then the candy bar was bought and split in half—that's just the way it's been." In response to a question about whether he and Damon knew when they were kids that they would remain good friends into adulthood, Affleck said this: "Matt and I had identical interests, so whether we ended up successful or making hot dogs at Dodgers games, we knew we'd end up doing the same sort of things. The remaining friends part was pretty consistent. We saw each other all the time, we talked on the phone all the time." Their comments today reveal both their close friendship and their tendency to kid each other, as shown in Damon's description of what Affleck was like as a kid. "I remember exactly what he was like: gregarious, outgoing. It was no surprise that he grew up into the totally obnoxious guy he is now."

EARLY MEMORIES

According to Affleck, he wasn't very popular with girls when he was young. In fact, he says he was awkward and socially inept. "As a kid, I was the kind of guy who got dumped a lot. I'd be talking on the phone for a week with a girl and I'd be like, 'I love you. Let's go out!' I became too needy," he recalls. And despite his movie star good looks today, he wasn't great looking back then. He was five feet, one inch tall when he started high school, and he grew a full foot during his junior year to his current height of six foot three. It was a painful year. "My knees and shins and elbows would just ache every morning," he recalls. By the end of high school, he was tall and gangly. "I don't think the ladies were saying, 'I'm looking for somebody awkward and beanpole-like, who doesn't have control of his own limbs.' My head was misshapen and lumpy, and I was way too sensitive."

EDUCATION

Affleck attended public schools in Cambridge. For high school, he attended Cambridge Rindge and Latin School, a prestigious and competitive public school that Matt Damon also attended. By that point, they had both already decided that they were going to be actors. In a joint session with a writer for *Interview* magazine, they described their high school years like this. Damon started out saying, "We used to have what we called 'business lunches' in high school, which meant we met at the smaller cafeteria and got a table" — and then Affleck jumped in to finish the thought — "and worked out some business plans. We were really nerdy." He also once said, "I guess you could say we were theater nerds, which certainly wasn't as cool as playing on the basketball team." Affleck continued to act throughout his teen years, making his network TV debut in the 1986 ABC Afterschool Special "Wanted: The Perfect Guy" and appearing in the 1987 TV miniseries "Hands of a Stranger." He graduated from Cambridge Rindge and Latin in 1990.

After graduating, Affleck followed his high school girlfriend to the University of Vermont. But he stayed there for only about a semester before dropping out. Next he transferred to Occidental College in Eagle Rock, California. While a student there he made his feature film debut in *School Ties* (1992), a drama about a Jewish student and football player at an anti-Semitic prep school. He and Damon, who also appeared in *School Ties*, played two wealthy prep school students who tormented the school football star, played by Brendan Fraser. Affleck only stayed at Occidental College for about a year before he decided to drop out of college again. By that point, he had decided to dedicate himself to acting.

FIRST JOBS

Staying in California, Affleck began living the life of a young, itinerant actor. He would get parts, get paid, live well, spend all his money, and end up broke again. He lived that way for about six years. During this time, he and Damon shared several different places around Los Angeles with a couple of friends from Cambridge or with other young actors. Sometimes Affleck would get a bedroom; sometimes he'd end up on the couch. In this way, he managed to scrape by with occasional parts in TV, movies, and commercials. For example, he made $20,000 for appearing in an NBC movie of the week, "Danielle Steel's 'Daddy'," but managed to spend most of it while laying around playing Sega. He made $30,000 for working on *School Ties*, but blew all of that, too. It was during this time that he and Damon began writing the script for *Good Will Hunting*.

Matt Damon, Minnie Driver, and Ben Affleck on the set of Good Will Hunting

At that point, no one in Hollywood considered Affleck leading-man material. His face still had a little-boy appearance, and he didn't fit the preferred look of the moment. He endured a lot of rejection. "Agents used to tell me, 'You have baby fat on your face,' and 'You're not good-looking enough.' For a long time the thing was blond and waifish, and that's not my thing. I was always getting characterized as 'beefy.' That's just not a flattering thing to say about anybody."

So Affleck took a different route, appearing in several independent films. These films, which are created without the backing or financing of a big Hollywood studio, give the filmmaker far more independence and control in creating offbeat story lines and in picking actors that might not match the current popular look. Of course, such films are also made on a shoestring budget, providing small salaries and few opportunities to move into a mainstream Hollywood career.

First up for Affleck was *Dazed and Confused* (1993), an unsentimental look at the last day of the school year for a group of Texas teens in the mid-1970s. Affleck played a high school senior, a football player and a bully who terrorizes freshman students on the last day before summer vacation. "After I had done *Dazed and Confused*," he says, "where I was the only unlikable character in a cast full of likable characters, everybody thought I was a [jerk], which is not much help when you're looking for a job. After that movie I was probably the poorest I ever was." He appeared next in *Mallrats* (1995), which was directed by Kevin Smith, who had recently made the indie hit film *Clerks*. Not as successful as its predecessor, *Mallrats* was an ensemble piece about a bunch of teenagers who hang out at a suburban mall. According to Affleck, "At the time I was interested in finding out how to make movies cheap, and I figured who better to talk to than the guy whose last movie [*Clerks*] cost $27,000. So I did [*Mallrats*] and ended up becoming friends with him." Affleck went on to make his debut behind the camera in 1995, when he directed a short film with the arresting title "I Murdered My Lesbian Wife, Hung Her on a Meathook, and Now I Have a Three-Picture Deal at Disney."

CAREER HIGHLIGHTS

The year 1997 marked the beginning of critical, popular, and financial success for Affleck. He appeared in three films that year, and garnered acclaim in each. His breakthrough role was in *Chasing Amy*, which was also directed by Kevin Smith. He played a charming cartoonist who falls in love with a woman who is a lesbian. In fact, Smith wrote the part with Affleck in mind. "He called me up and said, 'Hey, I'm writing this about a guy who falls in love with this woman who's gay and I want you to play the guy.' I said, 'Well, I'd love to.' He sent it to me as he was writing it. It was really nice to be involved from the beginning, for somebody to put that much faith in me." He also appeared that year in *Going All the Way*, based on the novel of the same name by Dan Wakefield. Affleck gave a nuanced performance as a former high school football star and sensitive veteran returning from duty in the Korean War. Both films premiered at Sundance, the renowned independent film festival organized by Robert Redford in Utah, which brought Affleck widespread attention from many insiders in the film world.

Writing a Screenplay

But what really brought Affleck fame and success was his part in creating *Good Will Hunting*. The movie first started out in the early 1990s as a single scene that Damon wrote for a playwriting class he took while a student at Harvard University. Affleck was visiting from California at the time, so Damon invited him to come to class and act out the scene with him. It was so good that they decided to start working on it together. They started writing in about 1993 and continued working on it sporadically for about three years, whenever they had time between their other film projects. Sometimes when they were off on location working on a movie they would write scenes and fax them back and forth. Sometimes they worked on the script together, with Affleck doing all the typing. They improvised and acted out the scenes as they wrote them, making sure that everything worked from the actors' perspective. As Affleck said, "Telling this story came naturally to us. It wasn't like we sat down and had a formula. It was much more like, 'Well, what would be fun to act?'"

They were motivated to begin writing the screenplay, according to both Affleck and Damon, because they weren't getting the types of roles they wanted as actors. As Affleck explains, "If no one else was going to give us the chance to do the kind of acting we thought we could do, we decided we'd just make this movie ourselves—however we could do it, low-budget, whatever. The whole idea was to have a videotape on the shelf at the end of the day and be able to say, 'We made this.'" Damon agrees, saying, "We wrote it right out of frustration. It was like, 'Why are we sitting here? Let's make our own movie. And if people come to see it, they come; and if they don't, they don't. Either way, it beats sitting here going crazy.' When you have so much energy and so much passion for it and nobody cares, it's just the worst feeling."

In late 1994, Affleck and Damon tried to sell their script. It incited a small bidding war, with various Hollywood studios trying to outbid

Affleck and Damon began writing Good Will Hunting *because they weren't getting the types of roles they wanted as actors. As Affleck explains, "If no one else was going to give us the chance to do the kind of acting we thought we could do, we decided we'd just make this movie ourselves—however we could do it, low-budget, whatever. The whole idea was to have a videotape on the shelf at the end of the day and be able to say, 'We made this.'"*

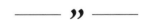

each other for the right to make their film. They finally went with Castle Rock, which paid them $300,000 each. "It was like we'd won the lottery," Damon recalls. The executives at Castle Rock also gave them some much-needed advice on how to rework their script, which by then had reached about 1,500 pages. The script had gone through many changes over the years that Affleck and Damon were working on it. They had tried out many different subplots, including several with spies. One draft had

Affleck, left, with his mother, Chris, and Matt Damon with his mother, Nancy, arriving at the 70th annual Academy Awards in Los Angeles, March 23, 1998

agents from the National Security Agency interested in recruiting the lead character for dangerous and dastardly missions. But the executives at Castle Rock urged them to write about what they knew: characters and relationships.

Good Will Hunting

Their final story, according to Affleck, is about "a kid from a working-class neighborhood in South Boston." Damon played that kid, Will Hunting, and here's how he describes Will: "He's an orphan, a born genius, who's discovered working as a janitor at MIT, and it's about him being caught between all these different worlds: the world of his friends [including Chuckie, played by Affleck]; the world of the therapist [Robin Williams] he comes in contact with; the world of this really amazing woman [Minnie Driver] he meets who challenges him; and then there's the lure of the world his genius introduces him to, which is represented by this math professor [Stellan Skarsgard]. So he has to face all these different forces that are at work. It's like a comedy and a drama and a coming-of-age story."

By late 1995 Affleck and Damon had a final draft of their script. They went back to Castle Rock, ready to begin filming, only to run into some creative differences. Chief among them was Castle Rock's decision to film the movie in Toronto, Canada, because it would be cheaper than filming it in the U.S. But Affleck and Damon were adamant that the movie had to be filmed in Boston, because they felt that the character of the city, especially South Boston (called Southie), was an integral element of the film. But Castle Rock balked, so the film went into turnaround. By the terms of their contract, Affleck and Damon had one month to convince another studio to pay off Castle Rock and purchase the rights to their film—or they would lose all control over what happened to their own script.

That's when their amazing luck kicked in. At that point Affleck was working with the director Kevin Smith on *Chasing Amy*, and Smith passed their script on to Harvey Weinstein, chairman of Miramax Studios. Weinstein loved it, agreed to film it, and bought the rights from Castle Rock. It came as a huge relief. "By then we would've done dog walking to get the thing made," Affleck jokes. "I still have to mow Harvey's lawn every Sunday morning." Next up to read the script was famed filmmaker Gus Van Sant, director of *Drugstore Cowboy, My Private Idaho*, and *To Die For*. By the time he was halfway through it, he called Affleck. "I said flat out I had to do it," Van Sant recalls. "We met at

"Agents used to tell me, 'You have baby fat on your face,' and 'You're not good-looking enough.' For a long time the thing was blond and waifish, and that's not my thing. I was always getting characterized as 'beefy.' That's just not a flattering thing to say about anybody."

Denny's in L.A. the week after I'd called him about the script. [Affleck] was just really, really excited. He was like a giant golden retriever with a ball." Then Robin Williams read it and asked to play the part of the therapist. At the time, Affleck and Damon were virtually unknown, so for them to hook up with so many accomplished people who wanted to make their film is a testament to their amazing luck—and to their incredible talent in creating such a superb screenplay.

Good Will Hunting was released in late 1997. The movie was a sleeper hit, winning legions of fans and excellent critical reviews. Many reviewers particularly praised the screenplay, like Janet Maslin in the *New York Times*. "Two young actors with soaring reputations have written themselves a smart and touching screenplay, then seen it directed with style, shrewdness, and clarity." *Good Will Hunting* also won many top awards. Affleck and Damon jointly won a Golden Globe Award in 1997 and an Academy Award in 1998 for Best Screenplay, and Robin Williams won the 1998 Academy Award for Best Supporting Actor for his work on the film. *Good Will Hunting* won nine Oscar nominations in all, including nominations for both Damon and Minnie Driver for Academy Awards for their acting.

———— **"** ————

"Ben's the real thing," says Jerry Bruckheimer, *the producer of* **Armageddon** *as well as* **The Rock** *and* **Con Air.** *"He's got that square jaw, that real American look, without being pretty. Women want to be with him and men want to be like him — which is what movie stars are made of."*

———— **"** ————

Armageddon

With his next big film, Affleck tried something completely new: he appeared in *Armageddon* (1998), a big-budget action-adventure film. In *Armageddon*, Earth is threatened with an asteroid impact that would wipe out the world as we know it. Affleck played A.J. Frost, a cocky, hot-shot oil driller. He is part of select crew that goes into space to try to drill a hole in the asteroid and plant a neutron bomb to blow it up before it can destroy the world. He co-starred in the film with Bruce Willis, who played his boss, and Liv Tyler, who played Willis's daughter and Affleck's love interest.

It was an arduous movie to film. Affleck did a lot of work on oil drilling platforms and on the "vomit comet," a NASA training simulator that recreates the feeling of being in space. He worked in a NASA space suit that weighed over 200 pounds and cost $10 million, which left him constantly terrified that he would wreck the thing. He also worked at NASA's Neutral Buoyancy Lab, an astronaut training center facility at the Johnson Space Center. There, he wore his heavy spacesuit in a huge tank of water, which Affleck found very nerve-wracking. "If it leaked, it would drop like a rock. That was scary," he recalled. But he overcame all these difficult conditions to give a performance that confirmed his future as a big star. "Ben's the real thing," says the movie's producer, Jerry Bruckheimer, who also produced such hits as *The Rock* and *Con Air*. "He's got that square jaw, that real American look, without being pretty. Women want to be with him and men want to be like him — which is what movie stars are made of."

Affleck, second from right, joins Bruce Willis in saving the planet in Armageddon

For some people it was a surprise for Affleck to appear in *Armageddon*. Because he had always worked in smaller, independent films, people assumed that he would be more interested in intellectual art-house films than in big-bucks action flicks. But for Affleck, it seemed very natural. "People say, 'How can you do this movie [*Armageddon*]? You're the indie guy.' I take it that they're conferring some kind of integrity on me when they say that. But when I was growing up, I liked *Star Wars* and *Lethal Weapon*. When I was growing up, I thought *Back to the Future* was the best film I saw that year. I am not a kid who was weaned on Fellini."

Shakespeare in Love

For many young actors, the typical career trajectory is to appear in ever-bigger films. So after winning fame first in several indie hits culminating in *Chasing Amy*, then following that up with the prestige of *Good Will Hunting*, then following that up with the big commercial triumph *Armageddon*, it might be expected that Affleck would follow that up with an even bigger and more successful film. But instead, he took a different course, as Amy Wallace wrote in the *Los Angeles Times*. "If you were building a prototype for a turn-of-the-century movie star, Affleck might be it. Hip and handsome, with a goofy charm that nicely masks his ambition,

Ben Affleck in Shakespeare in Love

Affleck is tampering with the time-honored Hollywood formula that equates an actor's star power with the size of his paycheck. . . . [He continues] to mix big films and small, supporting parts and cameos."

After *Armageddon,* Affleck went on to appear in *Shakespeare in Love* (1998), a fictional story set in 16th century England about the playwright William Shakespeare. In the movie, Shakespeare (played by Joseph Fiennes) is facing writer's block. He's working on a new play called *Romeo and Ethel, the Pirate's Daughter,* and he can't seem to write a word. He falls in love with a noble woman (played by Gwyneth Paltrow), who is betrothed to another man. Their infatuation and brief but doomed love affair become the basis of his new play, *Romeo and Juliet,* which he transforms from a silly farce into a romantic tragedy. In *Shakespeare in Love,* Affleck plays Ned Alleyn, a famous and conceited actor who Shakespeare needs in his play. According to Affleck, "I play this big star and I'm like a huge pain. I have this enormous ego and I'm very demanding, but Shakespeare has to have me in the play in order to get it produced." Affleck had only a secondary role in *Shakespeare in Love,* but it turned out to be one of the best films of the year. *Shakespeare in Love* won seven Academy Awards, including the award for Best Picture.

Recent Works

Affleck has appeared in several recent works. In *Forces of Nature* (1999), a big-budget romance, he had a starring role opposite Sandra Bullock. He played Ben, a practical, reliable, straightlaced, buttoned-down guy who is trying to get from New York to Savannah in time for his wedding. When his plane skids off the runway, he sets out on a road trip to Savannah. He teams up for the trip with another passenger, Sarah (played by Bullock), a sassy, free-spirited charmer. The two of them are constantly sidetracked by problems along the way, including hailstorms, hurricanes, and fires. They also seem to run into a constant stream of people who tell horror stories about the perils of marriage, all while Ben seems to be falling for Sarah. Also in 1999, Affleck appeared in *200 Cigarettes*. This ensemble romantic comedy featured a heavyweight cast of young actors, including Ben and his brother Casey, Dave Chappelle, Janeane Garofalo, Courtney Love, Gaby Hudson, Martha Plimpton, Christina Ricci, and Paul Rudd. The movie is set on New Year's Eve, 1981, in New York City's East Village, where a disparate group of unattached hip young people are looking for romance. Affleck had a small role in the film, playing a bartender who is romanced by several women. In addition, Affleck recently voiced the main character on the animated biblical film *Joseph*, a direct-to-video release. He did that project, he has said, in order to work with Jeffrey Katzenberg, an executive at DreamWorks. "He's really smart. That made it worth it."

Affleck once jokingly summed up his three rules for living. "Don't take yourself too seriously. Take what you do seriously, and find the humor in as much of life as you can. Those are my only three rules," he said, laughing. "Three nuggets, Confucius-style. Just put me under a tree and I'll fire out little bits of wisdom."

Affleck also has several new projects in the works. Coming up is *Dogma*, a religious farce that has been filmed but has not yet been released. Written and directed by Kevin Smith, the filmmaker who created *Chasing Amy* and other indie hits, *Dogma* features Affleck and Matt Damon as disgraced angels banished from heaven. With comedian Chris Rock as an apostle and singer Alanis Morissette as God, the movie's satiric approach to Christianity and organized religion is expected to be controversial. In the near future, Affleck also has plans to continue writing with Damon. The two are working on several projects together, including a screenplay called *Halfway House* about a pair of drug-abuse counselors in Boston.

Affleck once jokingly summed up his three rules for living. While he offered them partly in jest, they seem to epitomize his approach to life. "Don't take yourself too seriously. Take what you do seriously, and find the humor in as much of life as you can. Those are my only three rules," he said, laughing. "Three nuggets, Confucius-style. Just put me under a tree and I'll fire out little bits of wisdom."

HOME AND FAMILY

Affleck, who is unmarried, lives in New York and the Los Angeles area. He recently bought a 6,000 square foot home in the Hollywood Hills, complete with pool, spa, and stunning canyon views. Affleck remains very close to his brother and his mother; in fact, he and Damon each took their mothers as their dates to the 1998 Academy Awards ceremony where they won an Oscar.

SELECTED CREDITS

School Ties, 1992
Dazed and Confused, 1993
Mall Rats, 1995
Going All the Way, 1997
Chasing Amy, 1997
Good Will Hunting, 1997
Armageddon, 1998
Shakespeare in Love, 1998
Forces of Nature, 1999
200 Cigarettes, 1999

HONORS AND AWARDS

Special Achievement in Filmmaking Award (National Board of Review): 1997, for *Good Will Hunting* (with Matt Damon)
Broadcast Film Critics Association Award: 1997, for *Good Will Hunting*, for Best Original Screenplay (with Matt Damon)
Golden Globe Award: 1997, for *Good Will Hunting*, for Best Screenplay (with Matt Damon)
Academy Award (Academy of Motion Picture Arts and Sciences): 1998, for *Good Will Hunting*, for Best Screenplay (with Matt Damon)

Humanitas Prize (Human Family and Educational Cultural Institute):
    1998, for *Good Will Hunting* (with Matt Damon)
The Actor Award (Screen Actors Guild): 1998, for *Shakespeare in Love*, for
    Outstanding Performance in a Theatrical Motion Picture

FURTHER READING

Books

Brashares, Ben. *Ben Affleck*, 1999

Periodicals

Biography Magazine, Sep. 1998, p.93
Boston Magazine, Sep. 1997, p.68
Cosmopolitan, Apr. 1999, p.204
Current Biography Yearbook 1998
Details, July 1998, p.106
Entertainment Weekly, Feb. 13, 1998, p.20
GQ, Feb. 1998, p.148
Interview, Dec. 1997, p.118
Los Angeles Times, Nov. 30, 1997, Calendar section, p.3; Mar. 7, 1999,
    Calendar section, p.4
New York Times, Nov. 20, 1997, p.E1
People, July 20, 1998, p.121
Premiere, Aug. 1998, p.56
USA Weekend, June 28, 1998, p.4

ADDRESS

Miramax Films
Pearl Street Productions
7966 Beverly Blvd.
Los Angeles, CA 90048

WORLD WIDE WEB SITE

http://www.affleck.com

Jennifer Aniston 1969-

American Actress
Plays Rachel Green on the Television Series "Friends"

BIRTH

Jennifer Aniston was born on February 11, 1969, in Sherman
Oaks, California. Her father, John Aniston, is an actor best
known for his role as Victor Kiriakis on the soap opera "Days
of Our Lives." Her mother, Nancy Aniston, is a photographer
who was formerly an actress and model. Jennifer has an
older half-brother, John Melick, from her mother's first marriage. Aniston's family name was originally Anastassakis, but
her father changed it when he decided to become an actor.

YOUTH

Aniston's family moved from California to Greece when she was five years old. When they returned to the United States a year later, they settled in New York City. Before long, Aniston's parents began having problems in their relationship, and they were divorced when she was nine. "It was awful," she recalled. "I felt so totally responsible. It's so cliche, but I really felt it was because I wasn't a good enough kid."

From this time on, Aniston lived in a New York apartment with her mother and saw her father only on weekends. She and her mother had a good relationship, except when her mother pressured her to dress up and wear makeup. "My mother was someone who would say, 'Jennifer, please—before you go to the market, would you please put your eyes on.' I couldn't see my face as nice-looking without makeup," Aniston remembered.

Aniston often used her imagination to escape from her troubles. "From the minute she popped out, she was the queen of make-believe," her brother noted. "She was always walking her Barbies through scenes." Drama was an accepted part of her life as a girl. Both of her parents acted, and her godfather was Telly Savalas, star of the TV series "Kojak." Aniston first appeared on stage in a school play at the age of 11. But she only began to consider acting as a possible career after she saw the play *Children of a Lesser God* on Broadway. "I was sitting in the second or third row, and I was just so blown away," she recalled. "I walked out saying, 'That's what I want to do.'"

Surprisingly, Aniston's father discouraged her from becoming an actress. He stressed that acting was hard work, and said that it required commitment and patience to make it as an actor. "He gave me all the usual reasons," Aniston remembered. "'You don't want to deal with rejection.' 'It's competitive.' 'You can't always count on a steady income.' All that. And he did it in such a way that it was almost like making sure I was going to do it."

EDUCATION

Aniston completed her elementary and junior high school education at the Rudolf Steiner School in New York City. It was a progressive school where students designed their own textbooks and were discouraged from watching TV or seeing movies. Although she was a good student, Aniston often managed to get into trouble at the school. "I was always a little troublemaker. Nothing really criminal, but I'd always get reported for clowning or talking," she admitted. "I'd do things just to get both parents together in the principal's office. It was kind of like *The Parent Trap.*" She also shaved her hair above her ears and wore lots of makeup, earrings, and rubber bracelets. "I was just the ugliest thing," she recalled. "I was just a big poseur."

After graduating from the Rudolf Steiner School, Aniston was accepted into the Fiorella H. La Guardia High School for Music, Art, and the Performing Arts in New York City. Aspiring young actors, singers, and dancers from all over the city compete for a chance to go there. "That very tough four-hour audition process to get into the school told you what to expect," she remembered. "It was an amazing experience. Not only did we have to maintain normal academic levels—we also had this heavy schedule each day of drama, dance, and music. You always had to be prepared. You had to abide by the rules of the school. If you were late for class, if you were not dressed in the right clothes, if you didn't have your notebook and your rehearsal scene ready, you could be thrown out of the school. They teach you there that acting is a very serious profession, that you can't screw around. It's hard work."

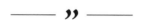

Aniston's parents divorced when she was nine. "It was awful," she recalled. "I felt so totally responsible. It's so cliche, but I really felt it was because I wasn't a good enough kid."

Aniston graduated from La Guardia High School in 1987. Rather than going on to college, she worked at a series of odd jobs in New York while trying to make it as an actress. She later admitted having some regrets about not attending college. "I missed out on that whole transitional phase in life that most people go through," she noted. She did enroll in some evening classes in psychology. "I'm trying to educate myself," she stated.

FIRST JOBS

Aniston worked part-time as a waitress while she auditioned for parts. She appeared in a couple of television commercials, then was offered a leading role in a controversial Off-Broadway play called *Dancing on Checkers Grave* in 1988. Her character was a young lesbian. Her friends warned her against taking the part because they worried she would be typecast. "But I felt the play was a wonderful opportunity," Aniston recalled. "It was important to me to prove that I could do it—that I could

The cast from the television series "Friends"

take on something so far removed from what I really was. After all that's what acting is all about—to tell stories and create characters that aren't yourself."

At the age of 20, Aniston moved to California to try her luck as an actress in Hollywood. She took part-time jobs as a telemarketer, messenger, and receptionist and attended auditions for parts in television series

29

and in the movies. During this time, she lived among other struggling young actors in the hills around Los Angeles and made lots of friends.

Aniston won roles in several TV sitcoms, including "Molloy" and "Ferris Bueller." She was usually cast as the bratty sister of the main character. She also appeared in the Fox comedy-variety series "The Edge." But none of these shows lasted more than one season. Aniston was disappointed every time a series failed to catch on with viewers. "You can't help relying on the belief that your show will become a hit, and when it doesn't, it's tough. It's not just the fact that you have to start all over again and attend auditions — it's that you miss the people. You miss the little family you've created." She made her first movie appearance in *Leprechaun,* a low-budget horror film released in 1993.

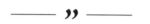

Aniston began to consider acting as a possible career after she saw the play **Children of a Lesser God** *on Broadway. "I was sitting in the second or third row, and I was just so blown away. I walked out saying, 'That's what I want to do.'"*

One day, Aniston's agent suggested that she might win more roles if she lost some weight. "My agent gave it to me straight. Nicest thing he ever did," she stated. "The disgusting thing of Hollywood — I wasn't getting lots of jobs because I was too heavy." Aniston changed from her usual diet of cheeseburgers and french fries to a healthier one. She also began exercising regularly with a trainer. As a result, she lost 30 pounds over the next year. While the weight loss did help her in auditions, she feels that the media has placed too much emphasis on it as the reason for her later success. "What bothered me about the tabloid stories was not what it said about me but that it might encourage young girls to think that they had to be that thin or they were nothing," she noted. "I don't think we should think that way. We all are valuable."

CAREER HIGHLIGHTS

"Friends"

In 1994, Aniston auditioned for a role on a new NBC sitcom called "Friends." Aniston won the part of Rachel Green, a spoiled rich girl who leaves her dentist fiancé at the altar and goes out on her own for the first time without the financial help of her parents. "It happened so fast," she recalled. "I went in, read the script, laughed out loud, got home and an hour later had the part."

The show follows the lives of six attractive people in their early 20s who live in New York City and hang out together. The other characters in "Friends" are Monica Geller (played by Courteney Cox), Rachel's uptight roommate who makes her living as a chef; Phoebe Buffay (Lisa Kudrow), a ditzy masseuse and musician; Ross Geller (David Schwimmer), a nerdy paleontologist who is both Monica's older brother and Rachel's main love interest; Chandler Bing (Matthew Perry), a smart-alecky young executive who lives across the hall from Rachel and Monica; and Joey Tribbiani (Matt LeBlanc), a dumb but loveable struggling actor and Chandler's roommate. Every week, the characters have comic adventures involving work, apartment life, the dating scene, and their evolving relationships with each other.

"Friends" debuted in 1994, and it turned out to be a big hit with viewers. In fact, just about everything connected with the show became wildly popular. Its theme song, "I'll Be There for You" by the Rembrandts, was played on radio stations across the country. Several other networks introduced "copycat" comedies about groups of young people. And thousands of young women adopted Aniston's hair style—a long, modified shag with wispy layers curving inward around the face and neck. It was known as "the Rachel." Aniston was amazed at all the attention she received for her hair. "I've hated my hair all my life," she stated. "It's always been curly and I wanted it straight. I've done all I could to have control over it, so all of a sudden, to have that happen was bizarre."

As "Friends" continued over the next few seasons, Aniston gained recognition for her acting ability and her comic timing. Her character gradually changed from a pampered princess who could barely handle a waitress job into a self-reliant young woman who holds a challenging position in the fashion industry. One of the recurring plot lines in the show involves the on-again, off-again romance between Aniston as Rachel and Schwimmer as Ross. At first, Ross admires Rachel from afar. Then, when Rachel finds out and begins to return his feelings, Ross becomes involved with another woman. They finally get together, only to break up over a misunderstanding. During the 1998 season, Ross was all set to marry someone else, but slipped and said Rachel's name instead during his wedding vows. Viewers continue to tune in to find out what will happen next.

For Aniston, appearing on "Friends" has been a great experience. She claims that the cast members are close friends in real life. "The minute

Ross and Rachel in a scene from "Friends"

we met doing the pilot, even before the show was picked up, we liked each other," she noted. "It's like an extended family. That's one of the reasons why the show is doing so well: The family is so nonexistent in our society, so your friends really do become your extended family." Aniston plans to continue working on the sitcom for several more years. "I think I would be crazy to leave. I get so much from that job. It's so fulfilling," she stated. "And we have this strong bond between us. We've had intense experiences together. We've had heartaches together. We've been through too much for it to just end before it's time. And it either goes on with all of us or none of us."

Expanding into Movies

Thanks to her successful role in "Friends," Aniston began receiving many offers to appear in movies. "I couldn't get a movie to save my life before 'Friends,'" she admitted. One of her early movie roles was as the unhappy wife of a womanizing stockbroker in *She's the One* (1996), directed by up-and-coming young filmmaker Edward Burns. "Everyone who's seen the film so far has been blown away by her performance," Burns said of Aniston. "It's nothing like her character in 'Friends.' The girl can act!"

Aniston received her first leading role in the 1997 romantic comedy *Picture Perfect.* She plays an ambitious advertising executive who is not taken seriously by her bosses because she is single. One day, she attends the wedding of a friend and has her picture taken with an attractive stranger. She then shows the picture to her co-workers and pretends that the man is her fiancé. She not only gets a promotion but also attracts the interest of the office playboy (Kevin Bacon). But the situation becomes complicated when the man from the photograph appears and wins her heart for real.

In 1998, Aniston took a more serious role in the romantic drama *Object of My Affection.* "I play this woman who falls in love with her best friend, who is gay," she explained. "She gets pregnant with her boyfriend, but she and the gay guy, played by Paul Rudd, want to raise the child together. It's very human and very compelling." In early 1999, Aniston appeared in *Office Space,* a dark comedy about work life written and directed by Mike Judge, the creator of *Beavis and Butt-head* and *King of the Hill.* Aniston plays a waitress, Joanna, in a chain theme restaurant. This satiric film really focuses on her boyfriend, Peter, a computer programmer who works in a corporate office.

Aniston receives many movie offers and plans to continue building her film career during breaks from "Friends." She has made the transition to film stardom more successfully than some of the other cast

> *The cast members on "Friends" have become close friends in real life. "The minute we met doing the pilot, even before the show was picked up, we liked each other. It's like an extended family. That's one of the reasons why the show is doing so well: The family is so nonexistent in our society, so your friends really do become your extended family."*

members of the popular TV show. Aniston believes that the phenomenal success of "Friends" created a backlash, so that some critics are eager for the stars to fail in their film projects. "Sometimes they were waiting and sharpening their knives to see who was going to fail first. I don't know why that is," she stated. "It's a sort of fascinating thing when people succeed really fast. They love you, they love you, they love you, you're great, and then they just have this really big party ripping you down. It's a very bizarre feeling because you don't know what you did wrong. You're just doing the same thing, the same job you've been doing the whole time."

Another problem of stardom for Aniston is the number of distorted or false stories that appear in the tabloids about her. "There have been some doozers," she admitted. "They said I had a cat fight with Sandra Bullock and one or the other of us had to go to the hospital. I forget which one. Then they said I was dating this masked wrestler named The Phantom and that no one knew who he was because he wore the mask. I've never met a wrestler in my life." For the most part, however, she accepts that talking to fans and signing autographs is part of her job. "It's sort of a wonderful compliment that people are so kind and generous as to approach you," she noted. "Of course you're human and there may be days when you're in a bad mood and keep the sunglasses on to avoid being recognized, but I've found people to be really nice, really gracious."

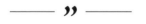

> *Aniston plans to continue working on "Friends" for several more years. "I think I would be crazy to leave. I get so much from that job. It's so fulfilling. And we have this strong bond between us. We've had intense experiences together. We've had heartaches together. We've been through too much for it to just end before it's time. And it either goes on with all of us or none of us."*

HOME AND FAMILY

Aniston has never been married. She lives alone in a three-bedroom house in the hills overlooking Hollywood. Her home features a swimming pool, a Jacuzzi, and lots of antiques. Aniston has been linked romantically with several celebrities over the years. For example, she once dated Adam Duritz, lead singer of the band Counting Crows. She also dated actor Tate Donovan for over two years, but they broke up in early 1998. Since then, she has been seeing actor Brad Pit, and their relationship is reported to be quite serious.

While Aniston claims that she would like to get married someday, she tends to be cautious in relationships and always tries to maintain her independence. "Men shouldn't be your whole life," she stated. "That's what I took from my childhood — that I will never depend on a man as much as my mom depended on my father. I have a full life, [my boyfriend] has a life of his own, and if we can merge, terrific. But a relationship isn't going to make me survive. It's the cherry on top."

Aniston remains close to her mother and to her brother, who lives in Los Angeles and is an assistant director of television commercials. She has also developed a close relationship with her father in recent years. "As best he could, my dad explained [about the divorce] and apologized, and it's enough. We've made up," she noted. "There's still parts that are hard for me, but I'm an adult. I can't blame my parents anymore."

HOBBIES AND OTHER INTERESTS

In her limited spare time, Aniston enjoys being with her dogs, hiking in the hills around Hollywood, surfing the Internet, and collecting antiques. She is an amateur artist and likes drawing, painting, and sculpting. She is also growing an herb garden in her yard.

CREDITS

Television Series

"Molloy," 1990
"Ferris Bueller," 1990-91
"The Edge," 1992-93
"Herman's Head," 1992
"Muddling Through," 1994
"Friends," 1994-

Movies

Camp Cucamonga, 1990 (TV movie)
Leprechaun, 1993
She's the One, 1996
Dream for an Insomniac, 1996 (released in 1998)
'Til There Was You, 1996
Picture Perfect, 1997
The Object of My Affection, 1998
Office Space, 1999

HONORS AND AWARDS

Screen Actors Guild Award: 1995, for Outstanding Ensemble
  Performance in a Comedy Series, for "Friends"

FURTHER READING

Books

Who's Who in America, 1999
Wild, David. *Friends: The Official Companion Book,* 1995

Periodicals

Boston Herald, July 28, 1997, p.25
Charlotte Observer, Sep. 2, 1995, p.C9
Cosmopolitan, Aug. 1997, p.172
Entertainment Weekly, Dec. 15, 1995, p.28
Mademoiselle, Apr. 1998, p.174
Newsday, July 27, 1997, p.C8
People, Dec. 25, 1995, p.92; Aug. 11, 1997, p.98; May 4, 1998, p.63; Mar. 8, 1999, p.120
Philadelphia Daily News, July 31, 1997, p.48
Redbook, Oct. 1998, p.132
Rocky Mountain News, Dec. 28, 1994, p.D12
Rolling Stone, Mar. 7, 1996, p.34; Mar. 4, 1999, p.54
Seventeen, Apr. 1998, p.122
TV Guide, July 26, 1997, p.16
USA Today, July 30, 1997, p.D2
Windsor Ontario Star, Oct. 22, 1990, p.B7

ADDRESS

"Friends"
4000 Warner Blvd.
Burbank, CA 91505

WORLD WIDE WEB SITES

http://nbc.com
http://friends.warnerbros.com

Maurice Ashley 1966-

Jamaican-American Professional Chess Player
World's First African-American Chess Grandmaster

EARLY YEARS

Maurice Ashley was born on March 6, 1966, in St. Andrew, on the Caribbean island of Jamaica. His father left home before Maurice was two years old, and he and his brother and sister were raised primarily by their mother and grandmother. The family was very poor, and he remembers that they couldn't afford shoes to wear to school. They lived in a neighborhood where, he says, "you considered yourself lucky if you didn't get shot on election day."

When his grandmother died, Maurice's mother took her three children to the United States. Maurice was 12 at the time, and they settled in the Brownsville section of Brooklyn. Chess was one of the many board games that he played with his siblings, in an apartment so small that he had to yell at his sister constantly to turn down the TV so he could concentrate on the game.

> *At the age of 14, Ashley was devastated when another player "totally destroyed" him in a chess game. "I'm a very confident and competitive person, and I tend to win most of the games that I play, so I was sure I could beat him. He crushed me. I was so stunned. I didn't have a chance from the beginning."*

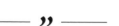

EDUCATION

When he started at Brooklyn Technical High School, Maurice was more interested in science fiction than he was in chess. But then one day when he was 14, a friend his own age challenged him to a game. Because he had always excelled at board games and was accustomed to winning, Maurice was devastated when the other boy "totally destroyed" him. "I'm a very confident and competitive person, and I tend to win most of the games that I play, so I was sure I could beat him. He crushed me. I was so stunned. I didn't have a chance from the beginning." Determined to salvage his pride, he immediately went to a local library and took out a book about chess. Filled with tactics and strategies used by chess players more than a century ago, the book changed Maurice's life. He studied it for hours and vowed that he would never let himself be humiliated in a chess game again.

Soon, though, the game began to take on a new meaning. "Maybe at the time I was thinking revenge, like I could learn some things and go beat that guy," Ashley says, "but instead, I was amazed. The whole majesty of the game, the strategies, plans, and ideas. . . . I just jumped in headfirst and fell in love." He goes on to say, "[What] actually happens on the chessboard is about one percent of the game. It goes on in the heads of the opponents, at almost a psychic level, and that's what makes it so absolutely intense. To me, it's like the golf shot that wins the Masters, or like

Michael Jordan taking the last shot to win the NBA finals. Chess has that kind of intensity from the first move."

Ashley started playing the game for three or four hours a day and reading every chess book he could find. But still, he didn't qualify for his high school chess team. So he started playing on his own in local tournaments. On weekends he would participate in "chess rumbles"—informal, nonstop competitions that would start Friday night and continue through Sunday. By the time he graduated from high school and enrolled in New York's City College, he was playing with members of the Black Bear School of Chess, a group of young African-American men who met regularly in Brooklyn's Prospect Park for chess matches. He also played for his college team, and he was team captain when his college chess club competed at the Pan-American Intercollegiate Championship in 1987. Like other chess players, Ashley accumulated points in competitions that allowed him to advance up the ranks, and during this time his ranking jumped from "expert" to "master" to "senior master" as he continued to improve his skills. Ashley had gotten a late start in chess, since most top players learned the game when they were only four or five. But by the time he graduated from City College with a degree in English, Ashley was well on his way to becoming a professional chess player.

MAJOR ACCOMPLISHMENTS

Teacher and Coach

Ashley's accomplishments caught the attention of the American Chess Foundation, which asked him to coach public school teams in the tough, crime-infested New York City neighborhoods of Harlem and the south Bronx. His passion for the game was an inspiration to his young students. Ashley was an outstanding teacher and coach, according to chess instructor Bruce Pandolfini, who participated in the program to teach chess in the schools. Pandolfini was also the real-life inspiration for the teacher in the 1993 film *Searching for Bobby Fischer*, the true story of a young boy in New York who is a chess prodigy. After seeing Ashley work with students, Pandolfini said, "It was more than just chess instruction. He practically lived with those kids. He showed them it was possible to start in the inner city and achieve greatness."

Ashley's student teams soon garnered a lot of attention from chess enthusiasts. His first team, the Raging Rooks, stunned the chess world when they won the National Junior High School Chess Championships in 1991, defeating some of the top private schools in the country. The team that

Ashley consulting with Ailinne Espinoza, 13, left, and Alexis Hernandez, 13, at New York's Mott Hall Middle School

Ashley started at Harlem's Mott Hall Middle School, the Dark Knights, also went on to win three national championships. These wins were a surprise to many. Chess, which is considered an intellectual pursuit, has historically been a predominantly white game. Ashley and his students have encountered prejudice from opponents who assumed that black people couldn't play chess because they weren't intellectually acute. But neither Ashley nor his students have let such ignorant attitudes stop them.

Ashley was excited to see kids who normally spent their time playing video games and watching MTV get hooked on chess. He knew that the game would keep them off the streets and out of trouble, especially in neighborhoods where they might otherwise fall prey to drug dealers. Teachers at the schools where he coached were very supportive, because they realized that the game was developing their students' thinking skills. "Children learn so much from chess; it's beautiful to watch. Problem-solving, goal setting, concentration, focus, patience . . . these are all the wonderful things you want kids to learn. Just getting a kid to sit and think for a little while is a miracle in some cases . . . to have them working out their ideas and focusing over long periods of time is great." Instead of presenting it as a slow-moving and largely silent game, Ashley taught his students to approach chess as a form of combat, with all the excitement and none of the danger involved in street fighting. He also taught them to play "speed chess," a fast-paced game that is popular on the streets of New York.

Ashley's success as a coach caught people's attention, and he was soon much in demand. In addition to his coaching, he created a CD-ROM chess tutorial and began flying around the world to become a play-by-play commentator for chess tournaments. But these activities, along with coaching young chess players, began to take their toll on Ashley's own game. The turning point came in a tournament in 1997, where he came in second-to-last. "My game took a nosedive. My dreams of being a grandmaster were undercut by all of the other things that I was doing. The player in me was screaming to come out . . . I decided I had to focus on one thing—playing."

Becoming a Grandmaster

In 1997 Ashley decided to stop teaching others and to devote himself entirely to competition. He started training to become a "grandmaster," the highest title in chess short of world champion. Of the 85,000 members of the U.S. Chess Federation, only 45 are grandmasters, and there are only 470 in the whole world. In order to become one, a player has to score a certain number of points in three rigorous tournaments or "norms" against top players within a seven-year period. Most of the norms are held outside the U.S. and are extremely difficult to win.

——— *"* ———

"Children learn so much from chess; it's beautiful to watch. Problem-solving, goal setting, concentration, focus, patience . . . these are all the wonderful things you want kids to learn. Just getting a kid to sit and think for a little while is a miracle in some cases . . . to have them working out their ideas and focusing over long periods of time is great."

——— *"* ———

With the support of his wife, Michele, Ashley took his young daughter, Nia, to pre-school each day and then spent six hours studying chess. He began downloading games off the Internet and playing chess once a week with a friend who was an international grandmaster. He also hired a chess trainer, who examined all of his past games and pointed out his weaknesses. According to his competitors, Ashley is an intense, cagey, aggressive opponent who never misses an opportunity on the board. "You feel that if you make the slightest mistake, you're going to get crushed," says his longtime opponent Jerald Times.

Ashley's approach to training for grandmaster was as thorough and disciplined as that of an athlete, and it paid off. Having already earned his first norm in 1993, he went on to achieve a second in 1997. Then, in March

1999, he beat Adrian Negulescu of Romania in a tournament at the Manhattan Chess Club. With that win Ashley became a grandmaster—the first African-American in history to do so. At the time, he said, "I'm numb from the neck down and giddy from the neck up."

How does he feel about being the first black grandmaster in chess history? "It is not significant to me to be the best black chess player in the world, although it is important to me to be the first," Ashley explains. He hopes that his success will open up the elite world of chess to minority players and send a strong message to young black people that they can excel not only in physical sports but in intellectual pursuits like chess. "The stereotype in this country is that African-Americans don't do well at things like chess. I know how brilliant black people are . . . and I feel like my achievement is a small drop to add to the wonderful intellectual greatness of our heritage."

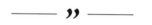

> "The stereotype in this country is that African-Americans don't do well at things like chess. I know how brilliant black people are . . . and I feel like my achievement is a small drop to add to the wonderful intellectual greatness of our heritage."

The Next U.S. Champion?

Ashley is currently involved in establishing a state-of-the-art chess center in Harlem where kids will be able to play against each other, study the game in a chess library, or play online with competitors around the world. But having achieved grandmaster status, he also dreams of being the first African-American to compete in the U.S. Chess Championships. He doesn't qualify right now, but he hopes to within the next couple of years.

In the meantime, Ashley is busy teaching his five-year-old daughter, Nia, to play chess. He wants to make sure that she doesn't go through what he went through at the age of 14. "When she goes to school," he says, "there won't be anyone who will crush her in a game of chess."

FURTHER READING

Chess Life, May 1999
Ebony, July 1999, p.30
New York Times, Mar. 17, 1999, p.B4

Newsday, May 11, 1999, p.B3
Sports Illustrated, May 30, 1994, p.9
USA Weekend, June 25-27, 1999, p.6

ADDRESS

U.S. Chess Federation
Publicity
3054 NYS Rte. 9, W.
New Windsor, NY 12553

WORLD WIDE WEB SITE

http://www.uschess.org

Kobe Bryant 1978-
American Professional Basketball Player
Star Forward for the Los Angeles Lakers

BIRTH

Kobe Bryant was born August 23, 1978, in Philadelphia,
Pennsylvania. He is the third child of Joe and Pam Bryant.
He has two sisters—Shaya, who is one year older, and
Sharia, who is two years older. Joe Bryant, whose nickname
was "Jelly Bean," was a former player in the National
Basketball Association (NBA). He was a flamboyant player
in the early 1970s, during the disco era in the United States.
He liked to wear outrageously colorful clothes off the court,

and on the court his undisciplined play sometimes got him into trouble. "His lack of attention to detail prevented him from having a better NBA career," recalls Los Angeles Lakers general manager Jerry West. "Joe didn't want to play, he wanted to style." But West notes that when it came to parenting, Jelly Bean was extremely focused. "Judge him as a parent," says West. "Anyone who has been around Kobe, and has seen the obvious closeness and love they have not only for him, but also his two older sisters, knows that Joe and Pam have been extraordinary parents."

YOUTH

Growing Up in Italy

Even as a youngster, Kobe Bryant's life was shaped by basketball. When he was five years old, his father left the NBA and moved the family to Italy, where he played in an Italian professional league. At first, living outside of the United States was not easy on Kobe or his sisters. "It was difficult at first because I couldn't speak Italian," he remembers. "So my two sisters and I got together after school to teach each other the words we had learned. I was able to speak Italian pretty well within a few months."

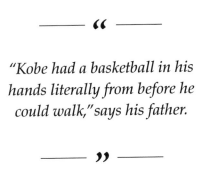

"Kobe had a basketball in his hands literally from before he could walk," says his father.

Over the next eight years, Kobe's father played on four different teams in Italy, which meant that the Bryant family had to move to a new city every few years. But while the family did not like moving so often, they enjoyed many other aspects of their life in Italy. For example, professional basketball teams in Italy play only once or twice a week, so Joe Bryant had lots of time to take his family to explore the countryside and the historic regions of Italy. "We all grew together there as a family," he says. "In Italy, you'd see whole families living in one big villa. That's what our kids saw. We would go have a meal and end up sitting at the table, eating and talking for three or four hours."

Whenever his family moved to a new neighborhood, Kobe would immediately seek out the nearest basketball hoop. "Kobe had a basketball in his hands literally from before he could walk," says his father, who encouraged his son's interest in the sport. Once he found a basketball court, young Kobe spent nearly all of his free time there. He was not always able to play for very long, however. The court was usually also a gathering spot for kids who played soccer, which is a far more popular sport than basketball in Italy. This meant that Kobe often had to practice alone and had to fight for court time. "After school, I would be the only guy on the basketball court, working on my moves," he recalls, "and then the kids would start showing up with their soccer ball. I could hold them off if there were two or three of them, but when they got to be 11 or 12, I had to give up the court. It was either go home or be the goal-keeper."

Joe Bryant made a point of taking his son to his team's practices whenever he could. There, Kobe would shoot baskets by himself off in a coner. As he grew older, however, he began to challenge his father's teammates to play one-on-one. "I used to set them up," Kobe remembers. "I'd say, 'Come on, you're playing a little kid.' Then it would come to game point, and they'd start getting serious, and I knew I had them. My father would be on the sideline talking trash: 'You're gonna let a little 10-year-old bust you up?'"

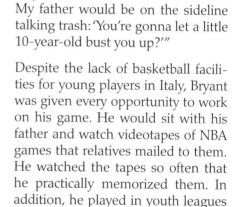

Gregg Downer, who was Bryant's coach in high school, remembers the first time he saw him on the basketball court:
"He was an eighth grader at Bala Cynwyd Junior High. I had heard about him, so I went to a practice. I watched him play for five minutes and I said to my assistant coach, 'This kid's a pro. He's going to be a pro.'"

Despite the lack of basketball facilities for young players in Italy, Bryant was given every opportunity to work on his game. He would sit with his father and watch videotapes of NBA games that relatives mailed to them. He watched the tapes so often that he practically memorized them. In addition, he played in youth leagues whenever he could. "In Italy, he played on club teams where he was given very good fundamentals," Joe recalls. "And he always had that dream. I didn't give it to him, and Pam didn't either. He just had it. He wanted to play at the highest level and more importantly, he was willing to put in the work."

Returning to the United States

When the Bryant family returned to the States in 1991, Joe and Pam and the kids resettled in Lower Merion, Pennsylvania, a wealthy suburb of Philadelphia. Joe took a job as an assistant varsity coach at a private school and also worked as a personal trainer. Kobe, meanwhile, decided that he wanted to see how the basketball skills that he had developed in Italy stacked up in the more competitive basketball environment of the United States. He played whenever he could, seeking out pick-up games and organized leagues alike. Within a matter of weeks, everyone in the area was talking about him. Gregg Downer, who was head basketball coach at Lower Merion High School, remembers the first time he saw Bryant on the basketball court: "He was an eighth grader at Bala Cynwyd Junior High. I had heard about him, so I went to a practice. I watched him play for five minutes and I said to my assistant coach, 'This kid's a pro. He's going to be a pro.'"

Downer worked hard to help Bryant develop various aspects of his game, and during the summer months he spent a great deal of time playing one-on-one against Bryant. After a while, though, the coach refused to play Bryant anymore. "I had to," he recalls. "I couldn't beat a 13-year-old."

As he grew older and stronger, Bryant was finally able to beat his father in one-on-one, too. But he remembers that the first victory was hard to come by. "I didn't beat him one-on-one until I was 16," says Bryant. "He was real physical with me. When I was 14 or 15 he started cheating. He elbows me in the mouth, rips my lip open. Then my mother would walk out on the court, and the elbows would stop."

EDUCATION

After the family returned from Italy to the United States in 1991, Kobe attended Bala Cynwyd Junior High School. In 1993 he moved on to Lower Merion High School, where he quickly emerged as the finest basketball player in the history of the school. But Bryant was not content to just play high school basketball. He also played in the Sonny Hill summer league, one of the best amateur leagues in the country.

By the time Bryant was 16 years old, he was so good that the head coach of the NBA's Philadelphia 76ers invited Bryant to play at his team practices. Bryant immediately accepted the offer, and proceeded to show that he was already capable of holding his own against NBA competition. In fact, rumors began to circulate that he sometimes dominated the action on the 76ers' practice court. "The buzz I heard," says former 76ers' coach Fred Carter, "was that Kobe was kicking so much butt in there that some days they had to get him out of the game. He was demoralizing guys."

From High School to the Pros

In 1996, Bryant's senior season, he led Lower Merion High to the state's Class AAAA title. He averaged almost 31 points a game during the season, and he was so dominant that he was named High School Player of the Year by both *USA Today* and *Parade* magazine. But despite Bryant's spectacular performances during his senior year, he caught everyone off guard when he announced that he was going to skip college and declare himself eligible for the NBA draft right after he graduated from high school in 1996.

This decision shocked many people, especially since Bryant's size (he is 6 feet, 7 inches tall and 210 pounds) is not that big for an NBA player. Members of the media claimed that his decision sent a bad message to younger players. Many of them argued that he was not ready for the high-pressure game of the NBA or the glitzy lifestyle associated with the league. They worried that he was too immature to handle the temptations that had ruined the careers of other young players. Journalists were not the only ones who felt this way. Most basketball fans thought he was making a mistake, too. They said that he was just too young to play in the top league in the world.

Some reporters wondered whether Kobe's father or his friends had pressured him to jump to the NBA. Coach Downer, however, insists that Bryant decided for himself after playing so well in the scrimmages against the 76ers. Bryant confirms that the decision was entirely his own. "I wanted to play against the best basketball players in the world," he said, noting that players like Michael Jordan, Charles Barkley, and Hakeem Olajuwon were nearing the end of their careers. "I wanted to get my crack playing against those guys before they were gone."

CAREER HIGHLIGHTS

Despite his youth, Bryant was selected 13th overall by the Charlotte Hornets in the first round of the 1996 NBA draft. He did not stay with the Hornets for very long, though. Even before his rookie season began, he came under attack from critics when he made it clear that he wanted to be traded to one of the NBA's high-profile teams, preferably the Los Angeles Lakers. He tried to handle the criticism as best he could. "My parents taught me that there would be criticisms out there all the time by many people, but you just got to do what you think is right." As a result of Bryant's demands, the Hornets did end up trading him to the Los Angeles Lakers (in exchange for Vlade Divac) before the start of the 1996-1997 season. Soon after the trade, the 18-year-old star

signed a three-year, $6.5 million contract. With such star players as the phenomenal Shaquille O'Neal, playing for the Lakers was a dream come true for Kobe, who as a baby had worn a Lakers jacket. It was also just what the Lakers wanted, since the team needed a shooting guard like Bryant.

As Bryant prepared for his rookie year, he also remained in the public eye. He took pop singing star Brandy to his high school prom, and he purchased a six-bedroom, six-bath ocean-view home in Pacific Palisades, California. He also joined the Screen Actors Guild, thought about getting into rap music, and became a teen idol.

Michael Jordan recalls this exchange with Bryant after the 1998 All-Star game. "I just hugged him and told him to keep going and stay strong because there are always expectations and pressures," said the Chicago Bulls star. "I know what too much pressure too soon can do to you and just wanted him to be aware. But he's a smart kid with bright future. He'll figure it out."

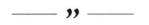

But Bryant made sure that he kept his sudden fame and wealth in perspective. His family joined him in his Pacific Palisades home, and they provided him with a positive atmosphere in which to adjust to his new life. "When Kobe came onto the team, we said, 'Oh my gosh, what are we going to have to do extra for this kid?'" Jerry West remembers. "'How are we going to watch over him?' But we haven't had to do anything. He's mature beyond his years, and he has his own clan with their own enclave."

Ups and Downs in the Pros

Out on the basketball court, though, Bryant struggled at times during his rookie season. He did not get a lot of playing time—in part because the Lakers had two other talented rookies (Derek Fisher and Travis Knight) and in part because star center Shaquille O'Neal was hurt for a large part of the season, which forced coach Del Harris to use his veteran players more so the Lakers had a better chance to win. Still, Bryant managed to average 7.6 points per game, even though he was the second youngest player ever to play in the NBA. In addition, he won the league's slam dunk competition during the season's All-Star game weekend with a variety of high-flying dunks that caught the attention of fans and players alike.

Nonetheless, Coach Harris says the transition to the pro game was a tough one for Bryant. "Kobe was a man among boys [in high school], but the game that he had in high school doesn't apply here. . . . All of a sudden, Kobe has to either continue and see if his stuff works or back off and adapt to the flow of a five-man game. He started out playing the only way he knew how. Well, it didn't work, and players didn't like playing with him. Then he gradually improved and got some playing time. He had some games where he was outstanding—but not against the top teams. He is extremely confident, and yet, it's been a real hard adjustment for him."

The Lakers made the playoffs at the end of Bryant's rookie season, and the prospect of competing in the postseason excited the young forward. But as it turned out, the 1996 playoffs ended in nightmarish fashion for Kobe. In a decisive playoff game against the Utah Jazz, Bryant put up three straight air balls at the end of the game, the last one coming as time ran out with the game tied. Once the game went to overtime, the Jazz won easily, ending the Lakers' season. Bryant was very disappointed with his poor play, but he later said that the loss might have been a blessing in disguise. "I know it sounds strange, but the way the season ended was exactly what I needed to get ready [for the next season]," he says. "It ended with me having to take a long look at my game and what I needed to improve it."

A Fan Favorite

Despite his limited playing time, Bryant was already a fan favorite around the league. Even though he was very young, his talent was unmistakable, and some people said that he was going to be "the next Michael Jordan." Such comparisons put tremendous pressure on Bryant, but instead of fighting the comparisons, he seemed to welcome them. In fact, he freely admits that he has tried to pattern his playing style after Jordan, who is recognized as the best player in NBA history. Bryant even copied the shot that Jordan is most famous for—the "fade-away" jump shot, in which he actually drifts back from the basket after he releases his shot. "It's a perfect move for me to have in my arsenal," Bryant says. "[Jordan and I are] the same body type, so we present some of the same problems for somebody trying to guard us."

On the shot, Bryant begins with his back to the basket. He then fakes either right or left, trying to make his defender guess wrong. After the fake, he spins to face the basket, jumps backwards, and shoots the ball, all in one fluid motion. He has been using the shot ever since he was a young player. Washington Wizards player God Shammgod remembers

*Bryant, bottom, battles for a rebound against
Greg Ostertag, left, and Chris Morris, right, from the Utah Jazz*

seeing Bryant use the move when they played together at a summer basketball camp. "He had a lot of confidence then, already. I used to tease him and say, 'Oh, Michael Jordan,' because he used to try to do everything like Mike."

Bryant's popularity also can be traced to his clean-cut appearance and his good manners. Unlike many other NBA players, he does not have tattoos or wear an earring. "I don't want any holes in my ears," he laughs. "No offense against anybody else, but it's not for me." Reporters, fans, and teammates, meanwhile, say that the young star is always polite, always signs autographs, answers media requests, and gets involved in charitable activities.

A Memorable All-Star Game Debut

In his second season with the Lakers (1997-98), Bryant improved his game. He still did not start for the Lakers, who were loaded with talent, but he became the team's "sixth man," the first substitute off the bench, who is expected to come in and provide an offensive and defensive spark. Fans seemed to recognize his raw talent and charisma and voted him in as a starter in the NBA All-Star game in February.

At age 19, Bryant was the youngest player in All-Star history. He rewarded the fans for their support with a dazzling effort. He finished the game with a team-high 18 points in 22 minutes on 7-16 shooting, with six rebounds and one assist. Some thought the older All-Stars would give Bryant the cold shoulder because he was so cocky and because he took so many shots, but most seemed to like him for three reasons: he backed up his talk with excellent play; he made it clear he respected the star players who came before him, and he showed a genuine love for the game. Coach George Karl said that Bryant earned respect because he "listened and learned."

After the game, Bryant even got to spend a special moment with his idol, Michael Jordan. "I just hugged him and told him to keep going and stay strong because there are always expectations and pressures," said the Chicago Bulls star. "I know what too much pressure too soon can do to you and just wanted him to be aware. But he's a smart kid with a bright future. He'll figure it out."

NBA Lockout

At the end of the 1997-98 season, Bryant said that he was prepared to take his game to the next level, but his career was put on hold when the NBA owners and players failed to agree on a new labor contract. This disagreement delayed the start of the 1998-99 season for months.

When the NBA season finally opened, Bryant found himself on the starting roster of a team that is off to its best start in years, with new coach Kurt Rambis, and the addition of superstar Glen Rice. Bryant also announced in January 1999 that he had signed a six-year extension with the Lakers, which is rumored to be worth over $70 million. The extension starts with the 1999-2000 season and will run through the 2004-05 season.

Bryant continues to be one of the most admired young players in the league. Other NBA players praise the young Laker as a budding superstar. "He amazes me," says Nick Van Exel. "I see him every day, and he still amazes me." Veteran forward Robert Horry, meanwhile, says that "Pretty soon, other players will have to fit in around him. Kobe is going to be the best player ever. . . . Kobe's got Michael's skills and Michael's will. But Kobe came into the league when he was 18, and he's going to be able to accomplish more."

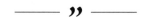

Bryant's family continues to be an important part of his life, according to his father. "We've been blessed. He's still a kid and a good kid. At home, we will play and wrestle on the floor. We all climb on the same bed, watch a movie, and eat popcorn. It sounds corny, but that's what we do."

Bryant recognizes that many challenges still await him in his NBA career. But he likes the idea of trying to live up to the high expectations that fans and players have for him. "Why would you even play if you didn't want to be the best player who ever lived?" he asks. "That's how I would think everyone would go into it. You want to be the man, you know, not the best of the moment, but the best who ever set foot on a basketball court."

HOME AND FAMILY

Bryant lives in Pacific Palisades, California, with his parents and sisters. He recognizes that he is young and that his parents are still an important part of his life. "If he goes somewhere [after a game], he calls and tells us where he is," says his father. "We've been blessed. He's still a kid and a good kid. At home, we will play and wrestle on the floor. We all climb on the same bed, watch a movie, and eat popcorn. It sounds corny, but that's what we do."

HOBBIES AND OTHER INTERESTS

Bryant loves to play video games, and one of his main opponents is Shaquille O'Neal. "Shaq is like my older brother," he says. "He makes my life easier. We have a great time." Bryant even has a video game named after him—"Kobe Bryant's NBA Courtside." Indeed, Bryant has become a popular figure in the world of celebrity advertising. In early 1998, he signed large endorsement contracts with Spalding Sports Worldwide and Adidas America. "Kobe basically embodies what the NBA is about right now: youth, excitement, charisma, and charm," says Spalding executive Dan Touhey.

HONORS AND AWARDS

High School Player of the Year (*USA Today*): 1996
Naismith High School Player of the Year: 1996
High School Player of the Year (*Parade*): 1996

Second Team All-Rookie Team: 1997
NBA Slam-Dunk Champion: 1997
NBA All-Star Team: 1998

FURTHER READING

Books

Egan, Erin. *SI for Kids Extra: It's Showtime, With Kobe Bryant,* 1998 (juvenile)
Layden, Joe. *Kobe: The Story of the NBA's Rising Young Star Kobe Bryant,* 1998
Schnakenberg, Robert. *Kobe Bryant,* 1998 (juvenile)

Periodicals

Advertising Age, Mar. 16, 1998, p.12
Los Angeles Magazine, May 1997, p.64; Jan. 1999, p.66
Los Angeles Times, Feb. 5, 1999, p.D1
Newsweek, Mar. 16, 1998, p.58
People, Sep. 21, 1998, p.11
Philadelphia Inquirer Magazine, Mar. 1, 1998, p.8
Sport, Mar. 1998, p.54
Sporting News, Dec. 8, 1997, p.66; Mar. 30, 1998, p.63
Sports Illustrated, Feb. 16, 1998, p.96; Apr. 27, 1998, p.42; Jan. 25, 1999, p.70
Sports Illustrated for Kids, Oct. 1997, p.28

ADDRESS

Los Angeles Lakers
Great Western Forum
3900 W. Manchester Blvd.
Inglewood, CA 90306

WORLD WIDE WEB SITES

www.nba.com/lakers
http://sports.latimes.com

OBITUARY

Sadie Delany 1889-1999 (above right)
American Teacher and Author

Bessie Delany 1891-1995 (above left)
American Dentist and Author

BIRTH

American society recently marked the passing of two remark-able women, Sarah Louise Delany, known as Sadie, and Annie Elizabeth Delany, known as Bessie. Each lived over 100 years, through a tumultuous time for African-Americans: from the post-slavery era in the South, to the days of the Harlem Renaissance in the 1920s in New York, through the Civil Rights Movement of the 1950s and 1960s, right up to the 1990s.

Sadie, the elder of the two sisters, was born on September 19, 1889, in Lynch's Station, Virginia, while her younger sister, Bessie, was born on September 3, 1891, in Raleigh, North Carolina. Their parents were Henry Beard Delany, the first black Episcopal bishop and the vice-principal of Saint Augustine's School in Raleigh, and Nanny James (Logan) Delany,

who was the matron at Saint Augustine's, making sure everything ran smoothly there. Sadie and Bessie were the second and third of their 10 children; their siblings were Lemuel, Julia, Henry (Harry or Hap), Lucius, William (Manross), Hubert, Laura, and Samuel.

The Delany sisters were intelligent, accomplished women who led fascinating lives, and they told their story in several books co-authored by journalist Amy Hill Hearth. Their most notable book was *Having Our Say: The Delany Sisters' First 100 Years*, a personal family history that the sisters told to Hearth, who recorded and organized their recollections. According to Jean-Claude Baker in the *New York Times Book Review*, "The Delany sisters tell more in these 210 pages than just their family's courageous history. They were witnesses

"Those were hard times, after slavery days," Sadie and Bessie wrote about their father's early years. *"Much of the South was scarred by the Civil War and there wasn't much food or supplies among the whites, let alone the Negroes. Most of the slaves, when they were freed, wandered about the countryside like shell-shocked soldiers."*

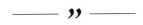

to no less than the struggle for this country's soul. Indeed, they were part of it, and their recollection of the journey, with all its humiliations and triumphs, is told simply, powerfully, humorously, and generously." It's also told in language that is sometimes surprising to modern readers. In talking about African-Americans, themselves and others, the Delanys use terms that are considered out-of-date and even offensive today. But the Delany sisters lived to be over 100 years old, and nobody expected them to change their terminology to please others. And their book is called *Having Our Say*, so most reviewers have felt that it was important to let these women do exactly that.

——— **"** ———

"Growing up in that atmosphere [at Saint Augustine's], among 300 or so college students, reading and writing and thinking were as natural for us as sleeping and eating. We had a blessed childhood, which was unusual in those days for colored children. It was the rare child who got such schooling!"

——— **"** ———

SOME FAMILY HISTORY

Family was central to the Delany sisters, and their family history, in particular, offers a fascinating look into America's past. Their father, Henry Beard Delany, was born a slave in 1858 in St. Mary's, Georgia. A mix of black, white, and Native American racial backgrounds, he was a house slave for the Mock family, who taught him to read and write. "They broke the law, teaching Papa to read and write," Sadie once said. "Papa always said those folks were as good as any people you could find anywhere. I know that sounds strange to feel that way about the folks that owned him."

Henry Beard Delany was only seven when the slaves were freed in 1865. "Those were hard times, after slavery days," Sadie and Bessie wrote. "Much of the South was scarred by the Civil War and there wasn't much food or supplies among the whites, let alone the Negroes. Most of the slaves, when they were freed, wandered about the countryside like shell-shocked soldiers." Henry's family fared a little better than that. They survived by eating fish and wild plants, and soon they were able to build a small cabin. "They were smart, but they were lucky, and they knew it. They could read and write, and they hadn't been abused, and their family was still together. That's a lot more than most former slaves had going for them." When he grew up, a white Episcopal priest encouraged him to enroll at Saint Augustine's, a college for African-Americans in Raleigh, North Carolina. Delany jumped at the opportunity. There, he excelled in his studies. He graduated as salutatorian of his class—second to the woman he would soon marry, Nanny James Logan.

Nanny James Logan was born free in Virginia in 1861. According to Sadie, "Mama was an issue-free Negro, born free but legally colored. Her mama was free, so she was born free." Nanny Logan's mother, Martha Logan, was black, but her father, James Miliam, was white. They lived in Virginia, where at that time it was illegal for blacks and whites to get married—in fact, interracial marriage was illegal in Virginia until 1967. Although they couldn't marry, Martha and James lived for years in two houses side by side with a walkway in between. That could have been dangerous, for in many situations a black woman might have been beaten by white townspeople for such behavior. But James Miliam was a big and tough man who was devoted to Martha, so nobody messed with her or their children.

Their daughter, Nanny Logan, was one-eighth black; there were other white ancestors in her background as well. Yet in the eyes of society and the law she was considered black. She was light-skinned enough to pass for white, but she was too proud of her heritage to hide it. A good student determined to get an education, she decided to attend Saint Augustine's School in North Carolina. But her mother, Martha, said she couldn't go alone. So Martha went too, splitting her time between her daughter in North Carolina and James Miliam in Virginia. Her mother's presence must have helped, because Nanny Logan graduated as the valedictorian, the top student in her class. Soon after graduation, she and Henry Beard Delany were married at the campus chapel, and they remained there at the school to work and raise their family. Proud, religious, and hardworking, Henry and Nanny Delany stressed to their children "self-improvement through education, civic-mindedness, and ethical living, along with a strong belief in God."

YOUTH

Growing up, Sadie and Bessie Delany lived in a cottage on the grounds of Saint Augustine's School, which was founded as a seminary and a teachers' college for black students. It was in many ways a privileged upbringing for African-Americans at that time. "Growing up in that atmosphere, among 300 or so college students, reading and writing and thinking were as natural for us as sleeping and eating. We had a blessed childhood, which was unusual in those days for colored children. It was the rare child who got such schooling!" Sadie and Bessie attended classes right on campus that were taught by teachers-in-training. Their school included neighborhood children as well as grown men and women who

Sadie and Bessie were always chaperoned when they left the school campus. "That's because things hadn't improved much since slavery days as far as the right of colored women and girls to be unmolested. If something bad had been done to us, and our Papa had complained, they'd have hung him. That's the way it was."

wanted to learn to read and write. Despite their relative comfort, the family never had any money. They wore hand-me-down clothes and carried water in from a well, since for years their home had no plumbing. Each night, their mother would fill a washtub 10 times so each of the children could have a bath with fresh water. But they always had a roof over their heads, enough food to eat, and enough to share with neighbors who needed help. Just 30 years after the end of the Civil War, many former slaves had barely enough to stay alive. In the Delany family, as their parents often reminded them, their motto was "Your job is to help someone."

Although Sadie and Bessie were sheltered, racism was a fact of life when they were growing up. The girls were always chaperoned when they left the campus, and sometimes even there, too. All young girls were chaperoned then, for their personal protection and safety. "That's because things hadn't improved much since slavery days as far as the right of colored women and girls to be unmolested. If something bad had been done to us, and our Papa had complained, they'd have hung *him*. That's the way it was."

Sadie's graduation photograph, Columbia University, 1920. She later earned a master's degree in education at Columbia in 1925.

"Jim Crow" Laws

But things got worse for the Delanys and other African-Americans in the late 1890s, as the result of a Supreme Court case called *Plessy* v. *Ferguson*. This important 1896 decision said that racial segregation was legal according to the Constitution. It paved the way for a series of "Jim Crow" laws, which formed the basis of widespread segregation in the South for over 50 years. (The name "Jim Crow" originally came from an African-American character in a popular song.) *Plessy* v. *Ferguson* established the policy of "separate but equal" public facilities—housing, transportation, schools, restaurants, bathrooms, drinking fountains, and more —for blacks and whites.

Although these separate facilities were called equal, in reality those for blacks were miserably inadequate. In effect, *Plessy v. Ferguson* legalized the way black people were already treated. "We knew we were already second-class citizens," Sadie once said, "but those Jim Crow laws set it in stone."

Even 100 years later, the Delany sisters remembered what life was like for African-Americans before and after Jim Crow. Sadie and Bessie were about seven and five years old when Jim Crow laws started to take effect in North Carolina. Their first experiences had a deep effect on them. One Sunday their family took the trolley to the park, and they went to sit up front in their usual seat so the breezes would blow through their hair. The trolley driver made them sit at the back, but the girls didn't understand why. At the park, they went to take a drink from a freshwater spring and found a

Bessie's yearbook photograph, Columbia University, 1923. Upon earning a Doctor of Dental Surgery degree, she became the second black woman licensed to practise dentistry in New York.

big wooden sign across the middle, with "white" on one side and "colored" on the other. When no one was looking, Bessie took a drink from the white side, but of course the water was just the same. Soon after that, one of their teachers took them to the drugstore for a limeade, a trip that they had made many times before. But this time, the man behind the counter said, "I can't wait on you."

Dealing with Prejudice

Those were just the first of many difficulties Sadie and Bessie would face because of race. The two sisters had very different ways of dealing with prejudice and other obstacles in life. They used to say that "Sweet Sadie" was the molasses and "Queen Bess" was the vinegar. Sadie could always find a way to get what she wanted without conflict, as she recalled here. "I'll tell you how I handled white people. There was a shoe store in

Raleigh called Heller's. The owner was a nice Jewish man, very nice. If you were colored, you had to go in the back to try on shoes, and the white people sat in the front. It wasn't Mr. Heller's fault; this was the Jim Crow law. I would go in there and say, 'Good morning, Mr. Heller. I would like to try on those shoes in the window.' And he would say, 'That's fine, Miss Delany, go on and sit in the back.' And I would say, 'Where, Mr. Heller?' And he would gesture to the back and say, 'Back there.' And I would say, 'Back *where?*' Well, I'd just worry that man to death. Finally, he'd say, 'Just sit anywhere, Miss Delany!' And so I would sit myself down in the white section, and smile."

Bessie had a more confrontational approach. In fact, one time she was almost lynched. She was waiting to change trains in Georgia, sitting in the station's colored waiting room. She had taken her hair down and was combing it out when a white man opened the door to the colored waiting room. "The white man stuck his head in and started, well, leering at me," Bessie later recalled. "He was drunk, and he smelled bad, and he started mumbling things. And I said, 'Oh, why don't you shut up and go wait with your own kind in the white waiting room?' What happened next was kind of like an explosion. He slammed the door and I could hear him shouting at the top of his lungs outside, 'The nigger bitch insulted me! The nigger bitch insulted me!'"

Bessie stayed where she was in the waiting room. But she could see a big crowd of white people gathering on the train platform, and she was sure that she was about to be lynched. Luckily, the train came around the bend just then, breaking up the crowd and giving Bessie a way out. "You know what Sadie says? Sadie says I was a fool to provoke that white man. As if I provoked *him!* Honey, he provoked *me!* Sadie says she would have *ignored* him. I say, how do you ignore some drunk, smelly, white man treating you like trash? She says,

>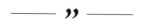
>
> *Bessie was almost lynched for the way she spoke to a white man. "You know what Sadie says? Sadie says I was a fool to provoke that white man. As if I provoked him! Honey, he provoked me! Sadie says she would have ignored him. I say, how do you ignore some drunk, smelly, white man treating you like trash? She says, child, it's better to put up with it, and live to tell about it. . . . She says I am lucky to be alive. But I would rather die than back down, honey."*

child, it's better to put up with it, and live to tell about it. . . . She says I am lucky to be alive. But I would rather die than back down, honey."

EDUCATION AND FIRST JOBS

Sadie completed her schooling at Saint Augustine's in 1910, and her sister Bessie finished up the following year. As each graduated, their father would give them the same lecture: "Daughter, you are college material. You owe it to your nation, your race, and yourself to go. And if you don't, then shame on you!" He also told them that he couldn't afford to pay for their schooling. But they shouldn't accept a scholarship, he said, because then they would be in someone else's debt. Instead, he told them to work and save up the money for school.

So in 1910, Sadie got a job working for the local schools as the Jeanes Supervisor for Wake County, North Carolina. The position was named after a white man named Jeanes who had started a fund to bring domestic science (home economics) lessons to black schools around the South. Sadie lived at home but traveled all over the area by train and by horse and buggy. She visited schools for blacks and taught classes in subjects like cooking, cleaning, sanitation, hygiene, nutrition, and taking care of children. Because she often stayed overnight in people's homes, she had a first-hand look at some of the desperate conditions in which people lived. "I know that I helped many people as Jeanes Supervisor, and I am very proud of that. I inspired many people to get an education, and quite a few went on to Saint Aug's," Sadie recalled. "They looked up to me, and I showed them it was possible to live a better life, despite what white people were trying to do to us." While Jeanes Supervisor she met Booker T. Washington, an influential black leader and educator who founded the Tuskegee Institute in Alabama. When Washington came to Raleigh, Sadie would drive him around in her brother Lemuel's car, showing him the local schools. Sadie continued as Jeanes Supervisor until 1916.

Meanwhile, in 1911 Bessie finished school, got the lecture from her father, and found a job to save money for college. Unlike Sadie, though, she left home and went to teach at a one-room school in Boardman, North Carolina. That was a tiny little town that had never seen someone like Bessie Delany, a young, pretty, educated, and self-confident black woman. "I remember walking through that town and the colored men would just stop and stare. They wouldn't say a word, they'd just take off their hats when I walked by. One time, I passed by several men and I turned and said, *'Just what are you looking at?'* They didn't answer. Finally, one of them said, 'Why, Miss Delany, we can't help it; you look just like a slice of Heaven.'

And I said, 'Well, I ain't *your* slice of Heaven, so put your eyes back in yo' *head.*' Honey, I meant business." After two years in Boardman, she was ready for a change to a bigger town. So in 1913 she took a new position in Brunswick, Georgia, at Saint Athanasius School, an Episcopal school for blacks. It was on her way to that job in Brunswick, in fact, that Bessie was almost lynched.

Moving to New York City

After several years both Sadie and Bessie had saved up enough money to attend college in New York City. Sadie moved there in 1916, and Bessie followed her about a year and a half later. They started out living in a boarding house. But several of their siblings moved to New York also, so soon they were all living together in an apartment. Eventually they were surrounded by family. While their oldest brother Lemuel, then a doctor, stayed in Raleigh, the other siblings all moved to Harlem, where the Delanys became a well-known and respected family. Sadie and Bessie were both young, smart, talented, and good-looking, and they had plenty of suitors. But both of them had already decided that they didn't want to get married. At that time, marriage would have meant sacrificing their careers, which they had no intention of doing.

Sadie started college at a two-year program at Pratt Institute in Brooklyn, then transferred to the Teachers College at Columbia University. She completed her bachelor's degree at Columbia in 1920. She then began teaching at Public School 119, an elementary school in Harlem. To earn extra money, she made sweets at home—cakes and lollipops—and sold them at school for a profit. After a while she even rented a loft in Harlem, called her business Delany's Delights, and started selling hand-dipped chocolates in stores all over the city. Sadie stayed in the candy business for several years, but she also continued her education, and in 1925 she earned her master's degree in education from Columbia University. Moving to the North hadn't changed anything about Sadie's approach to problems, according to one of her teachers. "That Sarah Delany. You tell her to do something, she smiles at you, and then she just turns around and does what she wants anyway."

Bessie also attended Columbia University. In 1919 she entered its School of Dental and Oral Surgery, becoming one of only seven blacks in the class, and the only female. She encountered her share of prejudice there. For example, after she received a failing grade on an assignment, she and a white student decided to see if the teacher was fair. The white friend re-

Equipment, furniture, and a sign from the dental practice of Dr. Bessie Delany.

submitted the assignment and earned a higher grade. When she graduated, Bessie was proud to be chosen to carry the flag at the commencement ceremony, until she discovered that she'd been given the honor only because no white student wanted to march next to her. Despite these obstacles Bessie graduated in 1923, becoming only the second black woman in history licensed to practice dentistry in New York.

CAREER HIGHLIGHTS

Sadie's Career

After finishing her master's degree, Sadie continued teaching in New York. But she wanted to move up to high school, which was considered a promotion and which paid better. At that time, she recalled, "High schools would boast that they did not have Negro teachers." Principals often refused to hire anyone with a Southern accent, which they claimed was bad for the children. "Of course, many black teachers had Southern accents, so it was just a way of keeping us out."

But Sadie found a way around those roadblocks. First, she took speech lessons to minimize her Southern accent. She also put her name on the waiting list for a high school position. When her name reached the top of the list, she received a letter asking her to come in for a meeting. But she knew that if she went to that meeting, they would see that she was black and would contrive an excuse for denying her the position. So instead, she said, "I skipped the appointment and sent them a letter, acting like there was a mix-up. Then I just showed up on the first day of classes. . . . Child, when I showed up that day—at Theodore Roosevelt High School, a white high school—they just about died when they saw me. A colored woman! But my name was on the list to teach there, and it was too late for them to send me someplace else. The plan had worked! Once I was in, they couldn't figure out how to get rid of me." That's how Sadie became the first black in New York to teach domestic science on the high school level.

> Sadie became the first black teacher in New York to teach high school domestic science by tricking the school offices. "I skipped the appointment and sent them a letter, acting like there was a mix-up. Then I just showed up on the first day of classes. . . . Child, when I showed up that day — at Theodore Roosevelt High School, a white high school — they just about died when they saw me. A colored woman! But my name was on the list to teach there, and it was too late for them to send me someplace else. The plan had worked! Once I was in, they couldn't figure out how to get rid of me."

Over the years Sadie taught at several schools in New York City, including Girls' High School in Brooklyn and Evander Childs High School in the Bronx. At Washington Irving High School in Manhattan, she taught night classes for adults who had dropped out of school. Often the only black teacher, Sadie was frequently lonely. Some of the white teachers acted friendly at school, but she didn't feel she could count on them to be real friends. Despite this sense of isolation, Sadie taught in the New York schools for about 40 years.

Bessie's Career

Bessie began her professional career as a dentist in 1923. She shared an office in Harlem with her brother, Hap, who was also a dentist, plus one other dentist. After a while they moved into a bigger office, which they shared with several other black professionals, including their brother Lucius, an attorney. Bessie charged $2 for a cleaning or for pulling a tooth, $5 for a silver filling, and $10 for a gold filling. She charged the same rates 25 years later, when she retired. At first, some of her patients were reluctant to see a female dentist. But once they sat in her chair they'd always come back, because she had a gentle touch.

Dr. Bessie, as she was called, became very well known in Harlem — so well known that she always received the vacation postcards that her patients sent addressed to "Dr. Bessie, Harlem." She would treat anybody, even people with infectious diseases that other dentists refused to help. And she never turned anybody away if they couldn't pay. She certainly never got rich, charging low rates and seeing many patients who couldn't afford to pay. In fact, she couldn't even afford to pay someone to clean her office. She used to get up at dawn, walk 10 blocks to her office, clean the office herself, walk 10 blocks home, bathe and dress for work, and then walk 10 blocks back to the office to start her day.

At that time, Harlem was the most influential black community in the country, the center of African-American artistic and intellectual life. Bessie and Sadie were living there during the Harlem Renaissance, a literary movement of the 1920s and 1930s that celebrated African-American culture. Bessie's dental office in Harlem became a gathering place, for the family and for others, particularly for black leaders and activists. They would meet there to plan protests against segregation. At one point the office even served as a campaign headquarters. Sadie and Bessie's brother Hubert, who was an assistant U.S. Attorney in New York and later a judge, ran for Congress. He based his campaign right in Bessie's dental office. Sadie and Bessie met a lot of interesting people over the years, at the office and elsewhere — they met the activist, historian, and sociologist W.E.B. Du Bois; the writer James Weldon Johnson ("Lift Every Voice and Sing"); the sociologist E. Franklin Frazier; the executive secretary of the NAACP Walter White; and the entertainers Alberta Hunter, Bill (Bojangles) Robinson, Ethel Waters, Bert Williams, Fletcher Henderson, Duke Ellington, Lena Horne, and Cab Calloway.

Retirement

In 1928 Sadie and Bessie's father died, and their mother came to New York to live with them. In the late 1940s they moved from Harlem to a cottage in the Bronx so their mother could have a garden. Soon their mother became ill and needed someone to take care of her. Sadie and Bessie took a look at their financial situation and decided that Bessie should retire — she didn't have a pension with her independent dental practice, whereas Sadie would qualify for a pension if she continued to

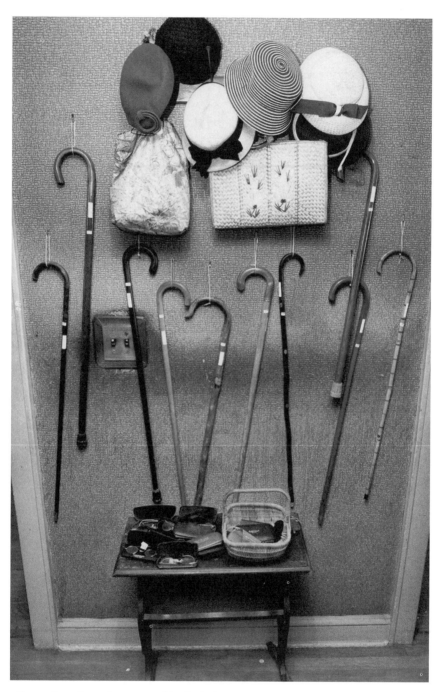

Possessions from the estate of Sadie Delany and Dr. Bessie Delany are displayed at their home during a public sale, June 4, 1999.

work until 1960. So Bessie retired from dentistry in 1950, staying home to take care of their home, their garden, and their mother. It was a difficult shock for both Bessie and Sadie when their mother died in 1956. Sadie, who always called herself "a mama's child," cried for weeks. A year later, they moved to Mount Vernon, which is just north of New York City. Bessie later admitted that she had planned the move to help Sadie get over their mother's death. They bought the last house on a dead-end street, with a view of New York City and room for a big garden. It was a two-family home, and they rented out the other side to their sister Laura and her husband.

After Sadie retired from teaching in 1960, the two sisters continued their quiet lives together. They woke up early every day. Sadie, the early bird, would wake up first with a smile and say, "Thank you, Lord, for another day!" Then she would go wake up Bessie, who would say, "Oh, Lord, another day?!" They would do yoga exercises and take a regimen of vitamins prescribed by Sadie, who kept current on news about nutrition. They ate their main meal at midday, including as many as seven vegetables each day. In the evening they would have just a milk shake for dinner, watch the "MacNeil Lehrer Report" on TV, say their prayers, and go to bed. They later said that they lived so long, in Bessie's words, because "we never had husbands to worry us to death!"

Having Our Say

Sadie and Bessie spent many years together, unknown to most of American society, before a newspaper story changed things. In 1991, a journalist named Amy Hill Hearth heard about these two sisters, each over 100 years old, and went to their Mount Vernon home to interview them. At first, Sadie and Bessie just didn't think they were interesting enough. But then they told her some stories about their lives. From those stories, Hearth wrote an article for the *New York Times*, which attracted the attention of a publisher. So she started visiting with the Delanys and recording their recollections of the past.

From those conversations came their memoir *Having Our Say: The Delany Sisters' First 100 Years*, which was published in 1993. The book became a bestseller and won the Delany sisters widespread fame and millions of admirers. They collected sacks of mail, received tons of interview requests from journalists, and appeared on several TV shows, including Oprah Winfrey. "We are having a ball!" Bessie said then. "I wake up in the middle of the night just to enjoy the excitement." In 1994 they published a second book called *The Delany Sisters' Book of Everyday Wisdom*. The following year, their first book, *Having Our Say*, was adapted into a Broadway play. Set in their Mount Vernon home, this dramatization featured the two sisters' nonstop conversations while preparing a meal celebrating their father's birthday. It was also adapted into a TV movie that appeared in 1999.

Sadie and Bessie were able to see the Broadway play in May 1995, just a few months before Bessie Delany died at home, in her bed, on September 25, 1995. She was 104. Losing Bessie was very difficult for Sadie; they had been together for over 100 years. She recorded some of the pain she went through in *On My Own at 107: Reflections on Life Without Bessie*, which was published in 1997. Sadie Delany died at home also, in her bed, on January 25, 1999. She was 109.

WRITINGS

By Sadie and Bessie:

Having Our Say: The Delany Sisters' First 100 Years, 1993 (with Amy Hill Hearth)
The Delany Sisters' Book of Everyday Wisdom, 1994 (with Amy Hill Hearth)

By Sadie:

On My Own at 107: Reflections on Life Without Bessie, 1997 (with Amy Hill Hearth)

FURTHER READING

Books

Delany, Sarah and A. Elizabeth. *Having Our Say: The Delany Sisters' First 100 Years*, 1993 (with Amy Hill Hearth)

Periodicals

Current Biography Yearbook 1995
New York Times, Sep. 22, 1991, Section 12, p.1; Sep. 8, 1993, p.C19; Sep. 23, 1993, p.B1; Sep. 26, 1995, p.B8; Jan. 26, 1999, p.A20
New York Times Book Review, Dec. 5, 1993, p.15
Newsweek, Nov. 1, 1993, p.54
People, Nov. 22, 1993, p.97; Oct. 9, 1995, p.48; Feb. 8, 1999, p.116
Smithsonian, Oct. 1993, p.144
Washington Post, Nov. 25, 1993, p.B1; Feb. 3, 1999, p.B6

Sharon Draper 1952-

American Author of *Tears of a Tiger* and *Forged by Fire*
1997 National Teacher of the Year

BIRTH

Sharon Mills Draper was born on August 21, 1952, in Cleveland, Ohio. She was the oldest of three children raised by Victor Mills, who worked as a hotel manager, and Catherine Mills, who held an administrative position with the *Cleveland Plain Dealer* newspaper for a number of years before turning to gardening.

YOUTH

Sharon Draper grew up in a black family that placed a high value on reading and education. Her mother often read stories and poems to Draper and her younger siblings, and both parents taught her that education was an important key to a happy and successful life. "Although my parents never went to college," Draper recalls, "they were educators. They read to me, helped me do homework, and were always there encouraging me to be a good student." As a result, Draper made frequent visits to the neighborhood library. By the time she was in the sixth grade, she had read all of the children's books and was ready to try more advanced materials. "I had to get a special card to go to the 'big side,' as we called it, and read the books there," she said.

Draper also liked to play games with other children in the neighborhood, but even then her love for learning was evident. One of her favorite games was to pretend that the steps of her front porch were a big school. Each of the seven or eight steps on the porch represented a grade of school, and she remembers that "you moved up the steps each grade to the top step." But instead of pretending to be one of the students, Draper preferred to take a different role. "I was always the teacher," she says with a smile.

EDUCATION

Draper attended A.J. Rickoff Elementary School in the Cleveland public school system. She was a terrific student blessed with tremendous enthusiasm for learning about the world around her, and her teachers quickly took notice of her intelligence and good study habits. Draper recalls that one teacher even "gave me O's for outstanding, saying an A wasn't good enough."

Draper's favorite teacher during her years in elementary school was Mrs. Mann, who taught her in fifth grade. Mrs. Mann challenged her fifth graders, giving them reading assignments that included the poetry of literary giants like William Shakespeare, Langston Hughes, Robert Frost, and Walt Whitman. "Because she had high expectations of us, we wanted to meet them," remembers Draper. "We didn't know we weren't supposed to be able to do that in fifth grade. She gave it to us and we loved it. It was part of making me the teacher I am today."

After completing elementary school, Draper moved on to John Adams High School in Cleveland, where she was one of the top students in her class. She skipped two grades over her elementary years, and as a high school student took a number of advanced courses, so she was able to graduate in the spring of 1967, three years early. She also was a National Merit Scholar, an honor given to the nation's top students.

In the fall of 1967, at the age of 15, Draper left Ohio to attend college at Pepperdine University in Malibu, California. Four years later she graduated with a bachelor's degree in English. Officials at Pepperdine immediately offered her a teaching position and free tuition to pursue a master's degree. But Draper decided to return to her home state of Ohio to continue her education. Soon after returning in 1971, she married Larry Draper and was offered a teaching position in the Cincinnati public school system. She accepted the job, but also continued to take classes as a student at night and during the summers at Miami University of Ohio in Oxford, where she earned a master's degree in education in 1974.

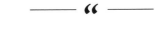

"I make that last quarter of their education something meaningful and memorable," states Draper, who passes out *"I Survived the Draper Paper" t-shirts to students who successfully complete the assignment. "They do not like [the research paper] at all and the reason they do not like it is, it's something demanding and they're ready to quit [high school and go on to college]. They don't like it, but when they get through it they are so proud. And they are so glad."*

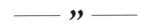

CAREER HIGHLIGHTS

Learning How to Teach

Draper knew that she wanted to be a high school teacher, and as she prepared for her first students, she was excited about showing them how wonderful reading, writing, and literature could be, just as her own parents and teachers had shown her. Those first months of teaching proved difficult, though, as she struggled to learn how to deal with students who misbehaved or acted like they did not care about learning. "I had a class my very first year of teaching that made me cry," she later admitted.

As time passed, however, Draper learned how to handle disruptive kids and developed ways to engage children who were on the verge of giving up on school. She became known around the high school as an instructor who challenged her students, but also as one whose classes were de-

———— " ————

*"I started writing
poetry because kids
didn't like the poetry
in the books, and we
started working on poems
together in class,"
Draper says. "If it's a
nice day we'll go outside
and sit under trees and
write poetry, and come
back in and read them."*

———— " ————

signed to bring out the best in her kids. Finally, Draper made sure that her students knew that she cared about them personally. "A teacher can't just go to school at eight and go home at three," says Draper. "A good teacher goes to the football games, the plays, and the things the kids are involved in. One of the things that endears a student to the teacher is, 'Wow, he came to my play.'"

In 1978 Draper joined the faculty at Walnut Hills High School, a primarily African-American school in the Cincinnati public school system specifically designed to prepare students for college. In the ensuing months, students who enrolled in her literature and composition courses discovered that Draper was not afraid to try unusual methods in order to stimulate their interest in their schoolwork. For example, she emphasized literature that she knew would interest her students rather than assigning books simply because they were regarded as "classics," and she was always trying out new innovations in her classroom. "I started writing poetry because kids didn't like the poetry in the books, and we started working on poems together in class," Draper says. "If it's a nice day we'll go outside and sit under trees and write poetry, and come back in and read them."

The "Draper Paper"

But in the hallways and locker rooms at Walnut Hills High School, Draper is most famous for the major research paper that she assigns to all of her students during the last quarter of their senior year. This assignment, which is known throughout the student body as the dreaded "Draper Paper," forces seniors to exercise the research, analysis, and writing skills that they will need to use when they move on to college. "I make that last quarter of their education something meaningful and memorable," states Draper, who passes out "I Survived the Draper Paper" T-shirts to students who successfully complete the assignment. "They do not like [the research paper] at all and the reason they do not like it is, it's something demanding and they're ready to quit [high school and go on to college]. They don't like it, but when they get through it they are so proud. And they are so glad."

Becoming a Writer

Draper had loved literature all of her life, and she enjoyed writing poetry. But she had never thought about devoting any serious amount of time to writing until 1991, when one of her students challenged her to enter an *Ebony* magazine short story contest. Draper recalls that he first pointed out that she was always encouraging her students to develop their writing skills, then handed her the contest application form and said, "Why don't you write something?"

Draper accepted the challenge, penning a story called "One Small Torch" that was inspired by a sad scene that she had recently witnessed. "I was in a grocery store and saw a lady screaming at a little boy, about three years old. I thought, what kind of life must he have? I went home and wrote a story imagining the life of the little boy."

A few months after submitting her story, Draper was stunned to learn that her story had been chosen as the winner of the contest, beating out 20,000 other entries. "One Small Torch" was published in *Ebony*, and she received $5,000 in prize money from the magazine. "Almost immediately after the publication in *Ebony*, things started happening," recalls Draper. "All of a sudden I was a writer. It changes other people's perceptions of you and changes your perception of yourself." A few weeks after the story was published, Draper received a letter from Alex Haley, the famous author of *Roots*, telling her how much he had enjoyed her story.

"Almost immediately after the publication [of "One Small Torch"] in Ebony, *things started happening. All of a sudden I was a writer. It changes other people's perceptions of you and changes your perception of yourself."*

A Second Career as Novelist

Encouraged by the *Ebony* award and the kind words of Haley and many other people, Draper decided to write a young adult novel featuring young African-American characters that would be recognizable to the students that she taught every day. Over the next several months she worked on the book whenever she could, toiling away in the evening, on

weekends, and even during study hall periods. The final result was *Tears of a Tiger*, a story about a young black teen who accidentally causes his best friend's death during a drunken driving episode. "[The book] is written for high school students—on their level, in their style, about their world," says Draper. "The main characters are African-American males, but it's written for all teenagers. The characters are just ordinary kids trying to get through high school."

Draper sent *Tears of a Tiger* to numerous publishing houses, only to be rejected time after time. But just as she was about to give up hope, the last of the 25 publishing houses that she had contacted accepted the book for publication. It was published in November 1994, and in the following months it received a great deal of attention for its sensitive treatment of teen drinking, racism, grief, and the various pressures that confront all teenagers. A reviewer for *Voice of Youth Advocates* called the book "as compelling a novel as any published in the last two decades," and the *Bulletin of the Center for Children's Books* remarked that *Tears of a Tiger* would "provoke lots of thought and debate among young adults." Draper's novel eventually was named an American Library Association Best Book for Young Adults in 1995, and it received the Coretta Scott King Genesis Award that same year.

"Tears of a Tiger is written for high school students—on their level, in their style, about their world. The main characters are African American males, but it's written for all teenagers. The characters are just ordinary kids trying to get through high school."

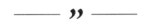

Writing for Younger Students

Gratified by the critical response to *Tears of a Tiger,* Draper was even more thrilled at reports indicating that the book was a big hit with teenagers. But she was also very happy with another book that she wrote in the months leading up to the publication of *Tears of a Tiger.* This book, a rip-roaring adventure tale called *Ziggy and the Black Dinosaurs* (1994), was specifically written to draw younger kids—and especially young African-American boys—to reading. Using the childhood antics of her two eldest sons as models, Draper spun an exciting tale that featured adventurous boys, buried treasure, secret club houses, and a dash of history.

The response to the *Ziggy* book—which ended up being published the same day as *Tears of a Tiger*—was so positive that Draper decided to feature Ziggy and his pals in further adventures. The first sequel was the 1996 book *Lost in the Tunnel of Time,* in which Ziggy and his friends be-

SHARON M. DRAPER

FORGED

BY

FIRE

Author of *Tears of a Tiger,*
Winner of the 1995 Coretta Scott King Genesis Award

come lost in an old Underground Railroad tunnel that was used to smuggle black slaves out of the American South before and during the American Civil War of the 1860s. Draper's tale was full of adventure and suspense, but it also taught young readers about the brave men and women who worked to help the many courageous blacks who tried to escape slavery. A third book featuring Ziggy and his friends, called *Shadows of Caesar's Creek,* was published in 1997. In this book, Ziggy and his pals (the so-called "Black Dinosaurs") learn about the history of friendship that exists between Native Americans and African-Americans.

Forged by Fire

In 1997 Draper returned to a young adult audience with *Forged by Fire,* a powerful novel about child abuse. The book tells the story of how Gerald Nickelby, a character from *Tears of a Tiger,* deals with horrible family problems when his previously secure life is turned upside down. After living with a loving aunt for several years while his mother was in prison for child neglect, Gerald must learn to live with her again, as well as a new stepfather, Jordan. The only comfort in the new family for Gerald is his new stepsister, Angel. When Gerald discovers that Jordan is sexually abusing Angel, he takes action. The book shows Gerald's growing bravery and maturity as he confronts and overcomes the terrors of his life. Draper, hoping the book would reach out to teens in similar situations and offer them hope, insisted that contact information for child abuse organizations appeared at the back of the book.

As with *Tears of a Tiger,* Draper's second young adult novel proved to be enormously popular with teens, and in 1998 it received the prestigious Coretta Scott King Award. Heather Caines, who was the head of the committee giving the award, called *Forged by Fire* "riveting, realistic, and hopeful. Draper ably tackles troubling contemporary issues, providing concrete options and positive African-American role models."

Teacher of the Year

By 1997 Draper was known as a popular author of books for children and young adults. But among Walnut Hills students and Cincinnati-area educators, she continued to be best known for her excellent teaching skills. Regard for her work in the classroom was so high that she won Ohio's Teacher of the Year Award in January 1997.

Draper's selection as Ohio Teacher of the Year automatically qualified her for consideration as the 1997 U.S. Teacher of the Year, and a few months later she won that award as well. The recognition thrilled Draper and her family, but it was no surprise to her students or her fellow teachers. "She's an excellent teacher with an engaging personality," said Walnut Hills High School principal Marvin Koenig. "She holds students to high expectations no matter how much of a fuss they put up."

Draper was subsequently honored at a White House ceremony attended by President Bill Clinton on April 19, 1997. "I am so proud to be a teacher," she said after receiving the award. "I am proud of all the students that I have had—students whose paths have crossed mine, students whose lives have changed mine. And to all those students, wherever you are, I want to say, thank you; and I want to say, I love you."

"I am so proud to be a teacher," she said after receiving the Teacher of the Year award. "I am proud of all the students that I have had—students whose paths have crossed mine, students whose lives have changed mine. And to all those students, wherever you are, I want to say, thank you; and I want to say, I love you."

In the year following Draper's selection as the nation's teacher of the year, she traveled around the country as a spokesperson for education. Everywhere she stopped, she encouraged young people to make the most of their educational opportunities. But she also used her appearances to heighten public awareness of the great job that most teachers do every day in schools from Florida to Alaska. "Reports like to focus on all the negative things in schools," she says. "Nobody ever covers the third-grade teacher loved by all the kids, and who sends the kids off to the fourth grade so well prepared. There are hundreds of these teachers all over the country who deserve recognition."

——— 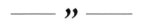 ———

"Teaching is not about the money. It's about what you want to do—what you want to give back, what you have that you can share with young people. . . . Some young people think teachers don't make enough money and don't get enough respect. I tell them I'll never make as much as Michael Jordan, but neither will you. I tell them if you want to make a difference in somebody's life, then go into teaching."

——— ,, ———

Draper's Thoughts on Teaching

Draper believes that educators perform a vital function in our society, even if they are not always paid accordingly. "Very little recognition or reward is given a job on which rests the knowledge of the past, the responsibility of the present, and the hope of the future," she once wrote. She noted that while professional athletes and entertainers make millions of dollars a year, "teachers, without whom the society would be unable to progress intellectually, are given a pittance and expected to appreciate it. A civilization that honors athletes over intellectuals, that lauds entertainment while denigrating education, that philosophically separates teachers from the ranks of professionals is a society in danger of destruction."

But Draper believes that the rewards of helping a child learn far outweigh the drawbacks. "Teaching is not about the money," she states. "It's about what you want to do—what you want to give back, what you have that you can share with young people. . . . Some young people think teachers don't make enough money and don't get enough respect. I tell them I'll never make as much as Michael Jordan, but neither will you. I tell them if you want to make a difference in somebody's life, then go into teaching."

MARRIAGE AND FAMILY

Sharon Mills Draper married Larry Draper, a fellow teacher in the Cincinnati school system, in 1971. They have four children, Cory, Damon, Wendy, and Crystal.

HOBBIES AND OTHER INTERESTS

Even during the summer and school-year weekends, Draper spends much of her free time helping kids or working on education issues. She is a community volunteer in programs that encourage disadvantaged children to read and write their own stories, and in 1997 she was named to the Board of Directors of the National Board for Professional Teaching Standards.

WRITINGS

Tears of a Tiger, 1994
Ziggy and the Black Dinosaurs, 1994
"The Touch of a Teacher" in *What Governors Need to Know about Education Reform,* edited by Marla Higginbotham, 1995
Lost in the Tunnel of Time, 1996
Shadows of Ceasar's Creek, 1997
Forged by Fire, 1997

HONORS AND AWARDS

Gertrude Johnson Williams Prize: 1990
Coretta Scott King Genesis Award: 1995, for *Tears of a Tiger*
Best Book for Young Adults Award (American Library Association): 1995, for *Tears of a Tiger*
Governor's Educational Leadership Award (State of Ohio): 1996
Ohio State Teacher of the Year: 1997
U.S. National Teacher of the Year: 1997
Excellence in Teaching Award (National Council of Negro Women): 1997
Coretta Scott King Award: 1998, for *Forged by Fire*

FURTHER READING

Books

Contemporary Black Biography, Vol. 16, 1998
Something about the Author, Vol. 98, 1998

Periodicals

Bulletin of the Center for Children's Books, Jan. 1995, p.164
Christian Science Monitor, May 5, 1997, Sec. 12, p.1
Cincinnati Post, Mar. 6, 1997, p.C1; Apr. 15, 1997, p.A1
Cleveland Plain Dealer, Apr. 28, 1997, p.A2
Columbus Dispatch, Aug. 22, 1997, p.F1
Ebony, Dec. 1990, p.138; May 1998, p.126
Jet, May 12, 1997, p.25
St. Paul Pioneer Press, Apr. 17, 1997, p.A14

School Library Journal, Mar. 1997, p.184
USA Today, Apr. 17, 1997, p.D4
Voice of Youth Advocates, Feb. 1995, p.338

ADDRESS

National Teacher of the Year Program
One Massachusetts Avenue, NW, Suite 700
Washington, DC 20001-1431

WORLD WIDE WEB SITE

www.ccsso.org/ntoy.html

Sarah Michelle Gellar 1977-

American Actress
Star of the TV Series "Buffy the Vampire Slayer"
and the Movies *I Know What You Did Last Summer*
and *Scream 2*

BIRTH

Sarah Michelle Gellar (pronounced Gell-are) was born on
April 14, 1977, in New York City. Her parents were divorced
when she was young, and she was raised by her mother,
Rosellen Gellar, a former teacher. Sarah has avoided discus-
sing her father in interviews, and she has made it clear that

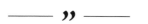

> *When Gellar was growing up she always felt like an outcast, different from the other kids. "I was always excluded from everything because I was different. That's difficult when you're a child."*

she considers some issues to be her private business, not public information: "I keep my private life private." She has said, though, that her parents split up when she was about six or seven and that she hasn't seen her father since then.

YOUTH

Gellar's whole life has been dominated by acting; as she says, "I was absolutely born to act." Growing up on the Upper East Side in New York City, she was discovered by a talent agent when she was still very young. "I was eating in a restaurant when I was three-and-a-half and some woman came up to my mother. I was the ultimate ham. A week later I was filming my first CBS-TV movie, *Invasion of Privacy.*" After that, Gellar started appearing in lots of commercials. While filming one Shake 'n Bake ad, she reports, she ate 98 pieces of chicken. At age four she appeared in a Burger King ad in which she criticized McDonald's for their meager hamburger patties. That was notable because it was one of the first commercials to directly attack a competitor and its products. McDonald's went on to sue both Burger King and Gellar, putting her in the difficult position of being called as a witness in a trial when she was only four years old. Ultimately, the case was settled out of court in 1982.

EDUCATION

Gellar started out attending private schools in the New York area. Later, her mother enrolled her in a public school. She was so busy working in commercials and TV movies that she was often absent from class, sometimes for months at a time. She even missed her eighth-grade trip to Busch Gardens because of an acting job. Throughout most of her youth, Gellar has said, she hated school. "I was miserable. I didn't fit in. They wouldn't let me leave school for auditions." She felt like an outcast, different from the other kids. "I was always excluded from everything because I was different. That's difficult when you're a child."

In 1992, she entered the Professional Children's School in Manhattan, which proved to be a far better fit. "One of my best friends was a fencer, and the other was a ballerina," she says. While attending school there,

Gellar did theater, commercials, and even modeled while still earning straight A's. She also practiced tae kwon do, a form of martial arts that would come in handy later. Gellar graduated early from the Professional Children's School, with honors, in June 1994.

FIRST JOBS

Gellar's first acting jobs came while she was still a child. In her first role, she appeared opposite Valerie Harper and Jeff Daniels in *An Invasion of Privacy,* a TV movie that was released in 1983. She went on to appear in a variety of roles in TV shows, TV movies, mini-series, feature films, and even theater productions, including *Over the Brooklyn Bridge* (1984), "Spenser for Hire" (1986), *The Widow Claire* (1986), *Funny Farm* (1988), *High Stakes* (1989), *A Woman Named Jackie* (1991), "Swan's Crossing" (1991-92), and *Jake's Women* (1992).

Gellar landed her first big role while she was attending high school. In 1993, she joined the cast of the long-running daytime soap opera "All My Children." For two years she played Kendall Hart, the abandoned daughter of Erica Kane, played by actress Susan Lucci. Despite her youth, Gellar won the part easily, as casting director Judy Wilson explains here. "As soon as Sarah walked in the door, I knew she was something special. She has that combination of possessing terrific range, being adorable, and having a little spice." Gellar needed that "spice" to play Kendall, the crazy, evil daughter of the ruthless and conniving Erica Kane. "It was amazing playing a psycholoony. I got to attempt suicide. I shot at people. It was *great.*"

At the time, there were many reports of a feud between Gellar and Lucci, including rumors about animosity between Lucci and her younger co-star. The tense situation couldn't have been any easier when Gellar won an Emmy Award, which Lucci has been nominated for 18 times but has never won. Then, just 24 hours after winning the Emmy, Gellar publicly announced that she was leaving

Casting director Judy Wilson explains here why Gellar was selected for her role on "All My Children." *"As soon as Sarah walked in the door, I knew she was something special. She has that combination of possessing terrific range, being adorable, and having a little spice."*

85

"All My Children." The timing of the announcement was questioned by many. Rumors circulated that she was leaving the show because she had been forced off or because she thought she was too good. In truth, Gellar and the show's executives had planned her departure months in advance.

CAREER HIGHLIGHTS

"Buffy the Vampire Slayer"

Gellar's breakout year was 1997, during which she appeared in a new hit TV series and two hit movies. Her TV series, "Buffy the Vampire Slayer," was based on a 1992 movie of the same name that featured light entertainment with a vain, stuck-up heroine. The TV show aimed for a very different effect, combining hip, ironic humor, typical high-school stories, and a dark, sinister tone. The ultimate effect, according to Gellar, was "'X-Files' meets 'My So-Called Life' meets '90210' meets 'Clueless.'"

"Buffy is a 16-year-old who just wants to fit in and be popular and be a teen-ager, but she gets saddled with the responsibility of saving the world while she also wants to go to the prom."

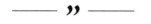

"Buffy the Vampire Slayer" follows the adventures of Buffy Summers, who is a "slayer." In each generation, we're told, one girl is born with the power to become the world's only vampire slayer, with the strength and skill to hunt vampires and other ghouls. The weekly show follows Buffy, who is alternately emotionally vulnerable and physically powerful, as she tries to combine her normal daytime high-school life with her role as a slayer, a martial-arts expert who spends each night fighting evil. Of course, that doesn't leave her much time to do her home work. As Gellar sees it, "Buffy is a 16-year-old who just wants to fit in and be popular and be a teen-ager, but she gets saddled with the responsibility of saving the world while she also wants to go to the prom."

After Buffy burns down her former high school, she and her mother, who knows nothing about her daughter's secret powers, move to Sunnydale. That turns out to be an unfortunate choice because Sunnydale sits near a Hellmouth, an entry point from the other world for vampires, mummies, and demons. According to Joss Whedon, the series creator, "This one community happens to be situated on a Hellmouth, which is a mystical porthole, and all different kinds of bad things like monsters, demons, and

The cast of "Buffy the Vampire Slayer"

giant insects gravitate toward it. It's not a very good place to go to school." At Sunnydale High School Buffy makes several close friends, including Willow and Xander, and becomes acquainted with Giles, the school librarian. Giles is a "watcher" charged with secretly guiding her activities as a slayer.

"Buffy the Vampire Slayer" was not an immediate hit when it debuted on the WB network in March 1997, but it soon built up a loyal and devoted following among teen viewers as well as TV critics. Many were drawn in by Gellar's portrayal of Buffy as a young woman who is attractive, self-reliant, and strong, particularly in scenes where she uses tae kwon do to fight the vampires. For other viewers, according to reporter Jancee Dunn in *Rolling Stone* magazine, "The show's appeal lies in the smart-mouthed writing and dark, anything-goes story lines."

But Joss Whedon offers another explanation. He says that the episodes "reflect a grotesque parody of actual high school experiences," using metaphors of the supernatural to depict all the pain and turmoil that are so common during these years. Buffy's terrifying encounters with vampires reflect the anxieties that many teens face. In effect, the scenes in "Buffy" can be seen as metaphors for the overwhelming experiences and feelings that teens contend with daily. "The show makes a myth out of people's teenage years, which is a very potent time," Whedon explains. "This is everything you wished your high school life had been like, and it's everything you went through, made to seem epic." Gellar agrees, saying "What makes the situations so horrific is that Joss bases them on reality. We have just taken real-life situations and put them on a grander or a more horror-level scale. But they are all situations we have faced." This real-life approach, together with the ironic humor, smart writing, and appealing lead character, have made "Buffy the Vampire Slayer" a huge hit among teen audiences.

> "What makes the situations so horrific is that [series creator Joss Whedon] bases them on reality. We have just taken real-life situations and put them on a grander or a more horror-level scale. But they are all situations we have faced."

Horror Films

In addition to her work on "Buffy," Gellar went on to co-star in 1997 in a couple of horror films created specifically for the teen audience. Although horror movies have been around for a while, new interest in the genre was sparked by the modern thriller *Scream*. Released in 1996, *Scream* tracks a series of brutal murders in the small town of Woodsboro, California. A group of high school students, including Sidney Prescott

Scream 2

(Neve Campbell), is being terrorized by a knife-wielding killer in a cape and Halloween mask. *Scream* was different from many earlier horror movies: it left the audience alternately cringing with terror and laughing at the funny one-liners. A clever, ironic, and unsettling send-up of old slasher films, it openly mocked the conventions of the genre. For example, a victim, cornered in the house by the killer, runs up the stairs rather than out the door, or a character who says "I'll be right back" never is. The movie was directed by Wes Craven, the famed director of *A Nightmare on Elm Street* and other horror movies. The screenplay was written by Kevin Williamson, who went on to write the thrillers *I Know What You Did Last Summer* and *Scream 2*, as well as the TV series "Dawson's Creek." Williamson has been credited with bringing the horror genre up to date, with witty dialogue, cute guys, and strong female characters. By earning more than $100 million, *Scream* created renewed interest in the genre among film makers and led to several similar new works.

Gellar's first movie in this genre was *I Know What You Did Last Summer*, based on the 1973 novel of the same name by Lois Duncan. Filming the movie was a real change of pace for Gellar. She had just finished working on her TV series, and she had to be reminded by the director, Jim Gillespie, that the character was different from Buffy. "When I first got down there, I was still in Buffy mode," she explains. "Like, here comes the bad guy. 'Give him your right, then a left!' Jim was like, 'Uh, Sarah, you're looking too athletic. This isn't a triathalon here.' I had to do things like untie my shoes or put pebbles in them when I'd run. I got a little more used to it, but I'm so used to being the aggressor in a fight scene, I couldn't see being defensive and then just flailing."

In *I Know What You Did Last Summer*, Gellar plays a teenage beauty queen. She and her co-stars, Ryan Phillippe, Jennifer Love Hewitt, and Freddie Prinze, Jr., play four teens who are out at a party one night. Driving home, they take a curve in the road too fast, hit a pedestrian, run away without telling anyone, and agree to keep it a secret. Then they get a note from someone who says, "I know what you did last summer," and the fun begins. This suspenseful thriller became a big hit with teenage fans. A sequel came out in late 1998 entitled *I Still Know What You Did Last Summer*, but Gellar didn't appear in that film.

Gellar's next movie, also released in 1997, was *Scream 2*. Like its predecessor, *Scream 2* was directed by Craven and written by Williamson. The film picks up the story two years after the Woodsboro murders. Sidney Prescott, again played by Neve Campbell, is now a Midwestern college student. Gellar has a smaller role as her friend at college, and other co-stars include Jada Pinkett, Rebecca Gayheart, Tori Spelling, and Heather Graham. *Scream 2* starts out with a movie-within-a-movie. The opening scene takes place at a movie theater, where students have come to see "Stab," a movie made from the best-selling book by journalist Gale Weathers (Courtney Cox) on the Woodsboro killings. The mask-wearing murderer who first stalked Sidney in *Scream* shows up at the movie where "Stab" is being screened. *Scream 2* is a spoof on sequels as well as on horror movies in general. The movie-within-a-movie scene makes fun of the original *Scream* while at the same time setting the mood for the murders that follow. The formula was successful again, making *Scream 2* a huge hit with teen fans.

Current Projects

Gellar continues to work on "Buffy," and she has expressed her desire to stay with the show in the future. In addition to the TV series, she has begun work on two films that are scheduled to appear in in 1999. In *Cruel Intentions*, a romantic drama that is a modern retelling of *Dangerous Liaisons*, Gellar plays a charming and conniving manipulator who ties to destroy anyone who gets in her way. She co-stars with Ryan Phillippe and Reese Witherspoon. In the romantic comedy *Vanilla Fog*, Gellar plays a young woman trying to keep her family's restaurant afloat after her mother's death. She co-stars with Sean Patrick Flannery, who plays a department store executive who tries to resist falling in love with Gellar, whom he believes has magical powers.

HOME AND FAMILY

Gellar, who lives in the Los Angeles area, is single. Her current working schedule, she has said, makes it difficult to have much of a personal life. "I've dated a couple of people recently, but with my job, dating takes a back seat," she said. "Sometimes I get upset and lonely, and it's sort of like, 'Wow, I'm the only single person left in America.' I can't commit to a serious relationship right now, but maybe it's because I haven't met the right person."

CREDITS

Television

An Invasion of Privacy, 1983 (TV movie)
"Spenser for Hire," 1986 (TV series)
A Woman Named Jackie, 1991 (TV movie)
"Swan's Crossing," 1991-92 (TV series)
"All My Children," 1993-95 (TV series)
"Buffy the Vampire Slayer," 1997- (TV series)

Movies

Over the Brooklyn Bridge, 1984
Funny Farm, 1988
High Stakes, 1989
I Know What You Did Last Summer, 1997
Scream 2, 1997

Theater

The Widow Claire, 1986
Jake's Women, 1992

HONORS AND AWARDS

Emmy Award (National Academy of Television Arts and Sciences): 1995, Outstanding Younger Actress in a Drama Series, for "All My Children"
Blockbuster Award: 1998, Best Supporting Actress, for *I Know What you Did Last Summer*

FURTHER READING

Books

Golden, Christopher, and Nancy Holder. *Buffy the Vampire Slayer: The Watcher's Guide*, 1998
Tracy, Kathleen. *The Girl's Got Bite: The Unofficial Guide to Buffy's World*, 1998

Periodicals

Parade, July 6, 1997, p.18
People, May 23, 1994, p.83
Rolling Stone, Dec. 25, 1997-Jan. 8, 1998, p.40; Apr. 2, 1998, p.40
Seventeen, Aug. 1994, p.140; Nov. 1997, p.126; Feb. 1998, p.79
Teen, Nov. 1998, p.50
TV Guide, July 1, 1995, p.32; Jan. 18, 1997, p.24; Aug. 2, 1997, p.16
USA Weekend, Oct. 23, 1998, p.10

ADDRESS

"Buffy the Vampire Slayer"
Warner Brothers Television Network
4000 Warner Boulevard
Burbank, CA 91522

WORLD WIDE WEB SITES

http://www.buffyslayer.com
http://www.wb.com

John Glenn 1921-
American Astronaut and Politician
First American to Orbit the Earth
Returned to Space at Age 77 to Become the
World's Oldest Astronaut

BIRTH

John Herschel Glenn Jr. was born July 18, 1921, in Cambridge,
Ohio, to John Glenn Sr. and Clara Sproat Glenn. John Sr. was
a railroad conductor and the owner of a heating and plumbing
business, and Clara was a homemaker. John had one sister,
Jean. The family moved from Cambridge to New Concord,

———— **"** ————

As Tom Wolfe points out in **The Right Stuff,** *Glenn emerged as a clean cut, honest slice of Americana, and the media loved him. In an early interview with the seven astronauts, he spoke feelingly and without guile about how much being an astronaut meant to him. "I think we would be most remiss in our duty if we didn't make the fullest use of our talents in volunteering for something that is as important to our country and to the world in general right now." "The guy had the halo turned on at all times!" commented Wolfe.*

———— **"** ————

Ohio, a small town in the southeastern part of the state, when John was two.

YOUTH

Glenn grew up during the Depression, a time when many people around the world were without jobs and money was scarce. Luckily, John Glenn Sr. was able to earn an income during the Depression, but the era was one of self-sacrifice and financial hardship. The Glenns were a close family, and the parents raised their children with their own firmly held moral beliefs. They valued honesty, hard work, patriotism, and devotion to family and church. They were active members of the local Presbyterian church.

John Glenn Jr. was a devout and earnest young man, like his father. The two would play taps each Memorial Day at the local commemoration in New Concord. He also showed the kind of staunchly moral approach to life that marked him as the "squeaky clean" astronaut he later became. He belonged to a group called the Ohio Rangers, which had vowed never to swear. Once, when the group was singing "Hail, hail the gang's all here," Glenn became upset when his fellow choristers sang the traditional phrase, "What the hell do we care." His old friend Edwin Houk, who later became a minister, recalled, "Well, I can tell you, it didn't sit well with Johnny. He came up to me, white-faced and righteous, and told me to stop. I think he was ready to knock my block off."

EDUCATION

Glenn attended the local public grade school, where he was an outstanding student. He also found time to play trumpet in the band and sing in the school and church choirs. In high school, he continued to do well in both academics and athletics, playing varsity football, basketball, and tennis. He also served as class president during his junior year and took part in high school plays. For spending money, Glenn worked as a lifeguard and washed cars. He graduated in 1939 from a high school that is now named for him.

Glenn went on to Muskingum College, which was located in his home town. There, he studied chemistry and started flying lessons, beginning a lifelong passion with flight. But his education was interrupted by World War II, and he never returned to college to finish his degree.

WORLD WAR II

During Glenn's junior year, the U.S. entered World War II. This international conflict, which began in 1939 when Nazi Germany invaded countries in Europe, expanded to the United States in December 1941. That's when Japan, an ally of Germany, attacked Pearl Harbor in Hawaii, destroying the U.S. fleet. The U.S. declared war on Germany and Japan, and John Glenn and many of his countrymen and women became part of the war effort.

Leaving college in 1942, Glenn entered the Naval Aviation Cadet Program and began training to become a fighter pilot. He joined the Marine Corps in 1943 and, as a first lieutenant, began to fly bombing missions in the Pacific. Over the next two years, Glenn flew 59 combat missions, earning two Distinguished Flying Crosses and ten Air Medals. After the war ended in 1945, Glenn stayed in the Marines, serving at bases in North Carolina, Maryland, and California, and building his career as a pilot and flight instructor.

MARRIAGE AND FAMILY

By this point in his career, Glenn was a husband and father. Soon after his enlistment, in April 1943, Glenn had married his high school sweetheart, Annie Castor. They had two children, David, born in 1945, and Lyn, born in 1947, who grew up on the many different bases where Glenn was stationed. Throughout their 55 years of marriage, Annie Glenn has been an important partner to her husband, during his careers as a pilot, astronaut, and politician.

THE KOREAN WAR

By 1952, Glenn had reached the rank of major. When the U.S. got involved in the Korean War, Glenn once again flew combat missions as a Marine fighter pilot. He was part of a mission that included troops from countries in the United Nations, which sought to preserve the sovereignty of South Korea in its conflict with North Korea. Glenn flew 90 missions during the Korean War, earning two more Distinguished Flying Crosses and eight additional Air Medals before the war ended in 1953.

BECOMING A TEST PILOT

After Korea, Glenn became one of America's finest test pilots. Already known as one of the best Marine pilots, Glenn wanted to match skills with other flyers. One of the most prestigious — and riskiest — assignments in the military during the 1950s was the test pilot program. As Tom Wolfe describes in his famous book on the early astronauts, *The Right Stuff,* this group of men, all of them military pilots from World War II and Korea, were testing the limits of the technology available at that time. They would push their planes to their limits, sometimes losing their lives, but also setting land and speed records and entering the history books for their efforts. They were brave, sometimes cocky, and obsessed with speed and their aircraft.

From the ranks of these test pilots came the first American astronauts, and one of them was John Glenn. As a test pilot, Glenn entered the record books for the first time on July 16, 1957, when he became the first man to make a nonstop, transcontinental flight from New York to Los Angeles. He flew at supersonic speeds in a time of 3 hours, 23 minutes, and 8.4 seconds. Once again, Glenn received a Distinguished Flying Cross, his fifth. Glenn's success in the air led to his appearance on a popular television game show of the time, "Name That Tune," where he won $12,500 for naming a song.

CAREER HIGHLIGHTS

The U.S. Space Program — Project Mercury

The modern age of space exploration began in 1957. That's when the Soviet Union launched Sputnik I, the first unmanned satellite, which inspired the U.S. to become serious about its space program. Both the Soviet Union and the U.S. had the rocket technology necessary to place an orbiting vehicle into space. That technology had been developed as part of weapons delivery systems used in World War II. After the war, the U.S. and the Soviet Union emerged as the two superpowers in the world. These two nations became locked in the conflict known as the Cold War — a war defined not by open warfare, but by escalating hostilities between the two nations and the division of the major world governments into pro-U.S. and pro-Soviet nations. With the Cold War raging, the two

The original seven Mercury astronauts. Front row, left to right, are Walter M. Schirra Jr., Donald K. Slayton, John H. Glenn Jr. and M. Scott Carpenter. Back row, from left to right, are Alan B. Shepard, Virgil I. Grissom, and L. Gordon Cooper Jr.

superpowers began what was known as the "Arms Race," in which the two nations were engaged in a potentially deadly competition to create ever more powerful weapons. The Arms Race led to the "Space Race," with the goal to be the first nation to land a man on the moon.

On April 9, 1959, Glenn was one of seven test pilots selected to be the first astronauts for NASA, the National Aeronautics and Space Administration. His fellow astronauts included Alan Shepard, Gus Grissom, Scott Carpenter, Donald "Deke" Slayton, Leroy Cooper, and Walter Schirra. The seven astronauts began their training immediately. They studied a wide range of scientific subjects, from astrophysics to astronautics, and took part in demanding physical training for their first flights into space. Glenn's area of specialty in the program was the instrumentation of the cockpit, an assignment he took to with his characteristic seriousness and zeal.

Glenn stands in his space suit, at Cape Canaveral, Florida, February, 20, 1962

As Tom Wolfe points out in *The Right Stuff*, Glenn emerged as a clean cut, honest slice of Americana, and the media loved him. In an early interview with the seven astronauts, he spoke feelingly and without guile about how much being an astronaut meant to him. "I think we would be most remiss in our duty if we didn't make the fullest use of our talents in volunteering for something that is as important to our country and to the world in general right now." "The guy had the halo turned on at all times!" commented Wolfe.

It's important to note in our modern, technologically sophisticated era, when the flight of the modern space shuttle doesn't warrant much news, that space flight was new and very dangerous during those early days. The astronauts went into space in a small capsule thrust into the atmosphere on top of huge, powerful, often unstable rockets. As Wolfe notes, "The main thing was: they had volunteered to sit on top of the rockets—*which always blew up!*" One of the journalists at that early press conference said, "Could I ask for a show of hands of how many are confident that they will come back from outer space?" Slowly, each man raised his hand. John Glenn raised both hands. The next day, the astronauts were hailed in the press as heroes, considered the "bravest men in America," according to Wolfe. "Henceforth, they would be served up inside the biggest slice of Mom's Pie you could imagine."

But America's bravest didn't make it into space first. Yuri Gagarin, a Soviet cosmonaut, was the first man to make that mark. He made a one-orbit flight on April 12, 1961, aboard the Soviet spacecraft Vostok. The Space Race was on, as the Americans rushed to assert their superiority to the Soviets. Less than a month later, Alan Shepard became the first U.S. astronaut to fly in space, as part of Project Mercury. Shepard was followed by Gus Grissom, whose flight took place on July 21, 1961. Glenn was scheduled to go next, and he was also the first American whose mission was to orbit the Earth. He received the news in November 1961, but because of delays, didn't make into space—and history—until several months later.

After one such delay, in January 1962, the NASA public relations department tried to invade the privacy of the Glenn home. John Glenn showed how fiercely independent and devoted to his family he could be. While Glenn sat in his capsule ready to be blasted into space, he was told that technical difficulties had delayed his mission one more time. Back at the Glenn home in Arlington, Virginia, the media were literally living in Glenn's front yard. Annie Glenn suffered from a severe stutter, and because of that she was very shy. She had agreed to talk to only one reporter, Loudon Wainwright from *Life* magazine, but then the NASA public relations people put pressure on her to accept a visit from then-Vice President Lyndon Johnson. Johnson wanted to take advantage of the moment to grab some media attention for himself, and he wanted to comfort Annie Glenn on television, in front of millions of viewers. Annie Glenn was terrified. The NASA public relations officials talked to Glenn as soon as he got out of the capsule that day, ordering him to tell his wife to talk to Johnson.

Glenn called Annie and told her, "Look, if you don't want the Vice President or the TV networks or anybody else to come into the house, then that's it as far as I'm concerned, they are *not* coming in—and I will back you up all the way, 100 per cent, and you tell them that. I don't want Johnson or any of the rest of them to put so much as *one toe* inside our house." The Glenns stood their ground, as a fuming Johnson was sent away from the home.

The Flight of Friendship Seven

Finally, on February 20, 1962, John Glenn entered history as the first American to orbit the Earth. Aboard his capsule, which he named "Friendship 7" in honor of his colleagues, he blasted off from Cape Canaveral for a three-orbit flight a-round the planet. He traveled 81,000 miles in just under five hours. As the world watched on televisions all over the world, Glenn entered the outer atmosphere and experienced weight-lessness for the first time. He uttered the famous words, "Zero-G and I feel fine," and described his view from the window of Friendship 7 as he watched three sunsets and noted the closeness and brightness of the stars. His capsule splashed down in the Atlantic Ocean, and he was picked up by a Navy ship.

> *As the world watched on televisions all over the world, Glenn entered the outer atmosphere and experienced weightlessness for the first time. He uttered the famous words, "Zero-G and I feel fine," and described his view from the window of Friendship 7 as he watched three sunsets and noted the closeness and brightness of the stars.*

Glenn returned to Earth an interna-tional hero. Unlike the previous So-viet launches, which had taken place in absolute secrecy, Glenn's flight had been broadcast around the world, with audiences able to listen in on his reports back to Earth. The success of Glenn's flight had done much to re-establish American confidence in its space program, even if the Soviets did make the first launch. His appeal was also part of the reverence we feel for those who dare to explore. As *Newsweek* magazine noted the day after his flight, "No satellite, no matter how ingenious or scientifically valuable, can match the ageless human drama of the individual—solitary, questing, vulnerable—facing the unknown."

*Glenn climbs into his Friendship 7 space capsule atop an
Atlas rocket at Cape Canaveral, Florida, February 20, 1962*

Glenn was treated to a hero's welcome, with parades in Washington, New York, and back in Ohio. He received a number of awards and citations from the U.S. and the United Nations, and he also spoke to Congress, urging them to support continued funding of NASA. Glenn was honored by the American Geographic Society, which asked him to add his signature to a special globe that includes the names of other explorers and fliers. He even got a little extra in his paycheck. In addition to his regular salary as a Marine and NASA pilot, Glenn received an additional $245 for the month of February 1962 — flight pay for his trip.

President John F. Kennedy was quick to embrace the new hero and to take control of Glenn's future. Unbeknownst to Glenn, Kennedy decided that the astronaut was too valuable as a national hero to allow him to take any risks, and he refused to allow Glenn to take part in any other space flights. "It was only years later that I read in a book that Kennedy had passed the word that he didn't want me to go back up," Glenn said. "I don't know if he was afraid of the political fallout if I got killed," but he was never able to discuss the topic with Kennedy, who died in 1963. Glenn was terribly disappointed. He didn't mind serving as a spokesman for the program, but he desperately wanted to go into space again.

Leaving the Space Program

In 1964, after two years of trying to get himself on another flight into space, Glenn resigned from NASA. He decided to enter the world of politics and ran for the U.S. Senate seat for Ohio. He chose to run as a Democrat, and in January 1964, he won the nomination. But shortly after that win, Glenn fell in his bathroom while shaving and seriously injured himself. He had damaged his inner ear, which profoundly affected his balance. He was forced to withdraw from the race.

After he recovered from his injuries, Glenn officially retired from the Marine Corps, and in November 1964, he entered the world of business. For the next several years he served as an executive for Royal Crown Cola. He also served as a director for the Questor Corporation and started other business ventures, including real estate purchases, that made him a very wealthy man. Glenn also hosted a TV series on explorers in the late 1960s.

Beginning a Life in Politics

In 1970, Glenn decided to give politics another try and once again ran for the Democratic nomination for the Senate. This time his opponent was Howard Metzenbaum, a wealthy businessman with strong political connections who was willing to spend part of his fortune to get elected. Although Glenn was a popular candidate, he lost to Metzenbaum in the primary, as Metzenbaum out spent him five to one.

In 1974 Glenn was ready to take on Metzenbaum again. He believed he had learned from his last defeat, and he tried to position himself in the state and in the party as the man to beat. He questioned Metzenbaum's ethics, showing that although Metzenbaum's worth was over $3.5 million, he had paid no taxes in 1969. Glenn didn't have the support of the state Democratic party, which was behind Metzenbaum. Nonetheless, many Democrats, including a large percentage of the labor vote, as well as some Republicans, supported Glenn. This time he defeated Metzenbaum by almost 100,000 votes in the primary to win the nomination for the Senate. In the Senate race that year, Glenn won against his Republican opponent, Ralph J. Perk. Glenn went to Washington as part of the first Congress elected in the wake of the Watergate scandal that had brought down the presidency of Richard Nixon. Glenn and other newly elected Democrats, including Senator Gary Hart of Colorado, Governor Mike Dukakis of Massachusetts, and Governor Jerry Brown of California, were seen as refreshing new voices in government, untainted by Watergate and Washington.

Glenn, 1998

Senator from Ohio

Glenn set about establishing himself as a hard working member of the Senate. He worked for lower taxes, an end to deficit spending by the Congress, and increased funding for health care initiatives and education. Over the next ten years, Glenn developed a reputation as an honest, diligent representative, distinguishing himself on committees devoted to nuclear nonproliferation, civil rights, and reducing military spending. In 1980, the Republican landslide that brought Ronald Reagan to the presidency didn't dent Glenn's popularity at home, where he was reelected in the largest plurality in Ohio history. As he had in earlier races, Glenn consistently underspent his competition, often by one-half, and won anyway.

In 1983, Glenn's name began to appear in a list of possible presidential candidates. That year, a poll put Glenn ahead of Reagan in a presidential preference race. Although some were concerned that Glenn either "would not or could not publicize himself," and although he lacked a formal campaign organization, he decided to run for the 1984 Democratic nomination for president.

Running for President

Glenn announced his candidacy in early 1984, and went on to run a campaign that was considered disorganized and inept. He was wooden, people said, and lacked a coherent message. The voters couldn't seem to figure out what Glenn stood for, and he did terribly in the early caucuses and primaries that determine the party's candidates. Some of his advisors blamed Glenn's poor showing on the effect of the film version of *The Right Stuff*, which had appeared earlier. They thought it portrayed Glenn in the only image that Americans could remember: "In the American mind he lives only on the tip of a booster rocket," said Sidney Blumenthal in *The New Republic*. In contrast, Glenn appeared on the stump as "stumbling, inarticulate, and boring." Glenn withdrew from the race in March 1984. Walter Mondale went on to win the Democratic nomination, but he lost the election to Ronald Reagan in a landslide.

The S & L Scandal

Reelected to the Senate again in 1986, Glenn once again settled into his work. He came to public attention again in 1987, named in a scandal that threatened to permanently tarnish his reputation. That year, Glenn and four other senators became known as the "Keating Five," for their relationship with financier Charles Keating. Keating was the head of a Savings and Loan, or S & L, known as Lincoln S & L. A Savings and Loan is similar to a bank. Keating had contributed a total of $1.4 million to the reelection campaigns of several key senators, including Glenn, Donald Riegle, Dennis DeConcini, John McCain, and Alan Cranston. Keating was under investigation by federal officials for allegedly stealing millions of dollars from his own bank and leaving the bank $2.5 billion in debt. In 1987 the senators known as the Keating Five met with the head of the Federal Home Loan Bank Board, Edwin Gray, and urged him to cease his investigation of Keating and Lincoln S & L. Gray later claimed that he found the senators' request "tantamount to an attempt to subvert the regulatory process."

Glenn claimed that as soon as he learned that Keating was under criminal investigation, he had nothing more to do with the financier. He tried to distance himself from the other senators involved in the scandal, claiming "we're not five peas in a pod." In 1990, the Keating Five were targeted in an inquiry by the Senate ethics committee. That is a Senate group that is responsible for investigating possible ethical abuses by members of the Senate. After a 14-month investigation, the committee found that Glenn and McCain had been guilty of "poor judgment." The other senators were reprimanded more harshly, especially Alan Cranston, who was charged with "impermissible conduct" and whose case was turned over to the full Senate.

Over the next several years, Glenn worked to erase the taint of the Keating scandal, focusing a lot of his energies on his work on the Senate Special Committee on Aging. After announcing in 1997 that he would retire from the Senate at the end of 1998, he focused his attention on parallels between reports coming out of the National Institute on Aging and reports coming out of NASA. While examining documents on the changes that take place in the body during the weightlessness of space flight, Glenn was struck by their similarities to the aging process. Changes in the blood and heart, loss of bone mass, and sleeplessness were just a few of the more than 50 changes that doctors had detected in astronauts over the years and that are also recognized as part of the process of getting older.

"I think it's safe to say I'm excited to be back," Glenn said in a moment of understatement. "I'm excited because I hope I can contribute to both NASA's and the National Institute on Aging's research on the human body."

Glenn was fascinated with the similarities and thought of a way to further research in space and aging. "I figured we could learn a lot if we sent an older person up, studied what the effects of weightlessness were, and tried to learn what turns these body systems on and off," he said. Thus Glenn began his effort to get himself back into space. He got in touch with NASA and, armed with scientific data, offered himself for a mission. He was told that he had to convince research scientists of the validity of his research and that he had to be able to pass the same physical required of every astronaut. Glenn succeeded in both areas. Scientists found his research credible, and NASA doctors cleared him for the mission.

The crew of Glenn's October 1998 flight. Seated are Curtis L. Brown Jr. and Steven W. Lindsey. Standing, from left to right, are Scott Parazynski, Stephen K. Robinson, Chiaki Mukai, Pedro Duque, and Glenn.

ANNOUNCING A RETURN TO SPACE

On January 15, 1998, it became official. Glenn announced that he would become the oldest person ever to fly in space. "I think it's safe to say I'm excited to be back," Glenn said in a moment of understatement. "I'm excited because I hope I can contribute to both NASA's and the National Institute on Aging's research on the human body."

Glenn began months of training for the mission, in which he would serve as a payload specialist. With characteristic modesty, Glenn insisted that his fellow crew members call him "John," not Senator. The differences between Glenn's first space craft and the mission were staggering. Friendship 7 was 36 cubic feet; the shuttle has more than 330 cubic feet for each of the crew members aboard. Glenn needed to learn a whole new attitude toward space flight. "We're teaching him how to live and how to sleep and how to clean up, just basic habitability in space," said one of his NASA trainers. "Now we go to space to work. We don't go just to survive." Glenn also had to combat negative comments in the press that he was going on the mission more for the publicity value than for the scientific value of the mission. Yet as launch time approached, Americans eagerly turned on their TV sets to watch Glenn enter the history books again—this time as the oldest man to travel in outer space.

THE FLIGHT OF DISCOVERY

After months of preparation, Glenn blasted off into space again on October 29, 1998, aboard the space shuttle Discovery. On hand at the launch at Cape Canaveral were 250,000 spectators and several of his old friends from the early days of the Mercury missions, including Scott Carpenter, who urged on his old colleague and seemed almost as excited as he was. As Discovery took off from the launch pad, Lisa Malone, countdown commentator from NASA, said, "Liftoff of Discovery with a crew of six astronaut heroes and one American legend." After a couple of hours in flight, the commander of the mission, Lieutenant Colonel Curtis Brown Jr., radioed back to Earth, "let the record show, John has a smile on his face and it goes from ear to ear." Glenn himself used an old phrase to relay his feelings: "A trite old statement: zero-G and I feel fine."

— " —

As Discovery took off from the launch pad, Lisa Malone, countdown commentator from NASA, said, "Liftoff of Discovery with a crew of six astronaut heroes and one American legend." After a couple of hours in flight, the commander of the mission, Lieutenant Colonel Curtis Brown Jr., radioed back to Earth, "let the record show, John has a smile on his face and it goes from ear to ear." Glenn himself used an old phrase to relay his feelings: "A trite old statement: zero-G and I feel fine."

— " —

In addition to Brown, Glenn's crewmates aboard Discovery were Steven W. Lindsey, pilot; Stephen Robinson, mission specialist; Pedro Duque, the first Spaniard to fly in space; Chiaki Mukai, a cardiovascular surgeon and the first Japanese woman in space; and Scott Parazynski, a doctor and specialist in space medicine whose job it was to monitor the changes in Glenn's physiology in space.

As part of the study on aging, Glenn wore a catheter in his arm during the entire nine-day mission. He began to refer to Dr. Parazynski as "Count Dracula," as the physician collected blood samples. "As much as I like Discovery, there's no place to hide when he comes after me," said Glenn. The tests run on Glenn measured many things, including the effects of weightlessness on the cardiovascular system, sleeping disorders, balance, and loss of bone density. But the Discovery mission scientists also did research in other areas. During the nine-day flight, they conducted experiments on astronomy, solar physics, insulation material, and artificial bone. They also did experiments in preparation for upgrades to the orbiting Hubble telescope, which continues to send back important information about space to scientists on Earth.

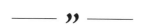

When Glenn was asked by an 83-year old reporter if there was hope for "people of my generation," he responded, "There's a lot of hope. You should run your life not by the calendar but how you feel, and what your interests are and ambitions. Old folks have dreams and ambitions too, like everybody else. Don't sit on a couch someplace."

The astronauts even appeared on network TV while in space. Host Jay Leno interviewed the astronauts for a spot on the "Tonight Show" and traded quips with commander Curtis Brown. Brown told Leno, "Jay, every time we fly by California, we see your chin." Leno told the crew, "This is the most amazing thing that has ever happened to me. I had to write a paper on Senator Glenn in the sixth grade, and I can finally turn it in."

On November 7, after a journey of some 3.6 million miles, including 134 orbits around Earth, John Glenn returned from space. He admitted he "didn't feel too hot," when he got out of the shuttle. "I was walking straddle-legged to keep my balance a little bit," he admitted. After a good night's sleep, he felt much better. He felt thrilled about being in space again, but also "a little let down that the whole thing is over." He stated that his second trip into space would be his last. His wife, Annie, hadn't been too keen on his trip into space, and, he said, "She's been through enough. I owe her some consideration at this point in my life." When Glenn was asked by an 83-year old reporter if there was hope for "people of my generation," he responded, "There's a lot of hope. You should run your life not by the calendar but how you feel, and what your interests are and ambitions. Old folks have dreams and ambitions too, like everybody else. Don't sit on a couch someplace."

Glenn and his wife, Annie, waving at his homecoming parade in New York, 1998

FUTURE PLANS

After his retirement in January 1999, Glenn plans to become involved in a new public-service institute founded in his name at Ohio State University, where he has also sent his papers. He also wants to be involved with fighting the cynicism about government he sees throughout the country. He's concerned about the bitter partisanship in Washington, in which members of the two political parties seem incapable of cooperating and working together. "Any major legislation has to have bipartisan support [the support of both political parties]. The more we work together, the better it is. We have different views, but when you get down to having so many political things in committee that are just irritants and are just partisan, that's not the way to go."

MESSAGE TO YOUNG READERS

In an interview with *Time* magazine, Glenn talked about his concern with the apathy he sees in many young people, and also about their importance to the political process:

"I don't think this country is ever going to get taken over by any resurgent Russia, China, or North Korea. But I worry about the future when we have so many young people who feel apathetic and critical and cynical about anything having to do with politics. They don't want to touch it. And yet politics is literally the personnel system for democracy. We've got the finest democracy in the world, but it's also one of the most complicated. Not everyone needs to run for public office, but every time someone drops out of the system it means they in effect give their franchise to somebody else. . . . If you say politics is so dirty you don't want anything to do with it, what you're really saying is that you don't want to get dirty from democracy. When I talk to young people, I try to get them thinking that politics is not only an honorable profession, it's one of the most honorable ones."

HONORS AND AWARDS

Distinguished Flying Cross (U.S. Military): five awards

FURTHER READING

Books

Carpenter, M. Scott, Cooper, L. Gordon, Glenn, John H., Grissom, Virgil I., Schirra, Walter M., Shepard, Alan B., Slayton, Donald K. *We Seven, by the Astronauts Themselves,* 1962
Cole, Michael D. *John Glenn: Astronaut and Senator,* 1993
Crocker, Chris. *Great American Astronauts,* 1988
Wolfe, Tom. *The Right Stuff,* 1979

Periodicals

Cricket, Oct. 1998, p.27
Current Biography Yearbook 1962; 1976
Life, Jan. 31, 1964, p.36A
New Republic, Feb. 13, 1984, p.13; Apr. 23, 1990, p.10
New York Times, Oct. 30, 1998, p.A1; Nov. 3, 1998, p.D3; Nov. 5, 1998, p.A20; Nov. 9, 1998, p.A12; Nov. 17, 1998, p.A27
New York Times Biographical Service, Jan. 1998, p.74

New York Times Magazine, Oct. 11, 1981, p.32
Newsweek, Jan. 29, 1962, p.72; Nov. 18, 1974, p.27; Oct. 26, 1998, p.30;
   Nov. 9, 1998, p.24
Time, Jan. 8, 1990, p.48; Nov. 26, 1990, p.35; Mar. 11, 1991, p.69; Aug. 17,
   1998, p.40
TV Guide, Oct. 24, 1998, p.15
U.S. News and World Report, May 20, 1974, p.36; Mar. 5, 1984, p.23
Washington Post, Mar. 17, 1984, p.A4

ADDRESS

Ohio State University
John Glenn
Bricker Hall
190 N. Oval Mall
Columbus, OH 43210

WORLD WIDE WEB SITE

http://spaceflight.nasa.gov/medialibrary
http://www.senate.gov/~glenn/

Savion Glover 1973-

American Tap Dancer and Choreographer
Creator of *Bring in 'da Noise, Bring in 'da Funk*

BIRTH

Savion Glover (pronounced SAY-vee-on GLOV-er) was born
in Newark, New Jersey, on November 19, 1973. His name,
Savion, is a variation on savior. His mother, Yvette Glover, is
a singer and actress who has also worked in various office
jobs to support her family. Less is known about his father,
whom Savion refuses to discuss and who left the family
when Savion was still a toddler. He has two brothers,
Carlton and Abron.

Glover was lucky to be born into a family with a history of athletic and musical talent. One of his great grandfathers, Dick (King Richard) Lundy, was a shortstop and a manager in the Negro Leagues, which were baseball leagues for African-American players before the major leagues were integrated. Glover's maternal grandfather, Bill Lewis, was a singer and pianist, and his grandmother, Anna Lundy Lewis, was a former minister of music at the New Point Baptist Church in Newark who performed gospel music with singer Whitney Houston.

YOUTH

Glover grew up in a housing project in Newark, New Jersey. He lived in a tough neighborhood, and his family didn't have much money. It would have been easy for him to get into trouble. But instead, he got into tap dance. As he says, "I would probably be stealing your car or selling drugs right now. I got friends who do that, but tap saved me."

Music, rhythm, movement, and noise have been central to Glover's life since the very beginning. According to his mother, Yvette Glover, "I noticed that Savion was gifted right from the womb. At the time of his birth, I was working as a computer operator, and when I was typing, in my womb, he would keep the rhythm of the keys." When he was just a baby, his grandmother

———— " ————

"I remember my first day [of tap dance class]. My mom couldn't afford dance shoes, so she put me in these old cowboy boots with a hard bottom so I could get some sound out. I used them for seven months. When I finally got real tap shoes, I was nervous. I kept moving my feet, thinking, 'Oh, so this is how it's supposed to sound.'"

———— " ————

picked him up one day when he was acting fussy. To calm him down, she started humming to him. He looked up at her, smiled, and started humming also. Yvette Glover recalls, "She and I looked at each other. She said to me, 'This baby's anointed. There is no doubt. He's anointed.'" As a toddler, he would pull out all the kitchen equipment he could reach. Using forks and knives, he would beat on different types of surfaces—on the pots and pans, on the walls—to see what different kinds of sounds he could make. With her background in music, his mother recognized his ability to recreate distinctive patterns of sound, what she calls his talent for "unusual, impeccable rhythm." She began helping him to develop this talent while he was still very young. "As a young boy of three or four," says Richard Ellner of the Broadway Dance Center, "he would sit around the kitchen and be banging on the table, banging on the walls, banging on everything in sight. His mother got really annoyed with that, . . . and she made him stop. So he transferred all that motion to his feet."

When Savion was just four, his mother enrolled him in violin lessons at a music school that specialized in the Suzuki method of instruction. He started his music training on the violin, but soon switched to drums. One day after class, his teacher came out and said to his mother, "Savion has got to go." Like mothers everywhere, Yvette Glover immediately assumed that he had done something to get in trouble, as she recounts here. "I said, 'Excuse me?' She said, 'He's got to go.' I said, 'Oh my God, what did he do?' She said, 'No, he doesn't belong. He is too far advanced for this class.'" The teacher arranged for Savion to have an audition at the Newark Community School of the Arts, where he soon became the youngest student in the history of the school to earn a scholarship. He started attending classes there when he was about four and a half.

STARTING TO TAP

Soon after that, Glover started performing with a band called "Three Plus" ("I was the Plus, on the drums"). When he was seven, he and the band played an opening at the Broadway Dance Center in Manhattan. Glover and his brothers started taking music and dance classes there on weekends. "I remember my first day," Glover says. "My mom couldn't afford dance shoes, so she put me in these old cowboy boots with a hard bottom so I could get some sound out. I used them for seven months. When I finally got real tap shoes, I was nervous. I kept moving my feet, thinking, 'Oh, so this is how it's supposed to sound.'"

Soon, Yvette Glover was driving her sons from Newark into Manhattan every weekend for dance and music classes. When Savion was eight years old, he saw an exhibition of rhythm tap by two veteran dancers, Chuck Green and Lon Chaney. Rhythm tap is a form of tap in which the whole foot, rather than just the heel and toe, is used to make sounds. After the performance, Glover turned to his mother and told her, "Mommy, this is what I want to do." From then on, he tapped everywhere he went, all the time: in his bedroom in the morning, in the bathroom, while walking to school. Since that time, tap has been a constant part of his life.

EARLY JOBS

Unlike most people who wait until adulthood to begin their career, Glover got started right away, combining childhood experiences, school, and jobs in the theater. He got his first big job when he was only about ten. In 1983, his teacher at the Broadway Dance Center told him about an upcoming workshop to prepare for a new stage show, *The Tap Dance Kid*. He was soon chosen to be the understudy for the lead in the Broadway show, and in late 1984 he assumed the lead role in what would be his first professional production.

The Tap Dance Kid was a Broadway musical and dance production about ten-year-old Willie and his family. Willie's grandfather was a famous tap dancer, but his father is a lawyer. He's worked hard to become successful and prosperous, and he wants his two children to follow him into the legal profession. But Willie wants to become a dancer, like his grandfather. Glover spent two years appearing as Willie in *The Tap Dance Kid*. While the show itself received mixed reviews, audiences and critics marveled at such accomplished dancing by such a young dancer.

For Glover, it was his first introduction to the world of show business. He gives a lot of credit to his mother for helping him to enjoy performing when he was so young, while still allowing him to act like a kid. "My mom always gave me my time to myself. She made it possible for me to chill out, have my life, be a kid, grow up." His mother always looked out for what was best for him, not just what was best for the show he might be appearing in. As his manager, or "momager," as Savion liked to say, she always went to the theater with him and traveled on tour with him when he was young. "When I was signing up for *The Tap Dance Kid*," Glover recalls, "the general manager took my mom into the office and said, 'Look, Savion can't ice skate, he can't ride his bike, he can't do this, he can't do that. No basketball.' And my mom said, 'Well, it looks like he can't be in *The Tap Dance Kid*, can he?' See, my mom allows me to be a kid. She doesn't want me to be [so] caught up in a movie set, or this theater, that I don't have time for myself or my family."

> "A lot of times, he'll do somebody's step. I know whose step it is. He'll do it, and he'll work it into his thing. It's like an homage — a real playful, respectful thing."
> — Gregory Hines

Savion visits Hoots the Owl on "Sesame Street"

EDUCATION

Glover received his education both through traditional schooling and through tutoring. He started out attending a Catholic school in Newark. But because he began performing professionally when he was very young, he had to combine his schooling with his work. When he was on the road touring with dance productions, he would be tutored privately each day. When he was appearing in Broadway shows in New York City, he would attend school in New York, which was about an hour away from his home in Newark.

In New York, Glover attended first the Professional Children's School and then the East Harlem Performing Arts High School in Manhattan. There, he was considered a nice kid who was particularly good at math. He would get up at 6:00 a.m., then head by train into Manhattan for the start of the school day at 8:00. He'd stay in classes all day, until about 3:00. When he was appearing in a show, he'd head over to the theater after school and stay in rehearsals until 6:00. If the weather was nice outside, he might have time for a little basketball before the start of the show at 8:00. After the show ended, sometime between 10:00 and 11:00 p.m., a limousine would take him home. He later also attended Arts High School in Newark, from which he earned a diploma in 1992.

SOME BACKGROUND ON TAP DANCE

Tap originated, people now believe, with the step-dances that slaves brought over from Africa to the New World. Those dances became even more important when slaves were forbidden by their owners to own drums, because they feared that drumming would incite revolt. With no drums, the percussive rhythms could only be created by the feet. Tap dancing evolved to combine these traditional African rhythmic dances with spirted Irish and English folk dancing. It developed in the 1800s, and by the early 1900s was being performed in minstrel shows and vaudeville acts. By the 1930s and 1940s, elaborate chorus lines of tap dancers became standard in Broadway shows and in Hollywood musicals, and the dancing of Bill "Bojangles" Robinson, Fred Astaire, Ginger Rogers, Ruby Keeler, and Gene Kelly filled movie houses. During that segregated era, most black dancers didn't find work in movies, but they did appear in live shows in nightclubs. Tap gradually became less popular in the 1950s and 1960s, and it looked at that point as if tap dance might be dying off. The dance form has made a resurgence in the 1980s and 1990s, spurred first by the noted dancer and actor Gregory Hines and later by Glover himself. In fact, many older dancers look to Savion to carry the tap dance tradition forward into the future by bringing in new, younger dancers who want to imitate him—just like he has imitated the older dancers.

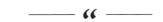

"Hoofing is dancing from your waist down. . . . People think tap dancing is all arms and legs and all this big old smile. No. It's raw, it's real, it's rhythm. It's us. It's ours."

When talking about tap, people generally talk about two styles of dance: Broadway (or show) tap, and rhythm (or jazz) tap. Broadway or show tap is the style of dance seen in a chorus line or in a Fred Astaire movie. Influenced by ballet and modern dance, this style of tap emphasizes posed arm movements, an erect upper body, and a light and graceful feel. Rhythm or jazz tap, for which Glover is known, is very different. In this improvisational form of tap, the dancer produces intricate percussive rhythms, treating the floor as the head of a drum. The way it sounds is just as important as the way it looks. The best rhythm or jazz tap dancers today are called hoofers, a rare compliment. "Hoofing," Glover says, "is dancing from your waist down. . . . People think tap dancing is all arms and legs and all this big old smile. No. It's raw, it's real, it's rhythm. It's us. It's ours."

One hallmark of modern rhythm tap is improvisation. Talented dancers learn basic steps and then create new ones and combine them in ever-changing new patterns. In this respect, according to Sally Sommer in *Dance Magazine,* a tap dancer is "like a jazz musician who ornaments a well-known melody with improvisational riffs." She goes on to say, "Among many tappers, improvisation is the most revered art, because it is about creation, demanding that imagination be turned into choreography instantaneously. Certainly it is the most difficult aspect of tap to master. The tap dancer has to have the brilliant percussive phrases of a composer, the rhythms of a drummer, and the lines of a dancer."

Another hallmark of rhythm tap is the challenge dance, a friendly competition in which dancers try to show up one another. "The toughest thing for any tap dancer is to get out there and improvise," Hines says. "Not only do you have to make it up, you've got to do something that tops the previous dancer. The challenge is a rite of passage. It's also one of the ways we kept the art form moving." Here, Hines describes one challenge dance with Glover. They were appearing together in a show, and Hines knew that Glover had been out late the night before, had performed an afternoon matinee show, and was exhausted. "So we get out on the stage, and we're doing it, but I can see he's not 100 per cent. I do my first step then he does a step. I pull something out, and I riff on it, so that even the people onstage are going, 'Ooh, ooh.' So now he blinks a couple of times, like he's a rhino that hadn't seen me and now he's spotted me. Now he reaches for something very interesting. But it's still not, you know, there. I finish off. I spin. I go up on both my toes, and I just stay there, and I come down with a flourish. And now I can see his nostrils flaring and his eyebrows wrinkling. His lips come pouting out like they do, and he does an amazing step — he spins around, goes up on *one* toe, and then he hops on the toe to some kind of percussive thing that pissed me off. And when he did that a roar went up like it was a bull-fight. The people onstage started laughing, because they knew I thought I had him."

LEARNING TO DANCE

Glover has had a unique approach to learning and practicing tap. Most dancers study for years in formal training and practice for hours each day to perfect their art. Not Savion. Glover doesn't attend a formal practice session each day; he considers any time he spends dancing, whether it's giving lessons or rehearsing for a show, to be practice time. And he quit taking regular dance classes when he was very young. Instead, he learned on his own and from other dancers.

In many types of dance, the rigorous physical requirements force people to retire before middle age. But in tap, dancers can continue performing throughout their lives, well into old age. And at the highest levels, tap dance is passed down from one dancer to the next. When performing together in shows, the older dancers tutor the younger ones between sets. That way, the best dancers learn by watching the older masters, picking up steps, adding them to their repertoire, and creating their own personal signature moves. Savion was able to develop his skills so quickly, in part, because he was able to imitate the styles and sounds of other dancers and because he had the opportunity to work with some of the best tap dancers of all time: Gregory Hines, Sammy Davis, Jr., Sandman Sims, Jimmy Slyde, Lon Chaney, Chuck Green, Harold Nicholas, Bunny Briggs, Steven Condos, and Arthur Duncan. According to Hines, "A lot of times he'll do somebody's step. I know whose step it is. He'll do it, and he'll work it into his thing. It's like an homage—a real playful, respectful thing." Glover has said that he feels a strong sense of duty to continue that history. "I feel like it's one of my responsibilities to keep the dance alive, to keep it out there, to keep the style." To that end, he teaches classes, holds workshops in cities where he's appearing on tour, and has trained and worked with several groups of young dancers.

> *"Tap is like a drum solo. I believe you can get so many tones out of using your foot. Your heel is like your bass drum. The ball of your foot is the snare. The side is like a rim shot. A regular tap dancer knows ball and heel; he doesn't know about the side of your arch, the side of your foot. We get sounds from the pinkie toe to all sides of the foot, back to the heel. . . . Drummers carry around their sticks; we carry around our tap shoes."*

DEVELOPING A PERSONAL STYLE

While Glover acknowledges a huge debt to earlier dancers, he has developed his own style as a dancer that is different from many earlier artists. He's fast, he's precise, he's athletic, and he's loud; in fact, he wears custom-made size 12½ EE Capezio tap shoes with an extra layer of metal under the taps to make the sounds even louder. He taps with all parts of his foot, often rising up on pointe, to create a variety of sounds. "Tap is

like a drum solo. I believe you can get so many tones out of using your foot. Your heel is like your bass drum. The ball of your foot is the snare. The side is like a rim shot. A regular tap dancer knows ball and heel; he doesn't know about the side of your arch, the side of your foot. We get sounds from the pinkie toe to all sides of the foot, back to the heel. . . . Drummers carry around their sticks; we carry around our tap shoes."

Glover calls his style "rough, funky, underground." Here, he describes what he calls "hitting," being able to express a personal style in tap: "Execute a rhythm to the fullest. If you gonna come up here and do something that you learned in class or that a teacher told you, that's cool and everything, but I wanna see what *you* got. I wanna see *you* hit. The complete expression of you in the moment. No restrictions. How you feel. How you hear the rhythms." Robert Sandla of *Dance Magazine* described his style as "the kind of rock-solid, so-fast-you're-not-sure-you're-hearing-it-right tap technique that has even blase dancers racing to catch up. He's a brilliant, even avant-garde tapper, kicking up sparks, rattling out torrents of sound dense with rhythm, sailing through more pointe work than Pavlova. What makes Glover a star is that he makes tap look so easy."

CAREER HIGHLIGHTS

For Glover, his career started when he was very young. He was just 11 or so when he started performing on Broadway in *The Tap Dance Kid*. His next big show was *Black and Blue*, in which he appeared first in France for six months in 1988 and again in the U.S. version on Broadway in 1989. The show was a celebration of black music and dance of the 1930s and 1940s that featured such veteran dancers as Bunny Briggs, Jimmy Slyde, Ralph Brown, and Lon Chaney. Glover earned a Tony nomination for his work in *Black and Blue*, becoming the youngest performer ever to be nominated for the prestigious Tony award. With this show, he was hailed by many as the future of tap dance.

Glover's next big credit was the movie *Tap* (1989), which starred Gregory Hines as Max, a down-on-his-luck tap dancer. Much of the movie is set in a dance studio where all the great old dancers hang out, and a challenge dance among the group is a highlight of the film. Glover plays the son of the woman who loves Max, and he also has a dazzling dance sequence. It was while working on these projects—*Black and Blue* and *Tap*—that Glover was able to trade steps with veteran tap dancers.

In 1991, Glover took a role as a regular character on "Sesame Street." He played Savion, a teen-age tap dancer. On Sesame Street, he found opportunities to share his love of tap dance all over the street, with human and with muppet characters. He danced with Elmo, talked with Gina, and hung out with Hoots the Owl at Birdland. What was intended as a three-day visit turned into a four-year stay; Glover appeared on the show through 1995.

It was while working on "Sesame Street" that Glover also appeared in the Broadway production *Jelly's Last Jam* (1992-94). It was a review of the life of jazz pioneer Jelly Roll Morton, his life story told in retrospect after his death while he is stuck in the Jungle Inn, "a lowdown club somewheres 'tween Heaven 'n Hell." In addition to straight biography, the piece mixes in social commentary on racism, specifically Morton's rejection of his black roots. Hines played Morton as an adult, with Glover taking the part of the younger Morton. The musical won glowing reviews.

———— " ————

"Savion is the best tap dancer that ever lived. He was doing things as a dancer at 10 that I couldn't do until I was 25. He has steps, speed, clarity, and an invention that no one else ever had. He's redefined the art form."
— Gregory Hines

———— " ————

In the 1990s, Glover began working in other formats, including choreography. In 1990, he created a piece for the "Rat-a-Tat-Tap" festival at the acclaimed Apollo Theater in Harlem. His number, "New Tap Generation(s)," featured 28 dancers, with Glover in a solo performance. In 1992, he received a National Endowment for the Arts (NEA) grant in choreography, becoming the youngest grant recipient in the history of the NEA. In 1993, he choreographed "Gettin' Hip to da Tap Hop" for the Jazz Tap/Hip-Hop Festival at the Strand Theater in Boston. In this work, 26 dancers were divided into two groups, with half doing tap dance and half doing hip-hop, until eventually the two groups came together and merged their styles. He also appeared as a guest artist in several programs in New York City and around the country in the early 1990s, solidifying his reputation as one of the greatest living tap dancers.

Bring in 'da Noise, Bring in 'da Funk

Glover's next work has become his signature piece. He was choreographing a show with director George C. Wolfe, with whom he had worked on *Jelly's Last Jam*. When Wolfe asked him what he wanted to do, Glover answered, "I just want to bring in the noise. I just want to bring in the funk." Together, they created the musical dance show, *Bring in 'da Noise, Bring in 'da Funk*. The show, which was unlike anything done so far, uses tap and "da beat" to celebrate the African-American experience. It blends together pieces from documentary, music, rap, dance, poetry, and percussion to tell its story, featuring Glover and three other dancers, two percussionists, a rap artist, and a singer. And the dancers used all types of dance to tell their story, in the words of Margo Jefferson in the *New York Times*: "plantation tap, ragtime tap, jazz tap, movie musical and film-noir tap, hoofer tap, gospel tap, rhythm and blues tap, reggae tap, and funk tap. Call it dance and music for what is past, passing, and to come."

Bring in 'da Noise, Bring in 'da Funk presents a series of vignettes from African-American history, featuring scenes from slavery, migration up north, Harlem during the 1920s, Hollywood in the 1930s and 1940s, and hard times today. One scene features Glover in a solo tribute to the veteran dancers who influenced him and served as his mentors: Chuck Green, Lon Chaney, Buster Brown, and Jimmy Slyde. Glover stands alone, as himself, back to the audience, facing a mirror, with a tape recording of his voice talking about his mentors. Laura Shapiro described the scene in *Newsweek* magazine like this: "As he describes them, he demonstrates what they've passed down to him, and what he's made of it. He calls his own style 'hitting'—'it's raw, it's rhythm, it's us.' And he shows off a gorgeous barrage of free-wheeling taps, grounded in the clarity, precision, and subtlety he learned from his mentors. Elsewhere in the show, he does amazingly expressive things with tap—it describes a lynching, a riot, and the despair of a whole community. But here Glover peels away story and text to show us the bare elements of his art."

Bring in 'da Noise, Bring in 'da Funk opened off-Broadway in November 1995 before moving to Broadway in April 1996. The show was a complete surprise to its audiences, most of whom had little experience with Glover's style of dance. Here, Shapiro describes what many felt when they first saw the show. "There you are awaiting an evening of tap, thinking pleasant thoughts about Fred Astaire and squadrons of smiling hoofers in spangly vests, when a blast of hip-hop/funk music rips through the theater and Glover rockets into view. He's leaning forward, his feet are slamming into the floor, his arms are sailing crazily, and he's wearing baggy bermudas, a giant T-shirt, and a huge, exhilarated grin. Three more tappers show up . . . and the stage explodes in a volley of hard-driving feet. Now Glover is on his heels, now he's on the inside of a foot, and now he's balancing on a pointed toe, while his other foot hammers the floor as fast and as precisely as the needle in a sewing machine. For all the cacophony, for all the heat of the street that fuels this number, there's no question about what's going on here: the best new choreography and the most glorious dancing Broadway has seen in years."

Shapiro's view was echoed and amplified by virtually all who saw Glover in *Bring in 'da Noise, Bring in 'da Funk*. With this show, according to Bruce Weber in the *New York Times Magazine*, "Savion Glover is almost all by himself reawakening a moribund dance language by combining a contemporary idiom — his feet speak street hip-hop, both the angry boom box and bluesy, incantatory varieties — with an almost supernatural physical gift. No tap dancer has ever heard the sounds he hears, at least no one who could transliterate them with his feet." *Bring in 'da Noise, Bring in 'da Funk* was a phenomenal success with audiences and critics from the very beginning. The show won four Tony awards, including the award for choreography for Glover. He danced in the show for two years, from 1995 to 1997, before relinquishing his role.

Recent Projects

Since leaving *Bring in 'da Noise, Bring in 'da Funk* in mid-1997, Glover has been involved in a variety of projects. He appeared as a soldier in Vietnam in a TV movie for the Showtime cable network called *The Wall* and tapped on a recording by jazz singer Abbey Lincoln, providing percussion on her recent CD called *Who Used to Dance*. He also hosted a TV special in late 1997, "Savion Glover's Nu York," that featured such performers as Puff Daddy, SWV, Stevie Wonder, Wyclef Jean, and Kirk Franklin. He's also in the process of setting up an official web site, to begin in late summer 1999. In addition, he and journalist Bruce Weber have been co-writing a book about his life, tentatively titled *Savion! My Life in Tap*. Due to be published in early 2000, the book combines biographical information on Glover's life with his own observations on dance.

Glover has also been working with a dance group he formed called Not Your Ordinary Tappers (NYOT), making appearances in New York, Washington, D.C., and Ohio. In these recent appearances, Glover is said to have found a new freedom, confidence, and maturity in his art. One of their pieces, called *Savion Glover/Downtown*, inspired Joan Acocella of the *Wall Street Journal* to write this. "Mr. Glover has no special secrets. He simply has, to a phenomenally advanced degree, what all tappers strive for. First, range. His small taps are smaller, his big taps bigger, than anyone else's. Second, articulation. Every sound, from the smallest to the biggest, is exactly that sound, with no soft edge muddling it into the next one. Third, speed. At one point, without lifting his foot more than an inch off the floor, he unleashed a flow of tiny taps that rippled off the stage like light off water. . . . At another point he took off into

"Savion Glover is almost all by himself reawakening a moribund dance language by combining a contemporary idiom — his feet speak street hip-hop, both the angry boom box and bluesy, incantatory varieties — with an almost supernatural physical gift. No tap dancer has ever heard the sounds he hears, at least no one who could transliterate them with his feet."
— *Bruce Weber*

the air, and though he was surely tapping—you could hear it—it was so fast that you never saw him land. All you saw was this happy man flying in the air while the sound geysered up beneath him. I burst into tears.

"Finally, Mr. Glover has, in spades, the thing that all those other skills are meant to serve, rhythmic fantasy. As with all great tappers, what he is is a great jazz musician. And so, as with Charlie Parker and the others, you go with him on a journey, from one pattern of sound to the next. . . . Sometimes it seems, incredibly, that the bass line is in the heel and the melody in the ball of the same foot, but most of the time the bass is in one foot, the melody in the other. . . . He seems to have gone inward to the point where he can now get out, and bring us what he has found. His pauses, his emphases, are intimate, personal, come-with-me. He is trying to tell us something. Once a marvel, he has become an artist."

MAJOR INFLUENCES

Here, Glover pays tribute to the master tap dancers who influenced him, people like Gregory Hines, Jimmy Slyde, Sandman Sims, Lon Chaney, and Bunny Briggs. "My biggest influence has been the great dancers who raised me, took me under their wings, taught me everything I know, allowed me to imitate them until I had my own style and my own voice. They challenged and encouraged me—Gregory Hines, Jimmy Slyde, and others—showed me that yes, tap is joyful, it's fun, that it can make you very happy. It is also a serious discipline and can express lots of feelings and thoughts—some sad, some blue, some angry, some thoughtful, some exuberant.

"And what I received, I love giving back. I love to teach, and to work with youngsters. And since the tap tradition was *almost* lost, I feel that it is my responsibility to keep passing it along."

HOME AND FAMILY

Glover, who is unmarried, lives in the New York area. One of the first things he did when he started performing was to buy a new house for his mother in New Jersey, outside Newark. He remains very close to his mother and brothers, one of whom, Abron, dances with NYOT.

CREDITS

The Tap Dance Kid, 1984-85 (stage)
Black and Blue, 1988 (stage; France, 1988; U.S., 1989)
Tap, 1989 (movie)
"Sesame Street," 1991-95 (TV)
Jelly's Last Jam, 1992-94 (stage)
Bring in 'da Noise, Bring in 'da Funk, 1995-97 (stage)
The Wall, 1997 (TV movie)
"Savion Glover's Nu York," 1997 (TV special)
Savion Glover/Downtown, 1998 (stage)

HONORS AND AWARDS

Martin Luther King, Jr., Outstanding Youth Award (Southern Christian
    Leadership Conference): 1991
National Endowment for the Arts Grant: 1992, for choreography
Choreographer of the Year (*Dance Magazine*): 1996
Tony Award: 1996, for choreography, for *Bring in 'da Noise, Bring in 'da
    Funk*

FURTHER READING

Books

Who's Who among African Americans, 1998
Who's Who in America, 1999

Periodicals

Biography Magazine, July 1997, p.71
Christian Science Monitor, June 23, 1992, p.13
Current Biography Yearbook 1996
Dance Magazine, Aug. 1989, p.38; Feb. 1993, p.73
Dramatics, Oct. 1992, p.22
Ebony, June 1989, p.88
New York Times, Feb. 20, 1989, p.13; Jan. 2, 1994, Sec. 2, p.32; Nov. 26,
    1995, Sec. 2, p.4; Apr. 26, 1996, p.C1
New York Times Magazine, July 28, 1996, p.28
New Yorker, Oct. 30, 1995, p.88
Newsweek, Apr. 22, 1996, p.68
People, June 24, 1996, p.134
Smithsonian, May 1997, p.86
Wall Street Journal, June 2, 1998, p.A20

ADDRESS

Morrow Junior Books
1350 Avenue of the Americas
New York, NY 10019

Jeff Gordon 1971-

American Stock Car Racer
NASCAR Winston Cup Champion in 1995, 1997, and
1998

BIRTH

Jeff Gordon was born on August 4, 1971, in Vallejo, California.
He was raised by his mother, Carol, and his stepfather, John
Bickford. Bickford, who worked for an auto parts manufacturer, first got Gordon interested in auto racing when he was
just a young boy. Gordon has an older sister, Kim, and an
older stepbrother, John Bickford Jr.

128

YOUTH

Gordon was fascinated by speed from a very early age. Some of his first memories are of rolling down a grassy hill near his home and then getting up quickly so he could run back to the top and do it again. It did not take the young boy long to discover that he could go faster on wheels than he could by rolling. "I rode my first bicycle when I was two-and-a-half or three years old," he recalled. "I remember those days. We had a big hill at our house, and I use to ride down the hill on my bike, skateboard, roller skates, whatever I had."

Gordon's stepfather soon noticed that he seemed to be unusually skilled at riding a bike despite his young age. As a result, John Bickford began entering his stepson in bicycle motocross, or BMX, races at the very young age of four. The competitors rode their bikes around obstacles and over jumps on dirt tracks. But Gordon's BMX racing career ended as soon as his mother saw how dangerous the races were. "At BMX events, they were hauling kids away in ambulances all the time," she remembered.

"I rode my first bicycle when I was two-and-a-half or three years old. I remember those days. We had a big hill at our house, and I use to ride down the hill on my bike, skateboard, roller skates, whatever I had."

Anxious to keep his stepson interested in racing, Bickford talked his wife into letting Gordon race small cars called quarter-midgets — six-foot-long miniature race cars with one-horsepower engines. He was only five at the time. She was still worried about her son, but soon realized that the quarter-midgets were a lot safer than the bikes. For Bickford, getting his stepson involved in auto racing was a dream come true. "I always wanted to race [professionally]," he noted, "but I couldn't afford it. I was living my dreams through Jeff. His being small made it obvious he'd never be a football player. So I taught him the only thing I knew, how to race."

Gordon spun out in his first quarter-midget race, but he soon found success on the track. Within two years, he had won 36 races. When he was eight, he won every race he entered at the two tracks near his home and earned his first national championship. Since Gordon was so good at it, racing became a full-time family event. His father served as coach and mechanic, and his mother often drove the truck to and from races. Most other racers his age might race 20 times a year, but Gordon raced every weekend, all year. "We raced 52 weekends a year, somewhere in the United States," his stepfather recalled. "We had eight or nine cars. We practiced two or three times a week. We were the Roger Penske [a successful professional race team owner] of quarter-midgets."

Moving Up into Higher Racing Classes

After winning the quarter-midget national championship, it was time for Gordon to move up to a new type of racing. He made the jump from one-horsepower midget cars to ten-horsepower go-karts. At age nine, Gordon was racing against boys seven or eight years older than him—and winning. Some parents of the other kids thought that he had to be lying about his age.

After winning all 25 go-kart races he entered, Gordon again moved up in class, racing higher horsepower go-karts against even older boys. The victories kept on coming. Another step up followed, this time to a division called superstock light that featured no age limit. As a nine- and ten-year-old, he was racing against grown men. "We were still winning!" according to his stepfather. "And those guys were going, 'There's no damn nine-year-old kid gonna run with us! Get outta here!'"

But Gordon soon grew tired of the controversy. He dropped back to the quarter-midget cars and won his second national championship at age ten. He kept racing midgets, but for the first time he began to feel the effects of burnout from too much racing. His life was different from that of other boys his age, and he knew it. Gordon did not get to hang out with friends after school or play sports. His schoolmates, he recalled, "had no idea what I was doing, except when we had a class project and I brought in my race car."

But Gordon eventually realized that the feelings he was having did not mean he was through with racing—he just needed a tougher challenge. When he turned 13, his family moved to Pittsboro, Indiana. Bickford had learned that there was a sprint car sanctioning body in the Midwest called the All-Star Series that did not have an age limit to keep young drivers out. "Nobody was fool enough to drive that young," Gordon recalled, "so they didn't think they needed an age rule." At age 14, he started racing a 650-horsepower (most cars on the road have less than 300 horsepower), 1300-pound, full-sized race car that cost $25,000 to put together. He was competing against men two and three times his age in races that were competitive enough to be shown on ESPN, the cable

*Gordon kissing the finish line after he won his second Brickyard 400
at the Indianapolis Motor Speedway, August 1, 1998*

television sports channel. It was unheard of for someone that young to race at that level.

One time, Gordon went to the corporate offices of Valvoline Oil to try to arrange a sponsorship deal. When he met with Valvoline executives to ask about sponsorship, they thought he was joking. One executive asked him how he got to their offices that day. "My mother drove me," Gordon replied with a straight face. "Now let me get this straight," the man said. "You drive a 650-horsepower sprint car on half-mile tracks and you had to get your mom to drive you down here?" "Yes sir," Gordon responded politely. "I'm not old enough to have a driver's license." He had to wait until he was 16 to drive legally on the roads in Indiana.

When he turned 18, Gordon joined the United States Auto Club (USAC) and began to race in its sprint car division, driving 815-horsepower open-wheeled cars. At the same time, he raced cars that were known as full midgets—lightweight, 320-horsepower cars. As usual, he was a winner, claiming the season championship in the full midget division.

EDUCATION

While most of his time was devoted to racing, Gordon did manage to attend Tri-West High School in Pittsboro. His high school years were far from normal, however. He often missed several days of classes at a time in order to travel to races. But he made sure he kept up on his school-work, always completing assignments in advance when he had to travel.

Gordon did find time to make friends while he was in school, although it took extra effort on his part. Most of the people at his school did not even realize that he was one of the most successful young auto racers in the country—they just knew he was a huge sports fan who was always on hand to cheer on Tri-West's teams. By his senior year, Gordon was one of the most popular students in the school and was even voted the king of his senior prom. He graduated from Tri-West High School in 1990.

> When he tried driving stock cars, Gordon immediately fell in love with them. "That first day, the first time I got in a [stock] car, I said, 'This is it. This is what I want to do.' The car was different from anything I was used to. It was so big and heavy. It felt very fast but very smooth. I loved it."

But Gordon knew that high school would probably be the end of his formal schooling. He already knew that his future belonged to auto racing. "I started to look at racing as a job," he remembered. "The night I graduated from high school, I finished fourth in a sprint-car race at Bloomington, Indiana."

When high school ended, Gordon realized he had reached a crossroads in his racing career. There are several types of car racing in the U.S., and he knew that it was time to choose the type he wanted: sprint cars, Indy cars, Formula One, drag racing, or stock cars. He did not really want to continue racing the open-style sprint cars or move into Indy-car style racing because obtaining sponsorship was often difficult. But he was not sure which avenue to pursue on the race track. His stepfather helped him out as much as he could. "My step-father made some connections and enrolled me in driving schools all over the country," Gordon stated. One of the schools he attended was op-erated by stock car racing legend Buck Baker. This experience would change Gordon's life.

CAREER HIGHLIGHTS

Gordon attended Baker's racing school in Rockingham, North Carolina, in the summer of 1990. The cars at Baker's school were stock cars—racing versions of cars you see on the road every day, such as the Ford Taurus and Chevrolet Monte Carlo. They were very different from the open-wheel sprint cars that Gordon had been driving, but the young champion immediately fell in love with them. "That first day, the first time I got in a [stock] car," he recalled, "I said, 'This is it. This is what I want to do.' The car was different from anything I was used to. It was so big and heavy. It felt very fast but very smooth. I loved it."

Gordon seemed to have a natural talent for stock car racing. He raced a few times in 1990 on the racing circuit called the NASCAR Busch Grand National Series. This series is one level below the NASCAR Winston Cup Series, which is the most popular form of auto racing in the United States. In 1991, team owner Bill Davis offered Gordon a full-time ride on the Busch Series, and Gordon jumped at it. As usual, he was successful. That first full year in stock car racing, he won the Busch Rookie of the Year award. In 1992, Gordon ended up winning three races and 11 pole positions (the starting spot in the race that a driver wins by having the fastest qualifying time). The 11 poles set a new Busch series record for one season.

Many people took notice of Gordon's success. At a race in Atlanta in August 1992, influential NASCAR team owner Rick Hendrick watched with great interest as the kid in the white car battled for victory against some of the biggest names in stock car racing. Although it looked like he might crash on every turn, Gordon maintained control and actually won the race, defeating such long-time NASCAR stars as Dale Earnhardt and Harry Gant. After the race, "I asked who the driver was," Hendrick recalled. "Somebody said, 'That's that kid Gordon.' I said, 'It's too bad he's got a contract because I see a lot of Tim Richmond [a former NASCAR star] in him, hanging his car out there like that lap after lap after lap.' His roommate said, 'He doesn't have a contract.' Two days later he did."

Gordon was happy to join the Hendrick Motorsports team because Hendrick was one of the richest, most powerful, and most successful owners in NASCAR's top Winston Cup Series. On the Winston Cup circuit, drivers accumulate points after each race according to their finishing position (175 points for first place, 170 for second place, etc.). At the end of the season—currently 33 races—the points are totaled, and the top 25 drivers receive prize money. The top point-getter becomes the Winston Cup champion and wins a substantial prize.

In 1993, Gordon began racing full-time on the Winston Cup tour. At the season-opening Daytona 500 in Florida—known as the "Super Bowl of stock car racing"—he stunned the racing world by winning one of the 125-mile qualifying races. At 21, he was the youngest man ever to win one of the qualifying races. He ended up finishing an impressive fifth in the race itself, a performance that was almost unheard of for a rookie driver. For the season, he finished seven times in the top five and eleven times in the top ten, good enough to win 1993 Rookie of the Year honors. "I looked at this year as a learning experience and as a chance to do some pretty good things," Gordon stated after the season was over. "We had a good year. I learned a lot and I had the opportunity to race with the best drivers in the world."

—————— **"** ——————

"Winning the [1995 Winston Cup] is just too good to be true," Gordon said. "There just aren't words to describe how I feel. It's been a spectacular year— better than we ever thought it could be."

—————— **"** ——————

The next year, Gordon broke through and won his first Winston Cup race, the Coca-Cola 600 at Charlotte Motor Speedway. Gordon was so overcome by emotion after the race that he burst into tears while being interviewed on national television. His dreams had started to come true. Later that season, he won again, this time taking the checkered flag in the Brickyard 400, the first-ever Winston Cup race to be held at the famous Indianapolis Motor Speedway (home to the Indianapolis 500). This victory was special to Gordon. Not only was it one of the richest races ever, but it took place only 20 miles from his teenage hometown of Pittsboro, Indiana. "To make history here in NASCAR is more than a dream come true," he said before the race. He was even more excited after the race. In fact, he had to take an extra lap after the race was over because he was crying tears of joy in his car, and he did not want to go on television like that and "be known as a crybaby all the time," he joked. The victory touched off huge celebrations in nearby Pittsboro.

Winston Cup Champion

Gordon's two wins in 1994 set the stage for an even more successful 1995 season. That year—with NASCAR fans all across the country taking notice of the superstar-in-the-making—Gordon won seven Winston Cup races. When the season ended, Gordon's strong finishing positions had earned him enough points to be declared the Winston Cup champion. At age 24, he was the second-youngest man to ever win the cham-

Gordon climbing out of his car at the Talladega Superspeedway after his qualifying attempt for the Winston 500, October 9, 1998

pionship. Counting the $1.3 million bonus he earned for winning the Cup, Gordon broke the record for most money won in a season with $4,347,343. "Winning the title is just too good to be true," Gordon said. "There just aren't words to describe how I feel. It's been a spectacular year—better than we ever thought it could be."

Gordon got off to a slow start in 1996 and was unable to win a second consecutive Winston Cup title. In the first two races of the year, Gordon finished 42nd and 40th, and people began to say that his 1995 season might have been a fluke. That talk ended in week three, when he won the race at Richmond, Virginia. Before 1996 was over, he had won 10 more races, the most of any driver. Only a late-season hot streak by veteran Terry Labonte kept him from his second title. If Gordon could not win the championship, he was glad to see his Hendrick Motorsports teammate Labonte win it. The two drivers had become friends, and Labonte had served as Gordon's mentor in 1995.

Losing the Winston Cup championship in 1996 only made Gordon want the 1997 title even more. The year started with a bang. Gordon won the Daytona 500 for the first time, leading a one-two-three parade of Hendrick Motorsports teammates across the finish line. Terry Labonte finished second, and Ricky Craven finished third. It was the first time three teammates had ever swept the top spots in stock car racing's biggest race. At age 25, Gordon became the youngest man ever to win the Daytona 500. "This is the big one, the Daytona 500!" he said after the race. "What a way to do it, 1-2-3 Hendrick, and I couldn't have done it without those guys [Labonte and Craven]. That was teamwork out there on the racetrack at the end."

For Gordon, the win was the start of a storybook year. He won 10 races for the second consecutive season, and this time his results were good enough to claim the Winston Cup championship. Along the way, he collected a $1 million bonus for winning three of the four major races on the Cup schedule (becoming only the second man to achieve that feat), and he held off veteran racers Dale Jarrett and Mark Martin to win the closest three-man race in NASCAR history. "This has been a very rewarding year and I really want to enjoy this championship," he said after the season ended. "I felt like [the championship in] '95 was just a whirlwind and I never got to sit down and relax, just enjoy it."

Success Brings Resentment

After winning two Winston Cup championships in three years, Gordon became the undisputed top name in stock car racing. He was young, good-looking, marketable, and a champion. Many fans loved him. But at the same time, there was a growing group of NASCAR fans who did not like Gordon. They thought he was a spoiled rich kid from California who always had the best car and the best crew. Many fans booed him and called him names at the track. Some people even created a Gordon Haters of America site on the Internet. But Gordon tried not to let some fans' resentment get to him. "How can I complain when people boo?" he asked. "Actually, it's a good thing because it means I'm winning. If I wasn't winning, you wouldn't hear any of that, so I'm not bothered by it, really. I just kind of smile, wave back at them, and walk away."

Ray Evernham, Gordon's longtime crew chief and one of the best crew chiefs in racing, talked about why so many people dislike Gordon so passionately. "He's 26, he's good-looking, he's talented, he's got a beautiful wife, and he's a millionaire," said Evernham. "If he wasn't my best friend, I'd probably boo him too. But in a world where a lot of sports heroes have rainbow hair and earrings and are getting locked up and have drug problems, I think he's good for our sport."

In 1998, Gordon gave the anti-Gordon crowd even more reasons to dislike him. He won a record-tying 13 races, including four in a row, and claimed his second straight Winston Cup championship. He had won three races before he went on his four-win streak in races 14 through 17 of the season. Only six other men had ever won four Winston Cup races in a row. It looked like Gordon would have no chance to win the fourth race, the Pepsi 400 at Michigan Speedway. But he pulled it off when a caution period with 20 laps to go let him make a pit stop and adjust his car so that he could pass leader Mark Martin. Gordon was still shaking his head after the race. "You can call me Houdini today because there was some magic out there," he said. "I'm scratching my head because this should not have happened. We shouldn't have pulled into Victory Lane today. That last set of tires and those adjustments made all the difference."

Ray Evernham, Gordon's longtime crew chief, talked about why so many people dislike Gordon so passionately. "He's 26, he's good-looking, he's talented, he's got a beautiful wife, and he's a millionaire. If he wasn't my best friend, I'd probably boo him too. But in a world where a lot of sports heroes have rainbow hair and earrings and are getting locked up and have drug problems, I think he's good for our sport."

Gordon won the last two races of 1998 to clinch the Winston Cup title and tie Richard Petty's record of 13 wins in a single season. To tie Petty was particularly exciting. "To end the season this way really puts icing on

Gordon beats Dale Earnhardt to win the Daytona 500, February 14, 1999

the cake for the entire year," Gordon stated. "To be able to do something that Richard Petty has done is a milestone and is something that I'm so thrilled and excited for this race team to be a part of." The season proved to be lucrative also. Gordon won over $6 million and earned, in total, over $9 million—in 1998 alone.

Gordon has continued his winning ways in 1999. Currently, he is driving a 1999 Chevy Monte Carlo. This 3,400 pound monster has a 358-cubic inch Chevrolet V8-SB2 engine that generates 700 horsepower at 8,000 r.p.m. With it, he won the Daytona 500 for the second time to open the 1999 Winston Cup season. Coming down the stretch, he held off Dale Earnhardt, one of his racing idols, to win the race. "This is a dream come true for me—to race Dale Earnhardt down to the final finish, all the way down to the line for the Daytona 500, it does not get any better," he noted.

In 1999, Gordon will attempt to become only the second driver to win three consecutive Winston Cup championships. He has the potential to set many new records and join the ranks of NASCAR legends. He is young enough that he might challenge Petty's record of 200 career victories. He also has a chance to beat the record of seven career Winston Cup championships held by Petty and Earnhardt. "I want to be in a position where I can be behind the wheel of the car and do my job to make it a winning car," Gordon explained. "I especially love being part of a winning team, because even on those days when we're not a winning combination, I still just like being behind the wheel and being challenged by that."

MARRIAGE AND FAMILY

Gordon met his wife, Brooke Sealey, at the Daytona 500 in 1993. She was that year's Miss Winston and was on hand to congratulate Gordon when he won one of the qualifying races. He knew immediately that he wanted to get to know Brooke better, but there was a rule that prohibited the drivers from having any personal contact with the Miss Winston models. Gordon ignored the rule and asked her to go to lunch the next day, and she accepted.

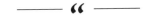

For the next year the couple hid their growing romance. They often attended the same NASCAR functions, but separately, not as a couple. Everyone wondered why the young and good-looking Gordon did not have a girlfriend, but he just smiled and kept quiet. "Hiding her for so long was so difficult," he admitted later.

Gordon has tried not to let some fans' resentment get to him. "How can I complain when people boo? Actually, it's a good thing because it means I'm winning. If I wasn't winning, you wouldn't hear any of that, so I'm not bothered by it, really. I just kind of smile, wave back at them, and walk away."

When Brooke's reign as Miss Winston ended at Daytona in 1994, they were finally able to make their relationship public. Gordon reserved the entire dining room of a fancy French

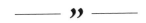

restaurant in Daytona Beach and asked Brooke to marry him. They were married on November 26, 1994. "It was really fun for me because now I'm married, I get to say wife," Gordon stated. "For so long, it's like girlfriend, fiancee. And I was finally able to say 'My beautiful wife.'"

HOBBIES AND OTHER INTERESTS

Off the track, Gordon is actively involved in charity work. He donates both time and money to organizations that fight leukemia and raise awareness about bone marrow donation and the National Bone Marrow Registry. He is also involved in the Motor Racing Outreach program, which is the auto racers' religious organization. He regularly speaks at churches and before other groups.

The fight against leukemia is a very personal one for Gordon. First, the son of crew chief Ray Evernham was diagnosed with leukemia when he was one year old. Then, shortly afterwards, team owner Rick Hendrick was also diagnosed with the disease. Gordon knew that he had to act. "I guess that's usually how it happens," he noted. "Something hits close to home and that's how it gets your attention. Unfortunately, you know, situations like that are what get most people's attention and if we could increase awareness to them out there, to the people who just want to give back and really make a difference — that's kind of our goal."

When Gordon is away from the track, he enjoys snow skiing, water skiing, racquetball, and video games.

HONORS AND AWARDS

National Quarter-Midget Championship: 1979, 1981
USAC Midget Series National Championship: 1990
USAC Silver Crown Division National Championship: 1991
Busch Grand National Rookie of the Year: 1991
Winston Cup Rookie of the Year: 1993
Driver of the Year: 1995, 1997, 1998
Winston Cup Champion: 1995, 1997, 1998
Man of the Year (True Value): 1996

FURTHER READING

Books

Brinster, Richard. *Race Car Legends: Jeff Gordon,* 1997 (juvenile)
Gordon, Jeff, and Bob Zeller. *Portrait of a Champion,* 1998
Mair, George. *Natural Born Winner: The Jeff Gordon Story,* 1998
Stewart, Mark. *Jeff Gordon,* 1996 (juvenile)
Who's Who in America, 1999

Periodicals

Detroit Free Press, Feb. 15, 1999, p.D1
ESPN The Magazine, Mar. 8, 1999, p.86

Forbes, Dec. 14, 1998, p.188

Los Angeles Times, Nov. 3, 1998, p.D1

New York Times, Aug. 8, 1994, p.C3; July 16, 1995, Section 8, p.2; Oct. 16, 1997; June 21, 1998, Section 8, p.1

Newsweek, July 28, 1997, p.54

People, May 12, 1997, p.152; June 30, 1997, p.73

Philadelphia Inquirer, Sep. 20, 1998, p.C1

Sport, Feb. 1995, p.31; Mar. 1998, p.86; Jan. 1998, p.55

Sports Illustrated, Apr. 24, 1995, p.46; Aug. 18, 1997, p.24; Aug. 10, 1998, p.80

Time, June 15, 1998, p.42

TV Guide, Aug. 2, 1997, p.22

USA Today, May 26, 1995, p.E18; Aug. 4, 1995, p.C1; Jan. 29, 1998, p.C3

Washington Post, Nov. 10, 1996, p.D1; Aug. 18, 1997, p.C1; Feb. 13, 1998, p.C11; Aug. 2, 1998, p.D1; Nov. 8, 1998, p.D5

ADDRESS

NASCAR
P.O. Box 2875
Daytona Beach, FL 32120-2875

WORLD WIDE WEB SITES

www.jeffgordon.com
www.hendrickmotorsports.com
www.nascar.com
www.thatsracin.com

David Hampton 1952?-

American Toy Inventor
Creator of Furby, the Animatronic Pet

BIRTH

Although little is known about David Hampton's family and the details surrounding his birth, he was born around 1952 in Ohio and grew up in Roseville, Michigan, not far from Detroit.

YOUTH

As a young boy, Hampton loved taking apart toasters and other small appliances. The basement of his family's home was filled with neighbors' broken radios, and he could often be found tinkering with them long after most boys his age were asleep. When he was 13, he began working in a television repair shop. He also rebuilt a World War II radar system, which ended up jamming the local police frequency, and put together a ham radio that broadcast his voice over the neighborhood's telephone wires.

EARLY MEMORIES

"When I was a boy, I had a green iguana lizard and I just loved it," Hampton recalls. "I remember all the awe I felt when I looked at the little pads on its feet and all the details of its body and personality. But in the end, I overfed it and it died." This early experience with owning a pet taught Hampton a lesson he never forgot. "With the Furby, I wanted to invent a toy that would come close to being a pet and that would teach children something about responsibility," he says.

FIRST JOBS

Hampton read in *Popular Mechanics* magazine that "the best electronics school was the Navy," so he enlisted right after he graduated from high school in 1970. He specialized in aviation electronics and traveled all over the world for eight years, learning to speak Japanese, Thai, Chinese, and Hebrew. When he got out of the Navy, he went to work in California's Silicon Valley, where one of his jobs included designing the video game Q-Bert. He also developed new products for Mattel, one of the largest toy manufacturers in the world.

CAREER HIGHLIGHTS

In 1990, Hampton decided to leave his job at Mattel and start his own design and consulting company. Among other successful projects, he designed the GeoSafari talking world globe and a hand-held device for Lionel, the toy train maker, that lets more than one train run on the same track. He also invented a medical nerve stimulator that blocks pain.

The Invention of Furby

In 1997 Hampton attended the Toy Fair in New York City, where toymakers exhibit the latest toys to buyers from all over the world. There, he encountered the Tamagotchi, an interactive, digital "pet" consisting of an alien creature on a tiny screen attached to a key chain. The pet's owner had to feed and clean up after it by touching a button or it would "die"—in other words, stop working. Although the Tamagotchi went on to become the year's top-selling toy, Hampton immediately noticed a flaw in its design: you couldn't pet it. He was confident that he could come up with something better.

Hampton returned home to California and began working on a toy he called Furball, a more life-like pet that wouldn't die. Furball began as a puff of fur that purred when its back was rubbed and laughed when Hampton tickled it. Eventually Furball became Furby, which looked like a combination of a penguin, a kitten, and an owl. Using a crude electronic board similar to the kits he had used as a child to build radios, Hampton gave Furby a voice. He enlisted the help of Caleb Chung, a former coworker from Mattel, to create the mechanics that would enable Furby to move and respond. It was Chung who decided that Furby should have large, expressive eyes and ears that could move like a dog's to show excitement or sadness.

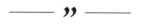

> "With the Furby, I wanted to invent a toy that would come close to being a pet and that would teach children something about responsibility."

Selling the Idea

Throughout the spring and summer of 1997, Hampton and Chung went from one toy manufacturer to the next, trying to drum up interest in their working model of Furby. Finally someone suggested they try Tiger Electronics, an Illinois company whose most recent success was the Giga Pet, a "virtual pet" similar to the Tamagotchi. Although Tiger wasn't known for making dolls or plush toys, company executives were immediately won over when they met Furby. Hampton and Chung signed a contract with Tiger in late November to produce a Furby prototype in time for the February 1998 Toy Fair, where it was proclaimed the season's "hottest new toy."

Although it normally takes a toy manufacturer about two years to make a new toy available to the public, Tiger Electronics had barely eight months to get the first million Furbies to the stores in time for Christmas. Hampton worked up to 17 hours a day, seven days a week to refine his working model. Then he spent about six weeks in China, where the factories that would actually make Furby were located.

Furby Frenzy

The first Furbies arrived at the F.A.O. Schwarz toy store on New York's Fifth Avenue on October 2, 1998. A white stretch limo pulled up to the store, and out walked six children carrying Furbies on purple pillows. Hampton was there to talk about the toy's history and language, and the entire event was broadcast live on the *Today* show. It was the beginning of "Furby Frenzy."

By Christmas 1998, Furby had become the top-selling toy in the U. S., as well as Canada and Great Britain. Parents started lining up at 4 a.m. in front of their local Wal-Mart when it was announced that a shipment of Furbies had arrived, and some were injured in the stampede when the doors were opened. "Toy scalpers" began collecting and selling Furbies, usually for much more than the standard $30 price. Some parents were paying up to $300 for the furry pets. This was very disturbing to Hampton, who deliberately designed the toy to be affordable.

What makes Furby so appealing? Just as Hampton had envisioned, Furby is an interactive computer game that can be snuggled and petted. It purrs when its back is stroked, snores when it sleeps, and says "Yum" when something is put in its mouth. Tilt sensors make Furby respond when it is moved. A microphone triggers responses to sound and music, and a light sensor reacts to changes in the environment. Unlike Tamagotchi, Furby won't die of neglect. If it is ignored for five minutes, the batteries shut down and it goes to sleep.

Best of all, Furby can talk. It speaks about 200 words and 1,000 phrases. In the beginning, its language is Furbish, a mixture of all the languages that Hampton learned when he was in the Navy. For example, "ay-lo," which is Furbish for "light," comes from the Hebrew word for God. Furby comes with a dictionary so the owner can translate what it is saying, but it is also programmed to learn English. Furbies communicate with each other by using a device similar to the remote control on a television. When Furbies meet, they greet each other in Furbish ("Da koodoh") and introduce themselves. If one Furby sneezes, its "cold" can spread to other Furbies within the four-foot range of its infrared sensors.

A Future for Furby?

Will Furby end up like Tickle Me Elmo, another "hot toy" that was fetching up to $500 on the black market a year ago but is now readily available in stores for $20? No one can say, nor will Hampton admit whether he is working on a successor to Furby. Tiger has released a number of Furby spinoffs, including Furby Babies and Special Limited Edition Furbies tied to the seasons, with Spring, Graduation, Autumn, and Holiday Furbies planned for 1999. Hampton thinks that there is definitely a future for interactive toys, and he predicts that the next generation of animatronic pets will be even harder to distinguish from real pets. Some owners are already claiming that their Furbies have learned foreign language phrases from watching TV and have cried over sad movies.

All this advanced technology has had one unexpected consequence, though. Recently, the National Security Agency (NSA) decided to ban Furbies from its offices. The NSA collects top-secret information for the federal government, and NSA staffers became concerned that Furby might be able to record their conversations. Tiger Electronics said that

Furby can't record conversations. It can only "learn" to say words and sounds that have already been pre-programmed into the toy. In fact, a spokesperson for the company said, "Furby is no spy."

And recently the Federal Aeronautics Association banned Furbies from domestic airline flights. It seems that Furby's programming can interfere with an airplane's own navigation and communication systems.

MARRIAGE AND FAMILY

Hampton lives with his wife, Cindy, and two sons—Mark, 13, and James, 10—in a farmhouse in California's Tahoe National Forest. The nearest town is 25 miles away, and the family gets their electricity from a gas-powered generator. Few of his neighbors know about Hampton's connection to Furby, and that's the way he wants to keep it. He prefers to work in privacy and isolation and rarely reads the newspaper or watches television.

It was Hampton's sons who helped him invent the Furby language. Mark came up with the idea that Furbies should be able to talk back and forth to one another. James, who was nine years old at the time, suggested that Furby should be able to burp.

FURTHER READING

Chicago Tribune Magazine, Dec. 13, 1998, p.12
New York Times, Dec. 10, 1998, p.B2
Newsweek, Oct. 19, 1998, p.66
People, Dec. 14, 1998, p.88
Scholastic News, Feb. 15, 1999, p.3
Time, Nov. 30, 1998, p.84

ADDRESS

Tiger Electronics
980 Woodlands Pkwy.
Vernon Hills, IL 60061

WORLD WIDE WEB SITE

www.furby.com

Lauryn Hill 1975-

American Singer and Rapper
Member of the Fugees and Creator of the Hit
Recording *The Miseducation of Lauryn Hill*

BIRTH

Lauryn Hill was born on May 26, 1975, in South Orange, New Jersey, which is near Newark. Her father, Mal, is a computer consultant and singer; her mother, Valerie, is a junior high school English teacher. Lauryn has one older brother, Malaney, who is now a lawyer.

YOUTH

Hill grew up in a stable and loving family, first in the suburb of East Orange and then in South Orange, where her family moved when she was in fifth grade. Her family lived in a tranquil suburban community with nice houses and green lawns. They were very comfortably middle class, but not wealthy. "I wasn't raised rich, but I never really wanted the things we didn't have. I think my parents instilled in us that we didn't need lavish things. As long as we had love and protection, we were always taken care of."

Hill has said that she grew up feeling part of two different worlds. Her neighborhood was right on the border of the slums in Newark. From her attic window she could see the projects, a grim block of buildings with public housing apartments. "[My] house is right on the borderline of the suburbs and the ghetto," Hill says. "I always had this duality. I went to school with a lot of white kids — it was really like a suburban environment — but I lived with black kids. Plus my whole family lives in Newark, in the city. So I grew up with two kinds of people in my life."

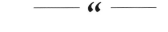

"I wasn't raised rich, but I never really wanted the things we didn't have. I think my parents instilled in us that we didn't need lavish things. As long as we had love and protection, we were always taken care of."

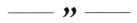

When Lauryn was growing up, everybody in the family loved music. "I don't remember my life without music," she says. Her father used to sing at weddings, her mother studied piano, and her brother played guitar, saxophone, and drums. Lauryn took violin lessons, and early on she showed an exceptional musical ability. "Her violin teacher kept telling us, 'I don't believe how musical she is,'" her mother recalls. "She just had this effect on people who listened to her."

But one of her first musical loves was old soul music. Her mom had amassed a huge stack of old 45s from the 1960s with classic soul hits from Motown, Stax, Atlantic, and Philly International, from artists like Marvin Gaye, Tammi Terrell, Gladys Knight, Curtis Mayfield, Roberta Flack, Donny Hathaway, Aretha Franklin, and Stevie Wonder. After her marriage, Valerie Hill had boxed up all her old records and put them in the basement. "One day little Lauryn found 'em," her mom recalls. "They all came upstairs. And thus began a journey. She started to play that music and loved it. One o'clock in the morning, you'd go in her room and you'd see her fast asleep with the earphones on. The Sixties soul that I'd collected just seeped into her veins." By the age of eight, Lauryn was an expert on old soul music. "I'd be the kid at family barbecues in the middle of Newark listenin' to the oldies station with the old folks," she recalls. "They'd go, 'Oh, that's Blue Magic!' And I'd go, 'No, it's the Chi-Lites.'"

EDUCATION

Hill's parents strongly emphasized the importance of education to their children. Even when she became involved in show business, her parents still considered schoolwork to be the top priority. "We made a deal, " her mother recalls. "I said that as long as her schoolwork came first, I would be happy to chauffeur her to auditions and showcases. And she kept up her end of the bargain." Lauryn heard the message loud and clear. While still in school she had several acting jobs and sang in a band, which evolved into the Fugees. But she was also an excellent student who earned straight As while getting involved in a wide range of extracurricular activities. A classic overachiever, Hill juggled a lot of different activities while attending Columbia High School: she founded a breakfast program for needy students, served as captain of the cheerleader squad and class president, ran on the track team, organized a gospel choir, took lessons in dance and violin, and still excelled in Advanced Placement (AP) classes.

When Hill graduated from Columbia High School in New Jersey in 1993, she applied to five top universities, and was accepted to all of them: Columbia University, University of Pennsylvania, Rutgers University, Spelman College, and Yale University. She selected Columbia in New York City because it was close to home and to her band. She attended Columbia for about a year before dropping out to focus on her music.

FIRST JOBS

Hill has loved to perform ever since she was a young child. She started out as a kid singing in front of the mirror, then graduated to the karaoke machine at Six Flags Great Adventure Park, a local amusement park. "That was my first studio," she says. When she was seven she went to see the movie version of the hit musical *Annie* with her mother, who says, "She was mesmerized. Her eyes were glued to the screen. After that, she learned every single song. I heard that every day—'Tomorrow, tomorrow.' I was so sick of 'The sun will come out tomorrow.'"

The Fugees — Hill, center, with Prakazrel (Pras) Michel, left, and Wyclef Jean, right

Hill got her first break at about 12 or 13 when she participated in Amateur Night at "Showtime at the Apollo" at the famed Apollo Theater in Harlem. She sang the old Smokey Robinson hit "Who's Lovin' You." Here, her mom recalls that night. "When the day came, we marshaled the forces, rented a big van, took a bunch of kids from her school for moral support, and went off to the Apollo. But when she started to sing, she was terrified, so she stood far away from the mike and the fans started booing. My brother-in-law screamed out, 'Get close to the mike!' and she grabbed the mike and sang that song with a vengeance, like, 'How dare you boo me.' She sang her heart out. At the end of the song, they were clapping and screaming for her. When we got home, she felt she had let herself down, and she started crying. I said, 'Lauryn, they're gonna clap for you one day and maybe not the next, but you gotta take it all. This is part of the business that you say you want to be in. Now, if every time they don't scream and holler you're gonna cry, then perhaps this isn't for you.' And she looked at me like I had taken leave of my senses. To her, the mere suggestion that this wasn't for her was crazy."

Joining a Band

Soon after that, Hill became part of a band with one of her brother Mal's friends named Prakazrel Michel (pronounced PRAZ-well, but just called Pras). They hooked up with another woman, Marcy, and called themselves Tranzlator Crew. At the time, they were working on something they called Tranzlator Rap, in which they rhymed in different languages. One day Pras's cousin, Wyclef Jean, dropped by when they were at a studio making a demo tape. Pras challenged Jean to rap freestyle over a song they were working on, and something clicked. Then Marcy left the group for college, and Jean joined up for good. While Hill was still in high school, the trio started playing at talent shows and neighborhood showcases. As she recalls, "We sang, we rapped, we danced. As a matter of fact, we were a circus troupe. Maybe we were a little overdeveloped in the sense that we did so much that we were just like, 'Yo, OK, I can do anything.' We were a piece of work, but you could see the talent."

Throughout her teen years, Hill worked on both her music and her acting. She started going to New York City for auditions and soon won a small part in an off-Broadway play. That part got her noticed by a talent agent, who helped her win a small part on the soap opera "As the World Turns" in 1991. She had a recurring role as Kira, a troubled teenage runaway. The following year she had a small role in the feature film *King of the Hill* (1992) as an elevator operator. Next she appeared as Rita Watson, a gifted but troubled and rebellious teen in *Sister Act 2: Back in the Habit* (1993), a sequel to the hit film with Whoopi Goldberg. Since then Hill was also cast in a small role in the independent film *Restaurant*, which is scheduled for release to theaters in late 1999. But for the most part, Hill has been devoting her time to music.

CAREER HIGHLIGHTS

Becoming the Fugees

While working on all these other projects, Hill was also hanging out in Jean's basement, where they were creating a studio called the Booga Basement. They changed the name of their band, first calling themselves Fugees—Tranzlator Crew, then just the Fugees. Their use of the word Fugees, short for refugees, was intended as a political statement. It refers to the plight of the many immigrants to this country from Haiti and else-where — both Jean and Michel's families emigrated from Haiti. "The group's name," according to Jean, "represents those who seek both mental and physical refuge from oppression and attempts to educate people in a country that perceives Haitians as 'refugees' and 'boat people.'" Michel also explains, "We decided to call ourselves the Fugees," he says, "because when we were growing up, people used to call us refugees — as if we were the only people seeking refuge from our land. What we're saying is that everyone is a refugee, whether mentally or physically, from your country, from your life. And it's in that sense that our music is re-fugee music." Refugee Camp was also the name of their production crew, a tight group of friends and musicians who helped create their distinctive sound.

The Fugees were developing new material with a new sound, combining hip-hop music with influences from the Caribbean islands of Jamaica and Haiti. They began playing different shows around New Jersey and started developing a core group of fans. Soon they attracted the interest of a manager, who helped them sign a contract with a record label, Ruffhouse Records, a division of Columbia Records known for its rap acts.

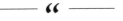

When Hill started putting her solo record together, there was a lot of resistance to her plan to hold full creative control. "Men like it when you sing to them. But step out and try to control things, and there are doubts. This is a very sexist industry. They will never throw the 'genius' title to a sister. They'll just call her diva and think it's a compliment. It's like our flair and our vanity are put before our musical and intellectual contributions."

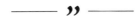

The Fugees started recording their first disk, *Blunted on Reality*, in 1991, when Hill was only 16, although it wasn't released until two years later. It featured a mix of freestyle raps, Afrocentric poetry, social and political commentary, and reggae rhythms. But the Fugees weren't altogether happy with the way *Blunted* turned out. To conform to current tastes, they were encouraged by their producers to create an aggressive, speeded-up, hard-core sound. "We had no clout," says Jean. "They was like, 'You got to be more aggressive, you got to scream.'" *Blunted on Reality* wasn't successful, but it paved the way for their next release.

The Score

After the release of their debut recording, the Fugees went back to the studio. For their follow-up, they knew they wanted a different approach. So the Fugees took control of production and went to work on *The Score*. Hill and Jean wrote and produced the songs, and Michel served as co-producer and manager. They recorded all of the tracks except "Fu-Gee-La" at Jean's house at the Booga Basement studio. "It's not chic, but it comes out good quality, because you feel like you're at home," says Jean. Then he adds, "it sort of gives you a Tuff Gong feeling," referring to the famed studio used by Bob Marley, the legendary Jamaican reggae musician.

The Score features an upbeat sound that's a mix of rap, reggae, soul, rhythm and blues, funk, and hip-hop, all overlaid with Hill's sultry and melodic alto. Here is how Alec Foege described it in *Rolling Stone*: "[The trio] concocted an hour-long opus on which no single track paints the whole picture. Slower and more textured than its predecessor, *The Score* drifts effortlessly from up-to-the-moment hardcore to reggae to old-school rap to '70s-style easy listening to Haitian-flavored acoustic folk. The glue that keeps it all together is the group's secret weapon: a killer live band with a killer live show to match."

The Score was released in 1996, and the Fugees toured relentlessly to support it. Their concerts featured a theatrical show underscored by a strong musical aesthetic. "We figured that even if hip-hop kids lost an appreciation for live music, we're going to bring it back and make them love it," says Jean. Their live shows and their recording — particularly their version of Roberta Flack's 1973 hit "Killing Me Softly," which saturated the radio airwaves — helped the Fugees develop a huge base of fans. *The Score* went on to sell 17 million copies, making it the all-time top-selling album by a rap group. It also won two Grammy Awards for the Fugees, for Best Rap Album and Best R & B Performance by a Duo or Group, for Hill's stunning version of "Killing Me Softly."

Solo Projects

After finishing *The Score*, Hill took a break to work on some solo projects. She took some time off from touring with the Fugees when she became pregnant with her son, Zion, who was born in 1997; her daughter, Selah, was born the following year. Their father is Rohan Marley, her longtime companion and the son of reggae musician Bob Marley. While taking a break from touring, she started doing some solo song writing. She wrote and produced the hit single "The Sweetest Thing" for the soundtrack of the film "love jones"; she wrote, produced, and arranged the single and

directed the video for the Aretha Franklin song "A Rose Is Still a Rose"; and she wrote and produced the song "On That Day" for gospel singer CeCe Winans.

Hill wrote additional songs, too, that she intended for other performers. But the lyrics were so intimate that she just couldn't give them away. Instead, she decided to create her own solo album. When Hill started putting it together, there was a lot of resistance to her plan to hold full creative control. "Men like it when you sing to them. But step out and try to control things, and there are doubts. This is a very sexist industry. They will never throw the 'genius' title to a sister. They'll just call her diva and think it's a compliment. It's like our flair and our vanity are put before our musical and intellectual contributions." Hill had served as executive producer with Jean of *The Score*, and she was ready to produce her album on her own. She knew what sound she wanted and she knew how to get it.

"I guess people figure [producing] is something that women don't really know about," she says. "But I was already a legitimate producer. It's just that my name was totally ignored because it was beside a man's." That view was echoed by Chris Schwartz, the CEO of Ruffhouse Records. "I don't think a lot of people gave Lauryn credit for how much she contributed to *The Score,*" he says. "A lot of people assumed that she was just a singer. I think when this new album comes out, she's really going to get her due as an artist."

> *Here, she explains what the title* **The Miseducation of Lauryn Hill** *means to her. "It's really about the things that you've learned outside of school, outside of what society deems appropriate and mandatory. I have a lot of respect for academia. . . . But there was a lot that I had to learn — life lessons — that weren't part of any scholastic curriculum. It's really our passage into adulthood when we leave that place of idealism and naivete."*

The Miseducation of Lauryn Hill

So Hill went to work on her solo album. She started recording at studios in New York and New Jersey, and then went down to Kingston, Jamaica, to Bob Marley's Tuff Gong studio. "The album was still in my head at that point," she says. "When I started recording the album in New York and New Jersey, lots of people were talking to me about going different routes. I could feel people in my face, and I was picking up bad vibes. I wanted a place where there was good vibes, where I was among family. And it was Tuff Gong." Hill knew she'd made the right choice when she started improvising a lyric over a drum-machine rhythm. According to Gordon Williams, her recording engineer, "It was our first morning in Jamaica, and I saw all these kids gathered around Lauryn, screaming and dancing. Lauryn was in the living room next to the studio with about 15 Marley grandchildren around her — the children of Ziggy and Stephen and Julian — and she starts singing this rap verse, and all the kids are repeating the last word of each line, chiming in very spontaneously because they were so into the song." For Hill, that moment was a turning point.

Hill set out, she says, to make "a hip-hop album that has the roots, the integrity, and the sound of an old record. I wanted the kids on the street to hear the hip-hop element and yet be exposed to the musicality, to realize that the two don't have to be mutually exclusive." To achieve a classic soul sound, she used live instruments on much of the album, a twist for hip-hop. "The first day in the studio, I think I ordered every instrument I ever fell in love with: harps, strings, timpani drums, organ. . . . It was my idea to record it so the human element stayed in. I didn't want it to be too perfect." As she explains, Hill was trying to get "a sound that's raw. I like the rawness of you being able to hear the scratch in the vocals. I don't ever want that taken away. I don't like to use compressors and take away my textures, because I was raised on music that was recorded before technology advanced to the place where it could be smooth. I wanna hear that thickness of sound. You can't get that from a computer, because a computer's too perfect. But that human element, that's what makes the hair on the back of my neck stand up. I love that."

Hill called her solo release *The Miseducation of Lauryn Hill*, a title that evokes the treatise *The Miseducation of the Negro* by Carter G. Woodson, a prominent African-American historian from the first half of the 20th century. Here, she explains what the title means to her. "[The] concept of 'Miseducation' is not really miseducation at all. . . . It's really about the things that you've learned outside of school, outside of what society deems appropriate and mandatory. I have a lot of respect for academia. . . . But there was a lot that I had to learn—life lessons—that weren't part of any scholastic curriculum. It's really our passage into adulthood when we leave that place of idealism and naivete."

An Anticipated Release

When *The Miseducation of Lauryn Hill* was released in 1998, anticipation was high. Some critics wondered whether she could make it as a solo artist, without the support of rest of the Fugees. Others wondered about her decision to forgo outside producers. Some critics wondered if the new album would be too mainstream for the hip-hop audience, yet too gritty for the pop audience. Ultimately, Hill ignored all the advice of marketers and focus groups and followed her own heart, creating an album that didn't fit into any of the traditional categories.

The Miseducation of Lauryn Hill was an immediate hit with both critics and listeners. Nominated for ten Grammy Awards in 1999, Hill won five Grammies for *Miseducation*, including Album of the Year and Best New Artist; she also won several other top awards. And Hill and her record were selected as the best artist or the best recording of the year by a surprisingly wide variety of publications, including *Rolling Stone, Spin, Details, Entertainment Weekly, Time, USA Today,* and the *New York Times*. It

Lauryn Hill holding four of her five Grammy Awards during the 41st annual Grammy Awards, February 24, 1999

quickly soared to No. 1 on the Billboard album chart and broke the record for first-week sales by a female artist, selling more than 400,000 copies in its first week alone. To date, *Miseducation* has sold ten million copies.

The Miseducation of Lauryn Hill has been described as an original, powerful, and deeply personal recording. Its 14 tracks—most of which were written, arranged, and produced by Hill—show a wide range of musical influences, yet the sound remains uniquely hers. She calls on a variety of styles, seamlessly fusing hip-hop with soul, R & B, reggae, and gospel. She uses both electronics and live instruments to tell the history of African-American music, with a dash of Caribbean soul for flavor. With her smooth, warm, expressive voice, she flows easily from singing to rapping. And her lyrics give a deeply personal account of her passage to adulthood, revealing the struggles along the road from innocence to maturity and independence. Some of the issues she confronts are religion and faith, family, motherhood, race, the cost of success, and the importance of love.

The intimate and introspective work reveals a political, social, and spiritual consciousness that is rare in the world of hip-hop music today, according to reviewers. "Not since such singers as Marvin Gaye and Stevie Wonder were at their peaks," wrote critic Kevin Powell, "have we heard a record so full of love, pain, healing, raw truth, and beautiful music as is *Miseducation*. In defining a generation and a gender, it also manages to overstep generations, gender, and group politics." Many reviewers gave Hill credit for elevating the culture of hip-hop music and bringing it into the mainstream of modern music. As Andrea Lewis wrote in *The Progressive*, "She is ushering in a new era of mainstream acceptance of hip-hop music that was unthinkable 20 years ago. And it's hip-hop with a heart, mind, and soul."

"Not since such singers as Marvin Gaye and Stevie Wonder were at their peaks," wrote critic Kevin Powell, "have we heard a record so full of love, pain, healing, raw truth, and beautiful music as is Miseducation. *In defining a generation and a gender, it also manages to overstep generations, gender, and group politics."*

Other Commitments

For such a young woman, Hill has been juggling a lot of different projects. But several things keep her grounded: her commitment to her family, including her parents, her brother, her companion, Rohan Marley, and their two children; and her commitment to her faith, because she is deeply religious. Hill considers herself blessed, as she says here: "I've been so successful because I respect the fact that my talent is a gift from God. It's cool if people give us kudos and accolades, but I know who is responsible for everything I do. All praise should be given to Him."

Equally important to Hill is her commitment to social activism, especially projects that help disadvantaged young people. She founded the Refugee Project, a nonprofit group that encourages social activism among urban young people. She also founded Camp Hill in New York and Refugee Camp in New Jersey, which are outreach and education camp programs for inner-city kids. She has also supported well-building projects in Kenya and Uganda and staged the first-ever benefit concert by a popular American group in Haiti, in order to raise funds for orphans and Haitian refugees who had been forced back home by the U.S.

HOME AND FAMILY

Hill, who is unmarried, lives with her longtime companion Rohan Marley and their two children, Zion and Selah. They live in South Orange, New Jersey, with her parents. When Hill first became successful, she bought a big house to share with her parents just a few blocks from the home where she grew up. She then turned part of her childhood home into a recording studio.

SELECTED CREDITS

Recordings

Blunted on Reality, 1993 (with the Fugees)
The Score, 1996 (with the Fugees)
The Miseducation of Lauryn Hill, 1998 (solo release)

TV and Movies

"As the World Turns," 1991
King of the Hill, 1992
Sister Act 2: Back in the Habit, 1993

HONORS AND AWARDS

Grammy Awards: 1997 (two awards, with the Fugees), Best Rap Album for *The Score* and Best R & B Performance by a Duo or Group for "Killing Me Softly"; 1999 (five awards), Album of the Year for *The Miseducation of Lauryn Hill*, Best New Artist, Best Rhythm and Blues Vocalist—Female, Best Rhythm and Blues Album for *The Miseducation of Lauryn Hill*, Best R & B Song for "Doo Wop (That Thing)"
Soul Train Music Awards: 1999 (four awards), Sammy Davis Jr. Award for Entertainer of the Year (with R. Kelly), Best R & B / Soul or Rap Album

of the Year for *The Miseducation of Lauryn Hill*, Best Female R & B /
Soul or Rap Album for *The Miseducation of Lauryn Hill*, Best R & B /
Soul or Rap Music Video for "Doo Wop (That Thing)"
Billboard Awards: 1999 (two awards), Best R & B Album for *The
Miseducation of Lauryn Hill*, Best R & B / Urban New Artist Video of the
Year for "Doo Wop (That Thing)"
Image Awards (NAACP): 1999 (four awards), Outstanding New Artist,
Outstanding Female Artist, Outstanding Album, and NAACP
Presidents Award
American Music Awards: 1999, Favorite New Soul / R & B Artist

FURTHER READING

Books

Nickson, Chris. *Lauryn Hill*, 1999
Shapiro, Marc. *My Rules: The Lauryn Hill Story*, 1999

Periodicals

Ebony, May 1999, p.60
Essence, June 1998, p.74
Entertainment Weekly, Oct. 2, 1998, p.26
Harper's Bazaar, Apr. 1998, p.204
New York Times, Feb. 26, 1999, p.1
People, Apr. 19, 1999, p.147
Rolling Stone, Sep. 5, 1996, p.40; Jan. 21, 1999, p.43; Feb. 18, 1999, p.46

ADDRESS

Columbia Records
550 Madison Avenue
New York, NY 10022

WORLD WIDE WEB SITES

http://www.laurynhill.com
http://www.lauryn-hill.com
http://www.ruffhouse.com

King Hussein (Hussein ibn Talal ibn Hussein) 1935-1999

King of Jordan

BIRTH

King Hussein of Jordan was born November 14, 1935, in Amman, Jordan. His name at birth was Hussein ibn Talal ibn Hussein. His parents were Crown Prince Talal and Princess Zein. Hussein had two younger brothers, Mohammed and Hassan, and a younger sister, Basma.

Hussein is from the Hashemite family of the Middle East. The Hashemites claim direct descent from the prophet Mohammed, the founder of the Islamic faith. As such, Hussein and his ancestors were the historic keepers of the most holy shrines in the Muslim faith, including the Dome of the Rock at the Al Aqsa Mosque in Jerusalem.

YOUTH

Despite his distinguished birth, Hussein grew up poor, in a house that had no heat. He remembered that when he was little, an infant sister died of pneumonia during a cold winter. When he was 10, he received his first bicycle as a gift from a cousin. But his mother had to sell it a few years later, when the family ran short of money. Money was so scarce that Hussein learned to sew when he was in elementary school. He'd ripped his school blazer, and knew that his parents couldn't afford a new one. He taught himself to sew so he could repair it himself.

EDUCATION

Hussein was educated at Victoria College, a school in Egypt, and at Harrow, a famous secondary school in England. He didn't care much for his classes, preferring sports, espe-

Hussein recalled that when an assassin shot his grandfather, King Abdullah, "Most of [his] so-called friends were fleeing in every direction. I can see them now, those men of dignity and high estate, doubled up, cloaked figures scattering like bent, old, terrified women. That picture, far more distinct than the face of the assassin, has remained with me ever since as a constant reminder of the frailty of political devotion."

cially soccer, cricket, and rugby. More important by far to Hussein's "education" was the influence of his grandfather, King Abdullah, the first king of Jordan. It was Abdullah who taught the boy the complex political alliances and the ways of the Arab world, where Hussein would one day play such a vital role.

A BRIEF HISTORY OF JORDAN

When Hussein was born, his grandfather, King Abdullah, was on the throne. Abdullah reigned over a country that had been carved out of the ancient lands of the Middle East by the British following World War I

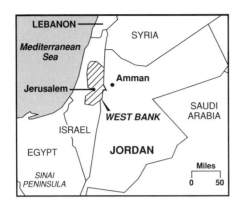

(1914-1918). He reigned over Jordan during a turbulent time in the history of the Middle East.

Prior to World War I, most of the land that makes up the modern Middle East was part of the Ottoman Empire, which had been ruled by Turkish sultans for centuries. When war broke out in 1914, the Ottoman Turks formed an alliance with the Germans. Germany and its allies were defeated in 1918, and the old empire crumbled. Under the directive of the League of Nations, England was given the task of governing sections of the Middle East. This area would eventually become 11 Arab states, including the new kingdom of Transjordan, created in 1920 with borders drawn by the British. It was the British government that installed Abdullah as king in 1921.

Abdullah was to a great extent "rewarded" with the kingdom of Transjordan. He had been loyal to the British cause after World War I, as they sought to consolidate their power in the Middle East after the collapse of the Ottoman Empire. The original kingdom of Transjordan, containing several of the ancient biblical lands of Gilead and Bethlehem, was mostly desert. The land is not rich in natural resources, nor in the oil that sustains many of the surrounding Arab nations. So during the years of his reign, King Abdullah relied on financial help from England.

The country became independent in 1946, known as the Hashemite Kingdom of Jordan, just as the Middle East became a hotbed of conflicting political unrest. Central to the problem was control of the holy city of Jerusalem and the displacement of the Palestinian people.

The Palestinians and the Creation of Israel

The Palestinians have lived in the area that is now Israel for more than 10,000 years. The area of modern Israel contains land that is sacred to three of the world's major religions—Christianity, Judaism, and Islam. Sovereignty over this land has been contested for centuries.

In the 19th century, Zionists, people of the Jewish faith who believed that a separate nation for Jews should be established in Palestine, began to immigrate to the area. In the 1920s, the conflict between Jews and

Arabs in the area of Palestine reached the point of armed conflict. Under the directive of the League of Nations, England was given the task of governing Palestine and trying to keep the peace among the warring factions.

In the 1940s, the British met with armed resistance from both Arab and Jewish groups. This situation worsened in the aftermath of World War II, when a huge mass of Jews immigrated to the area following the Holocaust. In 1947, the United Nations divided Palestine into separate Jewish and Arab states. The Jewish portion became the new nation of Israel; the Arab portion became parts of surrounding Arab nations. No new Arab nation in Palestine was ever created, making refugees of the Palestinian Arabs who left the area that became Israel. The Arab world declared war on the new Jewish nation, but in 1948, Israel won what it calls its War of Independence against Egypt, Syria, Lebanon, and Jordan.

After the 1948 war, Abdullah took control of two areas: the Old City of Jerusalem and the West Bank area, a prominent area west of the Jordan River in what is now Israel, and, then as now, a Palestinian stronghold. But unlike his Arab neighbors, Abdullah was pragmatic about Israel. He began secret meetings with the new Israeli leadership. These contacts, as well as his close ties to the British, led Palestinian radicals to view Abdullah as a threat. Plots against his life began to circulate.

"I had seen enough of Europe even at 17 to know that its playgrounds were filled with ex-kings, some of whom lost their thrones because they did not understand the duties of a monarch. I was not going to become a permanent member of their swimming parties in the south of France."

Abdullah and Hussein

Abdullah saw in his grandson, Hussein, the makings of his true heir. Hussein's father, Prince Talal, was mentally unstable; he would later be diagnosed as schizophrenic. Hussein loved and emulated his grandfather, who guided his political upbringing, introduced him to heads of state, and had him sit in on governmental affairs when he was just a teenager.

President Clinton looks on as King Hussein and Israeli Prime Minister Yitzhak Rabin shake hands after signing a joint declaration on the White House lawn on July 25, 1994, ending 46 years of hostilities between the two countries.

On July 20, 1951, with his beloved grandson at his side, King Abdullah journeyed to Jerusalem to worship at the Al Aqsa Mosque, one of the most holy Islamic shrines. Aware that there were plots against his life, Abdullah walked into the mosque that day and was assassinated by a Palestinian gunman. Hussein dove for the assassin, who shot him in the chest. "Is this what death is like?" he remembered thinking. In his 1962 memoir *Uneasy Lies the Head,* Hussein wrote, "I waited—but nothing happened; nothing, that is, except a miracle. I must have been standing at a slight angle to the man, for—we discovered later—his bullet hit a medal on my chest and ricocheted off. I was unharmed, and without doubt my grandfather's insistence that I wear my uniform saved my life."

The lesson of that day lived forever in the memory of the young prince. "Most of my grandfather's so-called friends were fleeing in every direction. I can see them now, those men of dignity and high estate, doubled up, cloaked figures scattering like bent, old, terrified women. That picture, far more distinct than the face of the assassin, has remained with me ever since as a constant reminder of the frailty of political devotion."

Abdullah's son, Prince Talal, left Switzerland, where he was being treated for schizophrenia, and returned to Jordan to assume the throne. But his mental illness was evident to everyone, so after serving less than one year, Talal abdicated in favor of his eldest son, Hussein.

BECOMING KING

On August 11, 1952, Hussein was proclaimed King of Jordan. He was 16 years old. After he was made king, he was sent to the famous British military academy at Sandhurst, to complete his military training before assuming the throne. On May 2, 1953, Hussein took control of a nation he would lead for 46 years.

CAREER HIGHLIGHTS

During his long reign, Hussein would become one of the most impor- tant leaders in the world and a prominent spokesman for peace in the war-torn Middle East. But as he took the throne, according to John Newhouse in *The New Yorker*, "The King and the country were alike — young, inexperienced, poor, and unpromising." For the new king, it was the end of childhood. "At 17, I knew the end of a dream. I would never be a schoolboy again. All my hopes were shattered."

Hussein also had to overcome the image many had of him as a fun-lov- ing playboy. He loved speed and danger and was often photographed skydiving, surfing, racing cars and motorcycles, and flying. It was time for him to change, he decided, and to dedicate himself to "discipline and hard work." In his autobiography, he wrote, "I had seen enough of Europe even at 17 to know that its playgrounds were filled with ex- kings, some of whom lost their thrones because they did not understand the duties of a monarch. I was not going to become a permanent mem- ber of their swimming parties in the south of France."

Learning to Lead

Instead, Hussein took a serious, pragmatic approach. As he came to power, he had to contend with the reality of Jordan's place in the Middle East. Oil had just been discovered in the surrounding Arab kingdoms of Saudi Arabia, Kuwait, Iran, and Iraq. Jordan had very little oil, which made it heavily dependent on its Arab neighbors. It was a time when a movement for Arab nationalism was galvanizing the Middle East, ex- pressed particularly in its unified animosity toward Israel. Jordan was also criticized for its continued close relationship with England, which was still pouring millions of dollars into the country each year. Even so,

Hussein decided to break most ties with Britain, which crippled the nation financially. He then sought for and won United States aid. The Central Intelligence Agency, or CIA, developed close contacts with Jordan at this time, and U.S. aid poured into Jordan for the next two decades.

To ward off opposition from within his country, Hussein solidified the loyalties of the army and the Bedouin tribes. The Bedouins, a nomadic people who still live in the desert areas of the Middle East, were fiercely loyal to Hussein. One of many political plots to unseat Hussein surfaced in April 1957, when a coup inspired by President Gamel Abdel Nasser of Egypt pitted army officers against him. Hussein went out to the troops themselves, saying, "I am one of you, and I am proud of you. If it is a matter of death, I would not worry as long as I have done my duty toward you. If you believe I am anything but what I say I am, go ahead and shoot." The soldiers, many of them Bedouins, declared their loyalty to their king. The coup was put down.

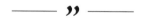

> *One of many political plots to unseat Hussein surfaced in April 1957, when a coup inspired by President Gamel Abdel Nasser of Egypt pitted army officers against him. Hussein went out to the troops themselves, saying, "I am one of you, and I am proud of you. If it is a matter of death, I would not worry as long as I have done my duty toward you. If you believe I am anything but what I say I am, go ahead and shoot." The soldiers, many of them Bedouins, declared their loyalty to their king. The coup was put down.*

Over the years, Hussein gained the nickname "P.L.K.," for "Plucky Little King." This referred both to his small stature (he was just 5'3") as well as to his indomitable spirit and willingness to fight those who would end his life and his reign. In 1958, while flying his own plane, Hussein was intercepted by Syrian jets, which tried to force his plane out of the air. In 1960, two members of his palace staff were found guilty of trying to poison him by putting acid in the nose drops he used for a sinus condition. Cats were sometimes found dead around the palace, victims of poisoning plots against the king. In dealing with his foes, Hussein showed tolerance and mercy. "The king was clever," says political scientist Abdul Hadi. "He didn't want there to be any martyrs or any heroes in Jordan other than himself."

In the early 1960s, Hussein began a series of secret meetings with Israeli officials, making clear his stand that Jordan would work for peace in the Middle East. At that time, the destruction of Israel was a common goal of other Arab states. It was a mark of Hussein's bravery and his commitment to trying to find a way for all nations of the Middle East to co-exist in peace that he pursued this goal, up to the time of his death.

Six-Day War

But for all his political craft and agility, Hussein could make terrible mistakes. His first major blunder came in 1967, when he joined forces with Egypt and Syria in fighting Israel in what became known as the Six-Day War. It only took six days for Israel to resoundingly defeat the three nations. For Jordan, the results were disastrous. They lost 15,000 men, their entire air force, and control of the West Bank, along with Jerusalem.

Palestinian Refugees in Jordan

As a result of the Israeli occupation of the West Bank, millions of Palestinian refugees fled into Jordan. These refugees were Palestinian Arabs who had lived in the West Bank when it was taken over by the Israelis. Hussein granted them Jordanian citizenship and gave them passports, so that they could travel freely. Yet the Palestinians created one of the most difficult problems Jordan has dealt with, a problem that continues to this day. The Palestinians wanted their own state. They did not want to belong to another country, or to live as refugees. Radical groups within the Palestinian community grew in power and authority in the late 1960s and worked actively to overthrow Hussein. Jordan became a base for Palestinian guerilla attacks against Israel. The situation gradually worsened with Palestinian Liberation Organization (PLO) leader Yasir Arafat (see entry in *Biography Today*, September 1994, and Updates in volumes dated 1994 through 1998). In 1970, Arafat challenged Hussein for control of Jordan and the Palestinians within it. Jordan faced civil war. Hussein remembered, "No one—adult or child—could be sure on leaving his house whether his family would see him again. Amman became a virtual battlefield."

Hussein sent troops to fight the radical Palestinian factions in a series of battles that became known as "Black September." Thousands of Palestinians lost their lives. During the fighting, Syria invaded Jordan on behalf of the Palestinians. Several days later, the Syrians withdrew, and the PLO, along with those Palestinians who remained loyal to them, retreated into neighboring Lebanon.

King Hussein climbs into an American F16 during his visit to an American base in Amman, 1996

Arab-Israeli War of 1973

In 1973, Egypt and Syria again went to war against Israel in retaliation for their losses from the Six-Day War of 1967. Hussein sent one tank command to the Israeli-Jordanian border, but refused to fight openly alongside Egypt and Syria. By this point, Hussein's secret meetings with the Israelis had been going on for 10 years. His purpose was to forge peace between the two nations, and to this end, he let the Israelis know of the build-up prior to the 1973 war. Yet the Israelis didn't heed his warning, and they suffered heavy casualties. Egypt and Syria failed to regain any of the territory they had lost in the 1967 war, and the war is generally considered to be a failure on both sides.

In 1974 the Arab League, the leading political entity of the Arab world, made an announcement that humiliated Hussein. They decided that the PLO was the only legitimate leader of the Palestinian people. Hussein, whose country still contained over two million Palestinian refugees, considered it a slap in the face. "It was a painful but not unexpected blow," he said. "I knew beforehand what the outcome would be." It was also further evidence of the volatility of political power in the Middle East. "What I didn't know was that Sadat [President of Egypt] and our Moroccan brethren [King Hassan] would be against me."

In 1978, Sadat surprised the world again when Egypt signed the Camp David accords. This plan, which was brokered by the U.S. and then-President Jimmy Carter, outlined conditions for peace between Egypt and Israel. Hussein was left out of the negotiations, at Sadat's insistence. "Let's be very clear," Hussein said after the agreement was made public. "I was never consulted or invited to take part." For Hussein, the Camp David accords did not bring any sense of overall commitment on the part of the Arab world to the peace process, or to a resolution of the fate of the Palestinians.

In 1988, Hussein renounced Jordan's rights to the West Bank, paving the way for full autonomy for the Palestinians, dispersed throughout Israel, Jordan, Lebanon, and other areas of the Middle East. His move was considered important, an endorsement of the legitimacy of the claims of the Palestinian people for nationhood.

And in the late 1980s, Hussein began multi-party elections, forging one of the only democratic, pluralistic governments in the Middle East. "The clock can't be turned back," he said. "Popular participation is the best way to achieve our political objectives."

The Gulf War

In 1990, King Hussein made the second major political blunder of his career. As Saddam Hussein sent Iraqi troops to invade the small, oil-rich country of Kuwait, King Hussein first sought peace between Saddam and the Arab nations. Then, as U.S. and other U.N. forces initiated the massive military operation known as "Desert Storm," King Hussein remained neutral. His actions angered the other Arab nations, who had sided with the United States and other Western powers in denouncing Saddam's invasion into a sovereign country.

Hussein was trying to preserve his relationship with Iraq, one of Jordan's most important trading partners and a major source of its oil. Yet he angered and alienated both his Arab neighbors and the U.S., which by that time was also providing the major source of Jordan's foreign aid.

> *On October 26, 1994, Hussein and then-Prime Minister Yitzhak Rabin of Israel signed a peace agreement ending almost 50 years of conflict between their two nations. The ceremony took place on a strip of land that lies on the border of Jordan and Israel. "This is without a doubt my proudest accomplishment: leaving my people a legacy of peace."*

In the ensuing war, Iraq faced a crushing defeat and was resoundingly driven back within its borders. Jordan suffered an influx of refugees again, as more than 300,000 Palestinians who had been living in Kuwait streamed in. The already strained economy of Jordan also had to deal with an economic crisis brought on when formerly friendly Arab states refused to send Jordan more than one billion dollars in financial aid.

In his defense, Hussein claimed, "I am pro-peace. I have backed nobody except my conscience and the interests of all in peace and security in this region." In 1992, Hussein changed his view of Saddam and called for an end to his rule of Iraq. This helped to renew a more cordial relationship with other Arab nations and the U.S.

A Diagnosis of Cancer

While working to repair his strained relationship with the U.S. and his fellow Arab states, King Hussein learned that he was suffering from cancer of the kidney. He flew to the Mayo Clinic in Minnesota, where he underwent treatment. He returned to Amman to a hero's welcome, as more than one million Jordanians lined the streets to greet him.

His bout with cancer had been a sobering event in the king's life. While buoyed by the warmth of his reception in Jordan, he also felt "an element of fear—of insecurity—about what might happen if I was not there, so I knew that I had to do everything I could, in whatever time I had left, to achieve peace and make it work."

Peace with Israel

Hussein redoubled his efforts to make peace with Israel, announcing in October 1992 that the two nations had agreed that they both wanted a formal peace agreement. That occurred on October 26, 1994, when Hussein and then-Prime Minister Yitzhak Rabin of Israel signed a peace agreement ending almost 50 years of conflict between their two nations. The ceremony took place on a strip of land that lies on the border of Jordan and Israel. "This is without a doubt my proudest accomplishment: leaving my people a legacy of peace," said Hussein.

Hussein's dream of peace throughout the Middle East was also aided by the surprise of an Israeli-PLO agreement in 1994, when Rabin and Yasir Arafat met in the U.S. and signed a pledge of peace on the White House lawn.

In November 1995, Hussein's partner in hammering out the peace agreement, Yitzhak Rabin, was assassinated in Jerusalem. Hussein wept at Rabin's funeral, saying, "It is peace that has been assassinated."

The next administration to come to power in Israel was that of Benjamin Netanyahu, whose right-wing party, Likud, had little commitment to a peaceful resolution to the Palestinian problem. Still, Hussein tried to work with the new Israeli head of state to promote the peaceful transfer of power in the West Bank to Palestinian hands.

King Hussein embracing his eldest son, Abdullah, age 37, in March 1998

In 1997, a crazed Jordanian gunman shot and killed several Israeli children on a field trip to Jordan. King Hussein went to the homes of the victims and knelt before the children's parents to ask forgiveness. Such actions led many Israelis to consider him, in the words of Deborah Sontag of the *New York Times*, "a larger-than-life figure who rose above the enmities of the region to forge with them a genuine peace."

Cancer Recurrence

In 1998, Hussein was diagnosed with lymphatic cancer. Once again he flew to the U.S. for treatment, which included a debilitating round of chemotherapy. Hussein addressed his people from his hospital bed at Minnesota's Mayo Clinic. "Rest assured, I am not over and done with yet," he told them. Still, he knew that his prognosis was grave. "There is life and there is an end to life, and that is the way with everyone."

The Wye Accord

In the fall of 1998, President Bill Clinton hosted the Wye summit talks between Yasir Arafat and Benjamin Netanyahu. The talks were aimed at ironing out the ever more rancorous relationship between Arafat and Netanyahu regarding Palestinian autonomy in the West Bank. The summit was not going well. Leaving his hospital bed to address the gathering, Hussein appeared, gaunt, weak, and bald from the chemotherapy. In a brief statement, the dying Arab leader made a final plea to those to whom the reconciliation process had fallen: "If I had an ounce of strength, I would have done my utmost to be there and to help in any way I can." He stressed to the combative Arafat and Netanyahu that there had been "enough destruction, enough death, enough waste." His stance was clear: "We have no right to dictate through irresponsible action or narrow-mindedness the future of our children or their children's children."

In a brief statement at the Wye conference in fall 1998, the dying Arab leader made a final plea to those to whom the reconciliation process had fallen. "If I had an ounce of strength, I would have done my utmost to be there and to help in any way I can." He stressed to the combative Arafat and Netanyahu that there had been "enough destruction, enough death, enough waste." His stance was clear: "We have no right to dictate through irresponsible action or narrow-mindedness the future of our children or their children's children."

A Change in Succession

In January 1999, Hussein returned to Jordan, thinking his cancer had been cured. That month, he released to the media a 14-page letter to his brother, Prince Hassan, in which he removed Hassan as his designated heir. He said that Hassan's supporters had tried to "destroy Jordan" both by spreading gossip to harm the king's wife and family and by creating divisiveness in the army and the government.

In the letter Hussein declared that his first-born son, Abdullah, an army officer, would succeed him after his death. Within days of his decision, Hussein was back in the United States. His cancer had recurred, and he sought urgent treatment for his condition.

DEATH

But Hussein's cancer had spread too quickly, and nothing could save him. On February 4, 1999, he returned to Jordan. He was unconscious when he reached Amman, where he died of heart failure on February 7. Abdullah was named king within hours of Hussein's death. King

King Hussein speaks in the East Room of the White House, October 23, 1998

Abdullah II addressed the Jordanian people: "Hussein was a father, a brother, to each of you, the same as he was my father," Abdullah said. "Today you are my brothers and sisters, and with you I find sympathy and condolences under God." One of Abdullah's first acts was to name his half-brother Hamzeh as Crown Prince, or next in line to the throne. This move was seen as further evidence that Prince Hassan and his family were not to succeed to lead the nation, and that subsequent leaders of Jordan would come only from Hussein's heirs.

Hussein's funeral was attended by hundreds of heads of states, including Presidents Clinton, Bush, Carter, and Ford. Millions of mourners lined the streets of Amman, weeping for their dead ruler. More than 80 percent of Jordanians had never known another leader but King Hussein.

LEGACY

"Even the sky is crying," said a commentator at Hussein's funeral. The nation, and the world, wept for a leader who had brought peace and stability to a region notorious for the lack of those things. Thomas Friedman wrote in the *New York Times* about the reason for this outpouring of affection and grief. "I believe it is because King Hussein ignited the same feeling in us that the late Israeli Prime Minister Yitzhak Rabin touched. It is the hope that is kindled when we see old men changing. There is something about watching these graybeards standing up, breaking with the past, offering a handshake to a lifelong foe and saying: 'Enough. I was wrong. This war is stupid.' It keeps alive the idea that anything is possible in politics, even in Middle East politics."

MARRIAGE AND FAMILY

Hussein was married four times. His first marriage, in 1954, was to Dina Abdul Hamid, who was a distant cousin. The marriage lasted only 18 months, and the couple had one child, a daughter named Princess Alia.

Hussein married again in 1961. His second wife was Toni Avril Gardiner, the daughter of an English colonel serving in Jordan. Toni took the Muslim name of "Muna," but refused to be called queen. She is still known as Princess Muna in Jordan. She and Hussein had four children: Prince Abdullah (now the new king), Prince Faisal, Princess Zein, and Princess Ayesha. That marriage ended in divorce in 1972.

In 1973, Hussein married his third wife, Alia Baha ud-Din Toukan, who was Palestinian and the daughter of a diplomat. She and Hussein had two children, Princess Haya and Prince Ali, and adopted a daughter, Abeer Muhaisen, before Alia's death in a helicopter crash in 1977.

Hussein's fourth wife is the former Lisa Halaby, an American with a degree in architecture from Princeton. She was working on an architectural project in Jordan when she met Hussein in 1977; they married in 1978. Halaby converted to Islam, and took the name of Queen Noor. She and Hussein had four children, Prince Hamzeh, Prince Hashem, Princess Iman, and Princess Raiyah.

HOBBIES AND OTHER INTERESTS

Hussein was always known as a man drawn to action, even to danger. He was featured in a *Sports Illustrated* article in the 1960s, with pictures of him surfing, skydiving, racing motorcycles, and flying, which was a favorite passion for him. He was also a great ham radio enthusiast.

WRITINGS

Uneasy Lies the Head, 1962

FURTHER READING

Books

Collier's Encyclopedia, 1997
Encarta Encylopedia, 1998
Hussein bin Talal. *Uneasy Lies the Head*, 1962
International Who's Who, 1998-99
Lunt, Maes D. *Hussein of Jordan: Searching for a Just and Lasting Peace*, 1989
Satloff, Robert B. *From Abdullah to Hussein*, 1994
World Book Encyclopedia, 1998

Periodicals

Boston Globe, Feb. 8, 1999, p.A1
Chicago Tribune, Feb. 10, 1999, p.A1
Current Biography Yearbook 1955; 1986
Houston Chronicle, Feb. 8, 1999, p.A1
Jerusalem Post, Feb. 8, 1999, p.1
Los Angeles Times, Feb. 9, 1999, p.A1
Miami Herald, Feb. 8, 1999, p.A1
New York Times, Feb. 8, 1999, p.A1, p.A27
New York Times Biographical Service, Oct. 1990, p.954; Sep. 1998, p.1448
New York Times Magazine, Nov. 6, 1960, p.30
New Yorker, Sep. 19, 1983, p.49
Newsweek, Aug. 10, 1998, p.38; Feb. 8, 1999, p.40
Philadelphia Inquirer, Feb. 8, 1999, p.A1
Sports Illustrated, May 8, 1967, p.42
Time, May 6, 1957; July 14, 1967, p.22
Times (London), Oct. 21, 1990; Feb. 6, 1999; Feb. 8, 1999
Washington Post, Sep. 27, 1987, p.D1; Feb. 8, 1999, p.A1

Lynn Johnston 1947-

Canadian Cartoonist
Creator of "For Better or For Worse"

BIRTH

Lynn Johnston was born Lynn Beverley Ridgway on May 28, 1947, in Collingwood, in the province of Ontario, Canada. Her parents were Mervyn Ridgway, a jeweler and watchmaker, and Ursula (Bainbridge) Ridgway, a self-taught illustrator and calligrapher. Johnston has one younger brother, Alan.

YOUTH

When Lynn was quite young, the family moved from Collingwood to Vancouver, British Columbia, where she grew up. According to Johnston, her parents didn't provide much emotional support. Her father was funny, but her mother was a strict disciplinarian. "They couldn't communicate except through jokes. They were very cold and very strict otherwise." They didn't show their feelings to their daughter, either. "All I really wanted was a hug," Johnston says, "I just wanted to be hugged." And they also didn't praise her. "My family would not compliment you. You could spend your life trying to please them. I had tremendous respect for my parents, but I didn't have that spiritual love for them that a kid should have."

Art was part of Johnston's life from her early childhood. "I started drawing when I was three. I found that whenever I couldn't handle the real world I would disappear into the paper. My grandfather was a stamp collector. Whenever he redid his albums, he would have these great pieces of beautiful heavy paper that he would just chuck out. My mother saved them for me. I used to draw in all those little squares and made up stories from square to square since I can remember. For me, drawing cartoons was my way of escaping. For example, if my mother and I were not getting along, then instead of having a fight with my mother I would have a fight between two characters on my paper. I could examine something visually and sort of work it out that way. Or if I had teachers I disliked, I would caricature them horribly and have a wonderful time doing it. Of course, I would get into trouble for showing them to people."

For Johnston, art became a way of dealing with some of those emotions that weren't expressed in her home. "I drew lots when I was mad," she says. "It helped me vent my anger. I was really an angry girl, even in elementary school. I wanted to be grown up. I'd fantasize and draw a picture of what I'd look like when I was old."

"I was angry, I think, until I was about 16, when I finally used the talents I was born with," she says. "That was when I got paid for my first piece of art. I was doing some babysitting for a friend of my father's who was a photographer, and he saw some of my sketches and had me do a pencil drawing of the Capitol building for a postcard for the government of British Columbia. I only got about $15 for the drawing, but it was wonderful to go into a shop on the mall and see my postcard. I think that was really the beginning of knowing that I could make a living doing what I do."

“

"I started drawing when I was three. I found that whenever I couldn't handle the real world I would disappear into the paper. My grandfather was a stamp collector. Whenever he redid his albums, he would have these great pieces of beautiful heavy paper that he would just chuck out. My mother saved them for me. I used to draw in all those little squares and made up stories from square to square since I can remember."

”

EDUCATION

Johnston's talent for drawing was apparent throughout her school years. She would draw pictures of Barbie dolls, but the boys in her class would erase the clothes and draw in the doll's private parts. The principal called Johnston in to reprimand her, but she argued that the private parts were drawn so badly that it was obvious that she hadn't done them. The principal believed her.

Johnston was not a great student. Throughout school, she often found her drawing more interesting than her class work. "It was often hard for me to take anything seriously," she once said. "[Even] though I enjoyed school, there were times, especially during math class, when I would rather draw than take part." Once, after she drew and doodled all over a math exam, she got an 'A' for the doodles and a 'D' for the math.

Johnston's parents recognized her talent for drawing, and they sent her to every art program that was available. After finishing high school in 1964, she enrolled in a fine arts program. "I went to the Vancouver School of Art and took very serious courses—mostly life painting and life drawing. . . . [That] was wonderful because I love the body and I love the rhythm of it and just what you can say with the position of the body." Johnston dropped out of art school in 1967, when she was about halfway through the program.

FIRST JOBS

After dropping out of school, Johnston went to work as an artist at an animation studio. "[For] the first time in my life I was with wacky people just like me. I just loved that environment. . . . [The] people were just so much fun." At about the same time she got married to a TV cameraman, although she hasn't given out a lot of information about him. Soon after they moved back east to Hamilton, Ontario. Beginning in 1968 or 1969,

Johnston worked for several years in the graphic arts department of the medical school at McMaster University. She did illustrations for the medical department, where she learned a lot about anatomy, and she also did illustrations for other departments at the university, like posters for student dances and cartoons for the children's ward at the hospital.

Soon, though, Johnston was doing cartoons even for her illustrations for medical school lectures. As she explains, "A lot of medical teaching is boring, boring stuff. It's charts and graphs showing how one amino acid connects to another; it's just endless diagrams. So I started doing cartoons with the graphs and charts. Instead of showing lines on a bar chart, for example, because it was called a bar graph, I would use different heights of bar stools in front of a bar and a different character on each one. People tended to remember the information in the charts with the comic illustrations. Eventually, when the other doctors found out that the students remembered that stuff better, that's all I got to do. It was the best job I ever had in my life. I think I've always had the gift for cartooning, but I didn't realize its potential until that job."

Johnston quit her job at the university when she got pregnant in about 1972. What should have been a joyous time in her life quickly deteriorated when her husband left her for another woman. With a young baby, no husband, and no job, Johnston was both emotionally and financially devastated. "I thought my world had collapsed. I had quit my job to raise my son. I was trying to start a graphic arts business at home." She worked as a freelance illustrator, but she had to rely on welfare to supplement her earnings. It was a really tough time for Johnston, but things soon improved.

CHOOSING A CAREER

Johnston became a professional cartoonist in rather an odd way. When she was pregnant with her son, her obstetrician was one of the doctors at

"For me, drawing cartoons was my way of escaping. For example, if my mother and I were not getting along, then instead of having a fight with my mother I would have a fight between two characters on my paper. I could examine something visually and sort of work it out that way. Or if I had teachers I disliked, I would caricature them horribly and have a wonderful time doing it. Of course, I would get into trouble for showing them to people."

For Better or For Worse: © Lynn Johnston Productions, Inc. Distributed by United Feature Syndicate, Inc.

the medical school who had enjoyed her humorous illustrations. "One day when I was lying on his examining table, bored because there was nothing to look at but the blank ceiling, I told him he should put some stuff up there, drawings or something. So he challenged me to do some work for that ceiling. During the time that I came in [to the office] on a regular basis, I did about 80 drawings about what it was like—for me, anyway—to be pregnant." She brought the one-panel cartoons into his office throughout her pregnancy and even after her baby's birth, and the doctor kept taping them up on the ceiling.

In the meantime, Johnston was struggling financially as a single parent. One day she got a call from her doctor inviting her to dinner. As she recalls, "I was totally thrilled just to go to dinner at my doctor's house. This was an honor for me. I showed up at his house with my baby on my hip. And he had all my drawings—80 of them—spread out on the floor. And he said, 'Lynn, you've got a book.'"

He was right. He helped her compile the drawings into book form and submit them to a publisher. Johnston's first collection, *David! We're Pregnant!* (1974), which featured cartoons about pregnancy and childbirth, sold over 100,000 copies. She soon followed that up with cartoons about the joys and tears of parenting during infancy and early childhood in *Hi, Mom! Hi, Dad! The First Twelve Months of Parenthood* (1975) and *Do They Ever Grow Up?* (1978). During the late 1970s Johnston's life improved in other ways as well. She got remarried, to Rod Johnston, a dentist, and she had her second child, a baby girl. Her family life became more stable, and her professional life did also.

CAREER HIGHLIGHTS

In the late 1970s Johnston's first cartoon books came to the attention of Universal Press Syndicate, which distributes comic strips to newspapers. Interested in her style of family humor, they approached her about doing a daily comic strip about family life. Johnston was pregnant at that point with her second child, and she and her husband were in the process of moving. With her moving boxes set up as tables, she did 20 sample cartoon strips featuring a family with a mother, Elly, who was also pregnant. She sent the sample strips off to the syndicate, worried that she wouldn't have enough ideas to produce a strip every day. Johnston was shocked when the syndicate offered her a 20-year contract. She spent the next six months creating the fictional universe of "For Better or For Worse," publishing the first strip in September 1979.

"For Better or For Worse"

For almost 20 years, Johnston has been creating the comic strip "For Better or For Worse." The strip runs seven days a week in newspapers all over Canada and the United States. In addition, the series has been republished in over 20 books to date, and it has been recreated in seven animated TV specials. "For Better or For Worse" features the Patterson family: the parents, Elly and John, and their children, Michael, Elizabeth, and April. Their stories offer many amusing and poignant insights into family life, often inspired by Johnston's own experiences.

In many ways, the Patterson family closely mirrors the Johnston family. Elly is named after one of Lynn's good friends from childhood. John is a dentist, like Rod. The two older children, who bear the middle names of Lynn's children, are each just a few years younger than their namesakes. Johnston is quick to point out these elements drawn from her life, yet she also makes clear that the strip is a work of fiction. "I use my life and surroundings as a source of inspiration, that's all." Only the youngest child, April, has no counterpart in the Johnston family. Lynn admits that she added April to the family at a time when her own children were growing older. As the mother of teenagers, she missed having young children around the house. She started to think about having another baby. But when she thought about all the trials a new baby would bring—messy diapers, teething pains, late-night feedings—she decided that Elly Patterson should have the baby instead.

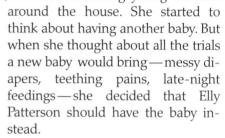

> *Johnston is quick to point out elements in "For Better or For Worse" that are drawn from her life, yet she also makes clear that the strip is a work of fiction. "I use my life and surroundings as a source of inspiration, that's all."*

Since the debut of "For Better or For Worse" in 1979, readers have watched the family grow, mature, and change over the years. And that, in fact, is one of the strip's most original features. Usually, in the comics, time stands still. Charlie Brown doesn't get any older, and Garfield doesn't seem to use up any of his nine lives. But that's not true of the Patterson clan. Fans have watched them experience many changes over the years. Elly and John have confronted the issues of middle age, Michael has grown from a young boy to a successful college student, and Elizabeth has matured into a high-school student with a boy friend. Even little April is now ready for school.

One of Johnston's greatest strengths is her ability to depict both the good and the bad moments of family life. Her strip mixes warm, family-style humor with a strong dose of realism to confront serious issues, including pregnancy, job-hunting, divorce, sibling rivalry, homosexuality, money problems, adolescent angst, menopause, and death. Johnston manages to introduce such topics while still incorporating the conventions of the comics, like slapstick humor, witty punch lines, and cute characters. "What sets Lynn's strip apart from the others," says Elizabeth Andersen, Johnston's editor, "is that her characters and readers are not spared mid-

life crises, financial hardships, or confrontations with prejudice, child abuse, and death. . . . That's Lynn's personal challenge — to bust out of the usual constraints of a comic strip, and to do it convincingly."

Controversial Stories

One way in which Johnston has "busted out" is in her use of controversial material. In 1993, she created a story about 17-year-old Lawrence Poirier, Michael's good friend since they were young boys. In a series of strips

185

that ran over several weeks, Lawrence reveals that he is gay, first to Michael and then to his parents. His parents respond with anger and dismay, and then they kick him out of the house. Johnston has said that the series was inspired by two people: by her brother-in-law, who is gay, and his experiences when he first came out to his family, and also by a gay friend who was murdered.

The series about Lawrence immediately provoked a storm of controversy. While some readers praised Johnston for her courage and integrity in dealing with an issue that affects many families, others felt that the strips condoned a way of life they deplored. They particularly objected to the topic of homosexuality showing up in the comics, which are widely read by children. Johnston and the syndicate received about 35,000 letters from readers about Lawrence's story. Many were angry, but about 70% supported her. Ultimately, while most newspapers ran the series, 19 papers canceled their subscriptions and 40 papers ran alternate strips to avoid the issue. But 56 new papers ultimately picked up the strip as a result of the story about Lawrence, and it won her a nomination for the Pulitzer Prize for editorial cartooning. Writing about the controversial issue of homosexuality was a big risk for Johnston, but her feelings on the subject are clear: "People should be judged by how kind and honest and trustworthy they are, not by their sexual orientation."

A similar storm of response from readers greeted another story in "For Better or For Worse." In 1995, the strip included a story in which April, then just a toddler, fell into a raging river while playing with a toy boat. Farley, the family's sheep dog, jumped into the river and held April's head up out of the water, while Edgar, Farley's son, ran and alerted the rest of the family. The story unfolded in the comics over several days, during which readers were unsure if April and Farley would survive. April did, but Farley was too old to overcome the cold and exhaustion, and he died. For Johnston, his death was a painful necessity to maintain the strip's realism. Because the strip progresses in real time, Farley was already 14 years old, the upper end of the life span for a sheep dog. "I didn't want him to die," Johnstons says, "but he was an old dog, and for the strip to stay true to his changing life, I had to let him go."

The impact of Farley's story was probably magnified because it took several days for readers to learn the outcome, but also because it appeared at the same time as the bombing of the Federal building in Oklahoma. That catastrophe was so deeply upsetting that it proved to be a difficult time for people to read about death in any form. The timing was a dreadful coincidence. Johnston works about six weeks in advance on her stories, so she has no idea what will be in the news when the comic appears in the newspaper. Again, she heard from her readers. While many were incensed that she would kill off a beloved character, others shared their own stories of grief over the death of a cherished pet and confided that the story helped them mourn their loss.

It's just these types of stories that have made Johnston so beloved by readers and so respected by other cartoonists. Her strip runs in about 2,000 newspapers around Canada and the United States, making it one of the five most widely distributed comics in the world. ("Peanuts" and "Garfield" are the top two, running in about 2,600 and 2,500 papers, respectively.) And when newspapers do polls of their readers to identify their favorite comics, "For Better or For Worse" consistently ranks at the top. Johnston has also won some top awards, particularly those from other cartoonists. In 1986, she became the first woman to win the Reuben Award for Outstanding Cartoonist of the Year from the National Cartoonists Society; in 1992, she was appointed to the Order of Canada; and in 1997 she was inducted into the International Museum of Cartoon Art's Hall of Fame.

MARRIAGE AND FAMILY

Johnston married her first husband, whose name is unavailable, in the late 1960s. They had one son, Aaron,

According to Elizabeth Andersen, Johnston's editor, "What sets Lynn's strip apart from the others is that her characters and readers are not spared mid-life crises, financial hardships, or confrontations with prejudice, child abuse, and death. . . . That's Lynn's personal challenge—to bust out of the usual constraints of a comic strip, and to do it convincingly."

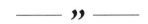

and divorced in the early 1970s. Aaron stayed with his mom after the divorce. In 1977 she married her second husband, Rod Johnston, a dentist and pilot. They have one daughter, Katherine (or Kate). Both Aaron and Kate are now grown. Aaron is a freelance cameraman, and Kate is a college student.

The Johnstons have lived in several different towns around Canada. Soon after their marriage they moved to Lynn Lake, Manitoba, a tiny copper mining town close to the Northwest Territories. It's about 700 miles north of Bismarck, North Dakota. Her husband was a flying dentist there—he

would treat people in town as well as fly his plane to visit those who lived too far away to come into town for treatment. "It was a tiny bush town, stuck in the arctic," she recalls. "People used dog teams to get around. It was an adventure. We'd fly our little plane to Winnipeg just so we could eat at McDonalds. We wanted fast food, movies, and actual shops."

On one flying trip they passed over a pretty lake and wooded peninsula in northern Ontario. The Johnstons fell in love with it. Coincidentally, some property there came up for sale just when they were ready to move. They bought the property in Corbeil, near North Bay, Ontario, about 200 miles north of Toronto. In 1984 they moved into a log cabin on the lake, surrounded by over 100 acres of woods, where Johnston has her studio.

Recently, Johnston was diagnosed with the neurological condition "torsion dystonia." It causes involuntary muscle spasms and shaking hands. Although it's not life threatening, it's also not curable. For Lynn, living with this neurological problem means it now takes her twice as long to do the art work for her comic strip. She continues to be the primary artist, but she has taken on an assistant to help. Johnston has said that she will continuing creating "For Better or For Worse" for about ten more years before retiring to enjoy life with her husband.

WRITINGS

Cartoon Books

David! We're Pregnant! 1974
Hi, Mom! Hi, Dad! The First Twelve Months of Parenthood, 1975
Do They Ever Grow Up? 1978

"For Better or For Worse" Collections

I've Got the One-More-Washload Blues, 1981
Is This "One of Those Days," Daddy? 1982
It Must Be Nice to Be Little, 1983
More Than a Month of Sundays: A "For Better or For Worse" Sunday Collection, 1983
Our Sunday Best: A "For Better or For Worse" Sunday Collection, 1984
Just One More Hug, 1984
The Last Straw, 1985
Keep the Home Fries Burning, 1986
It's All Downhill from Here, 1987
Pushing 40, 1988
A Look Inside "For Better or For Worse": The Tenth Anniversary Collection, 1989
It All Comes Out in the Wash, 1990 (contains reprints from other books)
If This Is a Lecture, How Long Will It Be? 1990
"For Better or For Worse": Another Day, Another Lecture, 1991 (contains reprints from other books)
What, Me Pregnant? 1991

"For Better or For Worse": You Can Play in the Barn, But You Can't Get Dirty, 1992 (contains reprints from other books)
"For Better or For Worse": You Never Know What's around the Corner, 1992 (contains reprints from other books)
Things Are Looking Up, 1992
There Goes My Baby, 1993
"For Better or For Worse": It's a Pig-Eat-Chicken World, 1993 (contains reprints from other books)
"For Better or For Worse": Shhh — Mom's Working! 1993 (contains reprints from other books)
It's the Thought that Counts . . . "For Better or For Worse" Fifteenth Anniversary Collection, 1994
"For Better or For Worse": Misery Loves Company, 1994 (contains reprints from other books)
"For Better or For Worse": Am I Too Big to Hug? 1994 (contains reprints from other books)
Starting from Scratch, 1995
Remembering Farley, 1996
Love Just Screws Everything Up, 1996
Growing Like a Weed, 1997
Middle-Age Spread, 1998

HONORS AND AWARDS

Reuben Award for Outstanding Cartoonist of the Year (National Cartoonists Society): 1986
Order of Canada: 1992
Best Syndicated Comic Strip (National Cartoonists Society): 1992
International Museum of Cartoon Art's Hall of Fame: 1997

FURTHER READING

Books

Authors and Artists for Young Adults, Vol. 12, 1994
Contemporary Authors, Vol. 110, 1984
Johnston, Lynn. *It's the Thought That Counts . . . "For Better or For Worse" Fifteenth Anniversary Collection,* 1994

Periodicals

Chatelaine, Mar. 1997, p.41
Chicago Tribune, Jan. 9, 1986, Section 5, p.3; July 12, 1987, Tempo Section, p.3
Current Biography Yearbook, Feb. 1998

Editor & Publisher, July 14, 1984, p.36; June 17, 1995, p.34; Sep. 30, 1995, p.30
Maclean's, Nov. 24, 1980, p.16
Ottawa Citizen, Sep.19, 1998, p.11
People, Sep. 15, 1986, p.121
Vancouver Sun, July 2, 1994, p.D12
Wall Street Journal, Mar. 30, 1987, p.17
Washington Post, Apr. 7, 1996, p.F1

Video

Life and Times, "Lynn Johnston: Lynn's Looking Glass," Sep. 9, 1998

ADDRESS

United Feature Syndicate
United Media
200 Madison Avenue
New York, NY 10016

WORLD WIDE WEB SITE

http://www.unitedmedia.com/comics/forbetter/index.html

OBITUARY

Shari Lewis 1934?-1998

American Puppeteer, Ventriloquist, Singer, Dancer, and Conductor
Creator of Such Beloved Characters as Lamb Chop, Hush Puppy, and Charlie Horse

BIRTH

Shari Lewis was born in New York City probably on January 17, 1934, although some sources list her year of birth as 1933. Her parents were Abraham and Ann Hurwitz. Shari had one sister, Barbara, who was nine years younger. Shari's name at birth was Phyllis Hurwitz. She changed her name from Phyllis to Shari when she was young because she thought it sounded more glamorous; Lewis was her married name.

YOUTH

If there was ever anyone who grew up destined to be a performer, it was Shari Lewis. Entertainment and performing were a vital part of life in the Hurwitz family while she was growing up. Her father, Abraham Hurwitz, was a professor of education at Yeshiva University. He had a deep concern for children, especially those on the edge of delinquency. Abraham Hurwitz believed in the then-revolutionary idea of education through entertainment: he thought children would learn more when they were having fun. He was also a professional magician, called Peter Pan the Magic Man, who was appointed the official magician of New York City by its mayor, Fiorello La Guardia. Her mother, Ann Hurwitz, was a music teacher, a music coordinator for the Board of Education of the New York public schools, and a conductor of youth orchestras.

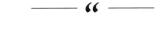

"One day Daddy walked by a closet and heard my sister screaming to be let out. She wasn't there. I'd thrown my voice. That's the first time we were both aware of the fact that I could do it."

Lewis had a unique and busy childhood, taking all types of lessons to learn to be a performer. "I once said to my mother, 'Why didn't you ever do needlepoint?' and she said, 'I did you.'" Her mother, in fact, was her first teacher. Shari started out with piano lessons beginning at about age two-and-a-half. She was so small at the time that she couldn't even reach the piano keys, so her mom put a potty seat up on the bench for her to use as a booster chair. By age four she was studying magic with her father. Throughout her childhood and teen years, Shari also took lessons in guitar, violin, accordion, dancing, acting, puppetry, juggling, ice skating, baton twirling, and ventriloquism.

Lewis first tried ventriloquism after she taught herself how to throw her voice, as she recalls here. "One day Daddy walked by a closet and heard my sister screaming to be let out. She wasn't there. I'd thrown my voice. That's the first time we were both aware of the fact that I could do it." Her dad seized the opportunity. He made her some puppets, including a little lamb. That one was really a bit of a joke, after he said "If Mary has a little lamb, why shouldn't Shari have a little lamb?" He also set up lessons with John Cooper, a 99-year-old former vaudevillian and legendary ventriloquist. Cooper and Lewis would sit on a bench in New York's Central Park, where he taught her all the old tricks.

EDUCATION

Lewis attended the public schools in New York City. At Herman Ritter Junior High School, she had a music teacher named Eta Morris who had a great influence on her. Morris believed that Lewis had the talent to attend Music and Art High School, a prestigious public high school in New York for students who are gifted in the arts. It is very difficult to get accepted into the school. According to Lewis, "[Miss Morris] said to me, 'You should go to Music and Art High School. If you bring a bag lunch every day this year, I will work with you to make sure that you get in.' And indeed, every lunch hour, Miss Morris and I sat at the piano. She taught me Carl Philipp Emanuel Bach's 'Solfegietto' and worked with me on theory (something I had never learned at the hands of my private piano teacher). She also introduced me to interpretation (*speed* was my specialty since I am dexterous and relatively high-strung). I got into Music and Art, and it turned out to be the most satisfying period of my entire life."

At Music and Art High School Lewis had another influential teacher: "Isadore Russ, the head of the violin department at Music and Art High School, became my idol. I had never really responded to the piano (it's too big, and you have to hit it). As soon as [Mr. Russ] put that violin under my chin, I felt an absolutely sensual connection to it and to the music I was making, and I practiced many hours each day, with no prodding." For Lewis, it was the first time she felt a real sense of passion for music. But it didn't prove to be her favorite thing. "In the seventh term, [the violin teacher] Mr. Russ came to me and said, 'You do many things. Unless you decide what you want to do and pursue one thing well, you will always scatter your energies. If you want to play the violin professionally, you ought to stop the daily dance lessons.' I made the opposite decision, but I have always been guided by his warning about the 'scattering of my energies.'" Instead of giving up dance, as her teacher had suggested, Lewis gave up violin.

Lewis graduated from Music and Art High School in about 1950 and went on to enroll at Columbia University in New York City. She spent just one year studying drama at Columbia before deciding to leave school to become an entertainer. After leaving school, she continued to develop her skills by taking additional classes in music, acting, and dance.

Lewis in 1961

FIRST JOBS

Of all of Lewis's interests, dancing was her favorite when she first started out. She longed to be a professional dancer, and she spent a year studying at the American School of the Ballet. She even landed some jobs dancing in the chorus lines of Broadway shows. But at just five feet tall, Lewis lacked the long legs and tall, willowy physique considered essential for a top dancer. She finally decided to switch from dance to puppets after an injury to her leg, as well as one to her ego. Lewis was a good dancer but not a great one, and she never won the leading parts. "I could never get out of the chorus line," she explained. "I didn't like that. So I came home and asked Dad, 'Where [are] the puppets?'" While convalescing from her leg injury, she practiced her skills as a ventriloquist and puppeteer. Now Lewis was ready for a new line of work.

She got her first big break in show business in about 1952, when she appeared on the TV variety show "Arthur Godfrey's Talent Scouts." With a

195

———— " ————

"[Treat children] to the very best entertainment. Don't play down to them. Give them good jokes, good music. The only concession is not to exceed their frame of reference. But I don't believe in programming which separates children from adults."

———— " ————

large ventriloquist's dummy, she performed the song "She's a Lady" and won a prize for her puppet show. In the mid-1950s she appeared on a variety of local shows in the New York area, including "Facts 'n Fun," "Kartoon Klub," "Shari and Her Friends," and "Hi Mom." These were variety shows, created for both children and their parents, that featured music, skits, and even informational segments, often written by Lewis.

CAREER HIGHLIGHTS

For over 40 years, Lewis entertained children and their parents with her adorable puppets and her perky, energetic, enthusiastic, and fun personality. With the writing and musical help of her long-time collaborators Lan O'Kun, Saul Turteltaub, Norman Martin, Bernard Rothman, and Stormy Sacks, she created TV shows, videos, books, live performances, and even CD-ROMs. Her work has amused generations of children—from her first audience back in the 1950s to their children years later. She loved music, and she always searched for ways to share that love with her young viewers. In all her work, she maintained this simple philosophy: "I have always believed in innocent excitement—magic, stunts, music, riddles—instead of explosions, crashes, and chases." Throughout her work, Lewis demonstrated her fundamental respect for children and their families. "[Treat children] to the very best entertainment," she once said. "Don't play down to them. Give them good jokes, good music. The only concession is not to exceed their frame of reference. But I don't believe in programming which separates children from adults."

Creating Lamb Chop and Friends

In about 1957, Lewis was invited to appear on the Captain Kangaroo show, a popular, long-running TV show for kids. Before she appeared, though, the producers came to her and said, "Your dummies are so big and clunky, you're five feet tall, don't you have anything that's dainty?" In fact, she did—the little lamb puppet that her father had made for her years before. So she tried a drama exercise that she had learned in an acting class. Here is how Lewis recalled her first conversation with Lamb

Chop. "I gave her something she wanted of me and a perfectly solid reason why she wanted it, and I gave myself an equally solid reason why there was no way she was going to get it. And then we improvised, and at the end of an hour of work in front of the mirror with her, I called my daddy and said: 'Hey Pop, this is it. You watch and see; this is it.' It was quite clear. She just came to life like no puppet I had ever worked before." Even Captain Kangaroo, played by Bob Keeshan, was impressed. "Lamb Chop was not a fantastic-looking puppet. It was just an old sock. But when she put it on her hand, your attention would be riveted—by Lamb Chop, not by Shari. She was genuine, she wasn't acting."

After creating Lamb Chop, Lewis went on to invent two more recurring puppet characters, each an individual in their own right: Hush Puppy and Charlie Horse. Here, she describes how they are all different, but all facets of her own personality. "We all have multiple personalities. Only I get to give them names and talk to them. It's very lucky for me. Lamb Chop is the vulnerable and the defensive and the innocent. Hush Puppy is the yearning for affection. Charlie is the wiseacre and smart-aleck. And they all exist within me." But Lamb Chop was always everybody's favorite. According to her collaborator Lan O'Kun, "We always though of Lamb Chop as being Shari as she would like to have been as a child."

Early Success on Television

Lamb Chop, along with Lewis's other puppets, proved to be a huge success—first on the Captain Kangaroo show, and then on other TV shows to follow. "Shariland," first broadcast in 1957, was a musical comedy show that included many features familiar to Lewis's current generation of fans, including songs, puppets, jokes, and games. Many shows also included a segment that showed her young viewers how to make a simple puppet from common household objects. "The Shari Lewis Show," from 1960 to 1963, was a musical sitcom in which episodes often dealt with a single silly situation. Shari herself once described it as "a musical comedy starring Lamb Chop, Charlie Horse, Hush Puppy, and what's her name."

According to Captain Kangaroo, played by Bob Keeshan, "Lamb Chop was not a fantastic-looking puppet. It was just an old sock. But when she put it on her hand, your attention would be riveted— by Lamb Chop, not by Shari. She was genuine, she wasn't acting."

From the 1997 PBS special, "Shari's Passover Surprise"

At that time, Lewis's TV shows were tremendously popular with viewers. "The Shari Lewis Show" was a particularly great success, and it even won a Peabody Award, one of the most prestigious awards in television. Still, it was canceled in 1963. That's when live-action TV for children made room for animation, and Lewis's show was replaced by the animated cartoon "Alvin and the Chipmunks."

New Career Directions

After the cancellation of her show, Lewis worked as an entertainer in a wide variety of formats. She tried a little bit of everything, usually with great success. She had two shows on television during that time, a syndicated show that was on briefly between 1975 and 1977 called "The Shari Lewis Show" (also called "The Shari Show") and a show in England on the BBC on Sunday nights called "Shari at Six" that ran from 1968 to 1976. She developed and starred in many different TV specials. She released over two dozen videos for kids that featured activities like magic tricks, secret codes, mysteries, and quick crafts, including the ever-popular "101 Things for Kids to Do" (1992). She appeared in the touring companies of *Bye Bye Birdie*, *Funny Girl*, *Damn Yankees*, and *Sweet Charity*. She developed a live nightclub act for adults and took it on the road to clubs in Las Vegas, Atlantic City, and elsewhere. For these performances Lewis sang, danced, told jokes, and worked with puppets, using material written for adults rather than children.

Lewis was perhaps most proud of her work with symphony orchestras. A strong supporter of music education, she believed that children should be exposed to different types of music—rock and roll, country, jazz, and classical music. She began conducting in 1977, when she was invited to appear with the Dallas Symphony. The people at the symphony were probably expecting a puppet show, but Lewis had something else in mind. "I'd been preparing for conducting from the get go," she explained. "My mother was a conductor, and I used to watch her lead very large children's orchestras, all the time. It never struck me as something I couldn't do. So when I was booked to perform with the Dallas Symphony, it occurred to me that this would be a wonderful opportunity to start conducting. I took two months off, canceled all of my engagements, and studied with my musical director, Stormy Sacks."

"I never violate classical music by kidding around with it. But I do violate the tradition of classical music that says that it is stuffy and that it has to be played by musicians who are aloof."

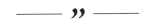

For her orchestra performances, Lewis created a family-oriented show, what she described as "a kind of cross between a symphony and a Vegas act for families." She might conduct the orchestra, either alone or with Lamb Chop, or join two life-size stuffed showgirl puppets in a dance, or have a kangaroo puppet play Brahms on the violin. Most of all, she tried to make classical music enjoyable for children and their families. "I never violate classical music by kidding around with it," she once explained. "But I do violate the tradition of classical music that says that it is stuffy and that it has to be played by musicians who are aloof."

In addition to performing, Lewis also turned to writing. She wrote over 60 books for kids on topics ranging from magic to origami, on which she was considered an expert. Her books include the series "One-Minute Bedtime Stories" so beloved by parents and small children. She and her husband even co-wrote an episode in the original "Star Trek" series. It was called "The Lights of Zetar," named after a chemical ingredient in her husband's anti-dandruff shampoo. The episode told the story of superior beings who transformed into electrical impulses and then caused problems for the crew of the Enterprise.

During this period Lewis also faced a personal crisis. In 1984 she was diagnosed with breast cancer. She underwent surgery and radiation, and she recovered beautifully.

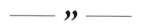

"We all have multiple personalities. Only I get to give them names and talk to them. It's very lucky for me. Lamb Chop is the vulnerable and the defensive and the innocent. Hush Puppy is the yearning for affection. Charlie is the wiseacre and smart-aleck. And they all exist within me."

"Lamb Chop's Play-Along"

In 1991, Lewis got the opportunity to create a new television series for kids. An executive from PBS (the Public Broadcasting Service) wrote an article in a Los Angeles newspaper asking people in the TV industry to submit creative ideas for new children's shows. That was all the motivation Lewis needed. She developed an idea, met with executives from PBS, and created a wildly successful new series.

"Lamb Chop's Play-Along," a half-hour program that ran on PBS from 1992 through 1996, featured Shari decked out in overalls with her menagerie of puppets and several children. The show included skits where the puppets acted out tough situations, like not being invited to their friend's party or feeling sad when their parents go out. The show was also filled with jokes, games, songs, and tricks—all silly and goofy and full of fun. The show was designed for kids aged two to ten, but many older children enjoyed learning the jokes and tricks and practicing them on their friends.

This "anti-couch potato show," as Lewis called it, constantly invited kids to join in and play along. For Lewis, one of the most important premises of the show was creating the opportunity for the audience to participate. "I was brought up doing audience-participation shows; my father did them in his magic act, and I knew that kids of all ages like to be part of the action." And the action on the show was very fast-paced, which kept her viewers up and moving.

From "The Charlie Horse Music Pizza"

The audience participation element was a big hit with young viewers, their parents, and TV critics. But another equally important component was the show's tone. It was sweet, silly, and enchanting, rather than hip or sophisticated. For Lewis, that was intentional. "If you get kids turned on by simple, wholesome stuff like riddles and magic tricks, you change their awareness of what is stimulating, and they discover they can enjoy something other than hostility, aggression, cynicism, sexuality, and violence."

"The Charlie Horse Music Pizza"

In 1998, Lewis went on to create a new series for PBS. "The Charlie Horse Music Pizza" is a half-hour musical comedy series devoted to music education for young children, ages three to eight. It is set in the Music Pizza, a pizza parlor on the beach that is the hangout for the neighborhood kids. The show debuted featuring Lewis as the owner of the pizza parlor, along with her side kicks Charlie Horse, Lamb Chop, and Hush Puppy, plus some new friends: Take Out, an orangutan who does gymnastic stunts while delivering pizza on his skateboard, and Fingers, a raccoon who lives in the garbage cans. There's also Cookie, the chef played by Dom DeLuise, and Junior, the assistant manager played by Wezley Morris. Each episode features a story and original songs, and games, activities, and crafts related to making music are also incorporated into the plot. Each episode also includes an element of music education that develops naturally from the storyline. "The Charlie Horse Music Pizza" provides an introduction to different musical styles and basic concepts like notes, pitch, harmony, and rhythm, plus samples of different instruments. In effect, the show provides a class in both appreciating music and making music.

> *Several years ago, when asked if she planned to continue working, Lewis said, "Until the day I drop. Oh yes, I have too much fun. There is nothing that I would do that would be more fun for me than what I do. I'm never bored because I work at play. I'm very lucky. I do the things that other people do for hobbies, but I do them for a living."*

"The Charlie Horse Music Pizza" debuted on PBS in January 1998. Lewis and friends shot 20 episodes to appear during that winter and spring, with plans to shoot another 20 episodes for the 1998-99 TV season. They had shot three of those new episodes when Lewis became sick in June. Diagnosed with uterine cancer, she was undergoing chemotherapy when she contracted pneumonia. Lewis died on August 2, 1998.

Lewis loved her work. Several years ago, she was asked if she planned to continue working. She said then, "Until the day I drop. Oh yes, I have too much fun. There is nothing that I would do that would be more fun for me than what I do. I'm never bored because I work at play. I'm very lucky. I do the things that other people do for hobbies, but I do them for a living."

AN APPRECIATION

Both children and their parents felt a sense of loss when Lewis died, as Sharon Waxman summed up in this appreciation from the *Washington Post*: "[Lewis's] show was a welcome respite from the inanity of children's programming. . . . She managed to poke fun at her characters without humiliating them, and she let them teach her as much as she taught them. Her humor was gentle. The education inadvertent. Political correctness unnecessary. Her manner warm but not cloying. . . . She never talked down to her viewers, and she kept the soul of a child alive within her—the playfulness, the curiosity, the openness.

"But the most delightful part was her relationship with Lamb Chop. From the moment Shari Lewis donned that white wool sock with a couple of false eyelashes and a pair of arms, Lamb Chop became a separate and unique personality, a charmer and a practical joker to whom Lewis gladly played the straight man. You never watched the show with an awareness that Lamb Chop was attached to her wrist. . . .

"I'll sure miss 'Music Pizza.' Give me some spicy, silly, sparkling Shari Lewis any day, singing that signature tune that makes no particular sense, but that neither my kids nor I can get out of our heads:

> This is the song that never ends,
> Yes it goes on and on my friends,
> Some people started singing it not knowing what it was,
> And they'll continue singing it forever just because,
> This is the song that never ends. . . ."

MARRIAGE AND FAMILY

Shari Lewis was married twice, although not much is known about her first husband. She was first married when quite young, probably during her teen years, to Stan Lewis, an advertising executive. Although they soon divorced, she kept the name Lewis. In 1958 she married Jeremy Tarcher, a television producer and book publisher. Lewis and Tarcher had one daughter, Mallory, who is now grown. Mallory is the only other person that Lewis would let do Lamb Chop.

People would often ask Mallory if she was jealous of Lamb Chop, viewing her as a rival for Lewis's affection. "As far as I'm concerned, Lamb Chop's a sock. I'm not jealous of my mother's footwear, either. I never had a problem with that. Lamb Chop is the perfect little sister. She works and earns a ton of money, she lives in a shoe box, [and] she gets no attention. . . . Now, who could want a sibling better than that?"

SELECTED CREDITS

Television Series

"Facts'n Fun," 1953
"Kartoon Klub," 1954
"Shari and Her Friends," 1954
"Shariland," 1957
"Hi Mom," 1957-59
"The Shari Lewis Show," 1960-63
"Shari at Six," 1968-76
"The Shari Lewis Show," 1975-77 (also called "The Shari Show")
"Lamb Chop's Play-Along," 1992-96
"The Charlie Horse Music Pizza," 1998

Television Specials

"A Picture of Us," 1973
"Shari's Christmas Concert," 1983
"Lamb Chop in the Haunted Studio," 1994 (also called "Lamb Chop's
   Spooky Stuff")
"Lamb Chop in the Land of No Numbers," 1995
"Lamb Chop's Special Chanukah," 1995
"Shari's Passover Surprise," 1997 (also called "Shari's Special Passover")

Videos

"Lamb Chop's Sing-Along, Play-Along," 1988
"101 Things for Kids to Do," 1992
"Shari's Christmas Concert," 1992
"Don't Wake Your Mom," 1992
"Let's Make Music," 1994

Writings

The Shari Lewis Puppet Book, 1958 (also published as *Making Easy
   Puppets*, 1967)
Fun with Kids, 1960
Folding Paper Puppets, 1962 (with Lillian Oppenheimer)
Folding Paper Toys, 1963 (with Lillian Oppenheimer)
Dear Shari, 1963
Folding Paper Masks, 1965 (with Lillian Oppenheimer)
The Tell It, Make It Book, 1972

Magic for Non-Magicians, 1975 (with Abraham B. Hurwitz)
One-Minute Bedtime Stories, 1982 (with Lan O'Kun)
Lamb Chop's Play-Along Storybook, 1983 (with Jacquelyn Reinach)
Abracadabra! Magic and Other Tricks, 1984
One-Minute Animal Stories, 1984
One-Minute Favorite Fairy Tales, 1985
One-Minute Bible Stories, Old Testament, 1986
One-Minute Bible Stories, New Testament, 1987

HONORS AND AWARDS

Emmy Awards: 1957 (two awards), best local program, outstanding female personality; 1958 (two awards), outstanding female personality, best children's show; 1959 (two awards), outstanding female personality, best children's show; 1973 (two awards), outstanding children's entertainer, outstanding achievement in children's programming; 1989 (two awards), outstanding female personality, best program; 1991, outstanding performer in a children's program; 1992, outstanding performer in a children's program; 1993 (two awards), outstanding performer in a children's program, outstanding writing in a daytime children's series; 1994, outstanding performer in a children's program; 1995, outstanding performer in a children's program
George Foster Peabody Broadcasting Award: 1960, for "The Shari Lewis Show"
John F. Kennedy Center Award for Excellence and Creativity: 1986

FURTHER READING

Books

Contemporary Theatre, Film, and Television, Vol. 19, 1998
Something about the Author, Vol. 35, 1984
Who's Who in America, 1998

Periodicals

Christian Science Monitor, Jan. 2, 1998, p.12
Current Biography 1958
Detroit Free Press, Aug. 28, 1995, p.E1
New York Times, Dec. 27, 1992, Section 4, p.9; Aug. 4, 1998, p.B7; Aug.4, 1998, p.A2
Newsweek, Apr. 25, 1983, p.16
Parents, July 1994, p.140

People, May 23, 1983, p.103; Oct. 19, 1992, p.154; Aug. 17, 1998, p.82
TV Guide, Oct. 29, 1994, p.49
Wall Street Journal, Dec. 18, 1991, p.A1
Washington Post, Aug. 4, 1998, p.B4; Aug. 5, 1998, p.C1

Video

Biography, "Shari Lewis and Lamb Chop," A & E Home Video, 1994

WORLD WIDE WEB SITE

http://www.pbs.org

Oseola McCarty 1908-
American Washerwoman and Philanthropist
Donated Her Life Savings to Help Kids Go to
College

BIRTH

Oseola McCarty was born on March 7, 1908, in rural Wayne
County, Mississippi. Her mother was Lucy McCarty Ziner-
man; her father died when she was very young. Oseola,
known as Ola to her family, had no brothers or sisters.

For much of her childhood, Oseola lived with her grandmother, Julia Smith McCarty, and her aunt, Evelyn McCarty.

Her mother, Lucy, had gotten remarried, and she and Oseola's stepfather moved from Mississippi to Chicago, Illinois, when Ola was about five. Like many African-Americans, they moved North hoping to find good jobs and to make a better life. Because both Lucy and her husband needed to work, Ola stayed behind so her grandmother and her aunt could take care of her.

LIFE IN THE SOUTH

McCarty grew up in a very poor black family in rural Mississippi. At that time and place—the early part of the 20th century in the deep South— life was very hard for African-Americans. Many white people felt a deep and abiding prejudice against black people. African-Americans were often treated as inferior, and they were expected to act subservient. When Mc-Carty was young, the South was still segregated under what were called "Jim Crow" laws. These laws forced the segregation of the races and created "separate but equal" facilities— housing, schools, bathrooms, drinking fountains, and more—for blacks and whites.

"There's a lot of talk about self-esteem these days. It seems pretty basic to me. If you want to feel proud of yourself, you've got to do things you can be proud of. Feelings follow actions."

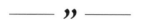

In reality, the separate facilities for blacks were miserably inadequate. African-Americans usually attended dilapidated, impoverished schools with underpaid teachers. After leaving school, their opportunities for work were often just as limited. Many African-Americans were able to find employment only in menial jobs at subsistence wages. Many men worked as laborers, and many women worked as domestics in the homes of white people, cleaning, cooking, and taking care of their children.

This was the society in which Oseola McCarty was raised.

YOUTH AND EDUCATION

McCarty grew up with her grandmother and aunt in the town of Hattiesburg, Mississippi. They lived in a small rented house that they kept immaculate; later, Ola's uncle bought the house, and he eventually gave it to her. Ola's family believed in hard work. Her aunt worked as a cook for white families in town, while her grandmother worked at home as a washerwoman, washing and ironing clothes for local white families. Her grandmother would wash and iron all day and into the evening, and her aunt would help out as soon as she got home from her job. They worked six days a week and rested on Sunday. Religion was important, too, including services on Sunday at the Friendship Baptist Church and prayer throughout the week. Still, Ola had time to play when she was young. She liked to make mud pies and create dolls out of grass and roots. But mostly she liked to help her grandmother.

When McCarty was six, she started attending Eureka Elementary School, the local school for black children. When she was in sixth grade, her aunt Evelyn became very sick. Evelyn was hospitalized for a while, but when she came home from the hospital she needed someone to take care of her. The grandmother, Julia McCarty, needed to keep working to support the family, so Ola left school to take care of her aunt. It wasn't unusual, at that time, for a child to drop out of school to help the family. Her aunt recovered, and Ola returned to school the following fall. But by then her classmates had moved up to the next grade, and she had been left behind. Although she had dreamed of becoming a nurse, Ola decided to drop out of school and help her grandmother at home. She learned how to press and straighten hair, charging her customers 75 cents each. She also picked up and delivered clothing to customers' homes and started helping her grandmother with the washing.

STARTING HER LIFE'S WORK

From that time on, for over 70 years, McCarty worked as a washerwoman. When she was about 20, her mother came to live there also, after the death of her husband. For years McCarty and her grandmother, mother, and aunt worked together.

How She Worked

Washing clothes at that time was very different then it is today. They had no washing machine or dryer, and it was hard work. McCarty and her relatives did the washing out in the backyard of their home. First, they would build a fire under a big cast-iron pot, heating water that they had carried from the hydrant out front. There was a bench in the yard with three big metal washtubs set up for washing and rinsing the clothes. They would first boil the clothes, then scrub them by rubbing them over a metal wash board. Then they'd rinse them, wring them out by hand, and hang them up on the line to dry. There weren't any wrinkle-free fabrics at that time, so everything had to be ironed, too. And they didn't use an electric iron, as we would today; instead, they used a heavy metal iron that had to be heated up on the stove before using it to press the wrinkles out of the clothes. They usually started their work by seven in the morning, took short breaks during the day to eat, and worked until about eleven at night. They took great pride in their work.

When she first started out, McCarty made about $1.50 per "bundle" of clothing, or all the clothes that could be wrapped up in a sheet. One bundle usually held about a week's worth of clothes for a family of four. Saving money was important to the McCarty family, and despite their very low income they always managed to set a little money aside each week. Ola's grandmother would wrap up her coins and bills in a handkerchief and then stash it under her mattress, or under the linens in the closet. Ola saved her money, too. She knew that one day her grandmother would be too old to work, and she wanted to make sure that she would be able to take care of her.

"I did have some advantages to saving money. My house was given to me by my uncle, and the people I worked for gave me clothes. I had to pay only for groceries and the other little things I needed. But I think my secret was contentment. I was happy with what I had."

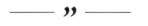

How She Lived

Ola's grandmother died in 1944, her mother died in 1964, and her aunt died in 1967. As they grew old and feeble, Ola cared for each of them in turn, and after that, she lived and worked alone. McCarty lived a very simple, frugal life. Her uncle had given her the house, so she owned it outright. She kept her home very tidy, although she didn't have a lot of fancy possessions. She never owned a car and never learned to drive; she walked wherever she needed to go in town. On grocery day, she pushed a shopping cart along the mile walk into town. She had an old TV set that didn't work too well, but she never really minded. She had a window air conditioner, but she didn't use it too often. She just really didn't want much—she didn't need many things. She spent much of her time in prayer and in reading her Bible. It was a quiet life of hard work, solitude, prayer—and saving money. As she commented in her book *Simple Wisdom for Rich Living,* a collection of her thoughts, "I did have some advantages to saving money. My house was given to me by my uncle, and the people I worked for gave me

OSEOLA McCARTY'S

Simple Wisdom

Words from the laundress whose $150,000 scholarship gift inspired the nation

for Rich Living

clothes. I had to pay only for groceries and the other little things I needed. But I think my secret was contentment. I was happy with what I had." The ever-frugal McCarty eventually got a washing machine for her work, but she gave it away because it didn't do as good a job as her own methods.

How She Saved

With the example set by her family, McCarty learned the importance of saving money early on. When she was a teenager, she opened a savings account at a bank in town. She was the first member of her family to do so. After that, she put a little money away each week. She couldn't save much, at first, but her fees gradually went up. By the late 1940s, she charged $10 per bundle of laundry, and she was able to save a bit more. She had several savings accounts at different banks around town. With compounding interest, and with her willingness to leave her money untouched, her savings grew. As she once confided, "The secret to building a fortune is compounding interest. It's not the ones that make the big money, but the ones who know how to save who get ahead. You've got to leave your investment alone long enough for it to increase."

McCarty certainly took her own advice. She left her savings alone for her entire lifetime. With time, her bankers noticed that her savings had started to add up. They advised her to put her money into safe investments like certificates of deposit and conservative mutual funds, which would earn more money for her. And they began to take a personal interest in her as well. They worried about what would happen to McCarty, and who would take care of her, when she was no longer able to work. In fact that time came in 1994, when McCarty was 86. Her doctor suggested that it was time for her to retire because of arthritis in her hands, which had been aggravated by years of doing laundry. McCarty knew that it was time to make a change in her life — but she had no idea what a big change it would turn out to be.

THE GIFT

By that time, simply by doing laundry, McCarty had saved $280,000, over a quarter of a million dollars. It's an astounding sum of money considering her low rate of pay and her frugal lifestyle. In early 1995, she started talking to her bankers and her lawyer about how to ensure that she would be cared for during her life and how to distribute her money after her death. Paul Laughlin, an officer at her bank, helped her set up her will. To explain percentages, he put out ten dimes. Then he asked her to divide up the dimes according to how she wanted her estate to be divided. She put one dime for her church, three dimes for some distant cousins, and the rest — six dimes, or 60 percent — for the University of Southern Mississippi, located right in Hattiesburg. According to Laughlin, "She was quite definite about wanting to give 60 percent to USM." For McCarty, it was a chance to give some child the education she never had. "I want to help somebody's child go to college. I just want it to go to someone who will appreciate it and learn," she said. "I'm too old to get an education, but they can."

In July 1995, McCarty signed an agreement called an irrevocable trust that gave the bank the responsibility for handling her finances today and outlined her wishes for the future. Currently, the money is essentially still being saved. The bank officers manage McCarty's investments and give her as much as she needs. At the time of her death, though, the remainder of the money will be turned over to the individuals and groups she has already picked out. The university planned to use the $150,000 donation to establish an endowed fund, the Oseola McCarty Scholarship fund, that would give college scholarships to needy students. Priority consideration would be given to deserving African-American students who demonstrate a financial need. But in the meantime, when word got out about McCarty's gift, people started sending matching contributions to the university. So USM used those donations to create the Oseola McCarty Scholarship fund right away, and McCarty's own money will be added later.

Officials at the university were deeply affected by her donation. "This is just extraordinary," USM president Aubrey Lucas said. "I don't know that I have ever been as touched by a gift to the university as I am by this one. Miss McCarty has shown great unselfishness and sensitivity in making possible for others the education she never had." That view was echoed by Bill Pace, the director of the USM Foundation, the university group that will administer her gift. "I've been in the business 24 years now, in private fund raising. And this is the first time I've experienced anything like this from an individual who simply was not affluent, did not have the resources and yet gave substantially. In fact, she gave almost everything she has. No one approached her from the university; she approached us. She's seen the poverty, the young people who have struggled, who need an education. She is the most unselfish individual I have ever met."

"The secret to building a fortune is compounding interest. It's not the ones that make the big money, but the ones who know how to save who get ahead. You've got to leave your investment alone long enough for it to increase."

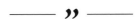

He went on to say, "We are overwhelmed and humbled by what she has done." When McCarty visited USM in August 1995, the first time she had ever visited a college campus, 1,000 teachers and other staff members stood up and cheered.

THE RESPONSE

It wasn't just university officials who responded to McCarty's generous gift. In fact, her donation touched people around the country. When word got out, she became a media sensation. Stories about her appeared in newspapers and magazines around the country, as well as on ABC, NBC, CBS, CNN, MTV, NPR, and the BBC. She was interviewed by several prominent TV hosts, including Oprah Winfrey, David Letterman, and Barbara Walters.

McCarty with the recipients of the Oseola McCarty Scholarship

Additional donations began to pour into the scholarship fund, first from local residents of Hattiesburg and then from people around the country. To date, people have contributed about $400,000 in matching funds. Many give credit to McCarty, saying that she inspired them with her generosity and selflessness. In fact, businessman Ted Turner, who owns a huge media empire, has said that her gift inspired his own decision to donate $1 billion to the United Nations. "I admire Oseola McCarty," he said. "She gave away her entire life savings. She did more than I did. I just gave away one third—I've still got about $2 billion left. She's the one who really deserves the credit."

McCarty began to get awards and invitations to speak, and she was soon traveling all over the country. The woman who had only been out of Mississippi once in her life has made almost 200 trips around the U.S. since then, often accompanied by Jewel Tucker, a USM administrator who has become a close friend. In 1995 she received an award from President Bill Clinton, and arrangements were made for a private plane to take her to Washington, D.C. But McCarty was afraid to fly, and she insisted on traveling by train. Unfortunately, though, all the seats on the train from Mississippi to Washington were already booked. So some phone calls were made, and soon Tom Downs, the president of Amtrak, arranged to have an extra private sleeping car added to the train, just for McCarty. Soon, though, she planned a trip to Colorado,

> *" "Some people make a lot of noise about what's wrong with the world, and they are usually blaming somebody else. I think people who don't like the way things are need to look at themselves first. They need to get right with God and change their own ways. That way, they will know they are making a difference in at least one life. If everybody did that, we'd be all right." "*

which would have taken over three weeks by train. That convinced her to start flying, if only for Jewel Tucker's sake. "The first time we flew," according to Tucker, "they put the table cloth over the tray and she looked at me and said, 'Jewel, you can eat on a plane?'"

THE RECIPIENTS

The first Oseola McCarty Scholarship was given out in 1995; to date, seven students have earned scholarships that have enabled them to attend college because of her generosity. Although her bequest will not actually go to the university until after her death, the USM Foundation decided to start funding the scholarship early with the monies given by other donors. The USM Foundation wanted McCarty to get a chance to meet the scholarship winners. The first recipient of the Oseola McCarty Scholarship was Stephanie Bullock. An honors student at Hattiesburg High School, she was a class officer, a member of the National Honor Society, an appointee to the Mayor's Youth Council, and an active member in her church. Yet she hadn't qualified for a scholarship to college, and her parents were worried about paying tuition and fees for both Stephanie and her twin brother, Stephen. "I was worried about how we could afford [college]," she said. "I told my parents that I don't like growing up because there's too much to worry about."

Because of McCarty's donation, Stephanie received a scholarship that eliminated those financial worries for the Bullock family. Stephanie was both elated and profoundly grateful, and she and McCarty have become close. "Oseola gave me much more than a scholarship; she taught me about the gift of giving. Now I know there are good people in the world who do good things. She worked her whole life and gave to others, and in turn she has inspired me to give back when I can. Eventually I plan to add to her scholarship fund," Bullock said.

"I want to give Oseola the family she's always wanted, so I've adopted her as another grandma. She even calls me her granddaughter. And when I graduate from USM [in 1999], she'll be sitting in the audience between my mother and my grandmother—right where she belongs."

HOME AND FAMILY

McCarty never married or had children. She lived for many years, first with her family and then on her own, in her small, neat bungalow in Hattiesburg. Currently, following surgery and some health problems, she is recovering in an assisted living facility near the University. She has her own room there, and she shares meals with other residents in the community cafeteria. Her favorite activity is reading her Bible, and she also spends time visiting with her many new friends.

WRITINGS

Simple Wisdom for Rich Living, 1996

HONORS AND AWARDS

Presidential Citizens Medal: 1995
Wallenberg Humanitarian Award (Wallenberg Foundation): 1995
Community Heroes Award (National Urban League): 1995
Avicenna Medal (United Nations Educational, Scientific, and Cultural
 Organization—UNESCO): 1995

Premier Black Woman of Courage (National Federation of Black Women
   Business Owners): 1996
Essence Award (*Essence* Magazine): 1996
Aetna Award (Aetna Foundation): 1996
Andrus Award (American Association of Retired People): 1996
Fannie Lou Hamer Award (National Council of Negro Women): 1997
Jefferson Award: 1997
Living Legend Award (National Association of Black School Educators):
   1997
Woman of Achievement Award (National Association for the
   Advancement of Colored People): 1997

FURTHER READING

Books

Coleman, Evelyn. *The Riches of Oseola McCarty*, 1998
McCarty, Oseola. *Simple Wisdom for Rich Living*, 1996

Periodicals

Chronicle of Higher Education, Aug. 11, 1995, p.A31
Detroit Free Press, Mar. 25, 1998, pC1
Ebony, Dec. 1995, p.84
Essence, May 1996, p.66
Family Circle, Apr. 22, 1997, p.52
Jet, Aug. 28, 1995, p.12
Ms. Jan./Feb. 1996, p.47
New York Times, Aug. 13, 1995, Section 1, p.1; Nov. 12, 1996, p.A1
People, Aug. 28, 1995, p.40; Jan. 13, 1997, p.71
Southern Living, Feb. 1998, p.32

ADDRESS

University of Southern Mississippi
Public Relations
Box 5016
Hattiesburg, MS 39406-5016

WORLD WIDE WEB SITE

http://www.pr.usm.edu/oolamain.htm

Mark McGwire 1963-

American Professional Baseball Player with the
St. Louis Cardinals
Holds the Record for Hitting the Most Home Runs
in a Single Season

BIRTH

Mark David McGwire, known to baseball fans everywhere as
Big Mac, was born on October 1, 1963, in Pomona, California.
He was the second of five sons born to dentist John McGwire
and his wife, Ginger. Like his brothers, McGwire was a big
baby who grew up to be a big adult — each of the McGwire

boys is over six feet, two inches tall and weighs more than 210 pounds. One of Mark's brothers, Dan, also went on to professional sports success as a quarterback for the Seattle Seahawks of the National Football League.

YOUTH

McGwire grew up in Claremont, California, a wealthy suburb of Los Angeles. "We grew up in a great cul-de-sac," or dead-end street, he recalls fondly. McGwire's father was busy with his dental practice, so his mother, a former nurse, had her hands full raising the five boisterous boys. McGwire remembers the tremendous amount of food his mother had to purchase to keep her growing boys from going hungry. "My mom used to spend about $200 twice a week at the supermarket," he recalls. "She really had trouble keeping the refrigerator full."

McGwire was interested in sports at an early age. Baseball and golf were the two sports he spent the most time on, although he was also a very good basketball player. His earliest memories are of caddying for his father when he was just five years old. McGwire's father encouraged his sons to enjoy sports, but when Mark approached him at age seven and requested permission to play Little League baseball, his father said no. "I'd heard too much about arguing, meddling parents and bad coaches," John McGwire explains. "I didn't want anybody to screw up my son. When I told him that he couldn't play, he cried and cried and cried."

A Young Star

A year later, however, Mark's father relented, granting permission for McGwire to play in a league where he would be facing boys up to 12 years old. That did not bother the young boy, as he made clear in his first Little League at bat. "His first at-bat, against a 12-year-old pitcher, Mark hit a home run over the right-field fence," remembers his father. "The surprising thing was he had an innate sense of how to play. He knew where to position players, he just knew. It was spine-tingling, his understanding of the game at such an early age. The old-timers who sat around the railroad tracks and talked baseball would say, 'This kid, he's something. He's going to light up the world.'"

But during his elementary school years, McGwire never really thought about making a career as a professional baseball player. "I played Little League and stuff," he remembers, "but I never thought about the big leagues until my junior year of high school, when some scouts started coming by. Then it hit me I had a chance to play major league baseball."

McGwire progressed through the various levels of youth baseball, moving from Little League to American Legion ball. He earned a reputation along the way as a great hitter and pitcher as well as the sort of youngster who would always look out for smaller, younger teammates. By the time McGwire had joined the local American Legion team, his exploits on the baseball diamond were already becoming legendary. Randy Robertson, a friend from his teen years, remembers that during one American Legion game, the big teenager literally hit a home run into the next county. It seems that Big Mac blasted one over the left-field fence and the street behind it, which happened to be the dividing line between Los Angeles and San Bernadino counties. "As he got older and more selective at the plate, he knew when he got his pitch," Robertson continues. "And he could hit it a mile."

> "His first at-bat, against a 12-year-old pitcher, Mark hit a home run over the right-field fence," remembers his father. "The surprising thing was he had an innate sense of how to play. He knew where to position players, he just knew. It was spine-tingling, his understanding of the game at such an early age. The old-timers who sat around the railroad tracks and talked baseball would say, 'This kid, he's something. He's going to light up the world.'"

EDUCATION

McGwire attended elementary school in the Claremont public school system, but during his freshman year in high school, he transferred from the Claremont public high school to Damien High School, a private, all-boys Catholic school with a reputation for strong academics and athletics. Damien baseball coach Tom Carroll still remembers the first time he saw McGwire: "His dad was with him. I saw this big old boy walking around—he was tall even then—but he seemed very shy. He always gave me the impression he was not cocky. He kind of kept to himself. Very polite, gentlemanly."

McGwire tried out for the baseball team, but did not make the varsity as a freshman. His sophomore season, he actually quit playing baseball to concentrate on playing golf full-time, a decision that seems hard to believe now but that was easy for him to make at the time. "I'd pulled a chest muscle, so it would be a while before I could really swing a bat, and

I'd have been playing JV baseball, which didn't excite me much," he says. "I'd been playing golf for years. My dad used to take me to the peewee courses when I was only six or seven, and I'd developed my own swing. I never had a lesson. I had a good year playing golf. I won several tournaments. But I found I missed baseball. I still play golf whenever I can . . . but I went back to baseball the next year."

Back on the diamond for his junior season, all the pieces fell into place for McGwire. He first made his mark as a pitcher. "His whole thing was he scared the hell out of the other kids," Carroll remembers. "He had that high kick and long stride, and it looked like he was nearly stepping on home plate as he was releasing the baseball." But McGwire was also the team's most dangerous hitter, and his performance swinging the bat convinced his coaches that they needed to make use of all of his abilities. During his senior season, McGwire played designated hitter whenever he was not pitching. He succeeded both on the mound and at the plate. He finished 5-3 with a 1.90 earned run average (ERA) as a pitcher and hit .359 with nearly a dozen home runs.

McGwire's performance caught the attention of pro baseball scouts during his senior season. In 1981 he was drafted in the eighth round of the major league draft by the Montreal Expos. He was excited about the prospect of playing professional baseball, but the team's signing bonus offer of $8,500 was far less than he had expected. After giving the matter a lot of thought, he decided to go to college at the University of Southern California, the only school that had offered him a scholarship. It was a decision he would never regret.

Joining the Trojans

The head coach of the University of Southern California (USC) Trojans baseball team was Rod Dedeaux, one of the legendary figures in the history of college baseball. McGwire's pitching ability deeply impressed Dedeaux, and he quickly made the freshman sensation an important part of his pitching staff. "He had that attitude, that determination you want to see in a pitcher," recalls Dedeaux. "He was an outstanding prospect." McGwire's teammates were impressed with the redhead's arm as well. "He threw really hard, had an incredible arm, a 90-plus mile per hour fast ball," remembers teammate Brad Brink.

McGwire pitched well his freshman season, compiling a 2.78 ERA. However, his life changed in the summer of 1982 when he traveled to Alaska to play in the Alaska Summer League, one of the top amateur leagues in the country. He was sent to play for the Anchorage Glacier Pilots so he

McGwire slugging his 62nd home run on September 8, 1998

could work on his pitching, but things did not turn out that way. When all three of the Pilots' first basemen did not show up for the season, McGwire volunteered to play the position, and the rest is history. From his first game he hit well, and when he did get in to pitch for the first time, he got hit hard and knocked out early. Back to first base he went, and he stayed there for the rest of the summer.

McGwire hit .403 with 13 home runs and 53 runs batted in (RBI) in just 44 games in Alaska and returned to USC a changed man. "Somewhere along the line up there in Alaska, it hit me," he remembers. "You know, I'd rather play every day than every fifth day. Then I started getting some hits. Ron Vaughn (an assistant coach at Anchorage), who's one of my biggest mentors as a hitter, pretty much started me and taught me everything I needed to know."

When McGwire returned to USC, Dedeaux at first resisted the idea of letting him give up pitching. He still believes to this day that the young man could have made it to the big leagues as a pitcher. However, McGwire laughs when he remembers what it was that changed his coach's mind. "Rod totally resisted it until he saw the three-run homers. Then he loved it." So did his teammates. As McGwire's playing time increased, he earned the reputation as an excellent hitter and team player, the guy his teammates wanted at the plate late in a close game. "When the game was on the line, it seemed like he always hit a home run or something," recalls Brink. "He was a clutch player, not just a home-run hitter. That's the sign of a great player."

McGwire hit 19 home runs his sophomore season after returning from Alaska, then blasted 32 as a junior, a single-season record at USC. Up to that point, the USC *career* record had been 32 home runs. Big Mac established a new career record also, and it was clear he was on his way to the pros. After his junior season, McGwire was selected to play on the 1984 U.S. Olympic team, although baseball was a demonstration sport that year, rather than a regular event. "The Olympics were a great experience," he said. "Playing with the caliber of players on that team was tremendous." The American team ended up coming in second in the Games.

That same summer McGwire was drafted by the Oakland A's, who selected him with the 10th overall pick in the first round. There was speculation that he was going to be the first player selected in the draft, but the New York Mets (who had the first pick) and other teams were afraid that McGwire was going to be too hard to sign so they passed on him. Eager to begin his pro career, McGwire left USC after his junior year and joined the A's minor league system. The decision was a hard one. Despite his early reluctance to go to college, he found it hard to leave. He called his decision to play at USC one of the best choices he had ever made. "I didn't think I'd enjoy it," he later admitted. "But I had a great time there. Those were the best three years of my life."

CAREER HIGHLIGHTS

Because of his college and Olympic experience, McGwire was far more advanced than the average minor league rookie. As a result, he ended up spending only two years in the minors. After starting at the Single A level, he quickly moved up to Double A ball and then to Triple A, which is just one step below the major leagues. In two full minor league seasons, he hit .298 and averaged 24 home runs and 109 RBIs. At the end of the 1986 season, the A's called him up and let him play in 18 games, in which he hit three home runs.

> *On the last day of the 1987 season, McGuire had a chance to become only the 11th player in major league history to hit 50 home runs. But he chose not to play because he wanted to attend the birth of his son, Matthew. "I got to the hospital just 45 minutes before the birth. I was in the delivery room so I got to see everything."*

Rookie of the Year

As the 1987 season approached, Oakland's coaches decided that McGwire was ready for full-time duty in the big leagues. McGwire started the 1987 season on the A's major league roster. It took him a few weeks to win the starting job at first base, but once he did, the job was his for good. He went on to have what is possibly the best rookie season that any hitter has ever had. During the first four months of the season, he was actually on a pace to challenge Roger Maris's legendary record of 61 home runs in a single season. In the final weeks of the season he cooled off, but he still finished the year with a rookie record 49 home runs, which was 11 more than any previous rookie had ever registered. He also hit .289, knocked in 118 runs, and led the American League with a .628 slugging percentage. "It's very surprising to me," McGwire said. "I've hit home runs throughout my career, in high school and college, but they never came in numbers like this. It's very surprising and I really can't explain it. It just happens."

After the season, McGwire became only the second player to be unanimously voted the American League Rookie of the Year (the first was Boston Red Sox catcher Carlton Fisk in 1972). The amazing year stunned even McGwire. "No, of course I didn't expect anything like that," he said after the season. "I've never set particular goals for myself, I just wanted to make the team. I went to spring training and worked my butt off. I hit well, and I think that opened the eyes of a lot of coaches."

The record-setting season provided McGwire a small taste of the media pressure that would follow him throughout his career. Baseball fans love home runs, and the public saw McGwire as the new king of the long ball.

"For three months," he recalls, "there wasn't a time when I came to the park that there wasn't somebody waiting for me at my locker. I like to get out to the park early and kick back for a while. But I had no chance to do that." By the end of the season, McGwire was struggling to deal with the pressure. "[The attention] bothered me," he admits. "It affected my concentration because I couldn't get in the right frame of mind. . . . It put pressure on me that I hadn't been putting on myself. I had a bad August (only three home runs), and I know that was the reason."

For the most part, however, McGwire handled the media attention gracefully, and as the year drew to a close he made a decision that further heightened the public's opinion of the young slugger. On the last day of the season, he had a chance to become only the 11th player in major league history to hit 50 home runs. But he chose not to play because he wanted to attend the birth of his son, Matthew. "I got to the hospital just 45 minutes before the birth," he said. "I was in the delivery room so I got to see everything."

Over the course of the next two seasons, McGwire continued to hit home runs at a remarkable rate. He teamed with outfielder Jose Canseco to form the Bash Brothers, a pair of young home run hitters who helped make the A's one of the best teams in baseball. From 1988 to 1990, the A's won the American League championship three straight times as McGwire proved that his early success was no fluke. In 1988 he followed up his sensational rookie year with a .260 batting average, 32 home runs, and 99 RBIs. The A's won 104 games that season, the most in the majors, but they were upset in the World Series by the Los Angeles Dodgers.

Triumph and Tragedy

In 1989, the A's were again the best team in baseball, and McGwire remained one of the major weapons in Oakland's line-up. While his batting average slipped to .231, he still managed to club 33 home runs and drive in 85 runs. The A's knocked off the Toronto Blue Jays to reach the World Series, where they faced the San Francisco Giants.

The 1989 Series between Oakland and San Francisco turned out to be one of the most memorable in history, but not because of what happened on the field. After splitting the first four games, the two teams were preparing to play Game 5 at San Francisco's Candlestick Park when a powerful earthquake shook the park and the surrounding city. Memorable video shot from the ballpark immediately after the quake showed the full extent of the quake's devastation—homes had been leveled, entire blocks were on fire, and the double-decker Bay Bridge had collapsed. The quake took a large human toll as well—nearly 60 people were killed, and hundreds more were injured. It was the worst earthquake in California in many, many years. Out of respect for the casualties of the quake, the Series was postponed for ten days. When it resumed, it was anticlimactic. The A's finished off the Giants by winning the next two games, but there was little reason to celebrate, as McGwire recalled in 1997: "We had to respect the people who died [in the quake]. We had to respect what happened in northern California. We didn't get to celebrate the way the Yankees got to celebrate [after they won the Series in 1996]. No champagne. No parade. We had a rally. There'll always be an asterisk next to our '89 championship."

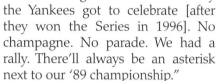

"It was a sweet, sweet run around the bases," he said after his 62nd home run. One of the first people to greet McGwire was his son Matthew, who was serving as the Cardinals' batboy. He lifted the boy in the air three times in an emotional scene that left many in tears. "When he picked up his son, it was the greatest moment I've seen since I've been in the major leagues," said manager Tony LaRussa.

With a World Series triumph under their belt, the A's wanted to use the 1990 season to establish themselves as a dynasty that would be seen as one of baseball's best teams ever. McGwire, as usual, did his part to help the A's win — he hit .235, with 39 home runs and 108 RBIs. Additionally, he won his first Gold Glove for fielding excellence, demonstrating that he was a multi-dimensional player.

The A's won the American League championship for the third straight season, and they were heavily favored to defeat the Cincinnati Reds in the World Series. But Cincinnati shocked the A's and the rest of the baseball world by sweeping Oakland in four straight games to win the championship. McGwire and the rest of his teammates played poorly in the Series, which angers the big hitter to this day. "Our team should have won three World Series rings in a row," he says. "But if you don't prepare yourself . . . I mean, what I know now I wish I knew then. There's no way I would let that happen."

A Slump for Big Mac

In 1991 the A's and McGwire suffered a sharp performance decline from previous seasons. The A's could finish no better than fourth in their own division, while McGwire saw his batting average plummet to .201 for the

McGwire lifting his son Matthew after hitting his 62nd home run on September 8, 1998

season. Even more surprising, he hit only 22 home runs and drove in just 75 runs. After the season, McGwire was so embarrassed by his performance that he told the A's to cut his salary, which they did not do. "Last year was not a lot of fun," he said in the off-season. "I wouldn't wish it on anybody. I had a down year. It's in the books. It's even on my baseball card. There is no escaping it. I'm not going to hide from it."

To bounce back from the disastrous 1991 season, McGwire rededicated himself to the weight room. While he was already an imposing 6 feet, 5 inches tall and weighed 215 pounds, he decided that he had not been taking care of his body. By lifting weights regularly several times a week, he added 25 pounds of muscle to his already strong body, extending his biceps to 17 and a half inches, which is the size of an average man's neck. "Weight training just makes you feel better about yourself," says McGwire.

In addition to the weight training, McGwire also sought help from a professional counselor. "I wasn't there as a person," McGwire recalls. "I truly believe that until you get to know who you are as a person, you can't do a lot of things in life. I think back to my early years, as a young kid, a young adult, as a ballplayer. I didn't know myself back then. I couldn't make a decision for myself. Because of what I've gone through in my life and the therapy I've gone through, I can do that now."

The combination of weight training and therapy seemed to work perfectly. One year after the frustrating 1991 season, McGwire bounced back with a fantastic year. He raised his batting average 67 points to .268, slugged 42 home runs, and knocked in 104 runs. McGwire was back in top form, and so were the A's, who won their fourth Western Division title in five years.

In 1992, however, injuries bothered McGwire for much of the season, and in 1993 and 1994, he played in a total of only 74 games because of a torn tendon in his left foot. The injuries frustrated McGwire, but he thinks they also helped him become a better ballplayer. "When I was injured in 1993, it was the first time in my career I had to sit back and watch the game," he recalls. "Instead of sitting back and feeling sorry for myself, I started watching the players, watching pitchers, watching how the game is played. It made me understand what the game is all about. In turn, it made me use my mind more than I ever have. It made me a better player. Now I'm convinced that this game is 99.9 percent mental."

In 1995, another foot injury, this time in his right foot, kept Big Mac out of the lineup at the start of the season. Once he got healthy in May, however, he tore up American League pitching. The 1995 season is best remembered because the major league players went on strike late in the season and forced the cancellation of the World Series. But Mac made it memorable, too. He hit 39 home runs in only 317 at bats, meaning that he hit one home run every 8.1 at bats, a new major league record. He also knocked in 90 runs and batted .274 in the shortened season.

The 1996 season showed that McGwire was healthier and a much more disciplined hitter than he used to be. He hit a career-high .312, slugged 52 home runs, and drove in 113 runs. In addition, McGwire drew 116 walks, which was also a career high to that point. The season was a disappointing one in one respect, however. The A's were in the process of rebuilding their team, and despite McGwire's star performance the club finished near the bottom of their division, well out of the pennant race.

A Move to St. Louis

In 1997 McGwire was at a crossroads of his career. It was the final year of his contract with the A's, which meant he would be free to sign with any team after the season was over. As the season unfolded, Oakland's management became convinced that it would be unable to re-sign McGwire to a new contract because he had become such a big star. As a result, the A's made the tough decision to trade McGwire to the St. Louis Cardinals during the middle of the season, even though he already had 34 home runs.

St. Louis general manager Walt Jocketty wanted to acquire a big name player for the Cardinals to help generate fan interest in the team. He had been talking to the A's about McGwire since the beginning of the season, but the deal was not completed until Jocketty offered Oakland a trio of talented young pitchers. Then Jocketty's real work started. He had to convince McGwire that St. Louis was the right team for him so the club could sign the superstar to a long-term contract. It did not take much to convince McGwire. He loved playing in front of the enthusiastic St. Louis fans, and within a month of arriving, he had signed a three-year contract with the Cardinals that was worth $30 million. "It was the fans that really got him excited about playing here. . . and staying here," remembers Jocketty. "He was here maybe a month, if that, and has his attorney call me about making a deal. That says a lot."

"I'm rooting for Mark McGwire," said Sosa in September, during the heat of the race. "I look up to him the way a son does to a father. I look at him, the way he hits, the way he acts, and I see the person and player I want to be. I'm the man in the Dominican Republic, he's the man in the United States. That's the way it should be."

The Cardinals are one of oldest teams in baseball, and over the years many excellent players have taken the field for St. Louis. However, the team has never had a power hitter like McGwire who can generate excitement every time he steps into the batter's box. In the remainder of the 1997 season, McGwire hit 24 more home runs as a Cardinal to finish with 58 for the season, only three homers short of Roger Maris's record of 61 homers in a single season.

Sammy Sosa hugging McGwire after his 62nd home run

Chasing Roger Maris

McGwire started off the 1998 season with a bang, hitting 11 home runs in the month of April, including three in one game against the Arizona Diamondbacks on April 14. By the end of May, he had 27 round-trippers. Fans around the country took notice, and it was clear the Maris record, which had been set 37 years before, was in jeopardy. McGwire remained calm, however. He had always told anyone who would listen that to break the Maris record, a hitter would need to have 50 home runs entering the month of September. That was the number he measured himself against.

McGwire made it to 50 well before September 1, hitting that magical number for the third time in his career on August 20. In fact, by the time September rolled around, McGwire already had 55 home runs, just six short of tying the record. All across the country, excited baseball fans said that the question was no longer *whether* McGwire would break the record, but *when* he would break it.

What made McGwire's record chase even more exciting was the fact that he was not alone in his pursuit of the magical single-season homer mark. Sammy Sosa of the Chicago Cubs was running neck and neck with McGwire. After starting the season slowly, the Dominican-born Sosa hit a record 20 home runs in the month of June to put himself in the running. All season the two sluggers dueled, tying for the league lead five times down the stretch. The competition was made even better because it was a friendly one—the two men respected each other immensely and became friends as the season wore on. "I'm rooting for Mark McGwire," said Sosa in September, during the heat of the race. "I look up to him the way a son does to a father. I look at him, the way he hits, the way he acts, and I see the person and player I want to be. I'm the man in the Dominican Republic, he's the man in the United States. That's the way it should be."

In the end, it was McGwire who reached the top first. On September 7, in the next-to-last game in the Cardinals home stadium before the team would leave on a long road trip, he hit number 61 to tie Maris. Playing in front of a national television audience and a capacity crowd that included baseball commissioner Bud Selig and the children of the late Maris, McGwire crushed number 61 as a gift to his father, who was celebrating his 61st birthday and was also in attendance.

Setting a New Record

Fans did not have to wait long for number 62. The very next night, on September 8, in a game against Sosa's Cubs, McGwire put his name in the history books with number 62, a low line drive that just barely made it out of the stadium. Ironically, it was his shortest home run of the season. "When I hit the ball, I thought it was a line drive and I thought it was going to hit the wall and the next thing I knew, it disappeared," he said after the game. "I was in shock, I was numb. *I did it!* I had all these things running through my mind, I was just in outer space. I can't even remember everything I did."

As McGwire watched his record-setting homer disappear, the slugger was so dazed by his feat and the crazed reaction of the stadium crowd that he had to be directed back to first base by first base coach Dave McKay because he missed the bag when he went by it the first time. He received congratulations from each of the Cubs' infielders as he circled the bases, then was mobbed by his teammates at home plate. "It was a sweet, sweet run around the bases," he said after the game. One of the first people to greet McGwire was his son Matthew, who was serving as the Cardinals' batboy. He lifted the boy in the air three times in an emotional scene that left many in tears. "When he picked up his son, it was the greatest moment I've seen since I've been in the major leagues," said manager Tony LaRussa.

The pandemonium inside the stadium continued as Sosa trotted in from right field to embrace his rival. Then McGwire jogged over to the stands and jumped into the seats where the Maris family was watching the game. As the capacity crowd cheered him on, McGwire hugged each of Maris's six children one-by-one in an unforgettable classy gesture. Roger Maris Jr. later said that he will remember that moment for the rest of his life. "It was such a crazy, emotional moment. I just remember him saying that my dad is always going to be in his heart. . . . For him to come over and greet our family and give us hugs and let us partake in his day the way he did was just so special. It's a moment that we'll never forget."

Finally, after the crowd had settled down a little, McGwire gave a short speech to thank the fans for their support. "After [the night before] doing what I did for my father and my son showing up just in time, I though what a perfect way to end the week . . . by hitting the 62nd for the city of St. Louis and all the great fans," he said as the Cardinals fans roared their approval.

Within a week of hitting number 62, McGwire was joined in the elite home run club by Sosa, who hit his 61st and 62nd of the year in an 11-10 win over the Milwaukee Brewers on September 13. McGwire was happy for his friendly rival: "I think it's awesome. I've said it a thousand times that I'm not competing against him. I can only take care of myself. Imagine if we're tied at the end. What a beautiful way to end the season."

Finishing a Record-Breaking Season

In the end, however, it was McGwire who pulled away with a final burst of power, hitting four home runs in the season's final three games to finish with an amazing 70 home runs for the season. Sosa would finish with 66, capping what many fans and writers called the best baseball season of all time. McGwire knows the chase captivated the fans' attention, and he feels a large part of the reason for that is because he and Sosa were such good friends. "That's why the country caught on to this chase," he said after the season. "They saw two people from two different countries get along and show great sportsmanship. You don't see that much in sports these days. Everyone who plays major league baseball should be really proud of what we did this year."

McGwire watching his 70th home run on September 29, 1998

Only one thing marred McGwire's magical, record-breaking season. In August it was reported that McGwire used a substance called androstenedione, a naturally occurring testosterone supplement that might enhance muscle mass and athletic performance. It also supposedly helps athletes recover from injuries by rebuilding damaged muscle tissue faster than normal. "Andro," as the substance is called, is banned in college sports, the National Football League, and by the International Olympic Committee, but it is legal in baseball. Many people criticized McGwire for using the substance, but his brother Jay, who is a physical trainer, defended him. "Mark takes so much pride in his body and is so worried about what people think of him that he would never do anything to damage his health or image. The key to anything is moderation, but that's not to say he's taking steroids, because he isn't."

McGwire knows the home run record is special, and that it might last as long as the 37 years that Maris's mark stood. But it was not until *after* he broke the record that he realized *how* important it was. "It's only been in these past few days after breaking the record that I've realized the impact I've had on people's lives," he said. "I've received telegrams, letters, and phone calls from Pete Rose, Johnny Bench, Joe Morgan, Cal Ripken, Jack McDowell, Brett Favre, Greg Norman, many of my former Oakland teammates and so many others. Ken Griffey Jr. hired an airplane to pull a banner saying congratulations when we were in Cincinnati. It's incredible."

———— " ————

Mc Gwire described his 62nd home run like this. "When I hit the ball, I thought it was a line drive and I thought it was going to hit the wall and the next thing I knew, it disappeared," I was in shock, I was numb. I did it! I had all these things running through my mind, I was just in outer space. I can't even remember everything I did."

———— " ————

MARRIAGE AND FAMILY

McGwire met his future wife, Kathy Williamson, while he was at the University of Southern California. She was one of the batgirls on the baseball team. They were married in December of 1984, and their son Matthew was born three years later in October 1987. Unfortunately, the marriage did not work out, and the couple divorced in 1988. McGwire has said that the two of them simply married at too young an age, and he noted that he and Kathy remain strong friends. In fact, McGwire often visits Matthew at her home, where she lives with her second husband, Tom. "I have a great ex-wife," says McGwire. "She has a great husband. I always see my son at her house. It's such a nice relationship, and the one who benefits from it is Matthew. He is so well-rounded. What he sees is that his mother is really happy with Tom. He also sees that his father is really happy with Matthew. He was raised in two happy households instead of one deteriorating household that is going to affect the kid throughout his life."

McGwire spends much of his free time with his son. "For the past few years we've taken a vacation together to celebrate our birthdays," McGwire said in 1998. "Last year we went to Mexico. This year we're going to a special place, which I'll keep quiet. I'm very sensitive about Matthew's being in the public eye. I understand people are going to look at me differently and place more demands on me. But, please, leave my son alone. Let him be a child."

HOBBIES AND OTHER INTERESTS

Off the field, McGwire is still an avid golfer who plays regularly. One of his best friends is professional golfer Billy Andrade, with whom McGwire has competed in a professional-amateur celebrity tournament. With the intense pressure of the 1998 home run chase, he was not able to play as often as he likes to, but he intends to change that in the off-season. "I want to play some golf," he said. "It's the sport I played first, since I was five years old—my handicap is 10 now, because I haven't been playing much, but it's been as low as four. My golf swing actually comes more naturally to me than my baseball swing."

McGwire also works on behalf of several charities that help prevent the sexual abuse of children and counsel victims of abuse. After he signed his $30 million contract with the Cardinals, he promised to donate $1 million a year for the next three years to the Mark McGwire Foundation for Children. Late in the home run race, when he was at 59 homers and under tremendous pressure, he took time out of his busy schedule to film a public service announcement for television speaking out against sexual abuse. "The sad thing is people don't want to realize that sexual abuse goes on and it is very, very sad," McGwire said. "I think if you want to bring America together, let's wake up and smell the coffee. It happens."

HONORS AND AWARDS

American League Rookie of the Year: 1987
American League All-Star Team: 1987-1992, 1995-1997
Gold Glove Award: 1990
Comeback Player of the Year (United Press International): 1992
Player's Choice Award (Major League Baseball Player's Association):
    1997, Man of the Year; 1998, Player of the Year
National League All-Star Team: 1998
Player of the Year (Associated Press): 1998
Sportsmen of the Year (*Sports Illustrated*): 1998, shared with Sammy Sosa

FURTHER READING

Books

Who's Who in America, 1998

Periodicals

Current Biography, July 1998
Inside Sports, Mar. 1988, p.44
Los Angeles Times, Aug. 25, 1998, p.C1
Maclean's, Aug. 24, 1987, p.36; Sep. 14, 1998, p.46
New York Times, July 5, 1998, p.22; Sep. 1, 1998, p.C28; Sep. 8, 1998, p.A1;
    Sep. 9, 1998, p.A1; Sep. 11, 1998, p.A27; Sep. 14, 1998, p.A1
Newsday, Aug. 9, 1998, p.C8
Newsweek, July 13, 1987, p.49; Sep. 14, 1998, p.54
People Weekly, Aug. 31, 1987, p.49
Sport, Oct. 1990, p.106; Apr. 1997, p.48; Aug. 1998, p.72; Jan. 1999, p.31
Sporting News, Sep. 2, 1996, p.9; Dec. 15, 1997, p.50; July 13, 1998, p.10
Sports Illustrated, July 13, 1987, p.42; Apr. 4, 1988, p.44; June 1, 1992, p.42;
    Aug. 26, 1996, p.32; Sep. 29, 1997, p.40; Mar. 23, 1998, p.76; May 11,
    1998, p.76; Sep. 14, 1998, p.28; Sep. 21, 1998, p.48
Sports Illustrated for Kids, May 1997, p.50; Nov. 1998, p.32
St. Louis Post-Dispatch, Aug. 18, 1996, p.F1; Aug. 10, 1997, p.F1; July 19,
    1998, p.F7; Sep. 3, 1998, p.D1; Sep. 8, 1998, p.C1; Sep. 9, 1998, p.A11;
    Sep. 10, 1998, p.A1,C1; Sep. 11, 1998, p.A6; Sep. 13, 1998, p.6; Sep. 17,
    1998, p.A19
U.S. News and World Report, Sep. 7, 1998, p.53
USA Today, Jan. 26, 1989, p.C2; Oct. 13, 1989, p.C4; Sep. 23, 1992, p.C4

ADDRESS

St. Louis Cardinals
Busch Stadium
250 Stadium Plaza
St. Louis, MO 63102

WORLD WIDE WEB SITES

http://players.bigleaguers.com
http://www.majorleaguebaseball.com/nl/stl
http://www.sportingnews.com//mcgwire

Slobodan Milosevic 1941-
Yugoslav President and Serbian Political Leader

BIRTH

Slobodan Milosevic (SLOW-beh-dahn mee-LOW-sheh-vitch) was born August 20, 1941, in Pozarevac, in the Serbian section of Yugoslavia. His parents, Svetozar and Stanislava Milosevic, were both born in Montenegro, a nearby province of Yugoslavia. His father, Svetozar, was an Eastern Orthodox priest who later taught Russian and Serbo-Croatian languages and literatures at the local high school in Pozarevac. When Slobodan was in elementary school, his father left the family and settled in nearby Montenegro. Some sources say that Milosevic's one sibling, a brother named Bora, left with the father and lived with him in Montenegro. In 1962, Svetozar Milosevic took his own life. Slobodan Milosevic's mother, Stanislava, was a teacher and ardent member of the Communist Party, which had come to power after World War II. She, too, died a suicide, in 1973.

YOUTH AND EDUCATION

Very little information is available about Slobodan Milosevic's early years. The few reports of his youth note that he had few friends, he didn't take part in sports, and he did very well in school. His mother made sure that he was always dressed in a shirt and tie, and she encouraged him to study and do well. His mother also encouraged him to become active in the Communist Party, and he joined the League of Communists in 1959.

In 1961, Milosevic entered the University of Belgrade to study law. While in law school, he befriended Ivan Stambolic, a man five years older than him from a powerful and well-connected Communist family. Milosevic graduated from law school in 1964. Under Stambolic's influence and patronage, Milosevic began his business and political career.

FIRST JOBS

Following in Stambolic's footsteps, Milosevic began to work for the state-owned gas company, Tehogas, where he rose to the level of director. In 1978, he again followed Stambolic, this time into banking. He was named director of Beobanka, the major bank in Belgrade, the capital of Yugoslavia, a position he held for four years. During this time, Milosevic traveled to New York on business, and he learned to speak English.

In 1982, Milosevic left the private world of business for a career in politics that has lasted to the present day. His first job in the political sector was as an employee of the League of Communists. At this point in its history, Yugoslavia was a Communist nation that had been led by the totalitarian ruler Josep Tito from 1945 until his death in 1980. Tito had kept peace among the several ethnic groups within the country by keeping an iron grip on all aspects of life within his Balkan nation, which had known ethnic warfare and strife throughout its history.

A BRIEF HISTORY OF YUGOSLAVIA AND SERBIA

The modern nation of Yugoslavia came into being after World War I (1914-1918). Yugoslavia is in southern Europe, in the region known as the Balkans. The Balkans include the countries of Albania, Bulgaria, Romania,

Croatia, Bosnia and Herzegovina, Yugoslavia, Macedonia, and parts of Greece and Turkey. Many ethnic groups populate the area, including Albanians, Bulgarians, Romanians, Serbs, Croats, Slovenes, Bosnians, Macedonians, Montenegrans, Greeks, and Turks. But unfortunately, the political boundaries in this region don't always correspond to its ethnic groups. For example, there are many Serbs living in Serbia, of course, but there are also Serbs living in Croatia and Bosnia, and Croats and Bosnians living in Serbia. The many different ethnic groups in the Balkans have lived there for centuries, and they have been ruled by a variety of political and national groups. Yet those various rulers have done little to dampen the strong feelings of ethnic loyalty among the peoples of the Balkans, and these loyalties have often led to war among the different ethnic groups, and between the groups and their rulers.

In a famous 1989 speech in Kosovo, Milosevic spoke of Serbia, then and now. "Today, heroism is still required. But we cannot exclude the possibility of further armed conflict. . . . Serbia has been exploited. Disunity has retarded the Serbian nature while the inferiority of Serbian leaders has humiliated the Serbian people."

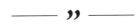

The Serbs first settled in the area now known as Serbia in the sixth and seventh centuries. For the next several hundred years, they fought with their neighbors — the Greeks, Bulgarians, and Hungarians — to control and expand their area of influence. Over the years, different Serbian rulers struggled for increasing control of more and more land. By the late 1300s, Serbia was a strong, independent state. But in 1389, Serbia lost its independence at the Battle of Kosovo Field, defeated by the armies of the Ottoman Turks. The wounded pride of the Serbs over the loss of Kosovo Field would fuel ethnic hatreds well into the 20th century and would contribute to Milosevic's rise to power.

Serbia remained under the control of the Ottoman Empire from the 13th to the 19th century. Turkish rule was harsh: the Serbian nobility was murdered and the Turkish Muslims treated the Christian Serbs like serfs. For nearly 500 years, the Serbs fought to throw out the Turks and regain their independence.

Just as Serbia was ruled by the Ottoman Turkish Empire until the early 20th century, other Balkan republics, including Bosnia and Herzegovina, were under the control of the Austro-Hungarian Empire. In the years leading up to World War I, Serbia led a movement to unify the different Balkan republics and throw out any foreign rulers. After World War I, the movement to unify the Balkan republics resulted in the formation of the Kingdom of the Serbs, Croats, and Slovenes. In 1929, the name of the country was changed to Yugoslavia. The six republics that originally made up the nation of Yugoslavia were Serbia, including the provinces of Kosovo and Vojvodina; Croatia; Bosnia and Herzegovina; Macedonia; Slovenia; and Montenegro. Each of these republics was largely divided by ethnic group. For example, the Serb people were the largest group in Serbia, the Macedonians in Macedonia, and so on. Yet for centuries there have also been large groups of ethnic minorities living in the republics, such as the ethnic Albanians who lived in the Kosovo section of Serbia, and the Serbs who lived in Croatia as well as Bosnia and Herzegovina.

Throughout the early years of the new country, ethnic tensions existed between the various peoples of Yugoslavia, and occasionally flared into violence. But at the end of World War II (1939-1945), when Josep Tito came to power, he banned ethnic conflict of any kind. He also tried to limit the power of the Serbs, who were the largest ethnic group in Yugoslavia, by granting autonomy to Kosovo, where the ethnic Albanians made up 90 percent of the population, and to Vojvodina, where ethnic Hungarians make up 60 percent of the population. These two provinces elected their own officials to state and federal political offices and also had their own civilian police forces.

When Tito died in 1980, his death prompted a power struggle within the Yugoslavian Communist Party. While Tito had banned ethnic hatreds during his years in power, they had continued to fester. These ancient hatreds now threatened to explode; economic problems in the country added to the strife. It was into this atmosphere that Slobodan Milosevic, a loyal employee of the League of Communists, entered politics.

CAREER HIGHLIGHTS

Entering Politics

Milosevic served as an undistinguished party bureaucrat for several years, once again using the influence of his mentor Stambolic to move up within the party. In 1984, he took over as head of the Belgrade Communist Party for Stambolic. In 1986, when Stambolic became President of Serbia, Milosevic was named head of the Serbian Communist Party. As he gained power, Milosevic began to portray himself as a Serbian nationalist. "Nationalism" is a political philosophy that encourages people to feel loy-

Milosevic and his wife, Mirjana Markovic

alty only to those of their individual nation or ethnic group. The Serbian nationalists promoted a "Greater Serbia" in an effort to unite the Serbs living in all the republics into one nation. Through his message of Serbian ethnic supremacy and passionate nationalism, Milosevic forged a political following that included communists and noncommunists alike, united in their vision of a Greater Serbia. The other ethnic groups within Yugoslavia, meanwhile, found Milosevic's rhetoric and threats to be frightening. What would happen to them as he and his political followers pursued their goal of a "Greater Serbia"?

The Famous Speech to the Serbians of Kosovo

In April 1987, Milosevic traveled to Kosovo, site of the battle with the Ottoman Turks that had stripped the Serbs of their kingdom in 1389. There, he made a speech that solidified his reputation as a champion of the Serbian cause. At that time, the majority population in Kosovo was Albanian, and Serbs were in the minority. The Serbs of Kosovo claimed they were being discriminated against by the Albanian majority. The Serbs rioted to protest their treatment and were being rounded up by the Albanian police force when Milosevic appeared and told them: "No one will dare beat you again!" Like lightning, the phrase traveled throughout Yugoslavia, becoming a slogan for the Serb nationalists.

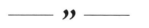

> "Yugoslavia today is a microcosm of the crisis of communism and [Soviet President] Mikhail Gorbachev's future nightmare: failed reforms, spiraling inflation, political impotence and resurgent ethnic rivalries." — Peter Millar, Times (London)

In December 1987, with his political star rising, Milosevic did what was to become a habit with him — he turned his back on his former mentor, Stambolic, and had him removed from office. He then began a purge of the Communist Party, removing anyone who could be considered a rival. In 1989, as he solidified his power, Milosevic moved against the autonomous provinces of Kosovo and Vojdovina, stripping them of their political freedoms, replacing their officials and police forces with Serbians, and rounding up and imprisoning any protesters.

In June of 1989, Milosevic made another famous speech, this time on the grounds of the Battle of Kosovo, to commemorate the 600th anniversary of the battle. Half a million Serbs cheered their hero as he ominously spoke of Serbia, then and now. "Today, heroism is still required," he told the crowd. "But we cannot exclude the possibility of further armed conflict." Declaring himself the true leader of a movement for a new, united

Serbia, he said, "Serbia has been exploited. Disunity has retarded the Serbian nature while the inferiority of Serbian leaders has humiliated the Serbian people." As Peter Millar wrote in the *Times of London* on the occasion, "Yugoslavia today is a microcosm of the crisis of communism and [Soviet President] Mikhail Gorbachev's future nightmare: failed reforms, spiraling inflation, political impotence and resurgent ethnic rivalries."

The Fall of Communism and the Yugoslav Federation

That same year, the Communist regimes of Eastern Europe began to fall. Before then, the governments of Eastern Europe had been largely controlled by the Soviet Union. But by 1989, the Soviet Union was on the verge of economic collapse. It could do little to stop the move for independence and democracy that took place in several former Soviet satellite nations, including Czechoslovakia, Bulgaria, Romania, Hungary, and East Germany.

At that time, Yugoslavia still included six republics: Serbia, Croatia, Bosnia and Herzegovina, Macedonia, Slovenia, and Montenegro. In 1990, the country began to come apart. First, both Slovenia and Croatia elected non-Communists to power. In Serbia, Milosevic renamed the Communist Party the Socialist Party, but his authoritarian powers remained absolute within his region and with Serbs all over Yugoslavia. He had placed Serbs in charge of the army, and when Slovenia, Croatia, and Macedonia declared their independence in 1991, Milosevic moved the army against the new nations, in the name of Serb unity.

Following the secession of Slovenia, Croatia, and Macedonia from the Yugoslav Federation, Bosnia and Herzegovina also declared its independence. These actions brought civil war to this area of the Balkans, which lasted from 1991 to 1995.

The Balkan Wars

The wars in the Balkans began in 1991, when first Slovenia declared its independence. Yugoslav troops, overwhelmingly Serb and controlled by Milosevic, fought to force Slovenia back within the federation. The fighting in Slovenia soon ended, and the former Yugoslav republic was independent. But in Croatia a protracted and bloody conflict began between Croats, who wanted their region to become independent, and Croatian Serbs, who wanted it to remain part of Yugoslavia. Next, Macedonia and Bosnia and Herzegovina declared their independence. Within each of the former republics, there were two factions: one representing Serbs, backed and financed by Milosevic, and one representing the ethnic majorities, including Croats in Croatia and Bosnian Muslims in Bosnia and Herzegovina.

The United Nations, which continued to try to broker a peace in the war-torn nations, placed sanctions on Serbia. That put even greater burdens on an economy strained by high unemployment, inflation, and scarce goods. The sanctions affected trade, oil imports, and air travel in Serbia, but did little to threaten Milosevic's grip on power. Instead, he used the sanctions to feed the nationalist fervor of the Serbians loyal to his cause. The Serb nationalists saw themselves as trying to right ancient wrongs done to them throughout history. They believed that the world was against the Serbs in what they saw as a fight for their very survival.

The war raged for three years, while United Nations representatives tried to find a peaceful way out of the conflict. By this point, with Yugoslavia torn apart, Milosevic declared himself head of the "new" Yugoslavia, consisting only of Serbia and Montenegro. The UN negotiated with Milosevic as spokesman for the Serbs. He always claimed that Yugoslavia was never officially at war with the rebellion republics, even though he was unquestionably orchestrating the war from Belgrade. In 1994, he turned his back on the Bosnian Serbs in an agreement with the UN that lifted sanctions against Yugoslavia in return for Milosevic's pledge to close his borders to Bosnia. He agreed and began a media campaign against his former allies, effectively destroying the Bosnian Serbs politically and making refugees of thousands of Bosnian Serbs who had looked to him for leadership and protection.

By 1995, the Serb militias had been unable to overcome the Bosnian Muslims, and retreated. In Croatia, the Croatian army swept most of the remaining Serbs out of their homeland and into Serbia.

"Ethnic Cleansing"

In a move that foreshadowed what they would later do in Kosovo, Serb troops began a campaign of "ethnic cleansing." That is, they used a systematic method of detention, torture, and murder to eliminate their enemies, people they hated solely because of their ethnic group. They forced non-Serbs, especially Muslims of Bosnia and Herzegovina, from their land, burning their homes and destroying their villages.

Observers note that atrocities were committed by all armies involved in the conflict. But according to Zarko Korac, a professor at the University of Belgrade, "Milosevic bears the greatest responsibility." The "cleansing" went on for years, culminating in the worst episode of mass murder in Europe since the Holocaust. In the city of Srebrenica, 8,000 Muslims lost their lives in July 1995. In all, some 250,000 people died in the Balkan wars of 1991-1995. As the world learned of the atrocities of the Bosnian war, and as Milosevic's role became clear, he became known as the "Butcher of the Balkans."

The Dayton Accords

Yet it was Milosevic who met with U.S. and European envoys in Dayton, Ohio, in 1995. He represented the Bosnian Serbs and signed the Dayton Peace Accords, which officially ended the Bosnia conflict. Milosevic thought of himself as an equal to the heads of state at the negotiations. "Yet he was no more a man of peace than he was a communist or nationalist," according to Johanna McGeary of *Time* magazine. "He simply did what he had to do to stay in power."

Indeed, over the years Milosevic has devised a number of techniques for staying in power. After the end of the Balkan civil wars, he began to lose political favor in what was left of Yugoslavia. And yet, as has happened throughout his career, Milosevic was able to hold on to power. Since he first came to power in the late 1980s, Milosevic has made sure that he controls the army, the police, and the media. He has complete control of the state-owned and operated television and radio broadcasts, and these have become virtual propaganda machines for Milosevic and have helped him retain power. In 1992, an American pharmaceutical executive born in Serbia, Milan Panic, took the post of Prime Minister of Serbia at the request of Milosevic. According to the *New York Times*, Milosevic hoped that "Panic would legitimize his Government and provide cover for the ethnic cleansing and territorial expansion the Serbs were supporting in Bosnia." But Panic wouldn't be used as a tool, and soon decided to challenge Milosevic for the presidency of Serbia. Panic soon learned how difficult it was to confront state-owned media, as he was completely unable to reach the Serbian people through coverage of his campaign on television or radio, to have his ads run, or his message heard. There was little or no opposition voiced from the U.S. or other nations, and few election observers. Milosevic purged voters from the rolls and used force to keep those most likely to vote for Panic from voting. He beat Panic, in an election universally viewed as a fraud. As the *Times* author noted, "the great tragedy is that, with a little outside pressure, Milan Panic could have won, possibly ending the most barbaric conflict Europe has seen in half a century."

When demonstrators take to the streets of Belgrade, as they did in 1991, Milosevic uses the strength of army tanks against his own people. When Milosevic's opponents win political elections, as happened in 1996, he virtually ignores the results and holds on to power. He even manipulates the constitution of his country. In 1997, after having served two terms as president of Serbia, he was unable to serve a third because of the laws outlined in the constitution. He had the government elect him President of Yugoslavia, a title he holds today.

Kosovo

In the summer of 1998, fighting began in Kosovo, a province of Serbia. The Kosovo Liberation Army, or KLA, made up of ethnic Albanians who wanted to win independence from Serbia, began a series of guerilla attacks against the Serbian leadership in Kosovo. Milosevic countered with a brutal offensive against all ethnic Albanians, designed to eliminate the KLA and all opposition to Serbian rule. As they had in Bosnia, Serb soldiers attacked civilians, forced them to leave their homes, and burned their villages and shops.

The remains of one of the Belgrade residences of Yugoslav President Slobodan Milosevic, which was struck in a pre-dawn NATO attack, April 22, 1999

NATO, the North Atlantic Treaty Organization, mindful of what had happened in Bosnia, decided to step in to protect the ethnic Albanians of Kosovo. NATO is a military alliance made up of the U.S., Britain, and many European nations. It was created after World War II to deal with threats against its member nations. As the problems in Kosovo worsened, NATO threatened Milosevic with air strikes if he didn't stop the fighting. Milosevic met with NATO officials in October 1998 and signed a cease-fire.

But the cease-fire didn't hold. In January 1999, Serb forces massacred ethnic Albanians in the village of Racak. The conflict raged. NATO again tried to broker a peace, telling both the Serbs and the KLA to back down. When talks broke off in February, Milosevic began another brutal offensive against the civilians of Kosovo.

The NATO Air War

On March 24, 1999, after warning Milosevic again and receiving no response, NATO began air strikes against Serbia, targeting military arsenals and convoy routes. By this point the Serbs had begun a mass expulsion of the Kosovo Albanians, forcing some one million people from their homes.

As they forced the Kosovars from their homeland, the Serb soldiers burned and looted their villages and massacred thousands. The refugees fled to neighboring nations, including Albania and Montenegro, and world relief organizations immediately mobilized to provide adequate food and shelter for nearly one million displaced people. Aid workers from all over the world brought food, medicine, and other aid to the Kosovars and set up networks to help them find relatives and friends who had been lost in the forced exodus from their homeland.

Meanwhile, Milosevic took refuge in his presidential offices in Belgrade. Not once did he address the Serbs, nor did he offer any official updates on the progress of the conflict. Belgrade itself became a target of the bombings, and soon the major infrastructure of the city and most of Serbia was destroyed. The air strikes destroyed the systems for water, electrical power, communication, and transportation, the backbone a modern society needs to exist. And yet the Serbian people stood behind their leader and remained defiant in the face of the world's condemnation and NATO's bombs.

> In 1995 Milosevic met with U.S. and European envoys in Dayton, Ohio, to sign the Dayton Peace Accords, which officially ended the Bosnia conflict. Milosevic thought of himself as an equal to the heads of state at the negotiations. "Yet he was no more a man of peace than he was a communist or nationalist," according to Johanna McGeary of *Time* magazine. "He simply did what he had to do to stay in power."

After 11 weeks of bombing, in June 1999, Milosevic agreed to NATO's demands and the bombing stopped. The terms of the ceasefire demanded that Serb forces pull back within the border of Serbia and that NATO soldiers monitor their departure and the peace in war-torn Kosovo.

Just before the war came to a close, Milosevic and two other Serbian leaders were indicted as war criminals by the International War Crimes Tribunal, an international legal organization set up by the UN after the civil wars in Yugoslavia. The War Crimes Tribunal is charging Milosevic and two other Serbian leaders with directing the mass murder and mass expulsion of the Albanian people from Kosovo. He is the only sitting chief of state in modern history to be so charged. What action will be taken against him remains unclear.

The Aftermath of the Bombing

After the bombing was over, the Kosovar Albanians returned to the rubble that used to be their homes. There, they uncovered hastily made mass graves that are providing evidence of the ethnic cleansing carried out by the Serbs in their efforts to rid Kosovo of Albanians. NATO forces tried to keep the peace between the returning Kosovar Albanians and the Serbs of the province, some of whom fled Kosovo for Serbia. The KLA agreed to disarm, but many Kosovar Albanians are demanding that Kosovo become an independent, Albanian state. Feelings of revenge are running high, and the return of a stable political and social structure in the area remains a dim hope at present.

Milosevic's Future

As the summer of 1999 drew to a close, Milosevic's fate was unknown. The Serbian Orthodox Church has called on him to resign, and in June a group offered five million dollars for his arrest on charges of war crimes. There are daily demonstrations in Serbia against Milosevic, by both mainstream and fringe political groups. Whether or not he will be able to hold on to power despite opposition from the outside world as well as within his own country remains to be seen.

MARRIAGE AND FAMILY

Milosevic married his high school girlfriend, Mirjana Markovic, in 1965. Markovic is a dedicated Communist and a professor of Marxism at the University of Belgrade. Markovic's mother was a former Communist partisan who was captured by the Nazis during World War II and forced to give up the names of comrades also opposed to the Nazi regime. She was killed when Markovic was just a few days old. Markovic considers her mother a great Communist heroine, and for years she has worn a plastic flower in her hair as a tribute to her mother.

Markovic is known as her husband's closest confidant and exerts a powerful influence over him. Over the years, she has published a newspaper column in which she has attacked her husband's political enemies. Often, these enemies find themselves stripped of power after being taken to task by the wife of Milosevic.

The couple have two children, Marija, 33, and Marko, 25. Both are active in the Belgrade social scene; Marko owns a disco and a recording company.

FURTHER READING

Books

Columbia Encyclopedia, 1993
Encyclopedia Britannica, 1999
International Who's Who, 1998-99
Rogel, Carole. *The Breakup of Yugoslavia and the War in Bosnia,* 1998
Who's Who in European Politics 1997
World Book Encyclopedia, 1998

Periodicals

Chicago Tribune, Oct. 17, 1988, p.A2
Christian Science Monitor, Oct. 18, 1988, p.A1
Current Biography Yearbook 1990
Foreign Affairs, Summer 1993, p.81
Los Angeles Times, Mar. 21, 1991, p.A18; June 6, 1992, p.A1; Dec. 26, 1996, p.A17
New York Times, Oct. 14, 1988, p.A8; Aug. 6, 1989, p.A1; Dec. 19, 1992, p.A1; Sep. 4, 1994, Section 4, p.3; Aug. 10, 1995, p.A8; Mar. 28, 1999; May 13, 1999, p.A1; May 29, 1999, p.A1; July 2, 1999, p.A1
New York Times Magazine, Sep. 1, 1991, p.19; Feb. 14, 1993, p.32
Newsweek, Apr. 5, 1999, p.36; Apr. 19, 1999, p.20; June 7, 1999, p.49
Reader's Digest, May 1999, p.177
San Francisco Chronicle, Sep. 15, 1990, p.A13; Nov. 26, 1993, p.A14
Times (London), July 31, 1988; Mar. 3, 1989; June 29, 1989; July 2, 1989; Aug. 11, 1991
Washington Post, Feb. 4, 1990, p.A1; June 15, 1997, p.D1

ADDRESS

Office of the President
Nemanjina 11
11000 Belgrade
Yugoslavia

Natalie Portman 1981-
Israeli-Born American Actress
Stars as Queen Amidala of Naboo in *Star Wars:*
Episode I, The Phantom Menace

BIRTH

Natalie Portman was born in Israel in the city of Jerusalem on
June 9, 1981. Her father is Israeli and her mother is American; because she was born in Israel with one American parent, she has dual citizenship. "Portman" is not her real last
name. Her parents, who are extremely private, have refused
to reveal her real name in order to protect Natalie, her career,
and their personal lives. They will not divulge many facts

about the family, including their names, the town on Long Island where they live, or the name of Natalie's high school. It is known that Natalie's father, who was born in Israel, is a doctor, and that her mother, a former artist, is now a full-time homemaker. Natalie is an only child.

GROWING UP

Natalie grew up in Israel until the age of three, when she and her family moved to the United States. Living on Long Island not far from New York City, she enjoyed attending school and taking dance classes. She also remembers that she liked to "direct performances" of the local talent. "I used to get the neighborhood kids and direct them, getting them to sing and dance, and then we'd charge admission."

GETTING "DISCOVERED"

When Natalie was 11, she was "discovered"in a pizza parlor in New York. An agent for a modeling agency approached her and asked if she had ever considered a career as a model. Portman recalls that he wanted her to model for Revlon cosmetics. "I told him I didn't want to model; I wanted to act. So he introduced me to some agents, and I started going out on auditions."

Her first role was as an understudy in the original Off-Broadway production of *Ruthless* when she was 12. Since then, she has gone on to become a major movie star, noted for her exceptional beauty and maturity in front of the camera.

CAREER HIGHLIGHTS

The Professional

Portman's first film role was in the 1994 movie *The Professional*, directed by French filmmaker Luc Bresson. She played Mathilda, a 12-year-old girl who apprentices herself to a hitman, the "professional" of the title, after her family is killed by corrupt drug agents. Most critics didn't like the film, but they thought that Portman did a good job in her role. Still, the film received an "R" rating for its brutal violence, and more than one critic was unnerved by the overtones of sex in the film. As Roger Ebert said in his syndicated column, the "heroine is 12 years old, and we cannot persuade ourselves to ignore that fact. It colors every scene, making some unlikely and others troubling." It was also ironic that Portman, only 13 when she made the movie, wasn't legally old enough to see the film in which she starred. It also seemed surprising that Portman's parents, who are supposedly so private and concerned with her privacy and welfare, would have let her make her film debut in such a questionable role.

Portman defended her role in *The Professional*, claiming that she "didn't feel exploited at all. I understood everything I was doing. It wasn't like some dirty old man was tricking me into something. The movie was simply about a little girl's crush on the first person who'd taken care of her."

Portman's next part was a minor role in the action film *Heat*, in which she played the troubled teenage daughter of the star, Al Pacino. Once again, critics noted her astonishing screen presence. The director of *Heat*, Michael Mann, said that when he met Portman, "you could tell she was kind of a prodigy. In the movie, she has a very short amount of screen time to believably communicate a child who is seriously dysfunctional without any overt hysteria or exaggerated dialogue, and she delivers. Only someone with serious talent can do that."

Portman was "discovered" at age 11 in a pizza parlor in New York by an agent for a modeling agency. Portman recalls that he wanted her to model for Revlon cosmetics. "I told him I didn't want to model; I wanted to act. So he introduced me to some agents, and I started going out on auditions."

Beautiful Girls

In Portman's next film, *Beautiful Girls* (1996), she played alongside such famous Hollywood actors as Uma Thurman and Timothy Hutton. In the opinion of most critics, she once again stole the show. In this film, she plays the role of Marty, a 14-year-old who has a crush on one of the main characters, Timothy Hutton. She plays a character wise beyond her years, especially in comparison to the adult characters, who are obsessed with the outward trappings of beauty. Her poise and intuitive acting ability—she has never taken acting lessons—was noted by Hutton. "The scenes with her were the scenes I looked forward to the most, because I knew there would be real clarity coming from her. She knew what she wanted, but she was also extremely free in the choices she made. Every take was different. Some people do the same thing over and over again, but Natalie really listens, so if I did something different in take two, she made these beautiful adjustments. To do that at the age of 44 is extraordinary, but at 13. . . ."

Lauren Holly, Portman, and Rosie O'Donnell,
posing at the opening of their film Beautiful Girls

After the success of *Beautiful Girls,* Portman received many film offers, including one to star as the lead of the new film adaptation of Vladimir Nabokov's *Lolita.* She turned down the role, because it would have required her to do a nude scene, which she refuses to do.

Portman next appeared in Tim Burton's 1996 sci-fi farce, *Mars Attacks!* In that film she played the daughter of the president, played by Jack Nicholson, with Glenn Close starring as the First Lady. Portman described her character as "dark and rebellious. I don't think this girl's like Chelsea."

In 1997, Portman appeared in a small role in Woody Allen's musical film *Everyone Says I Love You.* She appeared with such stars as Goldie Hawn, Alan Alda, Julia Roberts, and Drew Barrymore. Once again, Portman garnered praise for her small part. She said this about the Allen film: "It's an old-fashioned musical where people burst into song as they walk down the street. It was a little hard for me because my character wasn't clear-cut and I had to figure out who she was with relatively little information. Woody told us to think of the script as just a skeleton and said, 'If you can't think of anything to say, then say this, but feel free to say whatever you want.'"

The Diary of Anne Frank

In 1997, Portman decided to take a break from films to appear as Anne Frank in a new Broadway adaptation of Frank's famous diary. The story in the stage play is taken directly from Anne Frank's diary, telling of her life as an adolescent as well as the incredible trials of her Jewish family as they hide from the Nazis in a cramped attic above a house in Amsterdam during World War II.

Portman had deeply profound feelings for Frank and her plight; she is Jewish, and several members of her own family perished in the Holocaust. In an article for *Seventeen* magazine, she describes what it was like to prepare for the role of Anne Frank. Portman had read the diary for the first time when she was 12, while living in Paris with her mother and working on her first film, *The Professional*. "One weekend we went to Anne Frank's house in Amsterdam. I bought a copy of her diary there and began to read it at my father's urging. I became so entwined in her writing that I did nothing else for the next week until I finished it."

> **"[The Diary of Anne Frank]** *is the most honest book I've ever read because it is a true diary. It made me feels as if someone understood me. Anne Frank wrote about things that every teenager goes through but doesn't' really discuss openly. At the end, the family and the other people they hid with were caught and sent to concentration camps. This horrific ending brings even more meaning to her diary. Her faith in humanity, even when she was starving and sick in the attic — all because she was Jewish — has had a huge influence on me."*

"This is the most honest book I've ever read because it is a true diary," Portman says in her article. "It made me feel as if someone understood me. Anne Frank wrote about things that every teenager goes through but doesn't really discuss openly. At the end, the family and the other people they hid with were caught and sent to concentration camps. This horrific ending brings even more meaning to her diary. Her faith in humanity, even when she was starving and sick in the attic—all because she was Jewish—has had a huge influence on me."

Portman clearly remembers why she decided to do the play. "I am truly convinced that people need to be constantly reminded of compassion." She sees her own family's loss in the Holocaust in the same way. "I think that the world must acknowledge and understand how useless hatred and racism are, and fight against those problems. Every time I hear a racist, an anti-Semitic or any other hateful slur, I am reminded that people have not yet learned."

The Broadway production of Anne Frank met with mixed reviews, with some critics applauding Portman as "giving off a pure rosebud freshness that can't be faked," while others found the play to be unconvincing. One critic complained that the play "tried to force too much material into two acts." Another noted that the diary, when transferred to a stage, loses its power. "Reading the diary, you are inside Anne's mind and eyes. On stage Anne is part of a drama that sometimes appears as a familycom with Holocaust noises offstage."

Portman left *Anne Frank* in May 1998 to begin filming *Anywhere but Here*. The movie is based on a best-selling novel about a mother and daughter who leave their home in Michigan and travel cross-country to Holly-wood in search of fame. Her co-star in the film is Susan Sarandon, who had much praise for the young actress. "She's a really smart girl who has had a very rarefied upbringing, who has been raised with a lot of confidence and self-esteem, so she seems older that she is in many ways. I felt at all times that I was working with an equal. She has a natural grace that doesn't make her seem as if she's of her generation." The film is scheduled to be released in the fall of 1999.

> In 1995, when she was just 14, Portman was asked by George Lucas, the creator of the Star Wars movies, to play the part of Queen Amidala in **Star Wars: Episode I, The Phantom Menace.** "I wanted somebody who could be commanding, but who could still be young. I was looking for somebody who was smart and strong and a terrific actress, and Natalie met all those qualifications."

In May 1999, Portman appeared in one of the most anticipated films in years. It was in a role she had accepted years ago, and one that would bring her to the attention of millions of moviegoers around the world.

Portman as Queen Amidala of Naboo in
Star Wars: Episode I, The Phantom Menace

Star Wars: Episode I, The Phantom Menace

In 1995, when she was just 14, Portman was asked by George Lucas, the creator of the phenomenally successful *Star Wars* movies, to appear in his "prequel" to the first *Star Wars* trilogy, *Star Wars: Episode I, The Phantom Menace.* Lucas wanted Portman to play Queen Amidala, the mother of

Portman as Padmé Naberrie in
Star Wars: Episode I,
The Phantom Menace

Luke and Leia of the later movies. "I wanted somebody who could be commanding, but who could still be young," said Lucas. "I was looking for somebody who was smart and strong and a terrific actress, and Natalie met all those qualifications."

It was a tough decision for Portman to make. It involved not just the first film, but two more over nine years. And Portman hadn't even seen the previous *Star Wars* movies, so she really had no idea how popular they were, nor what a popular culture legend had grown up around them. She watched the films on video, and her friends let her in on the legend. Then she had to make up her mind. "I really thought about it before agreeing to do the film, because first of all it pushes you into the limelight and pushes you into the public more than any other film probably would do.

"Secondly, it was a huge commitment for a 14-year-old like myself to be deciding that I would be doing three films in the next 10 years. It's a huge decision to make at any point in your life — but especially when you're 14 and you don't know what you want to do with that life. I really thought about it and talked to my parents and other people I love and trust before I made the decision."

She did decide to take on the role, and spent the summer of 1997 filming in London and Tunisia. The weather was almost unbearably hot in Tunisia, where they filmed the desert scenes. One day, it was so hot that the cast actually fried an egg on the metallic covering of the lovable android R2D2.

In the film, Portman plays the brave young Queen Amidala, who must defend her people and her planet, Naboo, against the forces of evil. That evil is embodied in a group of aliens who have formed a Trade Federation to try to take over her planet. She is aided in her quest by two Jedi knights, Obi-Wan Kenobi, played by Ewan McGregor, and Qui-Gon, played by veteran actor Liam Neeson, as well as by a "cast" of thousands of androids, ingeniously created by Lucas and his special effects staff.

Amid an atmosphere of unprecedented hype, *The Phantom Menace* was released on May 19, 1999, and millions of fans have seen Portman's latest film to date. While some critics have found the acting in the film rather wooden, the movie's young fans have embraced it with enthusiasm. In its first five days, the film grossed more than $102 million dollars, and it had the biggest first day box office take in history. Portman's many fans are thrilled with her role as Amidala. They enjoy her character's bravery and ability with a light sword, as well as her many elaborate headdresses, hairstyles, and costumes. Portman herself was still a bit unready for the phenomenon that is *Star Wars*. "I was doing the Pediatric AIDS Carnival and this person asked me to sign something, and asked me to write, "The Force is God," she recalled recently. "I said, 'I can't write that,' and he settled for 'May the Force be with you.' But I think it was at that moment I realized exactly how deep this goes for some people."

On Playing Queen Amidala

Portman enjoys her role as Amidala, and sees the character as something of a role model for younger girls. "It was wonderful playing a queen with all that power," she says. "I think it will be good for young women to see a strong woman of action who is also smart and a leader."

She's scheduled to reprise her role as Amidala in the next two *Star Wars* epics, which will continue the story of the queen who marries Anakin Skywalker and gives birth to Luke and Leia, the prince and princess of the original *Star Wars* movies. She will begin filming the next segment in the summer of 2000; that film has a

> *"I really thought about it before agreeing to do [Star Wars: Episode I, The Phantom Menace], because first of all it pushes you into the limelight and pushes you into the public more than any other film probably would do. Secondly, it was a huge commitment for a 14-year-old like myself to be deciding that I would be doing three films in the next 10 years. It's a huge decision to make at any point in your life—but especially when you're 14 and you don't know what you want to do with that life. I really thought about it and talked to my parents and other people I love and trust before I made the decision."*

scheduled release date of 2002. Her last film for Lucas will be filmed in 2002, for release in 2004.

EDUCATION

Throughout her budding film career, Portman has attended public schools on Long Island, where she has always been an excellent student. She comes from a family that values education highly. "My parents have always stressed education over success, over money, over everything," she says. She recently graduated from high school with a 98.5 percent average following a curriculum that included advanced placement classes in physics, English, French, and math. She says that she "loves to learn," and looks forward to college. She'll be attending either Harvard or Yale in the fall, but plans to keep her college career as private as her high school life.

> "I think a lot of people my age are behind. They're less mature than they should be. A lot of kids I know have kind of been handed everything. I didn't come from a hard-knock life, but I've worked hard. Most of the people where I live get their car on their 16th birthday. Most of them don't really care about school. I see a lot of people who seem to have no interests. There's a lack of individualism. They're born into a world where you don't have to prove anything to anybody. . . . I've gravitated toward friends that are more rounded — toward people with ambitions."

ON HER GENERATION

Portman realizes that she is different from other kids she's grown up with. "I think a lot of people my age are behind," she says. "They're less mature than they should be. A lot of kids I know have kind of been handed everything. I didn't come from a hard-knock life, but I've worked hard. Most of the people where I live get their car on their 16th birthday. Most of them don't really care about school. I see a lot of people who seem to have no interests. There's a lack of individualism. They're born into a world where you don't have to prove anything to anybody. A lot of families have inherited their businesses; others have worked so hard they want their families to be comfortable, so they're not pushing their kids. I've gravitated toward friends that are more rounded — toward people with ambitions."

She doesn't see herself as a "goody-goody." "I would never say someone else is bad because they do something, but for myself, I'm kind of conservative. I've never tried smoking, I don't drink, I've never tried any drugs. I don't condemn people who do, I've just never wanted to."

FUTURE PLANS

Will Portman continue to act after college? "Right now, I like acting, but if something sparks my interest in college, I'll do that. It's so limiting to say, 'This is it for the rest of my life.' There are so many things that interest me — I love math, science, literature, languages."

HOBBIES AND OTHER INTERESTS

Portman is a vegetarian and has been since she attended a medical conference with her dad when she was eight. She couldn't stand the idea of animals being used for experiments, and she couldn't stand the thought of eating them any more, either. "They were talking about animal testing, and all I could think about was my dog, Noodles," she says. "I never ate meat again."

She doesn't consider herself much of a "social animal." "I don't really like high school parties," she says. She likes to spend time with her friends, but she also likes to spend time with her parents. "I'll hang out with my parents on a Friday night when my friends are going to a party I don't want to go to."

CREDITS

Movies

The Professional, 1994
Heat, 1995
Beautiful Girls, 1996
Mars Attacks! 1996
Everyone Says I Love You, 1997
Star Wars: Episode I, The Phantom Menace, 1999

Theater

The Diary of Anne Frank, 1997-98

FURTHER READING

Periodicals

Boston Globe, Oct. 26, 1997, p.D8
Harper's Bazaar, Nov. 1997, p.222
Interview, Mar. 1996, p.116
Los Angeles Times, May 10, 1999, p.A1
New York Times, Feb. 25, 1996, p.B11; April 25, 1999, p.B1; June 27, 1997,
    p.C2; Dec. 5, 1997, p.E1
Premiere, May 1999, p.93
Seattle Post-Intelligencer, May 11, 1999, p.D1
Seventeen, Jan. 1998, p.71
Toronto Star, May 8, 1999, p.A3
USA Today, Nov. 14, 1994, p.D4; Feb. 9, 1996, p.D1; Jan. 8, 1998, p.D2
Vanity Fair, May 1999, p.146

ADDRESS

ID PR
3859 Cardiff Ave.
Culver City, CA 90232

WORLD WIDE WEB SITE

http://www.starwars.com

J. K. Rowling 1965-
British Children's Writer
Author of the Award-Winning *Harry Potter* Novels

BIRTH

Joanne Kathleen Rowling (pronounced "rolling") was born outside of Bristol, a city in southern England, on July 31, 1965. She and her younger sister, Di, were the daughters of middle-class parents. Their father, Peter, was an aircraft factory manager, while their mother, Ann, was a lab technician.

YOUTH

As a child, Rowling liked to read books and tell stories. In fact, she wrote her very first story, about a rabbit who caught the measles, when she was only five or six years old. She continued to write stories throughout her childhood. But she admits that she rarely showed them to anyone because she was afraid someone might make fun of them.

———— `` ————

As a teenager, Rowling often felt awkward and unsure of herself. "I was quiet, freckly, short-sighted and rubbish at sports. My favorite subject by far was English, but I quite liked languages too. I used to tell my equally quiet and studious friends long serial stories at lunch-times.
They usually involved us all doing heroic and daring deeds we certainly wouldn't have done in real life."

———— ʺ ————

Rowling spent the first nine years of her life in an English town called Winterbourne. She and her sister used to spend hours outside playing with the other neighborhood children. Years later, she used the last name of a couple of her playmates in her writing. "[Two of the children] were a brother and sister whose surname was Potter," she explained. "I always liked the name, but then I was always keener on my friends' surnames than my own ('Rowling' is pronounced like 'rolling', which used to lead to annoying children's jokes about rolling pins)."

When Rowling was nine years old, she and her family moved to a small town called Tutshill in an area of England known as the Forest of Dean. "We were finally out in the countryside, which had always been my parents' dream," Rowling recalled. "And my sister and I spent most of our times wandering unsupervised across fields and along the river Wye."

As a teenager, Rowling often felt awkward and unsure of herself. "I was quiet, freckly, short-sighted and rubbish at sports," she remembered. "My favorite subject by far was English, but I quite liked languages too. I used to tell my equally quiet and studious friends long serial stories at lunch-times. They usually involved us all doing heroic and daring deeds we certainly wouldn't have done in real life."

When Rowling was 15, she learned that her mother had been diagnosed with multiple sclerosis (MS), a chronic, debilitating disease of the central nervous system that damages the spinal cord. "I had no idea that MS would hit her so quickly," she said. Rowling's mother finally died from the disease in 1990. "She knew I wrote, but she never read any of it," Rowling stated. "Can you imagine how much I regret that?"

EDUCATION

Rowling started school in Winterbourne, but received most of her elementary and high school education in the Tutshill school system. When she first attended classes at Tutshill at the age of nine, she had trouble adjusting to the curriculum. For example, when she took her first math test there, the quiz included fractions. Rowling had never learned fractions at her previous school, so she flunked the test. As a result, she remembers that her teacher, Mrs. Morgan, "sat me in the row of desks on her far right. It took me a few days to realize I was in the 'stupid' row. Mrs. Morgan positioned everyone in the class according to how clever she thought they were; the brightest sat on her left, and everyone she thought was dim sat on the right. I was as far right as you could get without sitting in the playground." Rowling eventually proved to Mrs. Morgan and her other teachers that she was a bright and intelligent girl. But she never forgot how Mrs. Morgan treated her during her first weeks at the school.

Rowling graduated from Wyedean Comprehensive School (the British equivalent of high school) in the early 1980s. She then enrolled in Exeter University, a college in southern England. She graduated a few years later with degrees in French and Classic Literature.

CHOOSING A CAREER

After graduating from Exeter, Rowling went to London to work for the Amnesty International organization. Amnesty International is a human rights group dedicated to helping people around the world who have been unjustly imprisoned or tortured for their beliefs or political activities. Several months later, however, she moved to Manchester, England, in order to be with her boyfriend at the time.

Soon after arriving in Manchester, Rowling found a job as a secretary. "Unfortunately I am one of the most disorganized people in the world and, as I later proved, the worst secretary ever," she recalled. "All I ever liked about working in offices was being able to type up stories on the computer when no one was looking. I was never paying much attention in meetings because I was usually scribbling bits of my latest stories in the margins of the pad, or choosing excellent names for the characters."

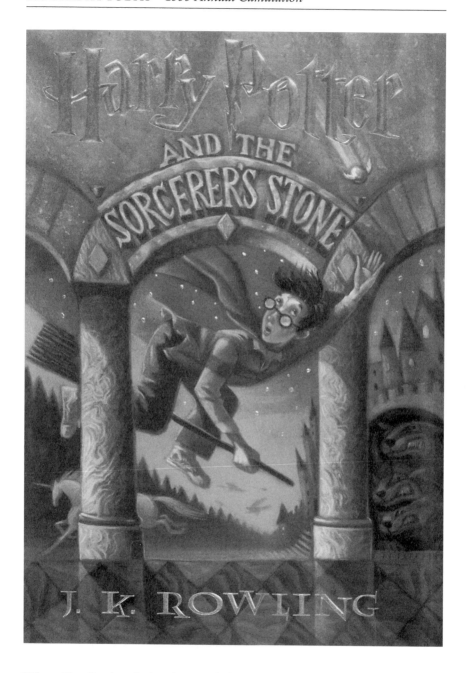

When Rowling's relationship with her boyfriend ended, she decided to leave her secretarial position and try something new. In 1990 she moved to Portugal, a country in southwestern Europe, to teach English as a foreign language. Within a few months of her arrival, she had settled into a pleasant and relaxed lifestyle. "I loved teaching English," she said, "and as I worked afternoons and evenings, I had mornings free for writing."

CAREER HIGHLIGHTS

Creating Harry Potter

The main story that Rowling worked on during her first months in Portugal was a children's tale about an unusual boy named Harry Potter. "I was on a train, staring out the window at some cows . . . and thinking of nothing in particular, and the idea for Harry just kind of fell into my head," Rowling remembered. "It was weird and wonderful when the idea hit me. I've always written and always wanted to be a writer, but I had never thought about writing for children."

During the course of her train ride, Rowling managed to create an entire story about Harry in her imagination. Over the next several months, she began writing her imaginative tale. She also continued with her teaching career and married a Portuguese television journalist. For a little while, it looked like her life was going perfectly. In 1993, however, Rowling's marriage crumbled, and she decided to return to the United Kingdom.

"I was on a train, staring out the window at some cows . . . and thinking of nothing in particular, and the idea for Harry just kind of fell into my head. It was weird and wonderful when the idea hit me. I've always written and always wanted to be a writer, but I had never thought about writing for children."

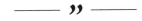

A Period of Struggle

When Rowling left her husband in December 1993, she had a daughter, Jessica, who was only four months old. She soon settled in Edinburgh, Scotland, where she worked to build a new life. "I had never expected to be in that situation," she stated. "The simple fact was that leaving my Portuguese husband meant leaving the country where I had set up home and the teaching career I had made for myself. My sister was in Edinburgh, but I had no friends. When I first arrived I was so completely lonely."

The next few years were very difficult ones for Rowling. She wanted to return to teaching, but found that she would not have enough money to provide her daughter with day care. She subsequently decided to care for

Jessica herself, even though this meant that she would have to rely on government welfare. "It's very very hard for a single mother in Britain, and I'm sure in America, to get out of the poverty trap," Rowling explained. "If you sink to a certain point, it's incredibly difficult to get out, because you don't have funds for child care. Without child care you can't work. . . . It's the most soul destroying thing. There were nights when, though Jessica ate, I didn't. Everything had gone wrong—with the exception of my daughter."

At times, Rowling felt very depressed about her situation. Despite everything, however, she never quit working on her Harry Potter story. In fact, she eventually recognized that writing about Harry and his adventures gave her a much-needed emotional boost. "While I was still writing I didn't feel like I had completely lost my identity," she said. "This book saved my sanity. Apart from my sister I knew nobody [in Edinburgh]. I've never been more broke and the little I had saved went on baby gear. In the wake of my marriage, having worked all my life, I was suddenly an unemployed single parent in a grotty little flat [ugly little apartment]. The manuscript was the only thing I had going for me."

> *Rowling's favorite places to write [Harry Potter] were little coffee shops or cafes. "The only way I could get my daughter to go to sleep during the day was to keep her moving. So I'd push her around the streets and the moment she dropped off [fell asleep] I would storm off to the nearest café [to resume writing]. . . . I spent a lot of time in cafes, and I quickly found the cafes in Edinburgh that were prepared to let me sit there for two hours while my daughter napped over one cold cup of coffee."*

Rowling's favorite places to write were little coffee shops or cafes located throughout the city. "The only way I could get my daughter to go to sleep during the day was to keep her moving," Rowling recalled. "So I'd push her around the streets and the moment she dropped off [fell asleep] I would storm off to the nearest café [to resume writing]. . . . I spent a lot of time in cafes, and I quickly found the cafes in Edinburgh that were prepared to let me sit there for two hours while my daughter napped over one cold cup of coffee." She also wrote late in the evening, after Jessica was asleep. "That's the bit I'm proudest of," she said, "the effort of will involved. It was proof positive of how much I wanted to write Harry."

Rowling finally finished her story, called *Harry Potter and the Sorcerer's Stone*, in 1995. She sent the manuscript to several publishers, and received several rejections. A literary agent named Christopher Little, who was delighted by the story, helped her find a publisher for the book. "It was a year after finishing the book before a publisher bought it," recalled Rowling. "The moment when I found out that Harry would be published was one of the best of my life."

Harry Potter and the Sorcerer's Stone

Harry Potter and the Sorcerer's Stone tells the story of Harry, who, left orphaned as a baby, is sent to live with an aunt and uncle who are mean to him. But there's something mysterious about Harry, too. "Harry [is] a boy who doesn't know he's a wizard, who has always been able to make strange stuff happen, but unconsciously—normally when he's scared or angry," she explained. "Unbeknownst to him, his name has been down at this amazing school for witchcraft and wizardry since birth. But he doesn't know this, because the relatives with whom he lives have hoped that if they're horrible enough to him, they'll be able to squash the magic out of him. They know what he is, but they've never told him."

On his 11th birthday, however, Harry is visited by a friendly giant who tells him about his magical powers. The giant then takes him to Hogwarts School of Wizardry and Witchcraft. Once he arrives at the school, Harry discovers that his real parents were legendary wizards. Joined by two school chums, he then has a series of great adventures involving baby dragon smuggling, battles against giant trolls, games of Quidditch (a game in which participants fly around on broomsticks and the game balls are alive), and a desperate search for a magical item known as the Sorcerer's Stone.

When Rowling's novel was published in June 1997, it caused an immediate sensation in the British book publishing world. Boosted by positive reviews from book critics and bookshop owners, *Harry Potter and the Sorcerer's Stone* became a runaway bestseller. A reviewer for the *Times* of London praised Rowling as "a sparkling new author brimming with delicious ideas, glorious characters, and witty dialogue," while the *Sunday Times* called the novel a "very funny, imaginative, magical story, for anyone from ten to adulthood." A reviewer in *The Scotsman* even wrote that "if you buy or borrow nothing else this summer for the young readers in your family, you must get hold of a copy of *Harry Potter and the Sorcerer's Stone*." British children loved it, too, and gave it the Children's Book Award, based on 60,000 votes by kids themselves.

Harry Potter and the Sorcerer's Stone also became a bestseller when it was released in the United States a few months later. Critics compared Rowling's style and talent to that of legendary children's writers like C. S. Lewis and Roald Dahl, and kids and adults alike praised the book for its clever style and exciting plot. Rowling was not that surprised that grown-ups liked the novel. "If it's a good book, anyone will read it," she said. "I'm totally unashamed about still reading things I loved in my childhood."

Still, the size of the critical and public response to Harry Potter's adventures amazed Rowling. "I never expected to make money [from the story]," she said. "I always saw Harry Potter as this quirky little book. I liked it and I worked hard at it, but never in my wildest dreams did I imagine large advances." As British and American publishers rushed to sign her to write additional books about Harry and his magical pals, Rowling realized that her days of poverty were over. "The main thing is this profound feeling of relief," stated Rowling, who agreed in 1997 to write a seven-book series about Harry. "I no longer have the constant worry of whether [Jessica] will outgrow a pair of shoes before I've got the money for the next pair. Until you've actually been there, you've no idea how soul-destroying it is to have no money. It is a complete loss of self-esteem."

> **"**
>
> *"I never expected to make money [from the story]. I always saw Harry Potter as this quirky little book. I liked it and I worked hard at it, but never in my wildest dreams did I imagine large advances."*
>
> **"**

As of the summer of 1999, *Harry Potter and the Sorcerer's Stone* was on the bestseller lists of both the *New York Times* and *Publishers Weekly*. Two years after its original publication, Rowling remains grateful for the warm reception the book has received. "I feel enormous relief that my daughter and I are now financially secure, and still slightly stunned that I am being paid to do the thing I love best in the world," she said. Nonetheless, she expressed annoyance about the way in which some magazines and newspapers described her rise to success. "When *Harry Potter* was published there seemed to be an aura of amazement that a single mother could produce anything worthwhile, which is pretty offensive," she said. "I would hope that other women would see what I've done as inspirational, but on the other hand I know I was very lucky. I had a 'saleable talent,' to put it crudely, and I also had an education, so even if I hadn't written the book I would have had the raw materials to rebuild my life."

Harry Potter and the Chamber of Secrets

In September 1998 Rowling published her second book in the Harry Potter series in England. In this sequel, titled *Harry Potter and the Chamber of Secrets,* Harry returns for a second year of wizard school at Hogwarts, only to encounter a terrible monster that has escaped from the Chamber of Secrets and is turning students to stone. Once again, Harry must confront the evil Voldemort, and he must live with some of his classmates' suspicions that he is responsible for the evil monster haunting Hogwarts. The book is funny, too, especially in characters like Gilderoy Lockhart, the egotistical new Professor of Defense against the Dark Arts, and Moaning Myrtle, a spirit who lives in the girl's bathroom. Once again, the bully Draco Malfoy makes trouble for Harry, and once again Harry champions Gryffindor on the Quidditch field.

Harry Potter and the Chamber of Secrets proved just as popular as the first Harry Potter book. In fact, it became the top-selling book in the United States when it was released in June 1999. Once again, readers of all ages and book reviewers agreed that the adventures of Harry Potter and the other inhabitants of the Hogwarts School of Wizardry and Witchcraft were wonderfully entertaining to follow. "Those needing a hit of magic, morality, and mystical worlds can do no better than opening *Harry Potter and the Chamber of Secrets*," stated a reviewer for *Newsweek*. "Rowling might be a Hogwarts graduate herself, for her ability to create such an engaging, imaginative, funny and, above all, heart-poundingly suspenseful yarn is nothing short of magical."

With the first two books in the Harry Potter series completed, Rowling turned her attention to writing *Harry Potter and the Prisoner of Azkaban*. This volume of the series covers Harry's third year at Hogwarts. In this book, he and his fellow students are menaced by the evil presence of Sirius Black, a cohort of Voldemort who has escaped from Azkaban, the prison for bad wizards, and is stalking Harry. To protect them, Hogwarts is patrolled by the sinister guards from Azkaban. As the story unfolds, Harry—and readers—learn more about Harry's parents. Once again Harry must confront the power of evil, and in so doing, learn more about his heritage—and himself.

The third volume had an interesting publishing history. The British edition was released on July 8, 1999, at 3:45 in the afternoon. The publishers wanted to make sure that British kids—who go to school in the summer months—wouldn't skip school to buy the book. The American publisher for the volume, Scholastic, hadn't planned to release the book until late September. But when they were confronted with anxious Harry Potter fans who were willing to buy the British edition from overseas booksellers, they decided to push up the U.S. publication date to September 8.

Young and adult readers alike expressed delight with the new book. Rowling, meanwhile, seems eager to write the remaining volumes of the series. She plans seven books in all about Harry, one for each of his years at Hogwarts. "The series is plotted in my mind," she says. "I always know what is going to happen next, and I've already written bits and pieces of each book."

Rowling told an interviewer on "CBS This Morning" "I've actually got the final chapter of book seven written, just for my own satisfaction so I know where I'm going." Her young fans are eager to know what the future holds. "Children—10, 11—come around to my house and start edging toward my study," she claims. She says that she likes the "comic potential" of magic. "And I like frightening people," she says. "The books are getting scarier and scarier as we go."

What kind of frights are in store for her loyal readers? "Without giving too much away, Harry's arch enemy is getting stronger," says Rowling, ominously.

Meanwhile, Rowling has sold movie rights to the first two novels to Warner Brothers for film versions to be produced in the next several years. She doesn't have any specific plans for books beyond the seven volumes on the wizards of Hogwarts. "It's going to break my heart when I stop writing about Harry," she says.

HOME AND FAMILY

Rowling continues to live in Edinburgh, Scotland, with her daughter Jessica. She refuses to discuss her relationship with her ex-husband, except to say that she is glad that she married him. "I don't regret the marriage, because it gave me my daughter—and I wouldn't want to change anything about her at all," she stated.

WRITINGS

Harry Potter and the Sorcerer's Stone, 1997
Harry Potter and the Chamber of Secrets, 1998
Harry Potter and the Prisoner of Azkaban, 1999

HONORS AND AWARDS

Children's Book of the Year (British Book Awards): 1997, for *Harry Potter and the Sorcerer's Stone*

Smarties Book Prize: 1997, for *Harry Potter and the Sorcerer's Stone;* 1998, for *Harry Potter and the Chamber of Secrets*

Best Book of the Year (*Publishers Weekly*): 1998, for *Harry Potter and the Sorcerer's Stone*

Best Book of the Year (*Parenting Magazine*): 1998, for *Harry Potter and the Sorcerer's Stone*

Best Book of the Year (*School Library Journal*): 1998, for *Harry Potter and the Sorcerer's Stone*

FURTHER READING

Boston Globe, Mar. 8, 1999, p.C7
Chicago Tribune, Oct. 19, 1998, p.1, Tempo section
Daily Mail (London), Oct. 10, 1998, p.17
Horn Book Magazine, Jan. 1999, p.71
The Independent (London), Nov. 21, 1997, p.19; June 15, 1999, p.7
New York Times, Apr. 1, 1999, p.E1
Newsweek, Dec. 7, 1998, p.77; Aug. 23, 1999, p.58
Publishers Weekly, Dec. 21, 1998, p.28; Feb. 15, 1999, p.33; May 31, 1999, p.94
The Scotsman, Nov. 20, 1997, p.15; July 9, 1998, p.7
Seattle Times, Oct. 21, 1998, p.E1
Sunday Times (London), June 29, 1997; July 26, 1998
Time, Apr. 12, 1999, p.86
Time for Kids, Apr. 30, 1999, p.8

ADDRESS

Scholastic Inc.
555 Broadway
New York, NY 10012-3999

WORLD WIDE WEB SITES

http://www.bloomsbury.com
http://www.scholastic.com/harrypotter/

OBITUARY

Frank Sinatra 1915-1998

American Singer and Actor

BIRTH

Francis Albert Sinatra was born December 12, 1915, in Hoboken, New Jersey. He was the only child of Martin and Natalie Garavanti Sinatra, called Dolly, who were both Italian immigrants. Martin was a fireman and Dolly was a politician and midwife.

Frank Sinatra was a big baby—nearly 13 pounds when he was born. His mother had a difficult time with the delivery.

The doctor had to use forceps, which left scars on Sinatra's head and burst his eardrum. The birth also left Dolly unable to bear any more children.

YOUTH

Dolly Sinatra was in many ways the major influence on her young son's life. She was enormously ambitious, for herself and her family. Frank was born in a working class world that was defined by social class based on wealth and ethnic background. In Hoboken, the white, Anglo-Saxon Protestants, or WASPs, were at the top of the class structure. Next in line were the German and Irish immigrants, followed by the Italians. Your background even defined where you could live — the neighborhoods were divided into Irish, German, and Italian communities. Dolly Sinatra didn't look Italian — she was blond and blue eyed, and she made the most of being able to "pass" for Irish. That allowed her access to better jobs and more money. She got involved in politics, then worked to get her husband a job with the fire department and her family a better house in the non-Italian part of town.

Because his mother was so busy, Frank spent a good deal of time alone or with his grandmother. Neighbors from his youth remember him as a lonely kid. During the Prohibition Era, when it was against the law to make and sell alcohol, Marty and Dolly Sinatra ran a bar, illegally, called Marty O'Brien's. Sometimes, Frank would hang out in the bar, and, as he remembered, "Occasionally, one of the men in the bar would pick me up and put me on the piano. I'd sing along with the music on the [player piano] roll." Once, he got a nickel for singing. "I said, 'This is the racket.' I thought, It's wonderful to sing. . . . I never forgot it."

EDUCATION

Sinatra attended grade school, junior high school and high school at local public schools in Hoboken. He never did that well in school. Even though his mother hoped he would be an engineer, he dropped out of high school after just a few months. He was faced with finding a job, so he decided to focus on his singing. "In my particular neighborhood in New Jersey, when I was a kid, boys became boxers or they worked in factories," Sinatra remembered. "And then the remaining group that I went around with were smitten with singing."

STARTING TO SING

In the early 1930s Sinatra attended a concert by the popular crooner Bing Crosby, and *he* was smitten. He knew from that point on that he wanted

"The Voice," in 1943

to become a singer. His mother was angry at first, but then she helped her son get singing jobs in the area. In 1935, Sinatra teamed up with three other boys from Hoboken, who were called the Three Flashes, and formed the Hoboken Four. At that time, a group made its name on radio, and the Hoboken Four appeared and won a prize on a local radio contest, "Major Bowes's Original Amateur Hour."

277

Sinatra toured with the group for a while, but he had ambitions to go out on his own. Back in New Jersey, he took a job waiting tables and singing at a road house called the Rustic Cabin. One night, the famous Big Band trumpeter Harry James heard him sing and hired him to perform with his band. In 1939, making $75 a week, Sinatra began a career in music that lasted six decades and made him one of the legends of popular culture.

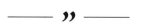

Sinatra learned from Dorsey how to take little catch breaths so that he could sing a full line, without taking a discernable breath, and maintain the meaning of the phrase. "I figured if he could do that phrasing with his horn, I could do it with my voice," Sinatra recalled.

CAREER HIGHLIGHTS

"Big Bands": Harry James and Tommy Dorsey

Sinatra broke into show business during the "Big Band" era of music. The Big Band era was characterized by full orchestrations of popular songs, often called "Swing" music, because of its danceable rhythms and tunes. These groups often had a major solo musician or composer as their leader, like Harry James or Glenn Miller, and a major vocalist to perform solo sections. Sinatra performed with James's band for six months. James remembers the youthful Sinatra's ambition and arrogance. "The kid's name is Sinatra. He considers himself the greatest vocalist in the business. Nobody ever heard of him, he's never had a hit record, he looks like a wet mop. But he says he's the greatest."

In 1940, he was invited to join Tommy Dorsey's big band. Sinatra leapt at the chance to work with the popular Dorsey. Over the next two years, from 1940 to 1942, Sinatra performed and recorded with Dorsey, making his first Number One hit with "I'll Never Smile Again."

Sinatra learned from Dorsey, too. The singer was always known as a terrific stylist, able to sing a song as if the lyrics were deeply meaningful. Most students of music know about "phrasing" — controlling breathing so that the musical thought can be given in one breath. This can be difficult if the line goes on for several measures. Sinatra learned from Dorsey how to take little catch breaths so that he could sing a full line, without taking a discernable breath, and maintain the meaning of the phrase. "I figured if he could do that phrasing with his horn, I could do it with my voice," Sinatra recalled.

He worked hard at the new technique. "I began swimming in public pools, taking laps under water and thinking song lyrics to myself as I swam holding my breath," he said. "Over six months or so, I began to develop and delineate a method of long phraseology. Instead of singing only two bars or four bars at a time—like most of the other guys around—I was able to sing six bars, and in some songs eight bars, without taking a visible or audible breath. That gave the melody a flowing, unbroken quality and that's what made me sound so different." It was a technique he used throughout his career and that helped make him one of the most accomplished singers of the 20th century.

Dorsey couldn't help but be impressed with the young singer. "You could almost feel the excitement coming up out of the crowds when that kid stood up to sing," he said. "Remember, he was no matinee idol. He was just a skinny kid with big ears. I used to stand there so amazed I'd almost forget to take my own solos."

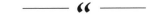

"You could almost feel the excitement coming up out of the crowds when that kid stood up to sing," bandleader Tommy Dorsey said. "Remember, he was no matinee idol. He was just a skinny kid with big ears. I used to stand there so amazed I'd almost forget to take my own solos."

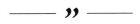

Sinatra, an often arrogant artist, thought he had the makings of a solo star. After two years with Dorsey, he was ready to go out on his own. But Dorsey insisted that Sinatra be held to the terms of his original contract, which allowed Dorsey to take 43 1/3 of Sinatra's income for the next ten years. It was a huge expense, but it bought Sinatra his freedom.

The Bobbysoxers

Frank Sinatra became the first big teen idol ever in 1942, when he did a show at New York City's Paramount Theater. George Evans, Sinatra's manager, had carefully orchestrated his client's image. Sinatra was tall and skinny, with long, curly hair and big bow ties. He projected a loveable, nonthreatening image that was wildly popular with young teens, who were called "bobbysoxers" for the heavy white socks they wore. Evans promoted the image of Sinatra as a loving husband and father—by

Frank Sinatra, Montgomery Clift, and Burt Lancaster in
From Here to Eternity, *1953*

this time Sinatra had married the first of his four wives, Nancy Barbato, and had a baby daughter, Nancy. With this wholesome image, Sinatra soared to popularity during the years of World War II, when there were plenty of lonely young women in the country, missing their boyfriends and husbands who had been sent overseas. Sinatra had a medical deferment due to his burst eardrum, so he was stateside. He described his appeal this way: "It was the war years, and there was a great loneliness. I was the boy in every corner drugstore who'd gone off, drafted to the war. That's all."

Sinatra's popularity continued to soar. He was the star on the popular and influential radio show, "Your Hit Parade." He was named most popular male vocalist by both *Downbeat* and *Metronome* magazines. He also began to appear in nightclubs, and his recordings began to sell in the millions. In 1944, when Sinatra returned to the Paramount for an extended engagement, 30,000 fans caused a near-riot in New York City. Manager Evans had hired girls to scream and swoon over Sinatra, "But hundreds more we didn't hire screamed even louder," Evans partner recalled. With the nickname "The Voice," Sinatra was a full-fledged teen idol.

Sinatra also began a film career at this time. His first film, *Higher and Higher*, featuring him as a singer, was dismissed by the *New York Times* critic as "a slapdash setting for the incredible unctuous readings of the 'Voice'." This film was followed by such hits as *Anchors Aweigh*, in which he sang and danced alongside movie great Gene Kelly. Sinatra won a special Academy Award for a short film he made in 1945 called *The House I Live In*, which featured him making a plea for religious and racial tolerance. At this time Sinatra was also a Democrat and fervent supporter of President Franklin Roosevelt, and he had been invited to the White House to meet Roosevelt, for whom he had campaigned during the 1944 elections.

A Career on the Rocks

But beginning in the late 1940s, a career that had seemed golden and indestructible began to crumble. Sinatra's manager, George Evans, had tried so hard to depict his star as a perfect husband and father. But that idealized image was losing out to Sinatra's true personality as an ambitious, womanizing star, obsessed with success and possibly involved with illegal activities. Although he and his first wife Nancy had three children, he was openly carrying on affairs with stars like Ava Gardner and Lana Turner. In the late 1940s such behavior wasn't easily tolerated by fans, who stopped buying his records and refused to attend his several forgettable films from the era.

In 1947, journalist Robert Ruark accused Sinatra of having ties to the Mafia, also known as the mob. The Mafia is reputed to be a widespread organization involved in many types of criminal activities, including drugs, gambling, and prostitution. Sinatra had traveled to Cuba, where he was photographed with Lucky Luciano, a noted gangster. It was the first of many accusations linking Sinatra and organized crime, and it devastated his image. Always a volatile man, Sinatra became incensed at the reports about his links to the mob. He took swings at members of the

Frank Sinatra from his Capitol Record years, 1953-1961

media reporting on the case, and developed a reputation as a tough guy, too often ready for a confrontation.

This period marked the darkest spot in Sinatra's career. In 1949, MGM studios released him from his film contract. His recording company, Columbia, also dropped him after several flops, including a recording called "Mama Will Bark" that featured another singer barking like a dog.

He had a short-lived TV show that was also canceled, and his long-time manager, George Evans, died. During this period, he even lost his voice, when he suffered a throat hemorrhage.

On the personal front, Sinatra and his first wife, Nancy, went through a much-publicized divorce, and he quickly married Ava Gardner, a major film star of the era. Their life together was volatile and unhappy, and Sinatra attempted suicide. They separated after only 11 months of marriage. Still, it was Gardner who pled with a studio president at Columbia pictures to get Sinatra a movie part he desperately wanted, the role of Maggio in the film *From Here to Eternity.* The movie is set at the beginning of World War II, and Sinatra played Maggio, the scrappy, pugnacious army punk who is beaten to death, with fervor and grace. He won an Academy Award for his role, and his career was back on track.

The LP allowed Sinatra and Riddle to form the first "concept albums," where the songs were selected to tell a story. In the words of Stephen Holden, this format let Sinatra bring his "remarkable introspective depth to the interpretation of lyrics, to make cohesive album-length emotional statements."

An Amazing Comeback

In addition to the film role in *From Here to Eternity*, Sinatra experienced a rebirth of sorts in his musical career. In 1953, he began to record for the Capitol label and to work with one of the legendary arrangers in the music business, Nelson Riddle. These early recordings, including *Songs for Young Lovers* and *Swing Easy*, were produced at the same time that a new recording medium, the long-playing record, or LP, came into existence. This allowed Sinatra and Riddle to form the first "concept albums," where the songs were selected to tell a story. In the words of Stephen Holden, this format let Sinatra bring his "remarkable introspective depth to the interpretation of lyrics, to make cohesive album-length emotional statements."

Riddle arranged lush orchestrations with inventive rhythmic underpinnings of songs by such greats as Cole Porter and George Gershwin, which Sinatra sang with depth and feeling. The collaboration between Sinatra and Riddle "virtually reinvented swing music for a more opulent era," according to Holden, and was tremendously popular with fans. Sinatra's many fans have most often cited his handling of ballads of love and loss as the key to his universal appeal. At this time in his life, still reeling from his relationship with Gardner, Sinatra poured himself into his music and created recordings that generations grew to love. According to Riddle, "It was Ava who did that, who taught him to sing a torch song. That's how he learned. She was the greatest love of his life and he lost her."

The Sinatra of this era is the favorite of many fans. With Nelson Riddle's magnificent accompaniments, Sinatra sang in a mellow, rich baritone that could reflect the eagerness of first love, or the anguish of love gone wrong. His voice could sweetly reflect on fairy tales coming true for "the young at heart." He could sing knowingly the complex, sophisticated Cole Porter lyrics of "grown up" love, of relationships that could tease and devastate the heart. And he could sing of feeling defeated by love, sitting in a bar at a quarter to three, wanting "one more for the road." Through all the years of his career, Sinatra was able to tap the emotions of successive generations of listeners, wooed by the beauty and poignancy of his voice.

"I do remember being described in one simple word that I agree with. The writer said that when the music began and I started to sing, I was 'honest.' That says it as I feel it."

For his part, Sinatra was not much given to self-analysis. He did say once that "Being an 18-karat manic-depressive, I have an over-acute capacity for sadness as well as elation." And, he thought, he was most himself in his music. "I do remember being described in one simple word that I agree with. The writer said that when the music began and I started to sing, I was 'honest.' That says it as I feel it."

Throughout the 1950s, Sinatra scored hits in both the musical and film world, winning his first Grammy in 1959 for *Come Dance with Me*. He also had many Top-40 hits, including "Love and Marriage," "All the Way," and "Witchcraft." His hit films included *The Man with the Golden Arm*, in which he played a heroin addict, *The Manchurian Candidate*, and the musicals *Guys and Dolls* and *Pal Joey*. He won special praise for *The Man with the Golden Arm*, portraying a man caught in the grip of addiction with such conviction that he astonished critics and audiences alike. He handled the songs and swagger of *Pal Joey* with characteristic aplomb, and fans loved it.

Rita Hayworth, Frank Sinatra, and Kim Novak in Pal Joey, *1957*

Chairman of the Board

Sinatra in the 1960s became the ultimate middle-aged swinger, surrounding himself with women and friends who loved to party. Nicknamed "The Chairman of the Board" by New York radio host William B.
Williams, Sinatra made successful films and recordings that brought in an

*"The Rat Pack," Frank Sinatra, Dean Martin, Peter Lawford,
Joey Bishop, and Sammy Davis, Jr.*

annual income estimated at over $4 million. He also became involved in the development of Las Vegas as a gambling vacation site, buying into the Sands Hotel and developing his entertainment empire.

The Rat Pack

Sinatra's companions in the swinging sixties included Dean Martin, Sammy Davis Jr., Joey Bishop, and Peter Lawford, actors and singers who together with Sinatra formed the "Rat Pack." The members of this group, who were known for their hard-drinking, hard-partying lifestyles, performed together in Las Vegas and even made movies together. Their films, generally dismissed as rather light-weight vehicles for the stars, included *Ocean's Eleven* and *Robin and the Seven Hoods.* Sinatra never took the movies very seriously. He was restless with the format and the endless "takes" necessary for each scene. He reserved his serious artistry for his music.

In 1961, Sinatra created his own record label, Reprise. Over the years, he produced such hit albums as *Ring-a-Ding-Ding, Sinatra-Basie: It Might as Well Be Swing,* and *September of My Years.*

Through his connection with the Rat Pack's Peter Lawford, who was married to John F. Kennedy's sister, Sinatra became involved with the presidential candidacy of Kennedy in 1960. He campaigned for Kennedy, and after he won, Sinatra put together his inaugural ball. But once again Sinatra's Mafia connections surfaced, and the friendship foundered. Sinatra had welcomed notorious mob boss Sam Giancana to his home in Las Vegas. But at that time, Kennedy's brother Robert Kennedy, who was serving as U.S. Attorney General, was leading an attack against organized crime. At his brother's urging, President Kennedy canceled a scheduled visit to Sinatra's home in Las Vegas. Sinatra never forgave him.

In the mid sixties, Sinatra tried marriage again. His third wife, the actress Mia Farrow, was just 21 when she married the singer, whose old friend Dean Martin quipped, "I've got Scotch older than she is." The marriage didn't last long; they were divorced in 1968.

In the late 1960s, the popular music scene was taken over by rock 'n roll, and Sinatra's music fell somewhat out of fashion. In 1967, reaching out to a younger crowd, he recorded the song "Somethin' Stupid" with his daughter Nancy, who had launched her own singing career. On his own, he had another big hit in 1969 with "My Way," seen by many as an anthem for his life and work.

Retirement/Return

But by 1971, Sinatra felt he had no more to offer the musical world. So he announced his retirement, ending his career at a concert in Los Angeles. The retirement proved to be short-lived, however. Within two years, he was back with a new album, titled *Ol' Blue Eyes Is Back*. For the next two decades, Sinatra toured and sang to packed houses all over the world. His aging fans loved him, and he filled sports arenas with admirers. Often accompanied by his old pals and established stars, like Sammy Davis Jr. and Liza Minelli, he performed his old classics for astronomical fees, making him one of the wealthiest entertainers in the country.

———— " ————

At the time of his death, tributes pored in from Sinatra's fans and friends. Actress Angela Lansbury, who had starred with Sinatra in **The Manchurian Candidate,** *remembered the effect of Sinatra on her generation: "In those years, one grew up, fell in love, fell out of love, all to the sound of his voice." Sinatra's own favorite singer, Tony Bennett, remembered him this way: "One of Sinatra's favorite toasts to make with glass in hand was, 'May you live to 100 and may the last voice you hear be mine.' The master is gone but his voice will live forever."*

———— " ————

By this time, the former fervent Democrat had become an equally committed Republican. Sinatra campaigned for former actor Ronald Reagan in his 1980 presidential bid. After Reagan won, Sinatra planned and hosted another inaugural ball. He remained a close friend of the Reagans throughout the 1980s and 1990s. Reagan awarded Sinatra the prestigious Presidential Medal of Freedom in 1984 for his contribution to American music.

Sinatra's last recordings were some of his best-selling. These included *Trilogy* (1980), which included "New York, New York." One of his final "signature" songs, it remains one of the songs for which he is best known. In 1993, he had a great success with *Frank Sinatra: Duets*, which featured him singing with some of the biggest stars of the modern musical era, including Tony Bennett and Barbra Streisand, but also recent stars like Luther Vandross and Bono. One unusual aspect of this best-selling recording was the way it was put together. Rather than actually singing with his duet partners, Sinatra recorded his takes separately, as did all the other singers, then the "duets" were mixed in the studio. But it didn't stop the fans from buying the record, and it introduced Sinatra to a new, and younger, audience.

"Chairman of the Board," 1990

In the 1990s, Sinatra, Tony Bennett, and other aging stars began to be embraced by young listeners, who were drawn to their "cool" style and swinging vocalizations. Although Sinatra's last concert took place in February 1995, he was still a top-selling recording star at the time of his death on May 14, 1998. He had been in ill health for some time, and he died of a heart attack at age 82.

LEGACY

At the time of his death, tributes pored in from Sinatra's fans and friends. Actress Angela Lansbury, who had starred with Sinatra in *The Manchurian Candidate*, remembered the effect of Sinatra on her generation: "In those years, one grew up, fell in love, fell out of love, all to the sound of his voice." Sinatra's own favorite singer, Tony Bennett, remembered him this way: "One of Sinatra's favorite toasts to make with glass in hand was, 'May you live to 100 and may the last voice you hear be mine.' The master is gone but his voice will live forever."

Sinatra's appeal to a younger generation was perhaps best given by Bruce Springsteen, in a tribute to Sinatra marking his 80th birthday in 1996. This icon of modern rock music, and another "Boss" from New Jersey, captured Sinatra's legacy to popular music this way:

> "My first recollection of Frank's voice was coming out of a juke-box in a dark bar on a Sunday afternoon, when my mother and I went searching for my father. And I remember she said, 'Listen to that, that's Frank Sinatra. He's from New Jersey.' It was a voice filled with bad attitude, life, beauty, excitement, a nasty sense of freedom, sex, and a sad knowledge of the ways of the world. Every song seemed to have as its postscript 'And if you don't like it, here's a punch in the kisser.' But it was the deep blueness of Frank's voice that affected me the most, and, while his music became synonymous with black tie, the good life, the best booze, women, sophistication, his blues voice was always the sound of hard luck and men late at night with the last ten dollars in their pockets trying to figure a way out. On behalf of all New Jersey, Frank, I want to say, 'Hail, brother, you sang out our soul'."

Many people felt conflicting emotions at the death of such a gifted musician who had also been such a difficult man, as Frank Rich writes here. "He was without question one of the greatest artists of any kind this country has produced. As a human being, he not infrequently resembled a thug. . . . It would be silly to pretend Sinatra's shabbiness didn't exist; to do so requires a sentimentality that is itself antithetical to the honesty that was the hallmark of his singing. In mourning, we should acknowledge who the man was, wonder at the inexplicable mystery by which art of such purity and power emerges from so flawed a vehicle, and then go right back to listening."

MARRIAGE AND FAMILY

Sinatra married four times. His marriage to his first wife, Nancy Barbato, with whom he had his three children, Nancy, Frank Jr., and Christina, lasted from 1939 to 1951. He married actress Ava Gardner in 1951, and they separated within a year; they divorced in 1957. In 1966, Sinatra married film star Mia Farrow; they divorced in 1968. In 1976, he married Barbara Marx, a former Las Vegas showgirl. She and his three children survive him.

HONORS AND AWARDS

Academy Award: 1953, for Best Supporting Actor, for *From Here to Eternity*

Grammy Awards: Album of the Year, 1959, for *Come Dance with Me;* 1965, for *September of My Years;* 1966, for *Sinatra: A Man and His Music;* Best Vocalist, 1959, 1965, 1966; Traditional Pop Performance, 1995, for *Duets*

Presidential Medal of Freedom, 1984

CREDITS

Selected Recordings

Songs for Young Lovers, 1953
Swing Easy, 1954
In the Wee Small Hours, 1955
Songs for Swinging' Lovers, 1956
A Swingin' Affair, 1957
Where Are You? 1957
Come Fly with Me, 1958
Come Dance with Me, 1958
Nice 'n' Easy, 1960
Ring-a-Ding-Ding! 1961
I Remember Tommy, 1961
Sinatra-Basie: It Might as Well Be Swing, 1964
September of My Years, 1965
Strangers in the Night, 1966
Francis Albert Sinatra & Antonio Carlos Jobim, 1967
Frank and Nancy, 1967
My Way, 1969
Ol' Blue Eyes Is Back, 1973
Trilogy, 1980
Frank Sinatra Duets, 1993

Selected Films

Higher and Higher, 1943
Anchors Aweigh, 1945
On the Town, 1949
From Here to Eternity, 1953
The Man with the Golden Arm, 1955
Guys and Dolls, 1955

High Society, 1956
Pal Joey, 1957
The Joker is Wild, 1959
Some Came Running, 1959
Ocean's Eleven, 1960
The Manchurian Candidate, 1962
Come Blow Your Horn, 1963
Robin and the Seven Hoods, 1964
Von Ryan's Express, 1965
Tony Rome, 1967

FURTHER READING

Books

Kelley, Kitty. *His Way: The Unauthorized Biography of Frank Sinatra*, 1986
Rockwell, John. *Sinatra: An American Classic*, 1984
Who's Who in America, 1998
Wilson, Earl. *Sinatra: An Unauthorized Biography*, 1976
Zehme, Bill. *The Way You Wear Your Hat: Frank Sinatra and the Lost Art of Livin'*, 1997

Periodicals

Billboard, May 30, 1998, p.21
Current Biography 1943, 1960, July 1998 (obituary)
Entertainment, Summer 1998, Special Sinatra Issue
New York, Apr. 28, 1980, p.30
New York Times, July 24, 1972; May 16, 1998, p.A1, A27
New York Times Biographical Service, Dec. 1990, p.1226
New Yorker, Oct. 4, 1982, p.142; Nov. 3, 1997, p.77; May 25, 1998, p.47
Newsweek, May 25, 1998, p.50
People, June 1, 1998, p.48; June 8, 1998, p.58
Rolling Stone, June 25, 1998, p.52
Time, May 25, 1998, p.67
TV Guide, May 30, 1998, p.12
Vanity Fair, July 1998, p.32
Variety, May 18, 1998, p.79

Gene Siskel 1946-1999

American Film Critic
Former Co-Host of the Popular Movie Review
Program "Siskel and Ebert"

BIRTH

Gene Siskel was born Eugene Kal Siskel in Chicago, Illinois, on January 26, 1946. His parents were Ida (Kalis) Siskel and Nathan Siskel, a store owner. Both parents died before Siskel was ten years old, however. With their deaths, Siskel and his two older siblings, Bill and Arlene, went to live with their

Aunt Mae Gray and her husband and three children in Glencoe, in the northern suburbs of Chicago.

YOUTH

Siskel was the youngest of the six children raised in the Gray household. The death of his parents had a significant impact on him, but his aunt and uncle made sure that he received plenty of love and encouragement after his arrival in their home. In addition, he got lots of positive attention from his brother and sister and cousins.

"One picture that made an impression on me [as a child] was A Star Is Born with Judy Garland. I remember the colors were richer than I had seen before. I remember being taken to a drive-in to see A Streetcar Named Desire. I remember being in the back seat and hearing people on the screen yell and scream. I grew up in a very happy home and didn't hear that. The movies, there was something potent there. It was adult."

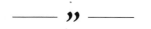

Siskel fell in love with movies at an early age. He spent countless weekend afternoons at the Nortown Theater, where he watched movies like *Peter Pan* and *Song of the South* over and over again. "I would walk eight blocks to the theater every Saturday with my friends," he recalled. The Nortown Theater was not like most movie theaters today. It was elaborately decorated in a Mediterranean theme with lighthouses and twinkling stars on the ceiling. It had expensive red velvet curtains and ornate plaster work on the walls. At that time, people didn't have the same home entertainment options they have today—no cable TV, VCRs, home movies, video games, or computers. Movie theaters were one of the few sources of entertainment outside of the home, and they played a very important role in the lives of both children and adults.

For Siskel, movies provided a window onto the world beyond what he encountered in his own neighborhood. As time passed, he realized that some films made him look at the world in new or different ways. "One picture that made an impression on me was *A Star Is Born* with Judy Garland," he recalled. "I remember the colors were richer than I had seen before. I remember being taken to a drive-in to see *A Streetcar Named*

Desire. I remember being in the back seat and hearing people on the screen yell and scream. I grew up in a very happy home and didn't hear that. The movies, there was something potent there. It was adult."

EDUCATION

Growing up, Siskel enjoyed school. He was bright and excelled in his studies; in fact, he was such a whiz at math that he was able to skip the third grade. After completing his elementary education in the Chicago area, Siskel attended high school at the Culver Military Academy in Indiana, a college preparatory schools for boys. At Culver, the staff stressed the principles of leadership, integrity, self-discipline, manners, and respect for self and others. Siskel was known there for being very self critical. He demanded a lot of himself and it showed in his behavior and work. Siskel probably graduated from Culver Military Academy in 1963.

Siskel then enrolled at Yale University in New Haven, Connecticut. He enjoyed his years at Yale, in part because of the friendships he made during that time. One of his best friends was George Pataki, who later became the governor of New York. "We played cards, Ping-Pong, and soccer in the basement of our dormitory at two in the morning," recalled Pataki. "Gene used to cheat [at Ping-Pong]. Not in a mean way, but by getting you laughing so hard you couldn't hit the ball back. . . . We were both thinking about law school. I actually went. I'm glad he didn't." Siskel earned a bachelor's degree in philosophy from Yale in 1967.

FIRST JOBS

After graduating from Yale, Siskel won a public affairs fellowship and went to California to work on a political campaign. He then joined the Army Reserve, where his responsibilities included writing press releases for the U.S. Department of Defense Information School. This experience kindled an interest in journalism. Before long he was helping publish a little newspaper at the Indianapolis military base at which he was stationed. Siskel left the Army Reserves in late 1968 and returned to Chicago to look for a job, determined to pursue a career in journalism.

CAREER HIGHLIGHTS

Siskel's career as a journalist and movie critic spanned over 30 years. Through the course of his career, Siskel rose from a neighborhood news reporter to one of the most famous movie critics in the world. His success has been attributed to his sheer passion for his work. Siskel loved movies

Siskel and Ebert

and he loved to talk and write about them. He once told a gathering of journalism students at Northwestern University in 1991, "Everything I want I get by writing."

Film Critic for the *Tribune*

On January 20, 1969, Siskel was hired by the *Chicago Tribune*, a daily newspaper, to work as a news reporter and staff writer. Siskel was grateful for the opportunity to develop his journalism skills, but he was also very ambitious. He kept an eye out for any job openings that might enable him to make a bigger mark at the newspaper.

About six months after joining the staff of the *Tribune*, Siskel learned that the newspaper was looking for someone to write reviews of new movies. Originally, the paper's editors planned to have several different staff writers contribute reviews, all using the same made-up name. But Siskel convinced them to let him write movie reviews and stories about the film industry all by himself. As a result, he became the film critic for the *Chicago Tribune* in 1970, at the age of 23.

Siskel was very excited about his new responsibilities. After all, he had loved movies ever since he was a small child. He knew that he was fortunate to be able to make a living writing about a subject that he enjoyed so much. But at the time Siskel secured his position as movie reviewer for the *Tribune,* people did not pay that much attention to movie reviews or to film critics. As the months passed by, Siskel began to think about ways to make himself better known to the public.

Teaming Up with Roger Ebert

In 1974 Siskel accepted an offer to provide movie reviews for WBBM-TV, a local Chicago television station. This new challenge excited Siskel, for it gave him a chance to build his career while still keeping his film critic job with the *Tribune.* A short time after Siskel's first reviews were broadcast on TV, executives at Chicago's local public broadcasting station approached him with an intriguing new idea. They wanted him to co-host a movie review show with Roger Ebert, the young film critic for the *Chicago Sun-Times.*

Siskel said this about his show with Roger Ebert: "We've always wanted viewers to feel as if they were just eavesdropping on a couple of guys who loved movies and were having a spontaneous discussion."

Siskel quickly agreed to take part in the program, even though he had doubts about teaming up with Ebert. The two reviewers had become distrustful of each other over the previous few years. As rivals working at competing newspapers, they deeply disliked each other and were constantly trying to outdo each other in their columns. Each man viewed the other as a potential threat to his career and professional security. Both men wanted to be known as the city's top movie reviewer, and they recognized that the other man was their most serious competition for that title. Still, both Siskel and Ebert recognized that the proposed show would give them a great opportunity to express their opinions and increase their visibility to the movie-going audience.

The first television show in which Ebert and Siskel both appeared aired in 1975. "Opening Soon . . . At a Theater Near You" included film clips and conversations between the two reviewers about four or five movies that were scheduled for upcoming release. "We wanted them to dispense tips to the average movie-goer," recalled one of the show's producers. "They weren't to discuss 'the cinema,' but give consumer advice." And that's just the approach they took, according to Siskel. "We've always wanted viewers to feel as if they were just eavesdropping on a couple of guys who loved movies and were having a spontaneous discussion."

To the delight of both Siskel and Ebert, the show was an immediate success. Viewers liked the program's relaxed format, which allowed the two critics to engage in entertaining arguments about the merits of the movies they reviewed. Viewers even liked a segment at the end of the show called "Dog of the Week," in which Siskel and Ebert used a dog sidekick to announce their selections for the worst new movie of that particular week (the dog was eventually replaced by a skunk and the segment was re-named "Skunk of the Week"). Finally, they enjoyed Siskel and Ebert's use of "thumbs up" and "thumbs down" signals to indicate whether they recommended the movie to their viewers or not. The show eventually became the highest-rated half-hour weekly series in the history of public television. By the late 1970s their show, now called "Sneak Previews," was appearing regularly on 200 public television stations across the country. Their success was easy to understand, according to Steve Rhodes in the *Baltimore Sun*. "The pair weren't pretty to look at — after all, they were newspapermen — and they didn't bring anything unique to the art of film criticism," said Rhodes. "But they made film criticism accessible to the general public with simple summaries and sophisticated opinions rendered in an intelligible, yet easy-to-understand way."

A Famous Duo

By the early 1980s Siskel and Ebert were as famous as many of the Hollywood actors and actresses that they talked about. Viewers seemed to like everything about their show, from the film excerpts from upcoming movies to their heated disagreements about the quality of the movies they reviewed. In fact, Siskel's prickly relationship with Ebert was often cited as a big reason for the show's success. "They are men obsessed," wrote writer Lawrence Grobel, "with movies, with themselves, with how they are perceived by others, with who is better, smarter, funnier."

As their fame increased, Siskel and Ebert appeared on late-night talk shows hosted by Johnny Carson and David Letterman in order to talk about new movies and argue with one another. They even co-hosted an episode of "Saturday Night Live." During this time, movie executives and film industry observers alike agreed that the two critics had become so well known that their opinions sometimes had an impact on a film's box office performance. In fact, enthusiastic "thumbs up" verdicts from Siskel and Ebert were credited with boosting the visibility and financial performance of a number of films. By 1982, when they left PBS to continue their partnership on a new program called "At the Movies" for WGN-TV in Chicago, Siskel and Ebert were regarded as the most influential movie critics in America.

Siskel and Ebert's partnership continued to roll along throughout the 1980s, as their show was syndicated to TV stations across the country. In 1986 their contract with WGN expired and they agreed to do their show for the Walt Disney Company. But this decision angered the owners of WGN, who also owned the *Chicago Tribune*. They punished Siskel for his decision to sign with Disney by removing him as the newspaper's primary film critic. He continued to write regular articles on the film industry for the newspaper, as well as little mini-reviews of new films, but he never regained his position as the *Tribune*'s main movie reviewer.

The *Tribune*'s actions angered Siskel, but he did not let the incident interfere with his career. Instead, he began contributing articles to magazines like *Saturday Review* and *Variety*, and he continued his longtime television partnership with Ebert. In fact, the two men had become such well-known TV personalities that their producers decided to call their show "Siskel and Ebert at the Movies," later shortened to "Siskel and Ebert." In 1990 Siskel's schedule became even busier when he began a six-year stint as film critic for the nationally televised program "CBS This Morning."

> "[Siskel and Ebert] definitely argue. They're certainly opinionated. They know movies and use that knowledge to win fights—and not just to show off. They insult each other. In short, they're entertaining. And they're informative. I may often disagree with both ... but I leave their show knowing what movies I want to see. That's a critic's job and they do it well."
> — *Jeff Jarvis*, **People**

Siskel's Continuing Love of Movies

Siskel often credited his undiminished love of movies as a key reason for his continued success as a film critic. He freely admitted that he had seen *Saturday Night Fever* almost 20 times, and that he once spent $2,000 at a

Jay Leno, left, gestures as he chats with Ebert and Siskel during the taping of
The Tonight Show With Jay Leno, *March 18, 1998.*

celebrity auction to buy the white disco suit worn by John Travolta in that movie (years later, he sold the suit at another auction for $145,000). Siskel also liked all kinds of movies, from historical dramas and adventure stories to romantic comedies and character studies. His favorite kinds of movies, however, were "films about innocence corrupted on a grand scale like *Citizen Kane* or comedies that are flat-out hysterical."

Siskel's continued passion for films also made it easier for him to ignore critics who charged that he and Ebert were more interested in insulting each other than in analyzing films. He pointed out that their show had always been intended to appeal to average moviegoers rather than film historians. "I think we do a lot of very good traditional criticism on our show," he said, "but the dominant interest of the audience is, "What should I go see?" In addition, Siskel noted that he and Ebert had challenged many troubling aspects of the Hollywood film industry over the years, from ugly depictions of violence against women to problems with the academy award nomination process. Other observers have rushed to the defense of Siskel and Ebert as well. "They definitely argue," wrote Jeff Jarvis in *People.* "They're certainly opinionated. They know movies and use that knowledge to win fights — and not just to show off. They insult each other. In short, they're entertaining. And they're informative. I may often disagree with both . . . but I leave their show knowing what movies I want to see. That's a critic's job and they do it well."

Struck Down by Illness

Siskel's thriving career came to a sudden halt in May 1998, when he underwent emergency surgery to remove a growth from his brain. Within two weeks of the surgery he was watching films from his hospital bed and phoning in film reviews for the "Siskel and Ebert" show. A few months later he rejoined Ebert on the program. But early in 1999, another tumor was found in his brain and he was forced to return to the hospital for medical treatment. This time, however, doctors were unable to save his life. He died in Evanston, Illinois, on February 20, 1999.

News of Gene Siskel's death triggered an outpouring of fond remembrances from friends and colleagues. "I knew the guy for 30 years," wrote *Chicago Tribune* columnist Bob Greene, "and I'm not sure I have ever encountered anyone quite as complicated. He was a true friend—and he was exasperating, brilliant, frighteningly ambitious, surprisingly sensitive to perceived slights, funny, frustrating, stern, staggeringly confident about his considerable skills but at the same time a critic who loathed the sting of being criticized, older than his years and younger than his children's years, loyal, suspicious, simultaneously certain of his many triumphs yet hungrier than a man who has never won anything at all."

After Siskel's death, Roger Ebert said this. "One question we were asked again and again was: 'Do you really hate each other?' There were days at the beginning of our relationship when the honest answer sometimes was 'yes.' It was unnatural for two men to be rivals six days of the week and sit down together on the seventh. But over the years respect grew between us and it deepened into friendship and love. . . . For the first five years that we knew one another, Gene Siskel and I hardly spoke. Then it seemed like we never stopped."

Siskel's longtime partner Roger Ebert, meanwhile, expressed deep sadness after learning of his death. "One question we were asked again and again was: 'Do you really hate each other?'" Ebert said. "There were days at the beginning of our relationship when the honest answer sometimes was 'yes.' It was unnatural for two men to be rivals six days of the week and sit down together on the seventh. But over the years respect grew between us and it deepened into friendship and love. . . . For the first five years that we knew one another, Gene Siskel and I hardly spoke. Then it seemed like we never stopped."

HOBBIES AND OTHER INTERESTS

In addition to being a passionate movie buff, Siskel was a dedicated fan of professional basketball and a fierce supporter of his hometown Chicago Bulls. Siskel owned season tickets for the Bulls' home games, and he attended every game that his hectic schedule would allow. Many Chicago players and team officials expressed sadness upon hearing of Siskel's death, "It's very sad, very sad," said Bulls center Bill Wennington. "Gene was a true fan. He wasn't there to be seen. He was there to enjoy the game, and he was very knowledgeable. He even talked about our offense. He knew exactly what was supposed to happen and the different options. He even knew it better than some of the guys on the team. He was special."

MARRIAGE AND FAMILY

Siskel married television producer Marlene Iglitzen in 1980. They had three children—Kate, Callie, and Will. They lived in a large apartment near Lincoln Park in Chicago. Siskel was known as a devoted husband and father and was widely admired for the time he spent with his family.

FAVORITE MOVIES

Siskel loved movies, of course, and he had many favorites. Some of his more recent selections include *Fargo, Babe, Hoop Dreams, Schindler's List*, and *Bull Durham*. But here are Gene Siskel's top ten movies of all time:

1. *Annie Hall*
2. *Casablanca*
3. *Citizen Kane*
4. *Pinocchio*
5. *City Lights*
6. *Red River*
7. *Singing in the Rain*
8. *Taxi Driver*
9. *Tokyo Story*
10. *2001: A Space Odyssey*

SELECTED CREDITS

Television

"Opening Soon . . . At a Theater Near You," 1975
"Sneak Previews," 1977

"At the Movies,"1982
"Siskel and Ebert at the Movies,"1986
"Siskel and Ebert,"1990

Writings

The Future of the Movies: Interviews with Martin Scorsese, Steven Spielberg, and George Lucas, 1991 (with Roger Ebert)

HONORS AND AWARDS

Clio Award: 1988, for *Siskel and Ebert at the Movies*

FURTHER READING

Books

Who's Who in America, 1998

Periodicals

Chicago Magazine, May 1987, p.120; Aug. 1996, p.56
Chicago Tribune, Feb. 22, 1999
Editor & Publisher, Feb. 27, 1999, p.25
Entertainment Weekly, Mar. 17, 1995, p.16; May 17, 1996, p.48; Mar. 5, 1999, p.18
Horizon, Sep. 1982, p.48; May 1984, p.68
Los Angeles Times, Feb. 21, 1999, p.B5
Ms., June 1981, p.21
New York Times, Feb. 21, 1999, p.46
Newsweek, Apr. 11, 1983, p.79
People, Aug. 20, 1984, p.61; Jan. 12, 1987, p.9; Mar. 8, 1999, p.64
Premiere, Apr. 1992, p.78
Seattle Times, Feb. 22, 1999, p.D7
Time, May 25, 1987, p.64; Apr. 5, 1993, p.67
TV Guide, Mar. 20, 1999, p.54
USA Today, Feb. 22, 1999, p.D1
Variety, Mar. 1, 1999, p.61

Sammy Sosa 1968-

Dominican Professional Baseball Player with the
Chicago Cubs
Home Run Phenomenon and Baseball's MVP for 1998

BIRTH

Sammy Sosa was born as Samuel Montero on November 12,
1968, in the city of San Pedro de Macoris in the Dominican
Republic, an island nation in the Caribbean. He is one of six
children, with three brothers (Luis, Jose, and Juan) and two
sisters (Raquel and Sonia). He was raised by his mother, Lu-
crecia (also known as Mireya) after his father, Bautista Mon-

tero, died when he was seven. He took his current last name, Sosa, after his mother remarried.

YOUTH

Sosa's childhood in San Pedro de Macoris was not an easy one. He grew up very poor in the city's Barrio Mexico section, often going barefoot and shirtless because of his family's lack of money. Other people in the neighborhood were impoverished as well. Few people could afford to buy even old and beat-up cars, and open sewers ran along the neighborhood's dirt roads.

To make money, Sosa's mother took in laundry and made food for factory workers. All of the children, Sammy included, did what they could to bring in money. He was forced to quit school at an early age so he could concentrate on work. Early jobs included selling oranges and washing cars. By the age of nine, he was working in a local plaza known as the Parque Central as a shoeshine boy. Even though he only received a few cents for each shine, Sosa worked so hard that he was often able to bring home nearly $2 a day.

Sosa lived in a town in which poverty was so great that many people turned to crime to make money. But Sosa always worked hard for what he earned. "He had to go out and create things to make money," said Omar Minaya, assistant general manager of the New York Mets, "but never anything illegal. He has a very moral, very right family." Sosa agrees that his family's support helped him resist a life of crime. "My family took care of me so that everywhere I would go, there was always someone with me, to make sure I didn't go the wrong way," he remembers. "When your family puts all their hopes in you, you don't want to disappoint them. I want to be there for them and make it for them."

Early Baseball Days

Sosa was an athletic child who grew up participating in two sports—boxing and baseball. Boxing was his first love, but baseball is almost a way of life in the Dominican Republic. Every single boy plays baseball as a child, and most dream of using the sport as their ticket out of the poor nation and into a spot in the major leagues in the United States. These youngsters are inspired by the growing number of Dominicans who have carved out careers in major league baseball in recent years. In fact, Sosa's hometown is one of the most famous in all of Latin America when it comes to baseball—it has sent more players per capita to the major leagues than any other city outside the U.S. Former All-Stars George Bell,

Tony Fernandez, Joaquin Andujar, and Ricardo Carty all hail from San Pedro. "I used to watch Andujar and Fernandez," remembers Sosa. "They had good cars and it made me feel good thinking, maybe some day I could have a car and give my mother a good house."

As a young boy, Sosa never had the nice equipment that American children take for granted when they begin playing sports. "I could not afford to buy a real glove," explained Sosa, "so I made gloves out of empty paper milk cartons. I would cut the bottom off the carton and stick my hand inside. Then I would tear holes for my fingers. My friends and I played catch with a rolled up sock, not a hardball." To make the ball, Sosa would put tightly wadded newspaper in the sock and then sew it shut.

> "I could not afford to buy a real glove," explained Sosa, "so I made gloves out of empty paper milk cartons. I would cut the bottom off the carton and stick my hand inside. Then I would tear holes for my fingers. My friends and I played catch with a rolled up sock, not a hardball." To make the ball, Sosa would put tightly wadded newspaper in the sock and then sew it shut.

As Sosa grew older, his baseball talent got him noticed. Eventually, Sosa's brother Luis convinced him to give up boxing and turn his attention to baseball full-time. "One day he grabbed me and said, 'You can play baseball,'" Sosa recalls. "When I was young, nothing else was in my mind than to be a baseball player. It was not like in the United States. The only way you can be a big person is to play baseball."

So, at age 14, Sosa played organized baseball for the first time on a team called the Braves in Barrio Mexico. The team was so poor that it could not even afford baseball caps, but that did not stop Sosa's talent from shining through. Teammate Pedro Sabino, who is now a radio broadcaster in San Pedro, remembers that Sosa's "swing was wild, but when he hit the ball, it always went for an extra-base hit." When the championship series came around, "The other teams complained that he was too good, and they would not let him play in the tournament. He had to play with older kids."

It did not take long for big league scouts to notice Sosa. Every American major league team has a scout in the Dominican Republic, and the competition for Sosa was fierce. He actually first signed a professional contract with the Philadelphia Phillies when he was just 15, but that contract was voided because Sosa was too young. He then went to play and practice with a team associated with the Toronto Blue Jays, but Minaya, who was then working as a scout for the Texas Rangers, literally stole Sosa away from the Blue Jays. "It's very aggressive down there," Minaya says. "I had someone wait for him by the bus stop by the Jays' camp, and when he got off the bus we shipped him three hours across the island and signed him to a contract with the Rangers." To Sosa, the added intrigue meant nothing. He just wanted to play baseball. "I did not care who I signed with," he recalls. "I only cared about signing and playing."

Sosa was given a signing bonus of $3,500, which he immediately turned over to his mother so that she would be able to buy groceries and clothing. Then, despite his lack of English skills and his young age, he was sent over to the United States. Once he arrived, he was assigned to the Rangers minor league team in Sarasota, Florida. On his own in a foreign country, Sosa was just 15 at the time.

CAREER HIGHLIGHTS

When Sosa moved to Florida, it was a big change for both him and his family. "I felt the biggest shock of my life when Sammy left to play ball," says his mother. "I really suffered. Fortunately, he would call almost every day and write, so I always knew how he was doing."

For Sammy, the biggest challenges in his new life were adjusting to American culture and learning the English language. "I did not go to McDonald's or Burger King because I didn't know how to say what I wanted," he recalls. "That was hard for me. But I knew I had to look for my future. This is my job. I only know how to play baseball."

Sosa spent the next few years learning English and perfecting his game in the minor leagues, where he showed an uncommon combination of power and speed. He progressed quickly through the minor leagues' Class A, Double A, and Triple A levels, and in 1989 he was called up to the Rangers' major league team. At 20 years and seven months, Sosa was the youngest Dominican to ever make it to the big leagues. In June of that year, he hit his first home run off future Hall of Fame pitcher Roger Clemens of the Boston Red Sox. But when the Rangers decided they needed a proven hitter in their line-up, the team traded Sosa and two other players to the Chicago White Sox for veteran slugger Harold Baines. The trade delighted Sosa, because he thought that he would have a better chance to play full-time in the major leagues with Chicago.

Sosa , 1996

The Big Leagues

In 1990 Sosa earned a starting job with the White Sox. He made the most of the opportunity. He drove in 70 runs that season, and was the only American League player to reach double figures in doubles, triples, home runs, and stolen bases. He finished seventh in the league in stolen bases with 32, and second in the league in outfield assists with 14.

Despite Sosa's promising season, all was not well between the young Dominican and the White Sox. Everyone agreed that Sosa had enormous potential, but the Sox were not pleased with his free-swinging style and his sometimes shaky defense, which led to many strikeouts. In addition, he was viewed as aloof and arrogant in the locker room because he did not speak to the media very much. People didn't realize that he was quiet because he couldn't speak English very well.

"When I was with [the Sox] I was very young and scared in those days," says Sosa. "I just hoped to stay in the majors. So, I tried to do everything I could to survive at the major league level." Minaya also pointed out that Sosa's batting style was a common one for a young man with his background. "You've got to understand something about Latin players when they're young—or really any players from low economic backgrounds. They know the only way to make money is by putting up offensive numbers," so Sosa was trying to swing at every pitch that came his way.

In 1991, the pressure to perform or lose his job seemed to get to young Sosa. The White Sox brought in veteran outfielder Cory Snyder, who took some of his playing time. Sosa's batting average hovered around the .200 mark all season, and in July, he was even sent back to the minor leagues for one month. The move was designed to shake Sosa out of his slump, but it didn't work. When he returned from the minors, he still hit around .200 and struggled to hit home runs. It was a lost season for Sosa. The White Sox were unhappy with his development, and he was unhappy playing only part-time.

When spring training arrived in 1992, the White Sox decided they had waited long enough for Sosa to develop. Anxious to add more punch to their batting order, they traded Sosa and Ken Patterson to the cross-town Chicago Cubs in exchange for veteran outfielder and former All-Star George Bell. Sosa was elated. "That made me real happy," he said. "Like getting out of jail."

The Cubs welcomed the arrival of Sosa, although they knew he needed work. "When he first got here, you could see he had great physical skills, but he was so raw," said Cubs first baseman and team leader Mark Grace. "He didn't know how to play the game. He didn't understand the concept of hitting behind runners. He didn't understand the concept of hitting the cutoff man to keep a double play in order. So many little things he just didn't know."

> *The loyal Chicago crowd went wild after number 62, chanting "Sammy! Sammy!" and cheering for several minutes while Sosa took three curtain calls to acknowledge his feat. After both home runs he gave the signal that had become his trademark, thumping his heart and blowing two kisses (one for his mother and one for his family and friends), his fingers in a "V" shape as a personal tribute to the late Harry Caray, the beloved Cubs broadcaster who died in early 1998.*

Sosa's first season with the Cubs was a frustrating one. He was injured twice—first a fractured hand and then a fractured ankle—and spent months on the disabled list, playing in only 67 games. He finished the season with eight home runs, 25 RBIs, and a .260 batting average.

Stardom for Sosa

In 1993 Sosa finally put all the pieces together and had a break-out season. The Chicago Cubs are one of the oldest teams in baseball, yet in the team's 118-year history, no player had ever hit 30 home runs and stolen 30 bases in one season—until 1993. In fact, the team had became almost legendary for being one of the worst teams in baseball. But with Sosa, the Cubbies' fate was about to change. He became the first Cub to achieve the rare combination of power and speed when he hit .261 with 33 home runs and 36 stolen bases. To Sosa, the sudden improvement was no surprise. "I started feeling more comfortable when I got here [to the Cubs]," he said. "I felt I had more of an opportunity here because they traded me here to play me every day."

Jim Lefebvre, who was the manager of the Cubs at the time, was quick to praise his budding superstar. "There are four things Sammy has going for himself," he said during Sosa's hot season. "Number one is great natural ability. The second thing is, Sammy has no fear of failure. The third thing is, he really wants to be great. He really does. And the fourth thing that all great players have—and he has it—is he loves to play."

Sosa had another strong season in 1994, hitting .300 for the first time with 25 home runs and 70 RBIs in just 105 games. Still, opposing players and managers continued to doubt his overall ability. Critics said he was a selfish player who tried to hit a home run every at bat instead of putting the needs of the team first. Cubs fans loved him, however, as he became the first player in nearly 15 years to lead the team in batting average, home runs, and RBIs.

Sosa took the criticism in stride. "I don't worry about nothing else," he said at the time. "I just want to play every day, do my best, and go home happy. . . . I can't make myself a hero to the people. I think they appreciate me. But all I can do is give everything on the field and try to help my team win. If I do my best and my teammates do their best, then we will win. In this game, you have to learn every day," he added. "The more you play, the more you learn. And when people say things like I don't hit the cutoff man, that's good for me. I know it's something I have to work on. People from the outside can see me better than I can see me when I'm on the field. It's good to learn."

Over the course of the next three seasons, from 1995 to 1997, Sosa proved that he did learn from his mistakes and that he could become a better ballplayer. In 1995 he repeated his 30-30 accomplishment of two years earlier, hitting 36 home runs and stealing 34 bases. His number of strike-outs remained high, peaking at 174 in 1997. But his offensive statistics became even better, reaching a level of consistency that only baseball superstars attain. He never hit higher than .273, but he hit 112 home runs and drove in 338 runs in the three-season span. By 1997 Sosa still had his critics. He was even left off the All-Star team that year even though he was leading the league in home runs at the time. But his supporters finally outnumbered his detractors by a large margin. One teammate seemed to speak for most people when he said that anyone who did not appreciate the way Sosa played the game was either "jealous or crazy."

As Sosa's performance continued to improve, the Cubs decided that they wanted to make sure that he would be wearing a Chicago uniform for a long time to come. They subsequently signed Sosa to a four year, $42.5 million contract. The size of the contract surprised some baseball observers, but the Cubs felt the decision to do what they could to keep Sosa was an easy one. As general manager Ed Lynch explained, the Cubs saw the situation this way: "We saw a five-tool player (hit for average, hit for power, run, throw, and field) who was coming into what are the prime years for most guys, and who probably couldn't find the trainer's room because he's never [hurt]. The one important variable was Sammy's maturity as a player. We were banking that he would continue to improve."

Sosa and McGwire

A Historic Home Run Race

As the 1998 season showed, the Cubs' decision to sign Sosa to a long-term contract would prove to be one of the smartest decisions ever in the major leagues. Sosa entered the season with the reputation of being a good home-run hitter, but no one thought that he would ever challenge the major league record of 61 in a season set by Roger Maris in 1961. Instead, all eyes were on Mark McGwire of the St. Louis Cardinals, who had hit 58 home runs in 1997 and was poised to make a serious run at the record.

During the first weeks of the 1998 season, it looked like Sosa was heading for a good but not outstanding season. On May 24, McGwire had already hit 24 home runs, and Sosa had hit only nine. On May 25, however, Sosa launched a power surge that was the best ever seen in the majors. In one stretch of 22 games, he hit 21 home runs, including 20 in the month of June alone. His 20 homers broke the major league record for most home runs in a single month. Suddenly, baseball observers realized that McGwire was not the only slugger with a shot at breaking Maris's single-season home run record.

Over the next several months of the regular season, McGwire and Sosa teamed for an assault on the home run record that captured the attention of the entire country. McGwire maintained a small lead over the Cubs slugger, but just when it seemed that the Cardinals' first baseman would pull away, Sosa would put on a burst and catch him. Five times Sosa managed to catch Big Mac, but only once was he able to pass him for the home run lead, and that was only for three innings on August 19. Still, Sosa kept the pressure on week after week.

The race to break Roger Maris's record was even more memorable because Sosa and McGwire demonstrated remarkable grace and style in handling the intense media pressure generated by the chase. As the season progressed, it also became clear that the two men genuinely liked each other. "I'm rooting for Mark McGwire," said Sosa in September, during the heat of the race. "I look up to him the way a son does to a father. I look at him, the way he hits, the way he acts, and I see the person and player I want to be. I'm the man in the Dominican Republic, he's the man in the United States. That's the way it should be."

"Sammy is showing a grace that blows my mind," said his agent, Tom Reich. "He is so intuitive. He draws everyone into his loop with his good will and generosity." For example,

McGwire was happy for his friendly rival. "I think it's awesome. I've said it a thousand times that I'm not competing against him. I can only take care of myself. Imagine if we're tied at the end. What a beautiful way to end the season."

McGwire was criticized by many people for admitting that he took the potentially dangerous but legal performance-enhancing substance called androstenedione. But Sosa eased some of the controversy by joking with reporters about the issue. He held up a bottle of Flintstone vitamins he kept in his locker and hinted that this was his performance enhancer. The reporters and the fans loved it.

As the season entered its final weeks, it was McGwire who first broke the home run record. McGwire hit the historic blast to pass Maris on September 8 in St. Louis, in a game against Sosa and the Cubs. One of the first players to congratulate McGwire after he crossed home plate was Sosa. The children of Roger Maris were also on hand for the amazing event, making it a truly memorable moment in baseball history.

Sosa was four homers behind McGwire at that point, with 58 home runs, but he did not take long to catch up. On September 13, in a wild contest against the Milwaukee Brewers, Sosa hit numbers 61 and 62 in the same game to help the Cubs beat the Brewers 11-10. Both home runs were mammoth shots, traveling more than 480 feet and landing on Waveland Avenue outside the Cubs' home park, Wrigley Field. The loyal Chicago crowd went wild after number 62, chanting "Sammy! Sammy!" and cheering for several minutes while Sosa took three curtain calls to acknowledge his feat. After both home runs he gave the signal that had become his trademark, thumping his heart and blowing two kisses (one for his mother and one for his family and friends), his fingers in a "V" shape as a personal tribute to the late Harry Caray, the beloved Cubs broadcaster who died in early 1998. "Who'd have ever thought that two people would [break the home run record] in the same year?" asked teammate Mark Grace after the game. "I hope that Sammy gets the attention he deserves."

After the game, Sosa was clearly overjoyed about his accomplishment. "I have to say that what I did is for the people of Chicago, for America, for my mother, for my wife, my kids, and the people I have around me," said the man the fans had nicknamed Slammin' Sammy. "I'm so emotional right now," he continued. "Mark, you know I love you. It's been unbelievable. I wish you could be here with me today. I know you are watching me, and I know you have the same feeling for me as I have for you in your heart."

McGwire was happy for his friendly rival. "I think it's awesome. I've said it a thousand times that I'm not competing against him. I can only take care of myself. Imagine if we're tied at the end. What a beautiful way to end the season."

As the final days of the season unfolded, baseball fans around the world waited to see which player would set the new single-season record. As it turned out, McGwire went on one of his famous hot streaks during the last weekend of the season, hitting four home runs in the final three games to finish with 70 homers, four more than Sosa registered. But Sosa still had one of the most amazing seasons in baseball history. He finished with 66 home runs of his own, batted .308, and led the major leagues with 158 RBIs. He also helped lead his team to a wild-card berth in the National League playoffs, where the Cubs were defeated by the Atlanta Braves.

Thanks to his historic season, Sosa has been showered with honors. The Cubs held Sammy Sosa Day at their game on September 29, handing out miniature Dominican flags before the game and bringing in a number of dignitaries, including Juan Marichal, current Secretary of Sports in the

Dominican Republic and a former major league All-Star pitcher. After the season ended, Sosa was the guest of honor at a parade in New York City, which is home to the nation's largest Dominican population. New York Mayor Rudolph Giuliani declared it to be Sammy Sosa Day in New York. While there, Sosa also threw out the ceremonial first pitch before a World Series game between the New York Yankees and San Diego Padres.

Perhaps the largest celebration took place in Sosa's Dominican homeland. Even though the country was in the midst of recovering from the devastating effects of Hurricane Georges, Dominican President Leonel Fernandez Reyna declared October 21 a Day of National Celebration as Sosa returned to a hero's welcome and victory parades. Sosa took an active role in the hurricane relief and recovery programs and donated a large amount of money to his homeland to help victims of the terrible storm.

After hitting his 62nd home run, Sosa was clearly overjoyed about his accomplishment. "I have to say that what I did is for the people of Chicago, for America, for my mother, for my wife, my kids, and the people I have around me."

In November 1998, Sosa was honored with the award for National League Most Valuable Player. The award was well-deserved, according to Cubs broadcaster and former Cubs All-Star third baseman Ron Santo. "I've never seen a season like this. I would say this has to rank, if you look at the MVP awards, as unique. Not only did he put up the numbers—and astronomical numbers—and bring the Cubs to the playoffs, but it was the way he handled himself."

"I don't recall anybody being an ambassador for baseball, even in my days, like Sammy has been," Santo continued. "Usually you're an ambassador after you get out of the game. But what Sammy has brought to the table is unique. There's not a lot of players who could handle what Sammy has handled—to go through that kind of pressure, to put up those numbers and to have fun doing it. It takes a very special person. This has to be the best MVP award I've ever seen presented to anybody."

Thanks to his 66 home runs and the grace and good humor with which he handled himself all season, Sosa's place in history is assured. To Sosa, however, fame is not the most important thing about what many fans call baseball's greatest season ever. "I do not want people to know just that

According to former Cubs third baseman Ron Santo, "I don't recall anybody being an ambassador for baseball, even in my days, like Sammy has been. Usually you're an ambassador after you get out of the game. But what Sammy has brought to the table is unique. There's not a lot of players who could handle what Sammy has handled — to go through that kind of pressure, to put up those numbers and to have fun doing it. It takes a very special person. This has to be the best MVP award I've ever seen presented to anybody."

Sammy Sosa hit a lot of home runs," he says. "I hope people will think of me not just as a good baseball player, but as a good person."

MARRIAGE AND FAMILY

Sosa met his wife Sonia in 1986 in the Dominican Republic. The couple has four children: Keisha, born in 1993; Kenia, born in 1995; Sammy Jr., born in 1996; and Michael, born in 1997. "They see me on TV and say, 'Papi! Papi!'" says Sosa. "I am very proud of them." The family lives in a new million-dollar home on Chicago's North Side. The house is sparsely furnished, with only a few mementos of Sosa's career, including a letter from Dominican President Reyna honoring Sosa for his record 20 home runs in June 1998. More telling is a plaque that Sosa has in a cabinet in the living room: "My home is small, no mansion for a millionaire," says the plaque. "But there is room for love and there is room for friends."

Sosa also maintains a winter residence in Santo Domingo, the capitol of the Dominican Republic, and owns a vacation home in Florida. He continues to look out for his family and has built two houses for his mother back in San Pedro.

HOBBIES AND OTHER INTERESTS

Off the field, Sosa does not flaunt his wealth. He loves automobiles, and owns nearly a dozen different cars. It is not something he talks about much, however, and about all he will say about the automobiles is that "probably the Rolls (Royce)" is his favorite.

Much of Sosa's time and money go to the charitable causes he supports. Back in San Pedro, he is known as "Sammy Claus" for the tour of children's

Sosa slugging his 66th home run of the season

hospitals that he made after the 1997 season. He annually gives away more than $500,000 to charity and recently set up a foundation, Sammy Sosa Charities, to manage his gift-giving activities. Back in 1994, he donated money to build a shopping and office center, called Plaza 30-30, in San Pedro. In the middle of the plaza is a statue of Sosa in his Cubs uniform called Fountain of the Shoeshine Boys to honor the other hardworking children who have not been as fortunate as Sosa. Coins thrown in the fountain are donated to local shoeshine boys.

Sosa is especially interested in giving the children of San Pedro more of an opportunity than he had as a child. Last Christmas, he gave 250 computers to Dominican schools, 21 of which went to San Pedro, and his latest endeavor is a baseball school for promising prospects in San Pedro and throughout the Dominican Republic. The school operates out of the first house he bought his mother and is intended for teens of "limited means." Students at the clinic are given scholarships, tuition, housing, food, and training, and they attend clinics that are often taught by Sosa himself. In just its second season, the academy has already seen five of its graduates sign professional contacts with major league teams. "The goal here is to produce major league players," says Ramon Espinoza, one of the school's instructors. "Sammy has ensured that they have what he did not have."

HONORS AND AWARDS

Commissioner's Historic Achievement Award: 1998
Jackie Robinson Empire State Freedom Medal: 1998
National League All-Star Team: 1998
National League Most Valuable Player: 1998
Player of the Year (*Sporting News*): 1998
Player's Choice Award (Major League Baseball Player's Association):
    1998, National League Outstanding Player
Sportsmen of the Year (*Sports Illustrated*): 1998, shared with Mark McGwire

FURTHER READING

Books

Who's Who in America, 1998

Periodicals

Chicago, Apr. 1997, p.18
Chicago Tribune, July 28, 1994, p.1 (Sports); Aug. 27, 1995, p.8 (Sports);
    June 20, 1996, p.3 (Sports); July 19, 1996, p.12 (Sports); Aug. 7, 1998,
    p.12 (Sports)
Maclean's, Sep. 14, 1998, p.46
New York Times, Sep. 1, 1998, p.C1; Sep. 8, 1998, p.C13; Sep. 9, 1998, p.A1;
    Sep. 14, 1998, p.A1; Sep. 15, 1998, p.1
Newsweek, Sep. 14, 1998, p.54
Sport, Jan. 1999, p.31
Sports Illustrated, June 29, 1998, p.35; Sep. 14, 1998, p.34; Sep. 21, 1998, p.48
Sports Illustrated for Kids, July 1997, p.58; Nov. 1998, p.32
St. Louis Post-Dispatch, Sep. 13, 1998, p.D8; Sep. 17, 1998, p.D1; Sep. 20,
    1998, p.A1
Time, July 27, 1998, p.46
TV Guide, July 25, 1998, p.30
USA Today, July 15, 1993, p.C5; Aug. 7, 1998, p.A1

ADDRESS

Chicago Cubs
Wrigley Field
1060 W. Addison
Chicago, IL 60613-4397

WORLD WIDE WEB SITES

http://players.bigleaguers.com
http://www.cubs.com
http://www.majorleaguebaseball.com/nl/chi
http://www.samsosa.com

OBITUARY

John Stanford 1938-1998

American Military Officer and School Administrator
Superintendent of the Seattle Public School System

BIRTH

John Henry Stanford was born September 14, 1938, in Darby, Pennsylvania. His father, Cecil Stanford, worked as a diesel locomotive engineer for a steel mill and as a night watchman. His mother, Beatrice Stanford, worked as a cook in neighborhood restaurants. John Stanford also had two sisters who were five and ten years older than him.

YOUTH

Stanford grew up in a household that placed a high value on ethics, personal responsibility, and education. "I learned about love from my family," he recalled. "My parents, who were not formally educated and had few material goods to give, nonetheless had an unending supply of love, and they used that love to make us feel richly endowed. My sisters and I believed that we could do anything: our parents' love gave us that foundation."

As Stanford grew older, his parents' encouragement gave him the confidence he needed to try new activities and perform well in school. They recognized that their young son would probably encounter racism at one time or another in his life, but they wanted to make sure that he never used prejudice as an excuse for failure. "Racism is an illness that your parents can instill in you," Stanford said later. "My parents never talked about race, or woe is me."

"My parents never taught me greed or hate or avarice or race. They taught me achievement," he said. "My parents would always say to me: Sonny, you can do anything you want to do. We're behind you. All we want you to do is try." The parents scrimped and saved so that John and his sisters could take piano lessons. There wasn't money for vacations, but musical education was always important.

"The most important tasks we will ever have as individuals is to be good parents — as a society, to educate and develop our children."

When Stanford was five years old, his family moved to Yeadon, Pennsylvania, a small town west of Philadelphia. They became part of a close-knit neighborhood of African-American families that came to feel like one big family to young Stanford. As he grew older, he became known around the community as a prankster and a natural leader. "I don't think I ever saw him down," said one childhood friend. "He was always upbeat and he always pushed others."

EDUCATION

When Stanford was a young student, no one would have predicted that he would go on to become a major general in the U.S. Army and the superintendent of a large school district. In fact, for a while, no one would have predicted much success for him at all. In elementary school, Stanford goofed off. He didn't pay attention in class and he didn't do his homework. At the end of sixth grade, his teacher, Miss Greenstein, came to his home. She wanted to have a "private conversation" with his parents. When they finished, Stanford could see the outcome on his parents' faces. Stanford failed sixth grade and had to repeat it the following year.

Stanford was devastated by that experience. He was embarrassed in front of his friends and neighbors, but most of all, he was ashamed because he had let his family down. His parents worked so hard to provide a good life for their family, even holding down two jobs. Neither of his parents had had the opportunity to attend school beyond the elementary level. They wanted their children to have better opportunities than they had, and they worked hard to provide those opportunities. Stanford's two older sisters took full advantage of their situation; they were both good students. As Stanford once said, "I felt like I was breaking their hearts."

> "I have a leadership philosophy: love 'em and lead 'em. I have an undying, unyielding faith in people. Leading means loving the people you lead so they will give you their hearts as well as their minds. It means communicating a vision of where you can go together and inviting them to join."

But the family didn't give up on him. During the next school year and from then on, his mother would call him several times every afternoon from her job, checking that he was doing his homework. She didn't have enough education herself to check the quality of his work. But she made sure that he got his homework done each day, and she kept in close touch with his teachers. Within a few years, that discipline started to pay off. "[My] work became regular, if only average; it wasn't until eighth or ninth grade that I felt any excitement about going to school. But the experience of failing sixth grade was pivotal. Miss Greenstein had recognized that I wasn't ready to move on—I was immature and unmotivated. I needed a kick in the pants—and her justified action provided it. The jolt of letting down my family, the shame I felt as my friends moved on, the embarrassment I felt in front of my neighbors, the message my retention sent to my parents: all forced me to take my schooling, perhaps my life, more seriously. At the time I was humiliated; I thought my life was ruined. Today I know the truth: I would not be where I am today if Miss Greenstein hadn't had the courage and love to do what she did." That experience had a profound impact on Stanford, and the courage and love that he felt from his teacher went on to guide his leadership philosophy as an adult.

He also took on greater responsibility at home. With his sisters in college and living out of the house, it was John's job to start dinner every day when he got home from school. Something about the loneliness of that time of his life stuck with him. He never liked being alone, and really hated eating alone in restaurants. "I neither like loneliness or solitude," he remembered. "Both of those are painful to me."

High School and College

After completing his elementary education in 1953, Stanford attended Yeadon High School. The students at the high school were mostly white, but he did not encounter much racism there. In fact, he was elected president of his class three out of his four years at the school. Stanford later recalled that at Yeadon High, "no girls got pregnant, no boys went to jail or hurt anybody. There was respect. There was lots of laughter and fun." He graduated from Yeadon High School in 1957.

Stanford's decision to continue his education at Pennsylvania State University delighted his parents. There, he participated in the armed forces program ROTC (Reserve Officers Training Corps), which trains students in schools, colleges, and universities to become officers in positions of leadership in the United States armed services. He also took flight training while in the ROTC, learning how to pilot an airplane. Stanford graduated from Penn State in June 1961 with a bachelor's degree in political science. Years later—in 1975—he also earned a master's degree in personnel management and administration from Central Michigan University.

CAREER HIGHLIGHTS

Success in the Military

In July 1961, after graduating from Penn State, Stanford resolved to build a career for himself in the U.S. armed forces. He enlisted in an officer training school of the U.S. Army. After completing his basic training, he was assigned to a base in Germany. Stanford spent the next three years in Germany as an air and battalion operations officer and as a platoon commander in a transportation division.

In January 1965 Stanford received a promotion to captain. He spent the next five years in Asia, working as a fixed wing aviator in Korea and serving two tours of duty in the Vietnam War. This war was a military struggle

Stanford shows his jumping ability after seeing a cheerleader perform at an activities rally.

for control of the country of Vietnam, located in Southeast Asia. It pitted the Communist rulers of North Vietnam against South Vietnam and its ally, the United States. The conflict lasted from 1959 to 1975, when U.S. forces pulled out and North Vietnam seized control of the entire country. The Vietnam War also created turmoil within the United States. Americans were deeply divided on the subject of U.S. involvement in Vietnam. Some people supported the fight against Communism, while others opposed U.S. involvement with what they viewed as a corrupt and undemocratic government in South Vietnam. The mounting casualty rate, as more and more Americans were killed, contributed to the strong protests against the war.

During the Vietnam War, Stanford flew on unarmed night reconnaissance flights to search for enemy troops. He also served as a commander of aircraft support during the conflict. His responsibilities included organizing military aircraft missions in order to support the activities of ground troops. He had no sympathy for the anti-war movement in the U.S. "I didn't know if it was a just war or not," he said. "I was just there, immersed in it. I did what I was asked to do."

In the spring of 1970, Stanford left Asia and returned to the United States. He spent the next few years taking military classes at the U.S. Army Command and General Staff College in Fort Leavenworth, Kansas, and fulfilling his duties as an officer in charge of personnel management. He spent part of this time in Michigan, where he completed his master's degree. He was promoted to lieutenant colonel in June 1975.

In 1977 Stanford was assigned to the Pentagon, the headquarters of the U.S. Department of Defense. He spent the next seven years working at the Pentagon, including a four-year stint (1981-84) as executive secretary to Secretary of Defense Caspar Weinberger, who served under President Ronald Reagan. From 1984 to 1991 Stanford commanded important military divisions in California, Virginia, and Illinois. During this time he also served as the director of logistics for the Persian Gulf War. This operation, also called Operation Desert Storm, was fought in Iraq and Kuwait in 1991. After Iraq invaded Kuwait in August 1990, a coalition of forces organized by the United States and the United Nations pressured Iraq's leader, Saddam Hussein, to withdraw from Kuwait. When Hussein didn't comply, the U.S. and U.N. forces began bombing Iraq. The war lasted just over a month, from January 17 to February 28, 1991. As director of logistics, Stanford was involved in moving 450,000 troops and all their equipment to the Middle East. It was a huge job, according to Stanford, "the equivalent of moving the entire city of Seattle—infrastructure, hospitals, housing, restaurants, transportation facilities, warehouses—to the middle of the desert, and then supplying it for an indefinite period of time."

Learning about Leadership

As his military career progressed, Stanford developed a leadership style based on caring and encouragement rather than intimidation. "As I was coming up through the ranks—as a lieutenant, a captain, a major, a colonel—I was constantly aware of the love my officers felt: love for me, for their jobs, for their peers," he explained in his book *Victory in Our Schools*, his assessment of how to improve public education. "They didn't talk about love; they didn't wear their hearts on their sleeves; but they lived it every day. We saw it in the passion they felt for the Army, and the pride with which they discussed our duties. We felt it in the way they looked us in the eye, deeply and respectfully, with genuine concern for how we were doing. We felt it in the way they worked hard to solve our problems. It was so different from the movie image of the military officer—the brusque commander barking orders without a smile. And as I watched these officers I realized that leadership was not a matter of dictating orders and commanding people to obey them. I realized that the very essence of leadership was love."

—————— " ——————

"As a superintendent, the best way I can love and lead my school district is to get the entire community jazzed about the public schools. I know that if I can get our community fired up about the schools, their excitement will infuse our district."

—————— " ——————

A New Challenge

Stanford retired from the U.S. military in 1991 at the rank of major general. He had enjoyed his long career in the Army, but decided that he was ready for a new challenge. After leaving the military, he accepted an offer to became the first African-American county manager for Fulton County, Georgia.

As county manager, Stanford was responsible for guiding all aspects of the county's health and growth. These responsibilities were very challenging. After all, Fulton County not only included rural areas and suburbs, but also the big city of Atlanta. In some cases, the needs and problems of these areas were quite different. Many suburban communities, for example, told their new county manager that their primary concerns included good roads and libraries and lower property taxes. The city of Atlanta, though, faced problems like poverty, unemployment, and high crime rates. Stanford's job was to address the needs of both suburbs and cities effectively without neglecting anyone.

Stanford spent the next four years as Fulton County's chief executive, managing an employee work force of more than 5,000 people and overseeing a budget of half a billion dollars. Just as his supporters had hoped, he proved to be a smart and effective manager of the county's resources. He reined in property taxes, increased spending for crime prevention, reduced county operating expenses, attracted new businesses, and instituted effective new welfare rules designed to put unemployed people to work.

Superintendent of Seattle Public Schools

In 1995, Stanford was asked to interview for the position of superintendent of public schools in Seattle, Washington. The job of superintendent of a large school district is similar to that of president of a large corporation. The superintendent oversees all the pieces that make the district run: the employees, the budget, the facilities, the transportation system, and the instructional component.

Stanford didn't go looking for the superintendent's job; they came looking for him. Still, he was intrigued by the idea of managing Seattle's

47,000-student public school system, even though many of the schools suffered from low test scores, crumbling buildings, drug abuse and teen pregnancy problems, and poor morale. Some in the Seattle community questioned his suitability for the job, since he didn't have any background in education. But he didn't see the role of superintendent as that of an educator; instead, he saw it as a position of leadership. He won over many doubters at an interview attended by school board members as well as teachers, parents, and the general public. "I told them confidently that I could lead their schools to success but I could not run the schools alone; I would need their help and I would actively invite their participation. I told them that the academic achievement of every child would be my highest priority, and that I would ask parents, businesses, and community groups to help us to raise the levels of achievement," he recalled. "I told them that despite the enormous problems the district was facing — aging buildings, declining test scores, a woefully insufficient budget, . . . despite all those things, *we can do it. We can reach and teach all children.*"

Stanford's leadership style and positive attitude impressed both administrators and parents in the Seattle area. They quickly offered him the job, only to learn that he was not sure that he wanted to leave Atlanta. Over the next few weeks, though, Stanford received hundreds of letters from Seattle parents urging him to take the superintendent's job. This outpouring of support convinced him to accept the position. "The most important tasks we will ever have as individuals is to be good parents — as a society, to educate and develop our children," Stanford said. "I'm not coming because I need a job. I have a great job. My coming out there is an opportunity to serve children and achieve something for children."

"If I can get parents to read to their children at night, if I can get the business community to provide resources to the schools, if I can get taxpayers to recognize the importance of voting for education levies, if I can bring all the city's resources to bear on education, then I will help my teachers, my principals, my families, and my students by creating the best possible public schools."

Stanford Takes Seattle by Storm

In September 1995, Stanford started his new job as school superintendent. He immediately impressed people with his upbeat attitude and forceful style. He routinely worked between 16 and 18 hours a day, traveling from school to school and talking with teachers, students, and community leaders about the challenges that the district faced. "He's going to set a new standard of morale, performance, and customer service," predicted one dazzled school board supporter.

For his part, Stanford expressed absolute confidence that he would be able to engineer a big improvement in the morale and performance in the city's public schools. "I have a leadership philosophy: love 'em and lead 'em. I have an undying, unyielding faith in people," he said. "Leading means loving the people you lead so they will give you their hearts as well as their minds. It means communicating a vision of where you can go together and inviting them to join."

> ──── " ────
>
> *One of Stanford's most notable defenders was General Colin Powell, a longtime friend. "Kids want to be loved and led, not lectured and left alone. They want to respect their adult leaders. They will if they are tough and fair and loving. Stanford understands this instinctively."*
>
> ──── " ────

With this philosophy in mind, Stanford approached Seattle-area businesses, universities, and government agencies in hopes of enlisting their help in building better public schools. "As a superintendent, the best way I can love and lead my school district is to get the entire community jazzed about the public schools. I know that if I can get our community fired up about the schools, their excitement will infuse our district," he explained in *Victory in Our Schools*. "If I can get parents to read to their children at night, if I can get the business community to provide resources to the schools, if I can get taxpayers to recognize the importance of voting for education levies, if I can bring all the city's resources to bear on education, then I will help my teachers, my principals, my families, and my students by creating the best possible public schools."

During Stanford's first year as superintendent, he implemented many changes in the Seattle public schools. Some of these changes were symbolic. For example, he changed the district's official motto from "Every student can learn" to "Every student *will* learn." But he also instituted important changes in school policies in order to improve the educational environment for Seattle's children. These changes included expanding and toughening tests given to students; installing new staff and programs

at struggling schools; reassigning more than one-third of the district's 100 principals; and creating a new administrative team to manage school programs. In addition, Stanford developed a citywide campaign to encourage reading, increased business and community commitments and donations to the schools, ended the school's outdated busing program, and called for parents and students to treat teachers with more respect. "The most important job title in the United States today is teacher," he stated. Finally, Stanford visited every school in the district, talking with students, teachers, and administrators alike to gain their impressions of the school system's problems and goals. Overall, Stanford tried in everything he did to focus on the academic needs of the students. As he said, "We would stop focusing on adults and begin focusing on children. Every action and every decision would be measured against a single inviolable yardstick: Is this in the best interest of children? Does this promote academic achievement?"

By the spring of 1996, Stanford had left an unmistakable mark on the Seattle schools. Some people raised concerns about his leadership, complaining that he emphasized test scores too much and that some of his ideas were impractical. But most members of the Seattle community praised their new superintendent. They viewed him as a tireless advocate for the city's children and claimed that his efforts to hold students, teachers, and principals more accountable for academic achievement were already showing results. Being a superintendent in a large school district is a tough job. It's hard for a superintendent to satisfy everyone—students, parents, teachers, other staff, community members, and business leaders. And school districts just don't have enough money to pay for all their competing priorities. So it was especially impressive that Stanford became such a beloved figure to so many throughout the Seattle community.

One of Stanford's most notable supporters was General Colin Powell, a longtime friend. "Kids want to be loved and led, not lectured and left alone," said Powell. "They want to respect their adult leaders. They will if they are tough and fair and loving. Stanford understands this instinctive-ly." Indeed, many observers noted that Stanford enjoyed an unusually good relationship with the students in the district. "What is different about him is his incredible charisma, how the kids know and love and re-spect him," said one retired teacher. "Everybody always talks about kids not respecting these days, but the kids know and respect him, and that's the greatest thing you can say."

"What is different about him is his incredible charisma, how the kids know and love and respect him," said one retired teacher. "Everybody always talks about kids not respecting these days, but the kids know and respect him, and that's the greatest thing you can say."

A Vote of Confidence

Stanford quickly became one of the best known education leaders in the United States. His passion for im-proving Seattle's public schools and his success in boosting both test scores and morale made him famous in education circles. In August 1996, his growing reputation as an educational innovator resulted in an invita-tion to give a nationally televised speech at the Democratic National Convention in Chicago. Stanford accepted the invitation and delivered a highly praised speech on the current challenges and future possibilities of education in America.

In the final months of 1997, however, the Seattle area was rocked by ru-mors that Stanford might soon leave the school district in order to take a leadership position with a major corporation. Speculation about his pos-sible departure became so great that a private foundation offered him $500,000 in return for a promise to stay as superintendent through June 2002. Stanford, though, turned down the money. He recognized that the students and teachers in Seattle's financially struggling schools would resent his acceptance of such a large payment. "That's good news," said one community activist after learning that Stanford refused the offer. "Because it underlines his message that what he's trying to do is focus everyone's attention on children."

Around the same time that he turned down the $500,000 offer, Stanford increased his efforts to secure more funding for the financially strapped district. He knew that students who were given access to good facilities and educational materials had a much greater chance of succeeding academically, so he led an effort to convince the city's taxpayers to set aside more money for the public schools.

In February 1998 the efforts of Stanford and other community leaders paid off, as Seattle voters overwhelmingly passed two school levies, or tax assessments. One of these levies was expected to generate $278 million for general school operations. The second levy secured an additional $150 million for facility improvements, including roof repair, power upgrades, improved science labs and performing arts facilities, improved gymnasiums, and new athletic fields. The passage of the levies also ensured that Seattle public school students would have greater access to computers and the Internet. "I'm really elated by this [vote]," said Stanford. "I think this sends a great message to our teachers and principals."

Diagnosed with Leukemia

In April 1998 Stanford received shocking news when he was diagnosed with a disease known as acute myelogenous leukemia, a kind of cancer. Leukemia causes an explosion of immature white blood cells, sometimes known as blast cells, which eventually crowd out the healthy blood cells necessary to supply the body with oxygen and fight infection.

News of Stanford's illness stunned the Seattle community. "Almost since the day he arrived in Seattle, John Stanford has been more than just a school superintendent," wrote reporter Jolayne Houtz in the *Seattle Times.* "He seems to crystallize something of parents' hopes and dreams for their children. People have invested their hopes for the future — of the schools, maybe of the community — in his leadership. When he was diagnosed with leukemia, it was more than just a personal crisis for him. It was also a blow to the community's collective aspirations for its children."

During the summer of 1998 Stanford took a leave of absence from his job in order to undergo two intense rounds of chemotherapy. The treatments made him very weak and ill, but he continued to follow the district's progress from his home. After a few months he returned to work, expressing great satisfaction with how the school system functioned during his absence. He explained that if the district had fallen apart or simply treaded water, it would have been a sign that he had not provided people with the tools they needed to operate on their own. The vision and goals that he introduced to the Seattle school system were meant to continue even in his absence, he said. Nonetheless, Stanford expressed great happiness when he received permission to resume his superintendent's duties. "I've had this vision of where I want to take this school district and what I want to get done," he said after returning to work. "I just don't know how much time I have to do it."

―――― " ――――

"The tears will not stop," said one Seattle Times editorial. "... Seattle's dazzling, well-loved school superintendent died early yesterday morning. A community is grieving. Stanford gave us leadership unseen in this town for years. He gave us strength through his stunning, positive attitude. He gave us a new sense of the possibilities of public schools, the heart and soul of this and any city. He could have gone off to a leisurely, monied, sunset career. Instead, he gave himself to the city's children. . . . The loss of John Stanford is enormous, but he leaves a legacy of accomplishment, hope, and love for the city's schoolchildren."

―――― " ――――

Leukemia Returns

Unfortunately, Stanford's leukemia returned a short time later, and he was forced to return to the hospital. Convinced that he could not withstand another round of chemotherapy, doctors prepared Stanford for a bone marrow transplant. Bone marrow, which is the tissue inside bones that creates blood cells, can be destroyed by leukemia. A bone marrow transplant is a fairly grueling procedure in which the recipient is given high doses of drugs to kill off the bone marrow. Then, doctors transplant the new, healthy bone marrow by injection. His sister offered to donate her bone marrow in hopes that her healthy cells could help Stanford fight off the disease.

Around this same period, the nonprofit foundation Alliance for Education announced the formation of the Stanford Book Fund. The foundation expressed its intention of honoring Stanford by raising enough money to buy a book for each of the district's 47,000 students. The foundation has raised about $600,000 so far. This effort was aided by the alternative rock band Pearl Jam. The band donated $78,000 from a concert for school library books and worked with Seattle radio stations to raise even more money.

Stanford greets a surprised crowd at a Seattle back-to-school rally in September 1998.

In September 1998 Stanford made a surprise appearance at a Seattle back-to-school rally. As he rose to the podium to address the crowd, the delighted audience roared their approval. "We all have created three wonderful years of growth," Stanford said. "We can reminisce about that. But it's time to get about rededicating ourselves, rededicating ourselves to doing more, to doing better—not to give up on each other, and never, ever give up on a child."

As the weeks passed by, Stanford repeatedly expressed his determination to triumph over his disease. "I'm still going to fight," he said in October 1998. "I intend to get well. I intend to get back. I intend to keep fighting and I have a team of doctors fighting on my side. There's so much that I want to do and I've got to do and push to get done so that we're not just a run-of-the-mill district doing what everyone else is doing. I am not letting cancer control my life."

Unfortunately, the various medical treatments could not stop the advance of Stanford's leukemia. He died on November 28, 1998, at Swedish Medical Center in Seattle. After his death, Stanford's family released a statement of thanks to the people of Seattle for their support: "His love affair with you was boundless and sincere, and the way you reflected that passion on him never ceased to amaze him."

Stanford's death stunned the entire Seattle community. "The tears will not stop," said one *Seattle Times* editorial. "Many parents, teachers and children are crying today because of everything John Stanford gave us. Seattle's dazzling, well-loved school superintendent died early yesterday morning. A community is grieving. Stanford gave us leadership unseen in this town for years. He gave us strength through his stunning, positive attitude. He gave us a new sense of the possibilities of public schools, the heart and soul of this and any city. He could have gone off to a leisurely, monied, sunset career. Instead, he gave himself to the city's children. . . . The loss of John Stanford is enormous, but he leaves a legacy of accomplishment, hope, and love for the city's schoolchildren."

MARRIAGE AND FAMILY

Stanford met Patricia Corley in March 1961, just as he was graduating from Penn State. "He was very popular and quite the charmer," remembers Pat, who was just a freshman when they met. Stanford, ever the hardworking guy, took off for Army basic training soon after. He was too busy to keep up on the dating front, so he wrote her lots of letters. She wrote back that she was seeing other guys. Soon he was back in Pennsylvania asking her to marry him. They got married in March 1994.

John and Pat Stanford had two sons: Steven, now an investment banker, and Scott, now a writer and field producer for TV news. To honor his father's memory, Scott has recently kicked off a drive to recruit volunteers for Big Brothers-Big Sisters. This organization, whose sole purpose is to help children, matches up adult volunteers with kids who could benefit from an adult mentor in their lives.

HOBBIES AND OTHER INTERESTS

During his lifetime, Stanford devoted much of his time and energy to his career and family. Nonetheless, he still pursued such hobbies as weightlifting, playing the piano, and restoring old cars during his free time.

WRITINGS

Victory in Our Schools: We Can Give Our Children Excellent Public Education, 1999 (with Robin Simons)

HONORS AND AWARDS

Master Army Aviator Badge (U.S. Army)
Distinguished Service Medal (U.S. Army)
Ranger Tab (U.S. Army)

FURTHER READING

Books

Stanford, John, with Robin Simons. *Victory in Our Schools: We Can Give Our Children Excellent Public Education,* 1999
Who's Who Among African Americans, 1998

Periodicals

Atlanta Constitution, June 27, 1991, p.E2
Business Week, Oct. 23, 1992, p.214 (Reinventing America special issue)
Christian Science Monitor, Apr. 30, 1996, p.1
Forbes, Sep. 23, 1996, p.66
Independent (London), Oct. 31, 1998, p.19
Jet, Aug. 28, 1995, p.23; Feb. 16, 1998, p.24; Apr. 27, 1998, p.55; Dec. 14, 1998, p.18
Los Angeles Times, Sep. 10, 1998
New York Times, Nov. 1, 1995, p.A1; Sep. 3, 1998, p.A18
Philadelphia Inquirer, Dec. 5, 1998, p.B3
Seattle Post-Intelligencer, July 7, 1995, p.C1; Aug. 27, 1996, p.A4; Aug. 30, 1996, p.A1; Jan. 6, 1998, p.A1; Feb. 5, 1998, p.B3; Mar. 6, 1998, p.A1; July 24, 1998, p.A1; Aug. 6, 1998, p.B2; Dec. 6, 1998, p.G1
Seattle Times, June 23, 1995, p.A1; July 23, 1995, p.B6; July 30, 1995, p.A1; Feb. 23, 1996, p.B1; July 2, 1997, p.A1; Aug. 24, 1997, p.B5; May 5, 1998, p.A1; May 10, 1998, p.A17; Nov. 29, 1998, p.A1; Nov. 29, 1998, p.B18
Times Educational Supplement, Nov. 29, 1996, p.15
Washington Post, May 5, 1997, p.A1
USA Today, Feb. 7, 1996, p.A1; Aug. 11, 1998, p.A3

Natalia Toro 1984-

American Student

Winner of the 1999 Intel Science Talent Search

EARLY YEARS

Natalia Toro was born in Boulder, Colorado, on August 21, 1984. Her parents, who emigrated to the United States from Colombia 20 years ago, are Dr. Gabriel Toro, a civil engineer, and Beatriz Toro, a homemaker with degrees in nursing and psychology. Raised to speak fluent Spanish, Toro showed an aptitude for science at an early age. Although her parents recognized their daughter's gift, they tried not to push her too much. They taught her to appreciate individual differences and to value everyone's talent equally.

EDUCATION

At an age when most of her friends were still struggling with addition and subtraction, Toro was studying algebra. At age 9 she moved on to calculus, and after skipping fifth grade, she enrolled in her first college-level math course. Toro begged her parents to let her jump directly from sixth grade to high school. They were hesitant, but they eventually agreed. So Toro skipped seventh and eighth grades and entered Fairview High School in Boulder at the age of 11.

Being an 11-year-old math and science whiz in a school where all her classmates were teenagers wasn't always easy for Toro. "I got picked on some," she explains, "but in general, when people get to know me before finding out my age, it doesn't make much difference." As a senior at Fairview, she took three courses at the University of Colorado in abstract algebra, analytical mechanics in physics, and chaotic dynamics in computer science. She graduated from Fairview High School in June 1999 at the age of 14.

MAJOR ACCOMPLISHMENTS

Intel Science Talent Search

In 1999, Toro competed in the Intel Science Talent Search, America's oldest and most prestigious science scholarship competition for high school students. The Science Talent Search (STS) was previously sponsored by the Westinghouse Corporation, until the Intel Corporation assumed sponsorship in 1998. Often referred to as the "Junior Nobel Prize," STS allows high school seniors from all over the country to compete for scholarships totaling $330,000. STS winners traditionally major in science at college, and more than 70 percent earn doctoral or medical degrees. Five former STS finalists have won Nobel Prizes, and two have won the Fields Medal, the highest award given to mathematicians.

Toro's project involved studying neutrinos, subatomic particles so small that scientists previously thought they had no mass at all. She analyzed a Japanese theory that said that neutrinos oscillate, changing from one type or "flavor" to another. Toro used equations from quantum mechanics, a specialized branch of physics, to predict neutrino counts. She then compared her findings with actual counts from a sophisticated neutrino de-

Toro with her exhibit at the Intel Science Talent Search

tector. She concluded that her results supported the hypothesis that neutrinos oscillate. If true, it would imply that neutrinos have mass and at the same time it would explain why it is so difficult for scientists to count them accurately. When asked about the implications of her research, Toro joked that "There are no direct implications for the real world. Neutrinos won't help you make a better cheeseburger." But understanding them could help scientists better understand the structure of matter and could have a fundamental impact on the study of high-energy physics.

When Toro entered the competition, she was one of more than 1,400 students from 49 states who submitted reports on their individual research projects. These reports were judged on the basis of research ability, scientific originality, and creative thinking. Toro was selected as one of the 40 finalists who would spend a week in Washington, D.C. There she would be interviewed by top scientists and experts from several different scientific disciplines to determine who would win the top prize, a $50,000 scholarship.

During her week in Washington, Toro was interviewed by J. Richard Gott, an astrophysics professor at Princeton University and the chairman of the judges. He asked her to tell him in what year there would be a 50 percent chance that humans will have become extinct, and to explain why. Afterwards, Toro didn't feel that she performed well in the interview. But she wasn't that upset, she later said, because she never expected to get as far as she already had.

Winning the Competition

The results of the Intel Science Talent Search were announced on March 8, 1999. Up on stage with the 39 other finalists, she listened to speeches and the announcement of the runners-up. "I was standing, thinking, 'It doesn't really matter.'" By that point she'd given up hope. "Then I heard, 'The winner,' there was a pause for suspense and I was trying not to giggle, 'at 14 years old' . . . and I realized I was 14 years old. I was so shocked." To her surprise, she was named the winner. At age 14, Toro became the youngest winner in the competition's 58-year history and only the second female in six years to walk away with the top prize.

In her home state of Colorado, March 30 was designated "Natalia Toro Day," the first of many honors to come her way. She also went on to win a $5,000 scholarship in the Lucent Technologies Global Science Scholars program last May, and to join the 25-member United States Physics Team as they competed against top students from 55 other countries at the International Physics Olympiad in Italy. Toro won a silver medal there.

Toro plans to enter Massachusetts Institute of Technology in the fall, where she hopes to earn a doctorate in physics. But science and math aren't her only interests. She enjoys tennis, swimming, and tutoring middle school students. She also plays the piano, and she rarely watches television.

Does she think of herself as a genius? "If you define genius as 99 percent perspiration and one percent talent, maybe I am," she admits. "But if you define genius as some incredible intellectual talent, I'm definitely not." According to Toro, she isn't any smarter than other kids—just more determined. "When I work on something, I'm really passionate about it," she explains. "If it means I have to miss a few meals or some sleep, it's worth it to me to do as well as I possibly can."

FURTHER READING

Denver Post, Mar. 9, 1999, p.A1
Denver Rocky Mountain News, Jan. 31, 1999, p.A28; Mar. 9, 1999, p.A5
New York Times, Mar. 9, 1999, p.A14
Newsweek, Mar. 22, 1999, p.81
Science News, Mar. 13, 1999, p.165

ADDRESS

Science Talent Search
Science Service
1719 N Street, N.W.
Washington, D.C. 20036

WORLD WIDE WEB SITE

http://www.sciserv.org

Shania Twain 1965-
Canadian Country Music Singer
Creator of *The Woman in Me* and *Come on Over*

BIRTH

Shania (pronounced shuh-NYE-uh) Twain was born Eilleen Regina Edwards on August 28, 1965, in Windsor, Ontario, a province in southeastern Canada. She was the second of three daughters born to Sharon and Clarence Edwards, with an older sister, Jill, and a younger sister, Carrie-Ann. Her parents split up when Shania was about two, and her mother became involved with Jerry Twain, an Ojibwa Indian. Sharon and Clarence Edwards divorced when Shania was about six.

The girls stayed with their mother, who married Twain. Shania has two half brothers from that marriage, Mark and Darryl. Her stepfather legally adopted her and her sisters, and they changed their last name from Edwards to Twain when they were still young. She changed her first name from Eileen to Shania, which means "I'm on my way" in Ojibwa, in about 1990 or 1991.

YOUTH

Controversy about Her Early Life

Some of the printed information about Shania Twain's early life is confusing, with conflicting versions of her childhood. Much of the confusion centers on her relationship with her stepfather, Jerry Twain. Shania and her sisters were adopted by Twain. As a result, they became members of his band, the Temagami Bear Island First Nation, and were granted First Nations status, meaning that they were considered a member of a recognized Native group. Shania was immersed in Native culture as a child. Jerry Twain's parents lived on the Mattagami Reserve, near Timmons, Ontario, where Shania grew up. She spent a lot of time on the reserve with the whole Twain family. Her grandfather took her into the woods to teach her how to track rabbits and to tell her old stories. Her grandmother sewed clothes for her to wear on stage when she first began performing.

Early in her career, Twain never mentioned her parents' divorce or her biological father, Clarence Edwards. Instead, she said that Jerry Twain was her father and that she was one-half Native American. She earned a lot of attention and respect for being a successful Native American, and she won several awards from Native groups. Then her biological father, Clarence Edwards, and his family came forward in 1996, after she was well-established professionally. They explained her true parentage, said that Edwards had stayed in touch with his children in the years since the divorce, and claimed that Shania had cut off all contact with the Edwards family after she made it big. She disagreed, saying that she had seen Edwards only a few times while growing up and that she had never had a relationship with him. Instead, she considered Jerry Twain, who had acted as her father in every way, to be her real dad, "the only father I have ever known; emotionally or in any other way. He was the only one who was there for me on a daily basis, thorough thick and through thin, until he died in 1987. . . ."

This whole issue created a big controversy. Some people felt that Shania had tried to deceive people and had used her Native background as a marketing tool to sell her image. Yet she was adamant that she had never meant to deceive and that she still viewed Twain as her father and his heritage as her own. "[As] the adopted daughter of my father Jerry, I became legally registered as 50 per cent North American Indian. Being raised by a full-blooded Indian and being part of his family and their culture from a young age is all I've ever known. That heritage is my heart and my soul, and I'm very proud of it." With all this inconsistent information, it's hard to be certain about the truth, and about Twain's motives.

Dealing with Poverty

Shania grew up in a couple of Canadian towns in Ontario, including Sudbury and South Porcupine, but she spent most of her childhood in Timmons, a mining town in northern Ontario. About 500 miles northwest of Toronto, Timmons, which is on the edge of the Canadian wilderness, calls itself "the gateway to the Northeastern Arctic and Greenland." Writing about Timmons in *Rolling Stone* magazine, Erik Hedegaard described it as "a medium-sized city in northern Canada, home to some of the largest gold mines in North America, 200 lakes, a year-round view of the sparkling northern lights, temperatures that can reach minus-40 degrees, many, many ice-fishing fanatics, a subpar educational system, and more than its share of unemployed."

"As a kid in school, I didn't have lunch a lot of times. I'd say I wasn't hungry or I forgot it. My father would notice me worrying about it, so he'd make me a mustard sandwich. He was so upbeat, he could make a meal of a piece of bread covered with shortening — and then smile. My parents taught me to be content with less but never satisfied. Still, it was hard being a kid without a lunch."

Jerry Twain often found himself among the ranks of the unemployed. He struggled to find steady work, and the family was very poor. "My parents were loving," Shania says. "We just didn't have any money." Her mother occasionally suffered serious bouts of depression, too, which made the tough times even tougher. Sometimes the heat would be turned off when it was 40 degrees below zero, because they hadn't paid their bills. They had to wear used clothes from second-hand stores that were completely worn out. Worse yet, they didn't always have even enough to eat. Sometimes they just ate bread, milk, and sugar heated up together in a

pot. Sometimes there was nothing to eat for breakfast, and nothing to take to school for lunch, either. Twain would pretend to teachers that she wasn't hungry, worried that welfare agencies might split up her family if they thought her parents couldn't feed all the kids. "As a kid in school, I didn't have lunch a lot of times. I'd say I wasn't hungry or I forgot it. My father would notice me worrying about it, so he'd make me a mustard sandwich. He was so upbeat, he could make a meal of a piece of bread covered with shortening—and then smile. My parents taught me to be content with less but never satisfied. Still, it was hard being a kid without a lunch."

"In my house," she recalls, "it was so wrong to take more than your share. If you decided to take an extra potato, someone didn't get a potato at all." She was shocked one time when a friend who was visiting poured a big glass of milk. "To us, eating like that was only on TV." Usually, Shania tried to hide her family's poverty from the kids at school. But, as she says here, "I recognized as a kid that I wasn't the worst off. My mother had a lot of pride. We never went to school dirty or in ripped clothes. . . . When I would see another kid that was dirty, I knew they didn't have the same loving parents I had." For Twain, even then, her values were clear. "No matter what we all went through, the bigger picture was always there: We were a family and we all cared about each other and we needed to stick together. I wasn't angry—I just dealt with it."

Getting Involved in Music

For Twain, making music soon became a way of life. By the age of three she could pick out melodies and harmonize with the country music her parents played on the radio at home. She grew up listening to Dolly Parton, Tammy Wynette, Willie Nelson, and Waylon Jennings. Twain started out singing at talent shows, community fairs, and other local events, later adding radio and TV. She was singing professionally by the age of eight. Her parents would wake her up after midnight and drive her to the Mattagami Hotel in Timmons. There, after the hotel bar was officially closed and no more liquor was being sold, she'd go up on stage with the country band and play a set with them. She'd earn $25 for her singing. By the age of ten, she started writing songs as well.

By her early teens, Twain was opening in concert for established Canadian country artists. At about the same time, she began to appear on Canadian TV shows, including "Opry North," "Easy Country," and "The Mercey Brothers Show." She also appeared on "The Tommy Hunter Show," a popular Canadian weekly variety show devoted to country music. For Twain, it became stressful to feel so much pressure to succeed. "Coming from a poor family," she says, "the only thing that's going to get your children anywhere is to just push like hell. And that's what my mother did." So Twain often used music as an escape. She would sit in her room, singing songs and picking at the guitar.

"I recognized as a kid that I wasn't the worst off. My mother had a lot of pride. We never went to school dirty or in ripped clothes. . . . When I would see another kid that was dirty, I knew they didn't have the same loving parents I had."

Twain has expressed mixed feelings about getting involved in show business while still so young. One time, she said, "I never liked any of that. I enjoyed singing, but I didn't understand why I had to get out of bed to sing in a bar in the middle of the night." She has also said, referring to her parents, that becoming a star was "their dream. I dreamed about being a kid." Another time, she had a different reaction to the whole experience. "It's not as if I were a prisoner of my parents' dreams. It's something *I* wanted." She has also said, "I think that starting young was a good thing, because if I hadn't started young, I don't know if I ever would have gotten the courage to go up on stage. By the time I was a teenager, it was second nature." Ultimately, it may have simply been a practical necessity for her family. "They weren't living vicariously through me or anything like that. I think the only desperation was to have a child that succeeded. It's like, if you have an Olympic athlete for a child, you are going to bite your fingers to the bone, wanting that child to succeed."

EDUCATION

Twain attended the Timmons High and Vocational School. She wasn't a very dedicated student, although she did participate in some school athletic activities, including basketball, volleyball, and gymnastics. But mostly, she was always working. She worked at a McDonald's, starting as a cashier, then working in the drive-through window, then training new employees. At night, she sang with different bands, playing '80s rock music like Journey, Cheap Trick, and Pat Benatar, as well as some of her own songs. For several summers she worked in a reforesting business that her father had started, clearing out areas and replanting trees for paper companies. Wielding an ax and a chainsaw, she served as a crew leader for a team of 13. She graduated from high school in 1983, but missed her graduation because she was working, on the road with her band.

> "
>
> *After her parents died, Twain took care of her younger siblings. "It's my nature to take charge. I did everything — maybe that's how I spent my grief. From the moment I got up I was cooking meals, doing laundry, cleaning house, cutting wood, making fires, driving them here and there, speaking to teachers and counselors. Then I'd go to work. I was in a fix-it state, trying to make everything normal. Now I know I can't fix everything. If I could do it over, I wouldn't try to be in such control."*
>
> "

FIRST JOBS

After high school, Twain continued to work in her father's reforestation business in the summer and spend the rest of her time playing in local bands and touring. She moved to Toronto and continued to sing there, while also working at a computer school. Then a serious tragedy struck her family that had a profound effect on her life.

A Family Tragedy

In November 1987, when Twain was 22, both her parents were killed in a car accident. They were driving the back roads doing reforestation work when they were hit by a fully loaded logging truck. They died instantly. For Twain, her personal feelings of loss were compounded by that of her younger siblings, who were still living at home and were left without parental support. Her older sister, Jill, had her own family to take care of.

So Shania stepped in to help out. She became the executor of her parents' estate and sold off their house and their business. With the help of Mary Bailey, a singer and family friend who had often given career advice to Shania and her mother, she got a job singing at Deerhurst Resort, located in Huntsville, Ontario. There, she performed in the lodge's dinner theater and musical revue. She bought a cottage nearby and became the legal guardian of her younger sister and two brothers, Carrie-Ann, 18, Mark, 14, and Darryl, 13. She took care of them during the day and worked at night. Times were still tough, and money was tight. The well for the cottage ran dry and they didn't have enough money for the laundromat, so they ended up washing clothes on rocks in the stream out back. Food was scarce, too. "I became Power Savior," she says. "It's my nature to take charge. I did everything—maybe that's how I spent my grief. From the moment I got up I was cooking meals, doing laundry, cleaning house, cutting wood, making fires, driving them here and there, speaking to teachers and counselors. Then I'd go to work. I was in a fix-it state, trying to make everything normal. Now I know I can't fix everything. If I could do it over, I wouldn't try to be in such control. I was babying my brothers too much."

Twain worked at Deerhurst from 1988 to 1991. She sang in a Las Vegas style nightclub revue, wearing a glittery costume and a feather headdress covered with rhinestones. Ultimately, working there proved to be a great experience for Twain, giving her an opportunity to try acting, dancing, and different types of singing, from show tunes to Motown. "It was almost like a musical education," she says. "It gave me a lot of confidence. I always had a dream of going to a performing arts school, and in some ways, that's what Deerhurst gave me." Deerhurst gave her something else that became important to her career: it was while working there that she adopted the name "Shania."

Signing a Recording Contract

By 1990, Twain's siblings had started moving out of her home, one by one, and she got ready to make some changes in her own life, too. Again, family friend Mary Bailey stepped in to help her through the transition. Bailey contacted a Nashville entertainment lawyer, Richard Frank, and invited him to come up to Deerhurst to hear a talented new country singer. He was so impressed with Shania that he offered to help her get started. Twain left Deerhurst and briefly returned to Timmons to work on her demo tape, while also working at the complaints desk at Sears. In the meantime, Frank made arrangements for her to come to Nashville to record a demo tape of her own songs, hoping to entice a record label to offer her a deal. Their approach worked, and in 1991 Twain signed a recording contract with Mercury Records in Nashville.

CAREER HIGHLIGHTS

Twain's first recording was the self-titled *Shania Twain*, which was released in 1993. It featured Twain doing cover versions of other people's songs. It didn't attract much attention from critics, who called it a decent if uninspired and bland debut effort. And sales were not impressive either, totaling about 100,000 copies. But it did have one huge, if unintended result—it led Twain to her future husband and producer, Robert John "Mutt" Lange.

Describing her stage show, Twain said, "Basically, the show will be a party, and I'm the hostess. It's not going to be that slick. Just high energy, great lights, and great sound."

Meeting "Mutt"

One person who liked the album—and especially the sexy video for the song "What Made You Say That"—was Mutt Lange, a successful rock producer from South Africa who has worked with such artists as Bryan Adams, Def Leppard, Billy Ocean, Foreigner, Michael Bolton, and the Cars. Lange, who was working in England at the time, called Twain's manager and asked to be introduced. Neither Twain nor her manager, Mary Bailey, recognized his name, so they sent him an autographed photo instead. But Lange persevered, and he and Twain eventually connected. He asked her if she had written any songs, and she was delighted to share the songs she had been working on for years. They started a working relationship by telephone, where she would prop up the phone on a pillow and play a song for him. He would record it over the phone, rework it, and play it back to her later, again over the phone. They finally met a few months later, in June 1993. Within weeks, in her words, "we knew we wanted to be together for the rest of our lives." They were married just six months later, in December 1993.

Since that time, they've set up a creative partnership. They have co-written most of the songs on her two subsequent recordings, and he has produced the music that she sings. The partnership seems to work out well. "[Creatively] we're really a team," Twain says. "We write our music together. We're in the studio together. We make the records together. I mean, he's the producer and my co-writer. So, we're very, very close. Not just as a man and a wife, but also creatively. So, we do pretty much everything creatively together."

The Woman in Me

Twain's second album, and her first to be produced by Lange, was *The Woman in Me* (1995). It contains a mix of ballads and upbeat tunes, written by Twain and Lange. The album closes with the *a cappella* lullaby "God Bless the Child" — an original song, not the Billie Holiday tune of the same name — which Twain used to sing to comfort herself and her siblings after the death of their parents. Her voice, according to Brian D. Johnson in *Maclean's* magazine, "has a melting twang, enough to conjure up country, yet more suggestive of the boudoir than the barn."

On *The Woman in Me*, Twain turned her back on traditional country music to create an original approach. The songs vary in tone and tempo, with a modern, New Country sound — what's been called county dance music — that clearly shows influences from pop and rock music. While they feature the twang of traditional steel guitars, fiddles, and haunting acoustic guitars, they also feature driving blues licks and strong rock beats. The lyrics in the songs vary as well, from conventional torch songs that lament lost love to sassy rockers that taunt and flaunt. These pieces show a strong, independent, feisty, and funny woman not willing to take any disrespect from a man. That was different from many earlier female country singers, as Donna McElroy from the Berklee College of Music explained in the *Milwaukee Journal Sentinel*. "Shania's a trail blazer. The status of the female country singer has been one of submission to her lot in life. . . . The poor singer is still in this dysfunctional situation. This girl [Twain] is saying, 'I ain't even going there. Don't even come to me with that stuff.'" She flaunted her proud attitude in both her lyrics and her delivery. Her image, in her videos and later in her stage appearances, was important to her growing popularity as well. Twain has been called a blend of country girl and city sophisticate. She's beautiful, and she shows off her great looks with tight, body-hugging clothes that always bare her midriff. As Karen Schoemer described Twain's approach in *Newsweek* magazine, "Shania has conquered country through a skillful strategy: pretend it's pop in everything but the sound."

The Woman in Me became a huge success. It has produced eight hit singles and has sold more than 13 million copies to date, a phenomenal figure for country music, making it the best-selling album ever by a female country singer. Yet Twain came in for a certain amount of criticism, especially in the world of traditional country music. Many wondered how much of Twain's success was due to her own talent, rather than her husband's skill as a producer and song writer. Others criticized the image she projects in her videos as too provocative, especially objecting to her flaunting her belly button. Others questioned why she decided not to go out on tour immediately following the album's release, which is the expected procedure. Twain herself said that with only one album to her credit, she didn't feel that she had enough original material to support a live show. Many doubted her, though. Perhaps unfamiliar with her history as a performer at a young age, they suggested that she didn't have the courage or the skill to perform live. Twain just scoffed at such suggestions. Many speculated, also, that she was a one-hit wonder who wouldn't be able to sustain her career. And the controversy over her Native heritage came to a head in 1996, as people learned the details of her family background and questioned her truthfulness. Taken together, all these issues created a backlash of negativity against Twain.

Come on Over

Twain silenced many of her critics with her next release, *Come on Over* (1997). It features 16 songs, again written by Twain and Lange, with just two ballads. Like its predecessor, the sounds range from rockabilly to classic rock to techno-Caribbean, while the lyrics feature an upbeat, witty, and confident take on male-female relations. "With *Come on Over*," Bruce Feiler wrote in the *New York Times*, "Ms. Twain firmly grasps the torch from Mr. [Garth] Brooks to become the dominant pop country voice in the late 1990s. She also moves closer to her goal of becoming a multimedia artist who uses Nashville as a launching point to achieve international stardom."

Come on Over, which has sold more than eight million copies to date, gave rise to Twain's first tour as a major country artist. This extended international tour, which began in Sudbury, Ontario, in May 1998 and was expected to continue through mid-1999, also squashed any suggestion that she didn't know how to perform live. "Basically, the show will be a party," Twain said at the start of the tour, "and I'm the hostess. It's not going to be that slick. Just high energy, great lights, and great sound." It was all that, and more. Backed by a nine-piece band, including three fiddle players, Twain sang with polish and firm command in a massive, energetic, high-tech show that featured multiple costumes changes, smoke clouds, fireworks, and big projection screens. As journalist Dave Tianen wrote in the *Milwaukee Journal Sentinel*, "she's a vibrant, flirtatious, open-hearted, high energy, immensely likable entertainer. . . . [To] truly appreciate her gifts, you need to see her in concert."

—————— " ——————

"[Twain is] a vibrant, flirtatious, open-hearted, high energy, immensely likable entertainer. . . . [To] truly appreciate her gifts, you need to see her in concert."
—*Dave Tianen*, **Milwaukee Journal Sentinel**

—————— " ——————

For Twain, the last few years have been wonderful, and she clearly has nothing left to prove. "The follow-up album [*Come on Over*] has been a terrific success," she says, "and no one can take that away from me now. Whatever happens from here on, it's irrelevant, in the sense of success or failure. I've succeeded as far as I'm concerned. . . . And I'm having more fun than I ever had before."

MARRIAGE AND FAMILY

Twain was married on December 28, 1993, to record producer Robert John "Mutt" Lange. They were married at the Deerhurst Resort, where Twain had performed before she made it big. Shania and Mutt started out in Nashville and then moved to Lake Placid, New York. There, they lived for several years on a 3,000-acre estate with a private lake in the Adirondack Mountains with their two dogs and two horses. Hoping for more privacy, they recently moved to a home outside Geneva, Switzerland, where they are building a recording studio.

CREDITS

Recordings

Shania Twain, 1993
The Woman in Me, 1995
Come on Over, 1997

TV Specials

"Shania Live,"CBC, 1998
"Shania Twain's Winter Break,"CBS, 1999

HONORS AND AWARDS

Canadian Country Music Association Awards: 1995 (five awards), Album of the Year, Female Vocalist of the Year, Single of the Year, Video of the Year, Song of the Year; 1996 (three awards), Entertainer of the Year, Female Vocalist of the Year, Video of the Year; 1997, Top-Selling Album; 1998 (six awards), Album of the Year, Female Vocalist of the Year, Single of the Year, Video of the Year, Fan's Choice Award, Top-Selling Album

Grammy Awards: 1996, Best Country Album, for *The Woman in Me*; 1999 (two awards), Best Female Country Vocal Performance and Best Country Song for "You're Still the One"(with Mutt Lange)

Academy of Country Music Awards: 1996 (two awards), Best New Female Vocalist and Album of the Year (with Mutt Lange)

Juno Awards: 1996 (2 awards), Entertainer of the Year and Best Country Female Vocalist; 1997 (two awards), Best Country Female Vocalist and Award for International Achievement; 1998, Best Country Female Vocalist; 1999, Best Country Female Vocalist

American Music Awards: 1996, Favorite New Country Artist; 1997, Favorite Female Country Artist; 1999, Favorite Female Country Artist

FURTHER READING

Books

Erlewine, Michael, ed. *All Music Guide to Country: The Experts' Guide to the Best Recordings in Country Music*, 1997
Gray, Scott. *On Her Way: The Shania Twain Story*, 1997
Hager, Barbara. *Honour Song*, 1996
Hager, Barbara. *On Her Way: The Life and Music of Shania Twain*, 1998
Who's Who in America, 1999

Periodicals

Chatelaine, May 1996, p.56
Cosmopolitan, Mar. 1998, p.198; Feb. 1999, p.123
Country Music, Nov.-Dec. 1997, p.34
Entertainment Weekly, Aug. 11, 1995, p.32
Interview, Mar. 1996, p.102
Maclean's, Aug. 28, 1995, p.54; Dec. 18, 1995, p.50; Mar. 23, 1998, p.48
McCall's Apr. 1998, 48
Milwaukee Journal Sentinel, June 28, 1998, p.1
Newsweek, Feb. 26, 1996, p.70
Parade, July 21, 1996, p.8
People, Sep. 4, 1995, p.61
Rolling Stone, Sep. 3, 1998, p.52
Toronto Star, Jan. 28, 1996, p.A1
TV Guide, Feb. 24, 1996, p.52
USA Weekend, Feb. 19-21, 1999, p.4
Washington Post, Mar. 3, 1996, p.G1

ADDRESS

Mercury Records
66 Music Square West
Nashville, TN 37203

WORLD WIDE WEB SITES

www.shania-twain.com
www.mercurynashville.com

Mitsuko Uchida 1948-
Japanese Classical Pianist

BIRTH

Mitsuko Uchida (METS-koh OO-shee-dah) was born on
December 20, 1948, in Tokyo, Japan. She was the third child
of Fukito Uchida, a diplomat, and Tasuko Uchida, a homemaker. Fukito had served in the Japanese diplomatic corps in
Europe during World War II, before Mitsuko was born. After
Japan lost the war, he was interned in the United States for
three months, then released and returned to Japan and his
job in the diplomatic corps.

YOUTH

Uchida grew up in a family that revered music. Her earliest memories of music are of listening to her father's extensive collection of recordings of the masters of European classical music, especially Mozart, Beethoven, and Haydn, played on a long-gone format, the old vinyl 78 rpm records.

Starting to Play the Piano

When she was just three years old, Uchida began to take piano lessons. Her parents never planned on their daughter becoming one of the finest pianists of the late 20th century. Instead, they saw it as part of a Japanese girl's "education," something all little girls of Japanese middle-class families did. "I suppose if my parents had any hopes for me it was that I would become an important piano teacher, get decently married, produce a child or two, and live within the framework of Japanese society," she remarked later.

From a very young age, her talent was unmistakable. Her proud father used to ask her to perform for guests. "How I loathed it!" she recalls. "It almost made me quit music. I hated being told to play even if I didn't feel like it. I would never ask any child to play unless the child wanted to."

> *From a very young age, her talent was unmistakable. Her proud father used to ask her to perform for guests. "How I loathed it!" she recalls. "It almost made me quit music. I hated being told to play even if I didn't feel like it. I would never ask any child to play unless the child wanted to."*

Reflecting on her early years, Uchida believes that "the hardest time for me was earliest childhood." "I grew up in Japan, where clarifying one's thoughts by projecting questions to teachers and parents is not an accepted behavior. Children are to do what they're told." For Uchida, this was a stifling atmosphere, and not just for a budding musician. "There were so many things I didn't understand about why things were as they were, in life as well as in music. But one was never really to ask, and I didn't have the habit of asking. So all these *whys* accumulated in me."

She believes that the Japanese approach to the teaching of music can be "antithetical to a true inner development. They believe in an instrumental or mechanical, rather than a musical, training. For them the teacher is sacred, a figure of unquestioned authority. Japanese pianists are always looking for the perfect teacher, someone who will unlock secrets you can only learn by yourself." She also views the status of women in traditional Japanese culture as an impediment to individual growth and development. "Women there are professional daughters or professional wives," she says.

Uchida's words about the composers she loves are almost as moving as her playing. About Mozart, she has said, "He had the quickest mind in music; he didn't chew things over and over like Beethoven. His music is full of unexpected corners, directions you couldn't have imagined him going in. You mustn't give them away to the listener—you must play as though you're *surprised."*

Moving to Vienna

By the time she was 12, Uchida was recognized as a gifted piano student of exceptional talent. But she wasn't going to develop that talent in Japan. Her father was sent to Vienna, the capital of Austria, to serve as Ambassador, and the family moved to Europe.

Uchida was terrified. "I didn't want to go, and when I got there I hated it. The change of language, of my style of life—it was absolutely terrifying." Not knowing a word of German, she was enrolled in the famous Vienna Academy of Music, where she studied from 1961 to 1968. Her teacher was Richard Hauser, who, she recalled, "demanded of me the same as from the 20-year-old students—you had to play by heart every new piece by the second lesson or you were out."

The work was hard, and she felt isolated. She says she's always been a loner, and that feeling was intensified by the atmosphere at her school. "I was an introverted kid, and I spent all my spare time reading everything in Japanese. Part of me wanted to learn German; the other part didn't." Still, she was able to immerse herself in the Western classical tradition in a way that would have been impossible in Japan. Vienna is the home of some of Western music's greatest composers, including those who became Uchida's favorites, such as Mozart, Schubert, Beethoven, and Schumann. And yet the Vienna Academy could be stifling, too. "Beethoven must be like *this*, Schubert like *that*; anything else is inadmissible."

Living Alone at 16

When Uchida was 16, her father was transferred to West Berlin. Uchida had to make a decision: "to go as a dutiful daughter or stay on my own and study music." She decided to stay alone in Vienna to continue her education. "I simply thought, what have I done all this work for? If I had gone with my parents, I would have just become the attractive ambassador's daughter who plays the piano terribly well."

For the next six years, she lived in a youth hostel and continued her studies at the Academy. "It wasn't easy: I *was* lonely," she said later. But she did it. Already a pianist of fierce individualism and determination, she knew she wanted to become a professional musician, and she knew that she needed to study and to explore as much of the piano repertoire as possible to find herself as an artist.

Although the focus of her education was clearly on music, Uchida also received a general education in Vienna. Like Julliard and other arts-based schools in the United States, the Vienna Academy offers students courses in areas outside of their main concentration. Uchida studied literature, math, science, and other subjects, graduating in 1968 with the equivalent of a Bachelor's Degree in music.

Starting to Compete

After graduation, Uchida prepared for her first piano competition. One year later, in 1969, she won the International Beethoven Competition in Vienna. The next year she placed second in the Chopin Competition in Warsaw, Poland. Winning two important competitions was a mixed blessing for Uchida. On the one hand, she was recognized as a significant new talent in Europe. But on the other hand, the atmosphere competitions create can damage the true potential of a player. "The premature exposure associated with such competitions can be disastrous. At 18 or 20 you are simply not ready, you can't have come to terms with yourself or have little beyond the most superficial notions concerning your artistic identity. Inevitably, the repertoire has been rapidly prepared, not chewed over and inwardly digested, learned, relearned, and relearned again."

Moving to London

By 1972, Uchida knew that she had to leave Vienna. She wanted to find her own musical identity, away from any musical community with an established way of playing music. In Vienna, "Tradition was all, tradition was always right. It was very good for me to know it because I had come

Uchida being conducted by Andre Previn, May 1996

from a country without tradition in Western music. And of course I learned German, which I think is essential for playing the great classical repertoire. But my god, it was such a mold! Especially about Mozart. It was all dos and don'ts. *Forte* was never to played really *forte*. Everything had to be done with good behavior—terribly dainty. Every phrase had to end with a little lift."

She decided to move to London, drawn to its open, independent musical and intellectual atmosphere. She spent the next several years studying and listening to music. "For the next five years I learned entirely on my own, which is the only real way. Things that are given to you are worth nothing." Immersed in the recordings of the great conductors and pianists of the 20th century, Uchida listened to Wilhelm Furtwangler, George Szell, Arthur Schnabel, and others. She found herself drawn especially to Fritz Busch's recordings of Mozart. She loved his "courage to be free—with taste. That is the most important thing. Without the courage of your own convictions, there is no performance." This led her to concentrate on Mozart's piano music, especially the sonatas (solo works for piano) and piano concertos (works for piano accompanied by chamber or full orchestra).

By 1975, she was preparing for competition again, and this time she placed second in the Leeds Competition in England. Around this time she began her concert career, playing in Britain and Japan, but mostly devoting herself to study and practice.

CAREER HIGHLIGHTS

In a career that has spanned 25 years, Uchida has established herself as one of finest pianists of the 20th century. She is considered one of the best interpreters of the works of Mozart, as well as other masters of the classical school, including Schubert, Beethoven, Haydn, Chopin, Schumann, and Debussy. This remarkable career started with a series of concerts she gave in London in the 1980s.

Wigmore Hall Concerts

It was as an interpreter of Mozart that Uchida first came to fame. In 1982, she gave a series of concerts at Wigmore Hall in London of the complete Mozart sonatas. The selection of these pieces was typical of Uchida's unique, fearless approach to the musical establishment. Many listeners had dismissed Mozart's sonatas as simplistic. But in Uchida's hands they were shown to be small masterpieces. Her thoughtful, intense, luminous performances of the sonatas captivated audiences. "The

Her practice routine begins each day with a Bach Prelude and Fugue, "a sort of cleansing or rejuvenating process. His music is surely the most perfect of all, the ultimate in spiritual harmony and balance; everything's included, nothing's in excess, a sort of paradigm of excellence," she says.

real incentive was that people had always said [the sonatas] were weak. It simply wasn't true! They are incredible pieces. They reveal his whole development, much more than the concertos."

Reviews from London and elsewhere were glowing. A critic from the London *Times* wrote that she is able to convey "an intense understanding of how music is made: the exact point at which to make a climax, the way a phrase rises towards its answer, the precise function to just one note in a theme. She does not sing the music; she exists in it."

Uchida's words about the composers she loves are almost as moving as her playing. About Mozart, she has said, "He had the quickest mind in music; he didn't chew things over and over like Beethoven. His music is full of unexpected corners, directions you couldn't have imagined him going in. You mustn't give them away to the listener—you must play as though *you're* surprised."

Three years after her groundbreaking interpretations of the sonatas, Uchida performed all 21 Mozart concertos, directing the English Chamber Orchestra from the piano. This concert series took place over a nine-month period, during the 1985-86 season. Once again, the music world was astonished by the depth and insight of her playing. One critic noted how her "incessant twists from major to minor and back were sharply expressive and nervy. The piano tacked between a tight, brazen *forte* and a trembling pianissimo. It was like hearing the music under brilliant strobe lights."

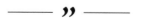

"*If you hear me play, you hear that I love playing the piano. Not just listening to musical technique, but I love the physical action of actually playing the piano. Don't you feel it? That's why I'm different from some other pianists. When they are free, they don't want to practice. I adore practicing. Even playing badly is wonderful. It's just such a pleasure.*"

International Acclaim

Uchida's recordings of the sonatas and concertos of Mozart made her reputation. Soon she was performing concerts all over the world and winning rapturous responses from concert-goers everywhere. Uchida is the first to describe her life as one totally devoted to music. She is an artist whose dedication, hard work, and seriousness are evident in everything she does. While she was preparing the 1985-86 concerts, she "couldn't read a book. I couldn't even listen to music at all. I simply felt I had to look at the score of Mozart concertos and then there is nothing to come between me and that piece of paper. . . . Mozart's music is like the air. When you are working on a lot of Mozart, he is everywhere."

In the 1980s, Uchida also performed and recorded the music of Chopin, again to wide acclaim. Once again, her thorough, thoughtful probing of a great classical composer resulted in performances that clearly articulated the beauty and depth of that creator's artistry. Will Crutchfield wrote in the *New York Times* of her Chopin performance, "In her care for musical purpose and fine shading of each phrase, her wonderful pointing of rhythm, her easily flowing legato and her understanding of balance and dynamic perspective, she is a true artist."

During the 1990 season, Uchida offered the piano music of another classical master, Beethoven, to the world. "Beethoven is the most intense compose that ever lived. It's frightening. But if I don't feel a struggle with Beethoven, I don't like it." As with her Mozart concerts, Uchida's Beethoven performances prompted rave reviews, and tickets sold out within hours in each city where she performed. One music specialist spoke for many when he claimed that Uchida was "one of those rare people who come along once in a generation and transform the ways we see the music."

Performing: Schedule and Preparation

Unlike other performing musicians, who might play 100 concerts each year, Uchida limits her concerts to just 50. She devotes herself to months, even years of preparation prior to concert series or recordings. During these times, she will practice for hours a day. Her practice routine begins each day with a Bach Prelude and Fugue, "a sort of cleansing or rejuvenating process. His music is surely the most perfect of all, the ultimate in spiritual harmony and balance; everything's included, nothing's in excess, a sort of paradigm of excellence," she says. She also takes several months off each year to practice, rest, and reflect.

"I try to be as accurate and honest as possible, in language and in music," Uchida says. The breadth of her language ability is nearly as astonishing as her playing. She speaks the three languages of the countries she has called home: Japanese, German, and English, and though she claims she is not, she is articulate, thoughtful, and perceptive in each. To this end, she studies the music and words of a composer, trying to glean the meaning behind a piece. "I am always very interested to find out how a composer thought; how he derived an idea, where he derived it from and how he gets to the final result. What does he use as the main motive? How does he turn the motives around? That is very interesting. It is my instinctive necessity to know all this."

Uchida has a very specific routine that she follows on concert days. She runs through her entire program, then eats "a big lunch. I always lose weight when I perform." Just before the concert she eats just "a corner of cake, a quarter of a banana. I learned that from watching the cyclists from the Tour de France." Then she arrives at the concert hall "before the public so I can sniff the air and set the position of the stool right. The stool is almost more important than the piano."

Uchida playing with the New York Philharmonic, May 1996

She presents a striking figure on the concert stage. She wears beautiful, colorful clothes, and she wears her long black hair free about her shoulders. As Charles Michener wrote in *Connoisseur,* "At the keyboard she is an intensely dramatic figure, her torso, arms, hands, and highly mobile face eloquently depicting her involvement with the music."

Uchida constantly challenges herself, to keep her music fresh and her performances meaningful. "I think one ought to be able to give always more, the older you get. If you live well, I think you ought to be able to give something different, and something stronger, the older you get." Her repertoire continues to expand. Although she knows that audiences "will go on perceiving me for a while as a Mozart specialist," she is performing more Schubert and Debussy now. Uchida has always loved the music of Schubert, a Viennese composer of the early 19th century, of whom she speaks with eloquence: "He was so incredibly adventurous in his compositions, even though he was technically less complete than Mozart and Bach. They were technically amazing. They could do anything they liked. With Schubert, you have the feeling he wanted to do something like that, but the beauty and strength of his music were the result of sheer genius, as if somebody else was holding his pen."

She also declares herself to be "passionate about the music of the Second Viennese School — Schoenberg, Berg, and Webern." Schoenberg, a modern composer who can be extraordinarily difficult for many modern listeners, is something of a personal cause for Uchida. She wants to introduce the beauty of his music to a modern audience. In 1997, she did a series of concerts in which she juxtaposed the classical, lyrical music of Schubert with the modern dissonances of Schoenberg. She wanted to challenge her listeners, the way she challenges herself. "By saying 'I understand Schubert but not Schoenberg' I believe people are misunderstanding the word 'understand'," she says. "What they are really saying is, 'that sounds pleasant to me because I got used to it, but that is just a noise because I refuse to hear it.' People remember what they can easily grasp, and what they can easily grasp, they like to repeat. We live in such an impatient age, an age of soundbite psychology and compilation albums — both of which I hate! Nothing in music is short!"

> "
>
> "'Success' is something you just can't stop to consider. If it comes then it's an added bonus, that's all. I mean the process of hopefully evolving into a performer of some sort of stature or consequence is so consuming, something that fuels and pervades your entire existence. It's really a question of seriousness. Is music your life's blood or not, does this quest for human and artistic significance obsess you entirely? If not then you have to do something else, and live a life less full of savage demands and sacrifices."
>
> "

Always looking for a new challenge, Uchida conducted the Cleveland Symphony for the first time in 1998, with rewarding results. One critic noted that their performance of a Mozart concerto showed "an unusually generous spirit of give-and-take between orchestra and soloist." That critic also noted the great admiration between the orchestra and Uchida. The musicians themselves were as generous in their applause of that night's conductor as was the audience.

Also in 1998, she was named the first woman director of the Ojai Music Festival in California. As director, she will help to plan and program the festival in the coming years. She will perform these duties in addition to her work as co-director of the Marlboro Festival, an series of annual concerts and workshops that take place in Vermont.

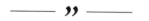

Uchida offers the following advice to kids who love to play and want to be musicians. "When youngsters talk to me, I tell them, 'Get rid of your teachers and take a long-term view. I don't want to influence you: you have to discover. If you're good enough, then one day somebody will notice. Because the world is not full of wonderful things and people are longing for good things."

FUTURE PLANS

At the age of 50, Uchida still has much to do. She is already preparing for a series of concerts she plans to give in 2018, when she turns 70. That year, she plans to perform Bach's Goldberg Variations and all 48 of his Preludes and Fugues. This music, some of the deepest and most profound ever written, will take her years to prepare, an experience she relishes. After nearly 50 years of playing, she still loves her instrument. "If you hear me play, you hear that I love playing the piano. Not just listening to musical technique, but I love the physical action of actually playing the piano. Don't you feel it? That's why I'm different from some other pianists. When they are free, they don't want to practice. I adore practicing. Even playing badly is wonderful. It's just such a pleasure."

ADVICE TO YOUNG MUSICIANS

Uchida is astonished at the lack of musical education available to most American school children. "The idea has to be put in your mind. Unless somebody does that, it's possible that many kids will never hear the most beautiful thing that the human race has ever produced."

She offers the following advice to kids who love to play and want to be musicians. "When youngsters talk to me, I tell them, 'Get rid of your teachers and take a long-term view. I don't want to influence you: you have to discover. If you're good enough, then one day somebody will notice. Because the world is not full of wonderful things and people are longing for good things."

For Uchida, the path of a young person hoping for a career in music is clear: dedication like her own. "'Success' is something you just can't stop to consider. If it comes then it's an added bonus, that's all. I mean the process of hopefully evolving into a performer of some sort of stature or consequence is so consuming, something that fuels and pervades your entire existence. It's really a question of seriousness. Is music your life's blood or not, does this quest for human and artistic significance obsess you entirely? If not then you have to do something else, and live a life less full of savage demands and sacrifices."

HOME AND FAMILY

Uchida lives in a house off the Portobello Road in London, with a separate studio that houses her five pianos: two Steinways, one Bosendorfer, a 1790 Longman, and a Broderip square piano. She has never married, although she lives next door to her companion of 20 years, Robert Cooper, a British diplomat. Uchida has never had children. She says that her career "would not have been possible if I had had a child. I would have made life hell for a child. And I would have been frustrated because I would not have had time for my music." Although she lives in London full time, she still retains her Japanese citizenship. She frequently performs in Japan, and she still keeps in close touch with her family.

HOBBIES AND OTHER INTERESTS

Uchida has very little time for activities not relating to music. Even her hobbies revolve around it. She reads voraciously, especially biographies, often of the composer whose work she is preparing. But she also likes comic strips, including "Calvin and Hobbes" and "The Far Side." She also loves the theater, especially Shakespeare. "It's like music — how to understand and interpret the words, and put it into an event that takes up a particular time span. Seeing how a great actor or interesting director sees the meaning of the words is very close to how I try to find the meaning of the notes."

She does enjoy bicycling in the South of France for a week or so each year. "The food is good and there's nothing to think about except the next hill—the perfect antidote to a performer's life." She also enjoys knitting. "It gives you something to do in lonely hotel rooms and airports and allows your mind time to dream and wander."

Still, Uchida's life revolves around her central passion. "Music doesn't lie. It is the truest friend. I spend all my time thinking about music. I wouldn't know what to do without it."

SELECTED RECORDINGS

Beethoven. *Piano Concertos Nos. 3 and 4,* 1996; *Nos. 1 and 2,* 1998
Chopin. *Piano Sonatas,* 1994
Debussey. *Etudes,* 1990
Mozart. *Complete Piano Sonatas,* 1988
———. *Complete Piano Concertos,* 1993
Schubert. *Impromptus Op. 90 & 142,* 1997
———. *Piano Sonatas Nos. 19, 10, 21,* 1998
Schumann. *Carnaval,* 1997

HONORS AND AWARDS

International Beethoven Competition: First Prize, 1969
Chopin Competition: Second Prize, 1970
Leeds Competition: Second Prize, 1975

FURTHER READING

Books

International Who's Who, 1998-99
Notable Twentieth-Century Pianists, 1995

Periodicals

Chicago Tribune, Nov. 29, 1992, Section 13, p.22
Connoisseur, Dec. 1988, p.120
Current Biography Yearbook 1991
Denver Post, Aug. 4, 1996, p.E1
Gramophone, July 1984, p.101; Feb. 1989, p.1275

Independent (London), Oct. 6, 1990, Weekend Arts, p.35; Mar. 24, 1997,
  Arts Section, p.14
Los Angeles Times, Oct. 24, 1991, p.F6
Music and Musicians, Nov. 1985, p.5; Oct. 1990, p.5
New York, Apr. 22, 1991, p.79
New York Times, Oct. 16, 1988, p.B27; Mar. 15, 1992, p.B57; Apr. 8, 1997,
  p.C9
Newsweek, Mar. 26, 1990, p.57
Stereo Review, July 1990, p.63
Times (London), Oct. 13, 1994
Vanity Fair, Dec. 1992, p.122
Wall Street Journal, Mar. 14, 1990, p.A16; June 16, 1998, p.A16
Washington Post, Apr. 3, 1991, p.C1; Nov. 17, 1995, p.F8

ADDRESS

AMG
150 5th Street
Room 845
New York, NY 10011

WORLD WIDE WEB SITE

www.phil.clas.polygram.nl

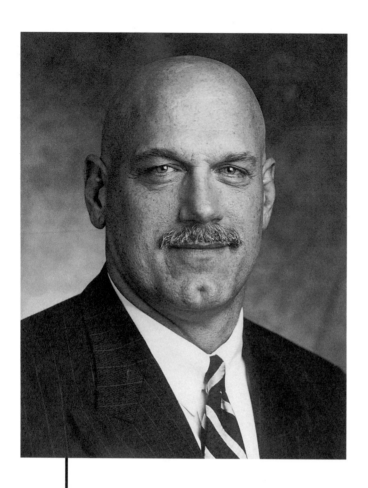

Jesse Ventura 1951-
American Politician, Entertainer, and Athlete
Governor of Minnesota
Former Professional Wrestler and Actor

BIRTH

Jesse "The Body" Ventura, former flamboyant professional
wrestler and now governor of Minnesota, was born James
George Janos on July 15, 1951, in Minneapolis, Minnesota.
His father, George W. Janos, worked as a steam fitter for the
city of Minneapolis, while his mother, Bernice M. (Lenz)
Janos, was a nurse anesthetist. They had two sons, Jan and

James. Known as Jim when he was growing up, he adopted the name "Jesse Ventura" in about 1974 or 1975 for his wrestling career and earned the nickname "The Body" soon after.

Both of Ventura's parents were military veterans who served in World War II. His father was a sergeant in the infantry who served under General Patton on a tank destroyer in North Africa, Italy, and Europe. He was a highly decorated vet who earned seven Battle Stars, but he never talked about his experiences during the war. His mother was a lieutenant and commissioned as an officer. She served as a nurse in North Africa. When they would have a fight, Ventura recalls, he would call her "the lieutenant," which really irritated her.

YOUTH AND EDUCATION

Ventura grew up in a blue-collar neighborhood on the south side of Minneapolis. He doesn't talk much about his early childhood. But it seems that many of his later interests were formed early on. Even when he was young, he would get into a lot of scrapes, and he knew that he wanted to be a wrestler. Childhood friend Kevin Johnson once told a story about an assignment they had in second or third grade to write about what they wanted to be when they grew up. "Most of us wrote about wanting to be a fireman or policeman. But he wanted to be a professional wrestler. He is probably the only one who went on to be what he had said."

Ventura once had to write a grade-school assignment about what he wanted to be when he grew up, according to childhood friend Kevin Johnson. "Most of us wrote about wanting to be a fireman or policeman. But he wanted to be a professional wrestler. He is probably the only one who went on to be what he had said."

Ventura's interest in politics was formed early, too, at family discussions around the dinner table each night. His father considered all politicians corrupt, and he would discuss current political figures and events with anger and contempt. It's ironic that Ventura ended up becoming a politician, according to another old friend, Steve Nelson. "I always though that if Jim ever ran for office," said Nelson, referring to Ventura's successful run for governor, "he'd have to answer to his father and do a good job. He'd better do it right."

In school, Ventura is remembered more for his athletic accomplishments than for his academic achievements. His favorite subject in school, he now says, was gym. He attended Cooper Elementary School and Roosevelt High School, where he played football and was captain of the swimming team. An outstanding swimmer, he held the local record for the 100-yard butterfly. Ventura graduated from Roosevelt in 1969. Several years later, he attended one year at a community college, but he never completed his college degree.

> *Journalist Kevin Dockery described Ventura's military training to become a Navy SEAL like this. "What they do is staggering — even witnessing it is hard. They grind you into the ground to let you show yourself that you're able to do 10 times more than you thought you could. At the end of it, they look like they've been through a train wreck. They smell so bad you can't get near them. But they have accomplished something very few men accomplish."*

MILITARY SERVICE

When Ventura graduated from high school in 1969, the United States was in the middle of the Vietnam War, a long-running conflict in southeast Asia. When the U.S. got involved in the late 1950s, it was essentially a civil war between North Vietnam and South Vietnam. The political makeup of these two countries contributed to the decision by the U.S. to get involved there. It was the Cold War at that time, a period of extreme distrust, suspicion, and hostility between, on the one side, Communist countries like the Soviet Union (now Russia), China, and their allies, and, on the other side, the United States and its allies. North Vietnam was controlled by Communists, and many people in the U.S. felt that it was important to support South Vietnam in order to stop the spread of Communism to other nations. In the late 1950s, the U.S. began sending in military advisers to help South Vietnam; in the early 1960s, the U.S. began sending in military troops to fight in the war. By 1969, when Jesse Ventura graduated from high school, U.S. forces had reached a peak of over 543,000 troops. They fought alongside about 800,000 South Vietnamese troops.

Initially, Ventura had no intention of joining the armed services after high school. He had enrolled in a local college and planned to start

Ventura shown in a photo taken from the
WWF's The Wrestling Album, *released in 1985*

school that fall. But his older brother, Jan, had joined the Navy SEALs (Sea, Air, Land), an elite special forces unit. Jan's stories had convinced one of Ventura's friends, Steve Nelson, to join also. Nelson asked Ventura to come down to the Navy recruiting office with him when he went in to sign up. By the time they left the office, Ventura had enlisted also.

Becoming a Navy SEAL

Ventura underwent a grueling 22-week training course, mostly in California. He started with the Navy's basic training, common to all new recruits, and then continued with the far more strenuous training to become a SEAL, like his older brother. He became adept at jungle warfare, parachute jumps, and diving (his record is 212 feet). He also qualified for and completed Basic Underwater Demolition training. It takes a phenomenal amount of physical strength, stamina, courage, mental toughness, and willingness to take risks to complete the training to become a SEAL. "What they do is staggering—even witnessing it is hard," said Kevin Dockery, who edited a book about the SEALs. "They grind you into the ground to let you show yourself that you're able to do 10 times more than you thought you could. At the end of it, they look like they've been through a train wreck. They smell so bad you can't get near them. But they have accomplished something very few men accomplish." The experience instills in each SEAL a profound sense of allegiance to the team, as well as a pretty cocky attitude about his skills. Ventura describes these fellow frogmen as "assassins, pirates, maniacs, and hell-raisers."

Ventura served in the Navy for six years. He spent four years on active duty as a SEAL and then completed two years in the Naval Reserves. While on active duty, he did two tours overseas, attaining the rank of Third Class Storekeeper. He was stationed at least some of the time at Subic Bay, a port in the Philippines, where at one point he played football on a Navy team. He may have also served in Vietnam; that part of his record is unclear. The SEALs were involved in many secret operations all over Southeast Asia that are still confidential today. Ventura refuses to disclose any details of his missions because, he says, of orders he was given by his commanding officer (CO): "I'm issuing all of you a directive right now that you should consider a direct order. You are to talk about nothing that you saw, nothing that you did, or anything that you heard about." For military personnel, and especially for the SEALs, following an order from the CO is mandatory, and Ventura took that order very seriously, as he explains here. "To this day, I still live by that order. I just don't tell war stories." That's all that he will say about his experiences in the military and whether he served in Vietnam. Ventura received his honorable discharge from the Navy in 1973.

FIRST JOBS

During his last months in the service, while stationed on a base in California, Ventura started working out with weight lifting, hoping to build his strength so he could play professional football. He also joined a motorcycle club called the Mongols. He continued riding with them for several months after leaving the Navy. But then a friend talked him into leaving California and returning home to Minnesota. "That was the right thing to do, looking back on it," Ventura admits. "Being in that club would have been nothing more than a one-way ticket to jail."

Back in Minneapolis, he enrolled at North Hennepin Community College on the GI bill, a federal program that pays for veterans to attend school. He earned almost straight-As there while playing on the school football team. He even fantasized about playing for the NFL. But, he says, after serving in the military, he no longer had the right attitude for college sports. "I soured on football real fast. I was a 22-year-old freshman, and after four years in the Navy, I'd played man's ultimate game, which is war. There is no way I could view football the way the coaches did—as a life-and-death-struggle." Ventura dropped off the team and focused instead on weightlifting.

Ventura played football in college after serving in the Navy. "I soured on football real fast. I was a 22-year-old freshman, and after four years in the Navy, I'd played man's ultimate game, which is war. There is no way I could view football the way the coaches did–as a life-and-death-struggle."

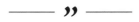

BECOMING A WRESTLER

While weightlifting at a local gym, Ventura met a former professional wrestler who offered to train him. He accepted, and spent seven months training before he was ready to turn pro. But first, he needed to develop an act for the ring. "If you're smart and you want to make money in wrestling, you have to develop a persona that will catch people's eye and make them remember you. I decided I wanted to be a rule breaker, which is what I am. I modeled myself after my hero in wrestling, Superstar Billy Graham [not the religious leader of the same name], who was the sport's first bodybuilder. He was an off-the-wall character, and I knew that was the key to success. I got my rap from him."

Even after doing all that training and developing a new persona, he still wasn't ready to wrestle. At this point he was still known as Jim Janos, and he felt he needed a new name to match his new persona. "I always liked the name Jesse, and since I was going to be a bad guy, I wanted to be identified as a Californian, because most Americans hate people from California. So I picked up a map of California and started putting 'Jesse' before the name of every place in the state. 'Jesse Ventura' had a great ring to it. Then I bleached my hair blond, because people dislike blond men, especially if they know their hair's been dyed. I wore my hair down to my shoulders and tried my best to look like a surf bum who did nothing but work out on the beach and chase women all day."

———— " ————

When Ventura started wrestling, he needed to develop an act for the ring. "If you're smart and you want to make money in wrestling, you have to develop a persona that will catch people's eye and make them remember you. I decided I wanted to be a rule breaker, which is what I am. I modeled myself after my hero in wrestling, Superstar Billy Graham [not the religious leader of the same name], who was the sport's first bodybuilder. He was an off-the-wall character, and I knew that was the key to success. I got my rap from him."

———— " ————

MARRIAGE AND FAMILY

During this same period, while he was preparing to become a wrestler, Ventura got involved with his future wife, Teresa, called Terry. In September 1974, she was a 19-year-old receptionist when they met at a bar called the Rusty Nail Tavern, where he was working as a bouncer. "I walked in, our eyes locked, and that was it," she recalls. They were married in July 1975. They have two children, Tyrel, born in 1979, and Jade, born in 1983. Before her husband's election, Terry Ventura raised and trained horses on a 32-acre spread in Minnesota.

CAREER HIGHLIGHTS

Professional Wrestling

In April 1975, Ventura turned professional. He headed to Kansas City in an old beat-up Chevy with $250 in his pocket. Often accompanied by Terry, his wife, Ventura spent the next ten years or so touring on the professional wrestling circuit. According to Ventura, professional wrestling is a mix of theater and sport. The matches are choreographed and tightly scripted. Even so, injuries occur. "I had knee surgery, I dislocated my shoulder, and I had my nose broken more times than I can remember. When you wrestle a full schedule, you spend every day of your life in pain."

Minnesota Governor Jesse Ventura yelling to the crowd at his inaugural "People's Ball" in Minneapolis, January 16, 1999

For his wrestling matches, Ventura created a persona with a look and an attitude to match. He developed an outrageous look, wearing a pastel scarf on his head, huge sunglasses, neon tights, and a feather boa. He also developed a reputation as one of the bad boys of wrestling, "a guy who'd beat the hell out of you and take your woman on top of it," he says. "I created that character. He wasn't *me*. . . . But I loved being a villain." And the fans loved to hate his obnoxious, arrogant, and condescending behavior and attitude. As he said at the time, "I've had knives pulled on me and been spit on, had cigarettes mashed into my skin, eggs thrown at me, my tires slashed, threats against my life. I took a BB shot near the eye once. That just pumps me up." In the ring, according to fellow wrestler Jerry "The King" Lawler, "Jesse was a brawling type, punch-and-kick kind of guy, and he had the big flying elbow drop." Ventura often worked with Adrian "Golden Boy" Adonis as a champion tag-team wrestler under the name East-West Connection.

Ventura has always been huge — six foot four, about 240 pounds, with a 52-inch chest. His nickname when he started out was "The Surfer," but wrestling fans soon gave him the nickname "The Body." His size contributed to one interesting sideline during his wrestling career. Sometimes, he would moonlight as a bodyguard, and in 1981 he worked part-time as a bodyguard on the Rolling Stones tour. That experience, perhaps more than any other, seemed to amaze people when Ventura ran for governor of Minnesota.

Ventura's wrestling career came to a sudden and unexpected end. The night before a WWF (World Wrestling Federation) championship bout against Hulk Hogan, with whom he had a long-standing rivalry, Ventura developed trouble breathing. His doctors told him he had pulmonary embolism (blood clots in his lungs), a very serious condition. The doctors were able to treat it with medication, but he retired from wrestling in the mid-1980s.

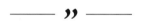

Ventura felt he needed a new name to match his new persona as a wrestler. "I always liked the name Jesse, and since I was going to be a bad guy, I wanted to be identified as a Californian, because most Americans hate people from California. So I picked up a map of California and started putting 'Jesse' before the name of every place in the state. 'Jesse Ventura' had a great ring to it."

Other Jobs

Ventura went on to several different jobs after that. He became a TV commentator for WWF matches, noted for his colorful, if biased, descriptions of events in the ring. "I became the first sportscaster to side with the bad guys, and I got more notoriety for my announcing than for my wrestling," he says. He also did some football announcing for the Tampa Bay Buccaneers' radio broadcast, again with a particular angle. "I try to make myself one of the guys sitting in the living room with all his buddies, drinking beer and eating chips, talking about the game. I try to do it from a fan's perspective." According to journalist George White, these announcing jobs gave Ventura the opportunity to improve his speaking skills. "So Jesse allows himself to be Jesse, still creating a character, but this time on the radio. In wrestling, the character was Jesse the Body. On the radio, it's Jesse the Fan."

He also began acting in films during this time. His first role was in *Predator*, starring Arnold Schwarzenegger. For the film, Ventura responded to an audition call for a six foot, four inch, 250-pound killer. "I just walked in there, with blond hair down to my shoulders, about six earrings, and a Fu Manchu mustache, and I didn't even read." As he recalls, the casting director "looked me up and down two times, then said, 'Let's go meet the producer.'" In *Predator*, where he became friends with Schwarzenegger, Ventura gave his most famous line, "I ain't got time to bleed."

After *Predator*, Ventura went on to appear in several other action films, primarily in small roles and often as a villain. He appeared in the films *The Running Man, Thunderground, Repossessed, Boxcar Blues, Abraxas, Ricochet,* and *Batman and Robin,* winning praise for these performances. According to Damian Lee, the producer of *Thunderground,* Ventura is "an incredibly solid performer. I don't think most people realize the depth he's capable of giving. There was a small intimation of it in *Predator* when he uttered the line, 'I ain't got time to bleed.' His delivery was so poignant, that line was memorable. . . . In this movie *[Thunderground],* he brings that same directness to the role of the major antagonist, and he also plays the cutting edge between sanity and madness with conservative delivery. That causes the audience and the other performers to wonder if he's putting them on or not. He can pontificate without sounding pompous, be philosophical without being boring, and be threatening with a smile on his face." On TV, Ventura appeared in an episode of "The X-Files" and served as host of a syndicated show called "The Grudge Match," in which contestants would come on the show to resolve their disagreements. They would start with a boxing match using huge oversized gloves, then continue with a fight using ridiculous weapons, like chocolate syrup, fruit pies, rotten tomatoes, or buckets of sludge.

Becoming Mayor

While continuing his announcing and acting careers, Ventura soon added one more job to his resume: mayor. In 1990, Ventura and his family were living in a suburb outside Minneapolis called Brooklyn Park. The city was planning to build a storm sewer near their neighborhood in a local wetland. Many people in the community were angry about the plan, and they tried to fight it. About 450 residents signed a petition to stop the plan, but the city voted them down. The neighborhood group tried to recruit Terry Ventura to run for mayor, but she refused. Then Jesse Ventura stepped in to run against the long-time incumbent, campaigning on the issues of less development, more recycling, and a two-term limit for city officials. He ended up winning the election in a landslide.

His record as mayor was mixed. During his tenure from 1991 to 1995, Brooklyn Park experienced a drop in crime, improved economic development, and greater access to city government for its citizens. But it's not clear how much credit Ventura can take for those improvements. As mayor, he didn't have a great deal of power to make decisions. He held just one vote on the seven-member city council, and he was frequently outvoted. He also came in for a lot of criticism because of his schedule. Often, he would fly into town for just a day or two in a week, and then fly back out for acting roles or announcing jobs.

Ventura did not run for reelection, and he left office in 1995. He took a job as a radio announcer and talk-show host on KFAN, a local talk-radio station. There, he was considered funny and articulate, refining the speaking skills that had served him well as a sports announcer and that would become even more important in his upcoming campaign to become governor of Minnesota.

Campaigning for Governor

In 1998, Ventura announced his candidacy for governor of Minnesota. He would be running on the ticket for the Reform Party, a political party that was created by businessman Ross Perot when he ran for president in 1992. As a running mate, Ventura chose Mae Schunk, an experienced teacher. His opponents were Republican Norm Coleman, the mayor of St. Paul, and Democrat Hubert (Skip) Humphrey III, attorney general of Minnesota. The Humphrey name is illustrious in both state and national politics. His father was the late Hubert H. Humphrey, former senator, vice president under Lyndon B. Johnson, and (unsuccessful) Democratic candidate for president in 1968.

Running under the slogan "Retaliate in '98," Ventura was motivated, he said, by the way the state was handling a $2 billion budget surplus in 1998. The legislature had chosen to return part of the surplus to the voters as tax relief, but to save some of it in state coffers. Ventura felt very strongly that the state should return all of the surplus to the taxpayers, who had paid the money in the first place. In general, he believes that government is too big and too intrusive. He campaigned on the issues of freezing state spending, creating tax cuts, and forcing school districts to cut class sizes. He refused to accept campaign contributions from political action committees, so-called "special interest money." He also made other pronouncements that were more controversial, like suggesting the legalization of drugs and prostitution and the elimination of financial aid for college students, the minimum wage, subsidized child care, and medical assistance for the poor.

At first, a lot of people didn't take his campaign very seriously, in part because he faced two very strong opponents with a history of public service in Minnesota. But it was also due to Jesse himself. Many political experts immediately discounted him because of the image and persona that he had created as a wrestler. He was big and bald. He campaigned wearing faded jeans and worn sneakers, sometimes with a camouflage or leather jacket. He was also funny, direct, and blunt; he said what was on his mind. He quoted from Jim Morrison and Jerry Garcia. He didn't look, speak, or act like a typical politician, and for that reason many political observers assumed that he couldn't get elected. But, in fact, a lot of voters liked both his style and what he had to say. They found his direct and honest approach a refreshing change from the usual vague political rhetoric. They also liked his refusal to

A poster with Minnesota Governor Jesse Ventura urging people to join the Reform Party in an Uncle Sam pose

accept money from special interest groups, which meant that he didn't owe any favors to anybody.

Winning the Election

On the eve of the election, people finally started to take notice. His rising poll numbers were helped by several irreverent, inventive TV ads that aired at the last minute. One featured two young boys playing with action figures: one of the toys (made from a Batman), which looked like Ventura, was fighting Evil Special Interest Man. On election day, his supporters turned out to the polls in droves. His tally was helped by Minnesota election law, which allows people to register to vote at the polls on the day of the election; most other states require people to register in advance, before voting day. This law allowed thousands of new voters, particularly young people, to decide to vote at the last minute. The result was a governor's race in which 61% of the eligible people voted, a very high turnout. Ventura won the race for governor with 37% of the vote.

Ventura's win led many political experts to try to understand what had happened. They wondered if his election was a sign of voters' deep-seated mistrust of government, or a referendum on campaign-finance reform. Or perhaps, they conjectured, people were simply disgusted by the political process because of the scandal that rocked President Clinton's administration during 1998. Experts also debated whether his win signaled the end of the two-party system. Many said his ability to reach so many in-different, unregistered, and young voters was a sign that these voters had chosen style instead of sub-stance. Essentially, these commentators tried to reduce his candidacy to a symbol, rather than accepting Ventura as the voters' choice.

———— " ————

According to **Rolling Stone** *magazine, "This is what the 38th governor of the state of Minnesota wears to his [inaugural] soiree: black jeans, a T-shirt bearing a likeness of Jimi Hendrix, a buckskin jacket, pink sunglasses, and cowboy boots. He also knows how to accessorize: Silver skull and hoop earrings dangle from each ear. His wife, Terry, is dressed like a heavy-metal babe in a black suede miniskirt and a leather jacket, with black knee-high boots."*

———— " ————

Becoming Governor

Ventura took the oath of office on January 4, 1999, becoming governor of Minnesota. Nearly 2,500 people braved the bitter cold—the temperature never reached zero that day—to attend an inaugural event that mixed elements of a pep rally, a carnival, and a solemn ceremony. To celebrate, he planned two weeks of events called "Voice of the People: Jesse Inauguration '99." These included a coffee break with Ford auto workers, a family fitness event with exercises led by Ventura, and a potluck lunch on a farm, where supporters were encouraged to bring a hot dish.

Typically, a governor's inaugural events would also include a formal evening event. But according to Ventura's wife Terry, "we did not want it to be a traditional, formal ball because we are not traditional, formal people." So they planned a party more to their taste, selling out the 14,000 tickets priced $10 to $20. The suggested attire for the "People's Ball," according to Terry: "Tux, tennis shoes, biker leather, whatever you feel comfortable wearing." They hosted a rock and roll party featuring

Governor Jesse Ventura presenting his first State of the State address to a joint session of the legislature, March 2, 1999, at the State Capitol in St. Paul

Jonny Lang, Warren Zevon, America, Delbert McClinton, Dave Pirner from Soul Asylum, and the Minnesota Vikings cheerleaders. According to *Rolling Stone* magazine, "This is what the 38th governor of the state of Minnesota wears to his soiree: black jeans, a T-shirt bearing a likeness of Jimi Hendrix, a buckskin jacket, pink sunglasses, and cowboy boots. He also knows how to accessorize: Silver skull and hoop earrings dangle from each ear. His wife, Terry, is dressed like a heavy-metal babe in a black suede miniskirt and a leather jacket, with black knee-high boots."

Since then, Ventura's time in office has been a mix of government business and controversy. He has appointed officials to serve as department heads throughout the state government, and he created and submitted a two-year state budget to the legislature. But he also went on the David Letterman show and made some jokes about the city of St. Paul and about the Irish that some people found offensive. He took out a permit for a concealed weapon and he suggested that his wife should be paid to be first lady, both of which caused some concern. He also got into a bit of a shouting match with some demonstrating college students at the state capitol, when he reproached them for seeking government aid for school. He also criticized single parents, saying "I don't want to sound hard core, but why did you become a single parent? Is it government's job to make up for someone's mistakes?" With comments like that, Ventura is sure to remain in the news throughout his term in office.

HOBBIES AND OTHER INTERESTS

Ventura and his family will be splitting their time between the governor's mansion, where they'll spend the week, and their 32-acre horse ranch outside the city, where they'll spend the weekends. In his free time, he enjoys riding his five waverunners, swimming, running, golf, and reading books about Navy SEALs and mystery stories. His favorite TV show is the soap opera "The Young and the Restless," his favorite movies are *Jaws, JFK,* and *Full Metal Jacket,* and his favorite foods are pizza, apple pie, and rigatoni. His hero is the boxer Muhammad Ali. He does charity work for the Make-a-Wish Foundation, which grants wishes to terminally ill children.

MAJOR INFLUENCES

Ventura has mentioned two people whom he admires and who have had an influence on his career. One is the wrestler Hulk Hogan. As wrestlers they were rivals, and in keeping with his wrestling persona, Ventura never said anything positive about him on the air. But in a subsequent interview he said this. "He's been the greatest champion in wrestling history. Hogan is synonymous with wrestling, and I'm happy for his success. . . . Many of us have ridden his coattails all the way to the bank."

Ventura also respects Arnold Schwarzenegger, whom he worked with in *Predator, Running Man,* and *Batman and Robin* and who taught him how to deal with Hollywood. "Arnold's my mentor; when I have a question about Hollywood, I go see Arnold. He's never lied to me, never. His honesty is impeccable, and in today's Hollywood, that's a rarity. And Arnold never forgets his friends."

CREDITS

Predator, 1987
The Running Man, 1987
Thunderground, 1989
Repossessed, 1990
Boxcar Blues, 1990
Abraxas: Guardian of the Universe, 1990

Ricochet, 1991
"The Grudge Match,"1991-92 (TV series)
Batman and Robin, 1997

FURTHER READING

Books

Dockery, Kevin, and Bill Fawcett, eds. *The Teams: An Oral History of the U.S. Navy SEALs*, 1998

Periodicals

Christian Science Monitor, Nov. 5, 1998, pp.1, 18; Nov. 6, 1998, p.1
New York Times, Oct. 31, 1998, p.A.10; Nov. 5, 1998, p.A1; Nov. 8, 1998, Section 4, p.4
Newsweek, Nov. 16, 1998, p.38; Feb. 15, 1999, p.30
People, May 24, 1982, p.85; Jan. 18, 1999, p.50
St. Paul Pioneer Press, July 19, 1998, p.A1; Nov. 8, 1998, p.A1; Jan. 3, 1999, p.A1
Time, Nov. 2, 1998, p.50; Nov. 16, 1998, pp.54 and 56; Jan. 18, 1999, p.38
Washington Post, Nov. 4, 1998, p.A1; Nov. 5, 1998, p.A.41; Jan. 5, 1999, p.A2

ADDRESS

Office of the Governor
130 State Capitol
75 Constitution Avenue
Saint Paul, MN 55155

WORLD WIDE WEB SITES

www.mainserver.state.mn.us/governor/about_the_governor.html
www.mainserver.state.mn.us/governor/for_kids_only.html
www.nga.org/Governor/Gov/Minnesota.asp
www.kfan.com/jesse/html
www2.startribune.com/stonline/html/jesse/

Venus Williams 1980-
American Professional Tennis Player

BIRTH

Venus Ebonistarr Williams was born on June 17, 1980, in Lynwood, California. She grew up, though, in Compton, a poor, predominantly black area of Los Angeles that suffers from high levels of crime and drug abuse. Her parents are Richard, owner of a private security company, and Ora-cene—who usually goes by the nickname "Brandi"—who was a nurse. Venus is the fourth of five daughters in the family. All three of her older sisters (Yetunde, Isha, and Lyndrea) are studying for professional careers in law or medicine. Her youngest sister, Serena, is a fellow member of the women's professional tennis tour.

YOUTH

Tennis has been a big part of Williams's life ever since she was a little girl. Her involvement in the game was due directly to the influence of her father, who decided to teach all his daughters how to play the game after watching the winner of a women's tournament receive a $48,000 check on television. Determined to instruct the girls himself, Richard Williams educated himself about the game by reading countless tennis magazines and studying dozens of instructional videos.

Richard Williams gave Venus her first tennis lesson more than a year before she entered first grade. "I was four and a half when I first picked up a racket," she recalled. "My sisters and I would each take turns hitting with my mom and dad. My entire family played almost every day." But whereas her oldest sisters never developed a deep love for the sport, Venus enjoyed every minute out on the court. She recalled that she would cry if her father did not allow her to hit every one of the 500 or so balls that he pushed around in a rusty shopping cart.

Learning to Play in Compton

During her elementary school years, Venus and her younger sister Serena spent hours and hours practicing their serves and backhands on neighborhood tennis courts under the watchful eye of their father. But unlike many other children, who learn how to play tennis on well-maintained courts at country clubs and nice school facilities, the Williams sisters learned how to play on the cracked and trash-strewn courts of their Compton neighborhood. Even though the Compton parks were often populated with street gang members and other shady characters, Richard Williams defiantly marched his daughters out to the park's tennis courts nearly every day.

The setting in which Venus and her sister learned to play, then, was occasionally dangerous. Williams recalled that when she was eight or nine years old, gunshots rang out across the park in which they were playing. The frightened girls dove to the ground, for they knew that street gang violence was an unfortunate reality in their neighborhood. But as time passed, Compton's street gangs began to leave them alone, and Venus and Serena were usually able to practice in relative peace.

By the time that Venus was ten years old, her father was regularly entering her in state tennis tournaments. Once in a while, she even found herself pitted against her sister Serena in a tournament. "The first time they ever played each other was in a tournament in Indian Wells, when we were living in California," recalled their mother. "Serena wasn't supposed to be in it, but she entered herself, filled out all the forms and everything. She was eight years old. She said she was in the tournament, and I said, 'No, you're not,' and she told me to check with the organizers. There she was, entered. Serena wound up losing to Venus in the final."

Indeed, Venus proved to be a seemingly invincible opponent in the junior tournaments that she entered. By age 12, Venus had compiled a 63-0 record in U.S. Tennis Association tournaments throughout southern California. Her performance caught the attention of many tennis experts, who marveled at her talent and sheer athletic ability. Certainly, Venus was becoming a terrific all-around athlete. For example, she was also a star track and field performer. Over the course of a couple years she went undefeated in 19 track meets as both a sprinter and a middle-distance runner.

> "I was four and a half when I first picked up a racket," she recalled. "My sisters and I would each take turns hitting with my mom and dad. My entire family played almost every day."

But as Williams added to her tournament championship total with each passing month, her father became alarmed at the sometimes overwhelming attention that she received. People started asking her for her autograph, and sports agents and sporting goods manufacturers were always approaching her. Richard Williams decided to cut both Venus and Serena off from these distractions by placing himself squarely between his daughters and the outside world. This arrangement stayed firmly in place for the next several years.

Instruction in Florida

By the early 1990s, Venus was regarded as an exciting young talent who had the potential to be a big star. In addition, members of the tennis establishment recognized that if she was successful, she might inspire many other black youths to give the white-dominated sport a try.

Around this time, Richard Williams decided that both of his daughters needed to receive professional coaching in order to continue to improve their games. He was very proud of his role in teaching tennis fundamentals to both Venus and Serena, but he recognized that there were other people who could teach them more. One of the first coaches that Venus's father contacted was noted tennis instructor Rick Macci, who had coached a number of star players over the years. Macci agreed to meet Venus, but initially he was unimpressed. "We started working out, doing some drills, and after about an hour, I thought I was wasting my time," Macci remembered. "Then Venus asks to go to the bathroom and as she walked out the gate, she walks at least 10 yards on her hands. I was stunned. Then she went into these backward cartwheels for another 10 yards. I'm watching this and the first thing I thought was: 'I've got a female Michael Jordan on my hands.'"

Macci agreed to coach both Venus and Serena, and within a matter of weeks he realized that both girls were loaded with talent. "I've seen a lot of good young kids all over the world, but it didn't stick with me that Venus and Serena were superstars until we got into competitive drills," he said. "It's scary the way they play against each other. No sister love or any of that. It's more like a street fight. Almost dangerous."

Both Venus and Serena Williams trained at Macci's Florida tennis academy from 1991 to 1995, except for a three-month stint at another tennis clinic in Florida. Since Macci's facility was across the country from their California home, their parents moved the family to the Florida community of Palm Beach Gardens. Their daughters' upbringing there was unusual in some ways—they were taught at home by their mother for several years, and they spent long hours honing their games—but in other respects, they were normal kids. They were given the same household chores that many other children have, and their parents encouraged them to pursue other interests and hobbies outside of tennis. "Venus and Serena are tough kids, but they are also incredibly polite and incredibly appreciative, and that's a tribute to the way Richard has raised them," said Macci.

For her part, Venus did not seem bothered by the fact that she did not always attend school with other children her age. "I never really had a lot of friends, so I don't miss out on *not* having them," said Williams. "Serena and I pretty much hang out together."

EDUCATION

Williams received home schooling for several years from her mother, who has college degrees in both education and nursing. Venus then enrolled in a private high school near the family's home in Palm Beach Gardens for her last couple years of high school. After graduating in 1997, she started taking classes at Palm Beach Community College. "Science is my favorite subject," said Williams. "Can you believe that in 1923 explorers found a prehistoric fish off the coast of Madagascar that was supposed to be extinct, like, 500 million years ago? Learning about that stuff is so cool."

Richard Williams has expressed pride that his daughters recognize the importance of knowledge in building a rich and fulfilling life. "I've told the girls they aren't leaving education behind for tennis," he said. "And I don't necessarily mean school education. Venus has gotten straight A's. Graduating from high school at 16 will be a piece of cake. But she's not in school just to learn, she's there to socialize and meet people. We've taught them at home, too. Finances, investments. My girls can tell you how to buy a home out of foreclosure. They need to learn these things. . . . So many times you see a great athlete at the end of the career, and they're sitting around saying, 'Look who I once was.' They're just a bunch of damn fools with nothing to fall back on. You don't hear a good answer when you ask, 'What are you today?'"

CAREER HIGHLIGHTS

During the early and mid-1990s Williams did not play in many tournaments, and she retained her amateur status. Richard Williams decided to keep Venus out of tournament play until she was older. This was partly based on race, he says. "When a white girl lost to my daughter, the parents would say, 'You let me down. How could you let that little nigger beat you?' I didn't want my kids growing up around that." Still, his decision was criticized by some members of the tennis community. They argued that she would never improve her game beyond a certain point if she did not play top-level players in a competitive atmosphere. Some even suggested that her father, who had gradually become known in tennis circles as a very opinionated and sometimes boastful man, was doing permanent damage to her career.

But many other tennis observers came to the defense of Richard Williams. They charged that some of the critics were motivated solely by the knowledge that the presence of Venus—a tall black girl who wore dazzling cornrows with multi-colored beads in her hair—would increase interest in the sport. Other people pointed out that several other teenage tennis stars of previous years had struggled to deal with the fame and pressure that came with a professional career. They said that Richard and Brandi Williams were simply doing their best to make sure that their daughters' careers did not unfold in the same way that former teen sensation Jennifer Capriati's had. Back in the early 1990s, a 14-year-old Capriati had charmed the tennis world with her talent and bubbly enthusiasm. But within a few years, the pressures of the professional tour had trans-

formed her into a deeply unhappy teenager whose career went into a tailspin after she was arrested for drug possession.

Richard Williams agreed that the memory of Capriati's sad decline was a major reason why he was bringing both Venus and Serena along slowly. "[Capriati] was a great kid at 14," he said. "At 15, she lost her smile. At 16, there were problems." For her part, Venus seemed to recognize that it was dangerous for her to attach too much meaning to the sport. "I just try to remember that tennis isn't the most important thing happening," she stated. "It can get larger than life. It's more of a job and a chore then. I try to keep it fun."

Venus Turns Pro

On October 31, 1994, Venus's long awaited debut as a professional tennis player finally took place. She entered the Bank of the West Classic in Oakland, California. In her very first match she faced Shaun Stafford, who was the 59th ranked women's player in the world. But if Williams was nervous, she didn't show it, because she beat her first pro opponent with a 6-3, 6-4 straight set victory. In women's tennis, a player wins a match by defeating her opponent in 2 out of 3 sets, while men must win

3 of 5 sets. The first player to win 6 games usually wins the set, but if their margin of victory is less than 2 games, the set is decided by a tie-breaker. Shorthand notation is often used to show the score of a tennis match. For example, 6-2, 4-6, 7-6 means that the player in question won the first set by a score of 6 games to 2, lost the next set 4 games to 6, and came back to win the match in a third-set tie-breaker.

> Tennis instructor Rick Macci agreed to meet Venus, but initially he was unimpressed. "We started working out, doing some drills, and after about an hour, I thought I was wasting my time. Then Venus asks to go to the bathroom and as she walked out the gate, she walks at least 10 yards on her hands. I was stunned. Then she went into these backward cartwheels for another 10 yards. I'm watching this and the first thing I thought was: 'I've got a female Michael Jordan on my hands.'"

"For her to be that good at 14 is awesome," Stafford said after the match. Williams's next opponent in the tournament was Arantxa Sanchez Vicario, who was ranked number two in the entire world. Many experts predicted that Sanchez Vicario would destroy her inexperienced opponent. But instead, Williams shocked both her foe and the stadium audience by winning the first set 6-3 and taking a 3-0 lead in the second set. Sanchez Vicario rallied to win the second set and went on to knock Williams out of the tournament, but the youngster's strong showing convinced many skeptics that her future was a very bright one.

In 1995, Richard Williams resumed coaching his daughters. Over the next two years, Venus only appeared in a few tournaments. But even though she did not win any of the tournaments that she entered, Reebok was so convinced that she was a future superstar that they signed her to a five-year, multimillion-dollar contract in 1995.

Williams made her first big splash in the world of professional tennis in the fall of 1997. She had an incredible season, moving up from No. 211 to No. 22 in the world rankings and advancing to the singles finals of the U.S. Open. The U.S. Open is one of the prestigious events that make up the "Grand Slam" of tennis, along with the French Open, Australian Open, and Wimbledon. Williams was the first unseeded player ever to reach the finals.

Prior to the tournament, Williams had not reached one final and only had a 10-9 record for the season. And she playfully announced before the tournament that her only goal for the competition was a very modest one: "My goal for this tournament is when I play my matches, for not one bead to fall out of my hair." But other observers noted that Williams actually entered the tournament with a lot of confidence. "She acted as if she were already the brashest of champions, predicting that she and her 15-year-old sister, Serena, would soon be battling it out for No. 1," wrote S. L. Price in *Sports Illustrated.*

Controversy at the U.S. Open

As the U.S. Open progressed, it became clear that the tall, athletic Williams was going to be a force to be reckoned with. Her booming serve, incredible power, muscular athleticism, and intimidating style overwhelmed many of her opponents, and she used her size, strength, and speed to tremendous advantage. Williams defeated Irina Spirlea in the semifinals to advance to the tournament final and gain the right to face top-ranked Martina Hingis. It was an astounding achievement for Williams to have made it so far in her first full year of professional play.

Unfortunately, an incident that took place during her match with Spirlea overshadowed her athletic performance. During a changeover late in their semifinal match, the two players collided with one another. Each player blamed the other for the incident, and Spirlea blasted Venus in a post-match interview as a smug and arrogant teenager. Richard Williams felt that the incident with Spirlea, who is white, could be traced to racism. He charged that his entire family had been victimized by racism in the tennis community over the years. But he then resorted to racial name calling of his own, calling Spirlea "a big, ugly, tall, white turkey."

Venus tried to ignore the whole controversy. "I've never been a person who is scared, fearful," she said. "I can't let that hold me back. I won't. This is a chance of a lifetime, the tournament of a lifetime. I wouldn't be angry if I didn't win. But I won't go out there and be afraid, because fear holds you back. I won't let it happen." Williams marched out to face Hingis with her usual determination, but her dramatic charge to the championship fell short. Hingis easily defeated Williams by a 6-0, 6-4 score to claim the U.S. Open title for her own.

At a press conference after the tournament, Williams was peppered with questions about her father's statements and her relations with white players on the tour. The whole tone of the media interrogation upset her, although she kept her poise. "I think this is definitely ruining the mood, these questions about racism," she finally told the reporters in exasperation.

Recent Events

As the beginning of the 1998 season approached, many members of the tennis community wondered if Williams would be able to duplicate her U.S. Open success. She responded by defeating Hingis in January 1998 to make it to the finals of the Adidas International in Sidney, Australia. Later that month, she won the mixed doubles event at the Australian Open, and advanced all the way to the women's singles final in that tournament before losing to Arantxa Sanchez Vicario.

Pointing to her fine performances in late 1997 and early 1998, many tennis fans thought that it was only a matter of time until Williams won her first singles tournament. "I think she's the best athlete the women's game has seen so far," said tennis star Andre Agassi. "Now it's a matter of how she puts it all together. She's going to beat 99 percent of the girls because of the athlete she is."

In early March 1998 Williams finally triumphed in a finals showdown. She beat number-two-seeded Lindsay Davenport to win her first professional singles title at the IGA Tennis Classic in Oklahoma City. In addition, she and her sister won the women's doubles event at the same tournament later that same day. Then, less than a month later, Venus defeated Anna Kournikova in the prestigious Lipton Championships final to take her second career title. During that tournament she unleashed serves of up to 122 miles per hour, the second fastest in the history of women's tennis.

"I just try to remember that tennis isn't the most important thing happening," she stated. *"It can get larger than life. It's more of a job and a chore then. I try to keep it fun."*

By winning the Lipton tournament, Williams served notice to the other players on the tour that she was a threat to win every tourney she entered. She completed her season by turning in an impressive win in the singles competition of the first German Open in October 1998. She beat Patty Schnyder of Switzerland 6-2, 3-6, 6-2 to earn the grand prize of $800,000. Following the German Open, though, she suffered from tendinitis in her left knee. In November she had to withdraw from the year-end Chase Championships in New York due to knee problems.

Williams's outstanding playing ability has sometimes been overshadowed by debate about the way that she and her family act. Her outspoken father remains a controversial figure in the tennis community for his provocative comments about other players, tour officials, racial issues, and his daughters' abilities. In addition, Venus has been criticized by some other players on the tour as a snob. Some opponents have charged that she is unfriendly and that she sometimes tries to intimidate other players.

Williams does not seem bothered by the criticism. "When I want to smile, I'll smile," she said. "If I don't want to, I'm not going to. I think it's a little bit peevish. Smiling—what does that have to do with anything?" Many other members of the tennis community agree. In fact, a number of players and commentators have charged that the young star is being criticized unfairly. Many feel that attacks on the Williams family are due to underlying racism in the predominately white sport. "The whole thing gets me upset," said former tennis star Pam Shriver. "What do people expect from a 17-year-old playing her first full year on tour? It took me a couple of years before I really felt accepted. Chrissie (Evert) and Tracy (Austin), when they had their game faces on, they were not approachable." Shriver also points out that the Williams family has been consistent in their priorities. "They've said time and again that their priorities are family, religion, and education. People thought it was lip service, but it isn't. Richard has been absolutely determined on those subjects. It's just that they've done it in an untraditional way." Other members of the world tennis community have pointed out that both Venus and Serena are known for being courteous to officials and reporters. "They've been doing something very, very right as a family, and I give Richard and Brandi a lot of credit for that," said WTA Tour chief executive officer Bart McGuire. "The Williams sisters are a huge plus for the tour off the court as well as on."

HOBBIES AND OTHER INTERESTS

Williams has a wide variety of other interests in addition to tennis. She enjoys playing guitar, surfing, rollerblading, playing basketball, and exploring the Internet. She has also taken tae kwon do lessons for several years, and loves to play with her three dogs. Finally, she and Serena are known for conducting tennis clinics in inner city neighborhoods in order to encourage other gifted young players from urban areas.

HOME AND FAMILY

Williams lives in a home on ten acres of land in Palm Beach Gardens, Florida, with her parents and her sister Serena.

HONORS AND AWARDS

U.S. Fed Cup Team: 1995
Most Impressive Newcomer (COREL Women's Tennis Association Tour): 1997
U.S. Olympic Committee Female Athlete of the Month: September 1997
10 Most Exciting Athletes to Watch List (*Sport* magazine): 1997
Lipton Championship, Women's Singles: 1998
German Open, Women's Singles: 1998

FURTHER READING

Books

Encyclopedia of Women and Sports, 1996
Who's Who Among African Americans, 1998-1999

Periodicals

Business Week, Sep. 29, 1997, p.140
Ebony, May 1995, p.68; Nov. 1997, p.42; Aug. 1998, p.38
Emerge, June 1997, p.64
Essence, Aug. 1998, p.78
Jet, Sep. 29, 1997, p.49
New York Times, Nov. 1, 1994, p.B10; Sep. 7, 1997, p.1(N); Sep. 14, 1997,
    p.28(N); Nov. 11, 1997, p.C28
New York Times Magazine, Mar. 16, 1997, p.28; Sep. 8, 1998, p.
Newsweek, Sep. 12, 1994, p.70; Dec. 26, 1994, p.114; Aug. 24, 1998, p.44
People, Nov. 21, 1994, p.162; Oct. 27, 1997, p.103; Dec. 29, 1997, p.134
Seventeen, Apr. 1996, p.54; July 1998, p.60
Sport, Jan. 1998, p.68; July 1998, p.70
Sports Illustrated, June 10, 1991, p.46; June 13, 1994, p.10; Oct. 17, 1994,
    p.22; Nov. 14, 1994, p.30; May 29, 1995, p.18; Sep. 15, 1997, p.32; Nov.
    17, 1997, p.31; Feb. 2, 1998, p.66; Apr. 6, 1998, p.64; May 11, 1998, p.22
Sports Illustrated for Kids, Jan. 1995, p.12; Aug. 1998, p.34
Teen People, May 1998, p.104
Tennis, Oct. 1992, p.38; Aug. 1993, p.46; Aug. 1994, p.26; Jan. 1995, p.112;
    Aug. 1995, p.68; Feb. 1997, p.31; June 1997, p.14; July 1997, p.46; Nov.
    1997, p.109; Mar. 1998, p.22; Sep. 1998, p.65
USA Today, Sep. 4, 1997, p.C1; Apr. 3, 1998, p.C13
Vogue, May 1998, p.270
Women's Sport and Fitness, Nov.-Dec. 1998, p.102

ADDRESS

Women's Tennis Association
133 First St., NE
St. Petersburg, FL 33701

WORLD WIDE WEB SITES

http://www.corelwtatour.com

Photo and Illustration Credits

Ben Affleck/Photos: CORBIS/AFP; CORBIS/Nubar Alexanian; AP/Wide World Photos; Frank Masi; Lauire Sparham.

Jennifer Aniston/Photos: Jon Ragel. Copyright © NBC, Inc.; Copyright © 1998-1999 Warner Bros.

Maurice Ashley/Photos: Librado Romero/NYT Pictures; AP/Wide World Photos.

Kobe Bryant/Photos: AP/Wide World Photos.

Sadie and Bessie Delany/Photos: Brian Douglas; Sadie Delany, 1889-1999, was the first African-American to teach domestic science on the high school level in the New York City public schools. Dr. Bessie Delany, 1891-1995, was the second African-American woman licensed to practice dentistry in New York State. The two sisters became famous after the age of 100 with the publication of *Having Our Say: The Delany Sisters' First 100 Years*, with the journalist Amy Hill Hearth; AP/Wide World Photos.

Sharon Draper/Photo: Sterling Roberts. Covers: FORGED BY FIRE copyright © 1997 by Sharon M. Draper and TEARS OF A TIGER copyright © 1994 by Sharon M. Draper, both Atheneum Books for Young Readers, an imprint of Simon & Schuster Children's Publishing Division.

Sarah Michelle Gellar/Photos: Frank Ockenfels; Kimberly Wright.

John Glenn/Photos: NASA; AP/Wide World Photos; AP/Wide World Photos; NASA; NASA; AP/Wide World Photos.

Savion Glover/Photos: Copyright © Kimberly Butler; Copyright © 1991 CTW. Sesame Street Muppets copyright © 1991 Henson. Photo by Richard Termine; Hassan Kinley; Copyright © Kimberly Butler.

Jeff Gordon/Photos: NASCAR; AP/Wide World Photos.

Dave Hampton/Photos: People Weekly copyright © 1998. Photo by Steve Labadessa; Tiger Electronics.

Lauryn Hill/Photos: Warren Du Preez; CORBIS/Dyane Leight; Cover: Courtesy of Columbia/Ruffhouse; AP/Wide World Photos.

King Hussein/Photos: AP/Wide World Photos. Map: NYT Graphics.

Lynn Johnston/Cartoons: Reprinted by permission of United Feature Syndicate.

Shari Lewis/Photos: CORBIS/Jim Spellman; UPI/Corbis-Bettmann; AP/Wide World Photos; Deb Halberstadt.

Oseola McCarty/Photo: Copyright © Steve Coleman. Cover: Longstreet Press.

Mark McGwire/Photos: AP/Wide World Photos.

Slobodan Milosevic/Photos: AP/Wide World Photos. Map: NYT Graphics.

Natalie Portman/Photos: AP/Wide World Photos; Copyright © Lucasfilm Ltd. & TM.

J.K. Rowling/Covers: HARRY POTTER AND THE SORCERER'S STONE jacket art copyright © 1998 by Mary GrandPré. Jacket design by Mary GrandPré and David Saylor; HARRY POTTER AND THE CHAMBER OF SECRETS and HARRY POTTER AND THE PRISONER OF AZKA-BAN jacket art copyright © 1999 by Mary GrandPré. Jacket design by Mary GrandPré and David Saylor.

Frank Sinatra/Photos: Reuters/Corbis-Bettman; AP/Wide World Photos; Ward, Baldwin/Corbis-Bettmann (*From Here to Eternity*); AP/Wide World Photos.

Gene Siskel/Photos: Bob Koyton; AP/Wide World Photos.

Sammy Sosa/Photos: Copyright © 1996 Chicago Cubs/Stephen Green; AP/Wide World Photos; Ronald C. Modra/*Sports Illustrated*.

John Stanford/Photos: Reprinted with permission, Seattle Post-Intelligencer.

Shania Twain/Photo: FMH/Barry Hollywood.

Mitsuko Uchida/Photos: Justin Pumfrey; Chris Lee.

Jesse Ventura/Photos: AP/Wide World Photos.

Venus Williams/Photos: COREL WTA TOUR; AP/Wide World Photos.

Appendix

This Appendix contains updates for selected individuals profiled in previous volumes of the regular series and the special subject series of *Biography Today*.

* TIM ALLEN *

After eight years as a top-rated show, Tim Allen's television comedy *Home Improvement* finished its run in May 1999. Allen decided to retire the show while it was still popular, before the series got stale. "It's been tougher to get the stories we want," said Allen. "There aren't as many young kids in the show, so some of the cuteness has gone out of it, and the contrast between adult issues and kids' point of view is gone." The final show of the series included flashbacks to the earliest days of the series, and *Home Improvement's* many fans tuned in one last time to enjoy the antics of Tim Taylor and his family and friends.

Allen and his wife, Laura Diebel, have started a new project, Tim Allen Signature Tools and project kits. Allen's tools, which he designed himself, are high quality precision tools and include drills, jigsaws, sanders, utility knives, screwdrivers, and hammers. His project kits are designed to help parents and kids work together to build household items, including a birdhouse, bird feeder, clock, toolbox, and treasure chest. All profits from the company go to charities, especially those benefitting children, as well as food banks, homeless shelters, the YMCA, and the Red Cross. Allen and Diebel have also funded the Target House in Memphis, a facility for the families of sick children who are receiving treatment in nearby hospitals. "Mostly I like challenges," Allen said of his new endeavors. "And it's a challenge to do a new business that everyone benefits from."

* BENAZIR BHUTTO *

Benazir Bhutto, the former Prime Minister of Pakistan, and her husband, Asif Ali Zardari, were convicted of corruption and sentenced to jail in April 1999. Bhutto was out of the country when the Pakistani court made its decision. She and Zardari were found guilty of accepting $9 million in kickbacks from foreign firms doing business in Pakistan. They were sentenced to five years in prison and a fine of $8.6 million. They are also banned from running for office again. Bhutto claims she and her husband, who is already in jail serving time for another sentence, are innocent. She charges that they are the victims of political enemies who want to ruin them and their reputations. Their case is currently being appealed.

* BILL CLINTON *

In December 1998, Bill Clinton became the second president in history to be impeached by the House of Representatives. The articles of impeachment, drawn up by the House Judiciary Committee, accused Clinton of perjury and obstruction of justice in charges arising from the Monica Lewinsky scandal. The Committee charged that Clinton had committed perjury in his testimony before the grand jury and had encouraged Lewinsky to lie to prosecutors to cover up their sexual relationship. According to the House Judiciary Committee, these actions warranted impeachment because they were "high crimes and misdemeanors," the grounds for impeachment outlined in the U.S. Constitution. The House voted on December 19 on the two separate counts to impeach Clinton. In the first vote, for perjury, 228 representatives voted for and 206 voted against impeachment. In the second count, obstruction of justice, 221 voted for and 212 voted against impeachment. The debate was characterized by partisanship on both sides. Throughout the proceedings, the votes split along party lines, with the Republicans voting for and the Democrats voting against impeachment.

As outlined in the Constitution, if the House votes to impeach, the president then faces a trial in the Senate on the charges outlined in the House's articles of impeachment. If the Senate finds the president guilty, he must leave office. On January 7, Bill Clinton's impeachment trial opened in the Senate. The Judiciary Committee members, known as the House Managers, presented their case against Clinton. Next, the White House lawyers presented the defense for the president. The Senate then debated the issues, and after five weeks, on February 12, 1999, the Senate voted on two counts brought against Clinton in the trial, one for perjury, and one for obstruction of justice. A two-thirds majority is necessary for conviction in the trial of a president. On the charge of perjury, 45 senators found him guilty, and 55 not guilty. On the charge of obstruction of justice, 50 senators voted for a guilty verdict, and 50 voted not guilty. Clinton was cleared of all charges.

The American public had consistently said in polls that they did not believe that Clinton's actions warranted impeachment, and were, in general, relieved by the verdict.

In the spring of 1999, Clinton authorized the use of U.S. air forces to aid the ethnic Albanian population of the Kosovar section of Serbia. As part of a NATO effort to protect the Kosovar Albanians, the U.S. led the offensive against Slobodan Milosevic, the president of Yugoslavia, whose forces were systematically trying to expel the Albanians from their homeland. (For more information on Milosevic see his entry in this volume of *Biography Today*.) U.S. involvement in the Yugoslav fighting was controversial, with some Americans favoring aid and forces in the region, and some not.

As Clinton embarks on his last year in office, he is concerned with the legacy he leaves, as well as with the upcoming elections in 2000, in which he hopes that his Vice President, Al Gore, will succeed him. It is also possible that his wife, Hillary Rodham Clinton, will run for the Senate for the state of New York, and the Clintons have bought a home in that state.

* HILLARY RODHAM CLINTON *

In the spring of 1999, Hillary Rodham Clinton announced that she would begin a "listening tour" of New York, with the possibility that she might run for the Senate from that state in 2000. If she does indeed decide to run as the Democratic candidate for the Senate from New York, her Republican opponent will most likely be Rudolph Giuliani, currently the mayor of New York City. In September 1999, Bill and Hillary Clinton bought a house in Chappaqua, north of New York City, where they will live after Clinton leaves the presidency in January 2001. The purchase fueled even more speculation that Hillary Clinton will formerly announce her candidacy soon.

* ELIZABETH DOLE *

In January 1999, Elizabeth Dole left her job as head of the American Red Cross to run for the Republican nomination for president. She is considered to be the first viable female candidate to run for president in U.S. history. Her campaign got off to a good start, but as of fall 1999, she was running a distant second in polls to George W. Bush, the son of former President George Bush. She was also far behind Bush in fundraising. Dole's agenda included improving the quality of public schools, fighting drugs, and building up America's nuclear defense system.

On October 20, 1999, Dole withdrew from the race for the nomination. She said she simply could not raise money fast enough to continue. "I've learned that the current political calendar and election laws favor those who get an early start and can tap into huge private fortunes or who have a pre-existing network of political supporters," she said. Of her two main rivals for the nomination she said, "Steve Forbes has unlimited resources. Governor Bush has raised over $60 million and has about $40 million on hand. . . . It would be futile to continue." At this point, she has not declared her support for either Bush or Forbes, and she would not discuss the possibility that she might be offered the Vice Presidential spot on the Republican ticket in 2000.

* JOE DUMARS *

After 14 years as a star forward for the Detroit Pistons, Joe Dumars retired from basketball on May 16, 1999. In his 14 seasons, Dumars was one of the most productive, and admired, men in the game. He twice led the team to NBA championships, in 1989 and 1990, and was named the MVP of the 1989 finals. The six-time All-Star scored more than 16,000 career points for the Pistons. Even though he retired as a player, Dumars will still help out with the Pistons' organization. As vice president of player personnel, he will advise the team on draft picks.

Dumars is also developing his business interests. In 1996, he founded Detroit Technologies, Inc., a company that manufactures automotive parts. He is also actively involved with children's charities. An avid tennis player, Dumars sponsors a celebrity tennis tournament that has raised more than $625,000 over the past few years to benefit children's charities.

* JOHN ELWAY *

John Elway, who played for 16 years with the Denver Broncos and led the team to two Super Bowl victories in 1998 and 1999, retired from the sport in May 1999. Although Elway had played brilliant football in has last years, injuries and age caught up with him, and he decided to leave the active roster. Always known as a quarterback who could muster his team late in the game, Elway engineered 47 fourth-quarter comebacks for the Broncos. His final Super Bowl performance won him the MVP honors for the game. But Elway may not be done with the game. In September 1999, he announced that he may become the president of a new NFL team in Los Angeles.

* NEWT GINGRICH *

Much to the surprise of his political friends and foes, Newt Gingrich retired from the House of Representatives in January 1999, following heavy losses for the Republicans in the November federal elections. Gingrich had wagered that the American people would be so disillusioned with the Democrats because of the Monica Lewinsky scandal that the Republicans could win a strong majority in the House and the Senate. When Gingrich's strategy backfired and the Democrats won a number of key races, Gingrich realized that his leadership was in jeopardy. In November, he stepped down from the post of Speaker, and in January he retired from the House altogether. The move surprised many, for the House was just about to begin the impeachment process of Clinton, who had long been a political enemy of Gingrich. Now a fellow at the American Enterprise Institute, a conservative think tank in Washington, D.C., Gingrich has begun a new consulting firm, whose purpose is to "help corporations shape their strategic visions years into the future."

* AL GORE *

After seven years as Vice President, Al Gore has decided to run for the presidency. He declared his candidacy in his home state of Tennessee in June 1999, and hopes to win the nomination from the Democratic Party in the summer of 2000. In announcing his candidacy, Gore said he would "take my own values of faith and family to the presidency." Gore had long been thought the favorite to win the nomination, but recent polls show his lead cut by challenger Bill Bradley, the former senator from New Jersey.

* WAYNE GRETZKY *

After 14 outstanding seasons in the NHL, Wayne Gretzky retired from hockey in April 1999. "The Great One" is acknowledged as the finest player the sport has ever known. *Biography Today* will publish a full retrospective of his career in 2000.

* KING HASSAN II *

King Hassan II, the ruler of Morocco for the past 38 years, died on July 23, 1999, of a heart attack at the age of 70. He was considered a moderate in the frequently turbulent world of Middle East politics, and he openly worked for peace with Israel. He was remembered by President Clinton, who said that Hassan "worked to break down barriers among the peoples of the Middle East, bravely opening a dialogue with Israel . . . seeking greater tolerance and stability in the region." Hassan was succeeded by his son, Mohammed VI.

* MICHAEL JORDAN *

Michael Jordan, considered to be the greatest basketball player that ever lived, retired from the sport in 1999. *Biography Today* will publish a full retrospective of Jordan's career in 2000.

* OSEOLA MCCARTY *

Oseola McCarty, a washerwoman who used her life savings to provide scholarships for needy students, died of cancer on September 27, 1999, at the age of 91. In 1995, the unassuming McCarty had come to the attention of people all over the world when she gave $150,000 to the University of Southern Mississippi for scholarships. She received accolades and honors she'd never dreamed of, nor sought. As something of a celebrity, she traveled the country for the first time in her life, and met the students she was able to help. So far, nine students have received scholarships, and three have graduated. One of the recipients, Stephanie Bullock, said this: "Heaven couldn't have gotten a better angel. She was an inspiration, a blessing, a treasure to the entire earth."

McCarty's selflessness moved people from all walks of life. Communications billionaire Ted Turner, after hearing of McCarty's gift, said, "If that woman can give away everything she has, then I can give a billion," and so endowed the United Nations with a gift of $1 billion.

* MARK MCGWIRE *

Mark McGwire of the St. Louis Cardinals was once again in the news in 1999 for another home run contest with his rival of last year, Sammy Sosa of the Chicago Bears. Once again hitting over 60 home runs in the regular season, McGwire went into the playoffs with 65 home runs, while Sosa had slugged 63.

* JULIUS NYERERE *

Julius Nyerere, the first president of Tanzania who led his nation from colonialism to self-rule, died of leukemia October 14, 1999, at the age of 77. He was remembered around the world as a ruler who championed independence for Africa. After being elected to the presidency in 1961, Nyerere was reelected three times, serving until 1985. Unlike many other African leaders of the mid-twentieth century, who rose to power though military might and maintained that power through force, Nyerere was known as an honorable man of peace and of principle. He stepped down voluntarily from the presidency in 1985, and continued to work for the betterment of his people. South African President Thabo Mbeki marked his death by saying, "It is a loss to the continent of Africa as a whole. He was one of the wise sons of Africa who guided our journey towards placing Africa in her rightful place in the world."

* DENNIS RODMAN *

The flamboyant Dennis Rodman was released from his contract with the Los Angeles Lakers in April 1999. The Lakers management found that he was a "distraction" to the team and its success. Since then, Rodman has appeared in movies and spent time on the professional wrestling circuit. "I'm just living my life the way I want to. I'm an entertainer," claimed Rodman. Still, he will be remembered for helping two teams, the Detroit Pistons and the Chicago Bulls, reach a total of five NBA championships, and he retires as perhaps the greatest rebounder of all time, leading the league in rebounds for seven consecutive seasons.

* BARRY SANDERS *

Top running back Barry Sanders, only yards shy of the all-time rushing record in professional football, abruptly retired from the sport on July 28, 1999, at the age of 31. His fellow players and the management of the Detroit Lions were stunned at the announcement, and Lions' fans were devastated. Many were particularly surprised by the timing of his decision, since Sanders was only 1,458 yards from becoming the all-time rushing leader in the NFL. After 10 seasons and 15,269 yards, Sanders claimed that "The reason I am retiring is simple. My desire to exit the game is greater than my desire to stay."

* SHEL SILVERSTEIN *

Shel Silverstein, one of the favorite children's poets of all time, died of a heart attack on May 10, 1999, at the age of 66. He was remembered for his funny, engaging verse that people of all ages enjoyed. Children's book critic Leonard Marcus called him the "troubadour king of American children's books." Of his ability to reach the kid in all of us, cartoonist Jules Feiffer said, "He imagined things the way kids do when they're little, and it goes away when they're older–only in his case it didn't go away."

* SAMMY SOSA *

As the regular baseball season drew to a close, Sammy Sosa of the Chicago Cubs and Mark McGwire of the St. Louis Cardinals were once again in a battle for the home run crown. Prior to the playoffs, Sosa had 63 home runs to his credit; McGwire had 65.

How to Use the
Cumulative Index

Our indexes have a new look. In an effort to make our indexes easier to use, we've combined the Name and General Index into a new, cumulative General Index. This single ready-reference resource covers all the volumes in *Biography Today*, both the general series and the special subject series. The new General Index contains complete listings of all individuals who have appeared in *Biography Today* since the series began. Their names appear in bold-faced type, followed by the issue in which they appear. The General Index also includes references for the occupations, nationalities, and ethnic and minority origins of individuals profiled in *Biography Today*.

We have also made some changes to our specialty indexes, the Places of Birth Index and the Birthday Index. To consolidate and to save space, the Places of Birth Index and the Birthday Index will no longer appear in the January and April issues of the softbound subscription series. But these indexes can still be found in the September issue of the softbound subscription series, in the hardbound Annual Cumulation at the end of each year, and in each volume of the special subject series.

General Series

The General Series of *Biography Today* is denoted in the index with the month and year of the issue in which the individual appeared. Each individual also appears in the Annual Cumulation for that year.

Special Subject Series

The Special Subject Series of *Biography Today* are each denoted in the index with an abbreviated form of the series name, plus the number of the volume in which the individual appears. They are listed as follows.

Adams, Ansel . . . . Artist V.1	(Artists Series)
Cushman, Karen . . . . Author V.5	(Authors Series)
Harris, Bernard . . . . Science V.3	(Scientists & Inventors Series)
Lobo, Rebecca . . . . Sport V.3	(Sports Series)
Peterson, Roger Tory . . . . WorLdr V.1	(World Leaders Series: Environmental Leaders)
Sadat, Anwar . . . . WorLdr V.2	(World Leaders Series: Modern African Leaders)

Updates

Updated information on selected individuals appears in the Appendix at the end of the *Biography Today* Annual Cumulation. In the index, the original entry is listed first, followed by any updates.

Arafat, Yasir . . Sep 94; Update 94; Update 95;
    Update 96; Update 97; Update 98
Gates, Bill . . . . Apr 93; Update 98
Griffith Joyner, Florence . . . . Sport V.1;
    Update 98 . . . .
Spock, Dr. Benjamin . . . . Sep 95; Update 98
Yeltsin, Boris . . . . Apr 92; Update 93;
    Update 95; Update 96; Update 98

General Index

This index includes names, occupations, nationalities, and ethnic and minority origins that pertain to individuals profiled in *Biography Today*.

GENERAL INDEX

419

Places of Birth Index

The following index lists the places of birth for the individuals profiled in *Biography Today*. Places of birth are entered under state, province, and/or country.

Birthday Index

BIRTHDAY INDEX